Theo Stammen

Political Parties in Europe

Translated from the original by
Gunda Cannon-Kern

John Martin Publishing Ltd, London

First published 1978 by Verlag C.H. Beck, Munich.
First published in English 1979 by
John Martin Publishing Ltd., London.

© 1980 by John Martin Publishing Ltd.

ISBN 0 906237 08 4

Printed in Great Britain by Glossary Print Productions

Preface

There are many books on political parties in Europe. They are usually written from a national point of view and sometimes from an academic one. As the movement towards European political unity gathers momentum, however, there is a need to broaden the national and academic vision by the study of European political parties in the European context. This is the purpose of this book. Originally written in German, the object of its publication in English is to bring this important contribution to political understanding to a wider — English speaking — readership.

In essence the book examines the historical development of political parties in Western Europe in the context of the present policy of European unification. The author also considers the possible structure of a European party system, highlighting common national political characteristics and the existing forms of international co-operation.

The book is primarily intended as a work of reference, which offers a comprehensive analysis of party political development on a national and European level.

To facilitate easy reference, the following sectional structure has been adopted:

1) A historical evaluation of European political integration, with particular regard to the first direct elections to the European Parliament.
2) An empirical analysis and comparison of national party systems in Europe.
3) A description of the existing transnational party relationships.
4) The presentation of a possible European party system drawn from parts 2) and 3).
5) European parliamentary statutes; European party manifestos and programmes.

This book was published originally in West Germany in 1978. Since this date the direct elections for the European Assembly have taken place. The new Parliament has begun the process of party alignment described in this book and to assert itself in seeking accountability of the 'executive' which has been a characteristic of Parliaments throughout the ages. To bring the reader up-to-date with events an Appendix has been provided setting out the results of direct elections and the composition of the new Parliament.

The evolutionary nature of the subject does not allow any precise predictions and forecasts or solutions to be offered; instead the reader is given the opportunity to view the subject as a whole in its historical perspective. We are left with live questions. In a political sense, how European are the Europeans? And, can our political parties' attitudes and thinking evolve to enable us to express our Europeanism?

Contents

ix

Section 2 : Documents relating to the political parties

FOREWORD
by Dick Taverne

As the 1970's draw to a close, the hopes of the founders of the European Community seem doomed to disappointment. A customs union has been achieved; but the Community has not developed a truly common market without major obstacles to internal trade. A common agricultural policy has been established; but its cost threatens to bankrupt the institutions of the Community. The Commission, the institutional voice of the Community interest, which is charged by the Treaty of Rome with the task of making proposals for the further development of the Community and which was once seen as the embryo government of a federal union, has declined in influence and standing. In the Council, national Governments have refused to accept majority voting on major questions, thus seeking to preserve their sovereignty intact, and on past form international crises seem to produce, not, as hoped, unity in the face of adversity, but tendencies towards disintegration.

One recent development offers new hope: the direct election of the European Parliament. This at least may inject a new political drive and could well lead to a renewal of a community spirit. For the first time it provides an opportunity of involving ordinary people more directly in the decisions that determine the future shape of Europe.

Why has the movement for a united Europe run into the sands? Many people point to a lack of popular enthusiasm for federalism. But in fact popular feelings have never played a major part in creating, or for that matter preventing, new developments. Only once were people in Britain asked to vote on a specific European question, namely British membership. This vote was strongly positive. Specific votes in other member countries have been equally rare. Nor has there been any other hard evidence either of a general widespread popular desire in favour of particular changes or a general hostility against them. Overall the impression one is left with is of a popular acquiescence in what were essentially the decisions of Governments. Political leaders, not popular movements, fashioned the institutions of the Community.

Why then do the hopes which moved these political leaders now seem so far from achievement? And why should the European Parliament make any difference?

To answer these questions one must go back to the origins of the Community. Many writers and thinkers had dreamed visions of a united Europe. Even when the visions were the same (and they seldom were) governments remained unmoved. However after 1945 the political and economic climate was ideally suited to new initiatives. All the original members of the Community had been occupied or defeated. The economic foundations of the original six had been largely destroyed. Then too, within a few years from the end of the war, a new threat appeared on Europe's eastern borders. With the unfortunate experience of past national rivalries behind them and the threat of domination by the Soviet Union looming over them,

1

it was natural that the governments of Europe should wish to work together in ways which had never appealed to them before. Indeed, it is noteworthy that the one large European country which refused to join in these moves was Britain which had neither been occupied nor defeated and saw itself playing its world role on a very different stage. When Britain finally did seek membership, it was only because it was realised that neither the Commonwealth nor a special relationship with the United States could give Britain a major role in the world and because its relative economic strength had started to ebb away.

The original impetus for creating a new Community was therefore a strong one and at the time the biggest obstacle to its creation, namely a self-confident nationalism, did not exist in the founder States.

It is however worth remembering that the historical conditions which created other federations were absent in Europe. There was no war of independence as in the United States. There was no common history based on a common culture as with the evolution of the older members of the British Commonwealth like Australia. There is no distinct European culture based on a common language. Indeed, one of the greatest problems of enlargement may well be that building Europe will end up like building the Tower of Babel. And the past history of the European States was mainly one of mutual conflict.

The European Community was then primarily a governmental and not a popular conception. Monnet's grand design was, as it were, progress by planned anomaly. The institutions with which the Community started could not work unless further steps were taken which would require further institutions. A common agricultural policy, like a fully effective customs union, would eventually be incompatible with varying exchange rates. They would therefore require congruance of economic growth and a monetary union, which would in turn require further institutions and stronger central management. This in turn would lead, in a democratic setting, to an effective European Parliament. And so on. A popular Parliament was not the base but the coping stone of the edifice. Necessity would be the mother of unity, not the irresistible will of the people.

But what the founders saw as an irreversible logical process has worked out differently. The old driving forces have disappeared. New ones have not replaced them. It is true that external crises arose, economic crises like the quadrupling of the oil price in 1973 and successive waves of monetary crises caused by the weakening first of the pound then of the dollar. But whatever new impetus these crises provided towards unity proved insufficiently strong to outweigh the inclinations of national governments to go it their own way. National self-confidence had been re-established in France and in Germany. Britain's was declining but far from extinguished.

Central to this weakening of the community impetus, as compared with the nationalist impetus, was the decline of the Commission. Partly this reflected a changed environment; partly this sprang from internal causes.

The Commission in its heyday had a clear purpose and function, on which all member States agreed. Even when De Gaulle attacked the Commission for exceeding its jurisdiction and sought to confine its role within clearly defined boundaries, all member states agreed that the Commission was the instrument through which the EEC could achieve the customs union and establish a common agricultural policy. However, after 1969, when both these tasks had been accomplished, the Commission was given no similar clear role on which all the member States were agreed. It sought to create such a role for itself. Hence its enthusiasm for a monetary union. If it could have achieved agreement on the goal of an economic and monetary union, it would have had a third great task. But the Werner plan of the early 1970's proved abortive. And while the Florence speech of the President of the Commission, Roy Jenkins, with its renewed call for a monetary union, may have played a part in the emergence of the European monetary system, the EMS essentially represents a number of limited steps on a long road. Roy Jenkins had called for "a pole vault", not for a long march.

Without proposals from the Commission, the Council cannot deliberate. The Commission is the motor of the Community. At the moment the Council, particularly the European Council with its meetings of Heads of State, provides the steering. But off-the-cuff initiatives by the Heads of State, however useful, are not likely to produce carefully worked-out proposals which provide Community solutions to Community problems. The Heads of State and their lesser colleagues in the Council are served by national administrations. However farsighted these may be, they start from the base of their own national interests. Where these conflict with other national interests, the tendency is to look for the lowest common denominator of agreement, not for the optimum solutions which are designed for the interests of the whole, even if they may benefit some more than others.

When the Commission of the Community lacks influence and power, the Community as a whole is stalled. It fails to speak with an effective voice in the Councils of the world. The bargaining power of individual European nations acting separately is overwhelmed by that of the powerful economies of the United States or Japan or indeed of groups like OPEC. The growth of each part of the whole is somewhat diminished if each part acts separately.

The main cause of the Commission's decline was then, external. But even within limitations imposed on it from outside, there seems little doubt that the Commission could have functioned more effectively. But it is itself to some extent affected by the same national disease. Too many individual Commissioners pursue their own political tasks conscious of their own political future in the member States. The Commission has failed to convey a clear sense of priorities or convince national administrations with the quality and logic of its proposals. Individual Commissioners, ploughing their own furrow, produce a battery of particular suggestions, which sometimes irritate national susceptibilities without particularly promoting the Community aims. Members of the Commission's civil service look to national lobbying for promotion. The Berlaymont is in danger of being nationalised.

So the balance of power has shifted. The European Council has become the most

3

important single influence in the Community. The Council of Ministers has lost some influence to the European Council but has gained some at the expense of the Commission. It has, as it were, cowed the Commission into seeking compromises for its proposals from the start. Instead of starting by stating the Community interest, which may later have to be modified in the light of national objections in the Council, the Commission starts by negotiating with individual countries before its proposals see the light of day. In fields like energy which cry out for Community initiatives, the voice of the Community is almost silent.

Not that the Commission is useless or powerless. Its influence on negotiations in GATT and its forthright attempts to promote reform of the CAP still demonstrate that the Commission has a vital role. The fact that Roy Jenkins has secured the presence of the Commission not only at meetings of the European Council but at the economic summits of the western world has re-asserted the political role of the Commission.

But when all is said and done, the Berlaymont today is not the centre of the new Europe as it was in the days of Hallstein. The Commission, like the Community as a whole, needs an injection of new life. If the Community stands still, it is likely to disintegrate. Yet national Governments do not have the will and the Commission does not have the power to move the Community forward.

Why should we expect a new impetus from the European Parliament when national Governments, who reflect the balance of power in their own countries, have been the main cause for this lack of progress? First, the elections of June 1979 hardly showed an overwhelming public interest. Voters clearly had no great expectations from their representatives. Next, the parties at Strasbourg are the same parties which have created the Governments in Paris, Bonn and Whitehall. The only difference is that the representatives of Strasbourg have less power. Lastly, how much can one expect from the party groups, when within each group national interests are likely to clash and their languages, backgrounds and political traditions are so very different? It is comparatively easy to make out a case that the European Parliament is no more than a collection of powerless, divided, disparate and unrepresentative MP's who will have little influence on the Commission, less on the Council and none on the gatherings of the Heads of State.

I believe, to the contrary, that like all Parliaments, the European Parliament will not be content to remain a walking shop; that it has the means of extending its powers; that in extending its powers it will restore the Commission to some of its former influence; and that inevitably, by its very nature, Parliament will pursue the Community interest before national interests.

MP's in all countries thrive on conflict with the Executive. The more that the Executive seeks to control the influence of Parliament the more Parliament will use every means at its disposal to fight back. The same will happen between the European Parliament and the Council.

Relations with the Commission are very different. Often Parliament and Commission will clash. But both will realise that they are allies of necessity, united by a common antagonist who seeks to diminish them both. It is primarily at the

4

Council's actions that the fire of the European MP's will be directed.

The Parliament does not lack weapons with which to fight. The history of Westminster shows the crucial part played by control over government funds. Time after time Westminster used this control to extend its powers. The European Parliament starts with a considerable say over the funds of the Community since it controls its discretionary spending. If these funds are withheld the Community cannot function and the member states suffer.

In addition, despite the low turn out at the elections last June the European Parliament has a certain moral weight on its side which can certainly be exaggerated but which cannot be altogether ignored. The fact is that national Parliaments cannot in practice control their Ministers in the Council. Because these have to negotiate and must sometimes yield their national viewpoints, they cannot be mandated before decisions are reached. Nor can they be effectively held to account after the Council has made its decisions, if these are forced on the Minister by external circumstances. (However powerful the right of veto, it cannot be used on every occasion without becoming self-defeating). Democratic control over the Council is therefore remote and, at best, secondhand. The European Parliament by contrast is directly accountable.

Let me turn next to the relations between the new Parliament and the Commission. The Commission's life will certainly be made more difficult. Already Commissioners express apprehension at the increased burdens which they will have to bear to serve the Parliament; but the Commission has nothing to fear from a stronger Parliament. The Commissioners' problem is a lack of legitimacy. They are appointed by governments once in four years and have almost total security of tenure for that period. Their accountability to anyone is virtually non-existent, since the right of Parliament to sack the whole Commission is virtually an unusable power. They can only too easily be categorised as bureaucrats whose claim to be heard rests solely on their technocratic skills.

But what if individual Commissioners were to become liable to be dismissed by Parliament? Or if Parliament were to scrutinise the Commission's proposals before they go to Council? If it is wise, the new Commission of 1981 might voluntarily yield such powers to Parliament in practice even if the Treaty is not altered. It could also submit itself for endorsement by the Parliament after its appointment by Governments. In any event, Parliament might well virtually arrogate some of these powers to itself. Nothing could prevent it from expressing strong disapproval of the actions of particular Commissioners and this could hardly be ignored. Nothing could prevent it from debating the issues on which the Commission is about to make proposals.

All such developments can only improve the standing of the Commission. It will provide some of the legitimacy which it now lacks. It will make the Commission more like Ministers and less like civil servants.

Finally, the very nature of the coming conflict between Council and Parliament is bound to affect the posture of the Parliament and the causes which it promotes. The Council represents the interests of the nation states. By contrast the Parliament

5

will become the champion of the Community. The Council will defend its sovereignty, that is the sovereignty of individual countries. The Parliament will seek to over-rule this sovereignty and extend the powers of the Community. And, despite the different make-up of the national parties within the party groups at Strasbourg, all the pressures will tend to make them act as groups, since the influence of each group in the Parliament will depend on its unity. And in so far as there is unity, this will be because the groups look at the issues on Community lines not national lines.

That is why I believe that the Parliament offers hope of new life to the Community. That is why those who are concerned with the future of Europe must now look more closely at the parties of other countries represented in Parliament. And that is what this book is about.

9th October 1979   *Dick Taverne*

Dick Taverne is at present a member of the five-man Independent Review Body set up to examine the functioning of the European Commission. In 1972 he resigned as the Labour MP for Lincoln and won the ensuing by-election as a Democratic Labour candidate with a majority of 13,000.

INTRODUCTION

It is obvious today that the objective of achieving the first direct elections to a European Parliament within the European Community in 1978 was unrealistic. Yet it is important to see the initiatives taken in 1976 by the political leaders of the EC countries and the joint decision of all EC Foreign Ministers as meaningful steps towards the revival and continuation of a policy of European integration. These initiatives resulted in the European direct elections which took place in June 1979. Such initiatives were long overdue, as they had been anticipated for many years by the normative clause of the EEC Treaty of 1957 (and analogous clauses of the other Treaties of the Community), "the Assembly shall draw up proposals for elections by direct universal suffrage in accordance with a uniform procedure in all Member States". (Article 138 of the EEC Treaty).

Direct elections and integration

Any suggestions from members of the EC Parliament to remedy this were met with attitudes ranging from delaying tactics to open rejection, particularly from the Council of Ministers.

Action to bring elections about can be traced from 1974, when the political leaders agreed (we will see later for what reasons) "to hold general elections, as stated in the Treaty, as soon as possible". This was followed at various summit meetings in the course of 1975 and 1976 by further moves towards the staging of these first European direct elections.

European resolutions

Agreement was reached regarding the number of delegates to be elected in each country. Then in September 1976 a formal treaty was signed which specified further details of the electoral process: "Act concerning the election of the representatives of the Assembly by direct universal suffrage". These agreements and resolutions at top level opened the way to the first direct elections of the European Parliament — over twenty years after the signing of the Rome Treaties (1957). The fact that in 1977 difficulties and obstacles emerged which were mainly domestic matters and which hampered the European countries in their legislative preparation for the elections (so that finally the date of the elections had to be postponed for two years) did not lessen the importance of the 1976 initiatives. The postponement is more indicative of the fact that the realisation of something that has been delayed for a considerable period cannot be achieved overnight.

In 1976 the relevant electoral laws (in each EC country) did not exist, for a uniform electoral system as required by the EEC Treaty (Art. 134) had not yet been worked out. Furthermore, the political parties which influence political thinking within the European Community had only just begun to establish themselves on a transnational level.

The essential conditions for the successful holding of the elections had in the meantime been created — each national Parliament separately considered and passed its own specific electoral bill, and the European political parties constituted themselves as "European" parties and issued their relevant manifestos. Thus it was possible prior to these elections to view them more optimistically and confidently than in 1976. However, it was apparent that although they open up a range of far-reaching possibilities and opportunities for the further development of the European Community, they also carried a considerable number of risks which were difficult

Possible development of the EC

to anticipate. Hope and confidence in the long-awaited progress towards a united Europe was mixed with a feeling of concern about whether the population of the EC countries would regard the elections as a genuine opportunity for Europe and, more importantly, whether they would seize this chance to positively advance political integration.

Regardless of how one looks at the first European direct elections one must consider them as a genuine "test", which — whether it proves successful or not — will have considerable repercussions on the future of Western Europe.

In this book I do not speculate on the consequences of these first elections — such consequences are easy to imagine, yet difficult to predict with precision; the focus of attention is on factual matters of importance. Direct elections to the European Parliament create a number of political, legal and above all organisational problems which it is imperative to solve satisfactorily for a successful outcome.

Importance of political parties

Of these factors the *political parties* are of utmost importance. It is the functioning of political parties more than anything else that determines the success of elections. From the experiences of all Western democracies, we know that the development of political thinking is difficult to imagine without a real contribution from the parties. Taking this one step further and transposing *national* experience onto a *transnational* level, one may conclude that in the process of European integration political parties will play an essential role. One must at the same time be aware of the fact that up to now all political parties in Europe have been merely *national* parties. The term 'national' is used as denoting a political party which restricts its activities within the boundaries of a single national community (Germany, France, Great Britain). In other words: *European parties and a European party system as such have never before existed.*

If one acknowledges the importance of parties and a party system in democratic elections, then it is clearly necessary to consider in relation to the first European direct elections what the *conditions and possibilities* are for the formation of future *transnational European parties* and a *European party system*. The primary task of the book is to give an answer to this question.

Objective

To begin with, we must approach the subject by a examination of its key issues, and consider them individually. The questions can be differentiated as follows:

1. Present condition of national party systems

— (1) What is the present condition of parties and party systems in the individual European countries at the time of the first direct elections to the European Parliament? Can common or similar structures be found, and do they allow conclusions as to the form of possible transnational parties within the framework of a future political system in Western Europe? These questions refer to the *actual situation today* (national parties and national party systems) and are considered in relation to their repercussions on the European direct elections and to the further development of European integration.

2. Transnational party connections

— (2) Which transnational connections between individual national parties or party groups of a given political conviction exist in Europe? To what extent have these connections already become formalised? What is their political importance with regard to the European direct elections and the political integration of Europe?

8

Which organisational arrangements and guidelines for political co-operation on a European level have these parties so far been able to develop? These questions attempt to explore a *"secondary" level of reality*. The rudimentary stages of this area already exist and it is developing relatively fast; it is also of particular practical importance to the successful outcome of the European elections.

— (3) Is it already possible to trace the outlines of a transnational European party system through these different aspects? If so, what shape will this European party system assume in the future? These last questions aim at a final evaluation of the various points discussed. Their results can be combined to form an overall picture which looks beyond the first direct elections and raises some ideas about the further political integration of Western Europe.

3. Outlines of a European party system

The book has been divided into the following parts:

Structure of the book

Part 1: The first part sets out an historical approach to the problem of the development of European integration up to the present ime and evaluates the importance of direct elections to the European Parliament in this context.

Part II: The second part presents an empirical analysis of the national party systems in Europe. It compares them systematically in order to establish common and constant features of the national European party systems which may be relevant for the foundation of all-European parties and of an all-European party system.

Part III: The third part describes and analyses the already existing transnational party connections in Europe and discusses them from an organizational, institutional and programmatic point of view.

Part IV: The fourth and final part attempts to form a (provisional) overall picture of a transnational European party system from aspects dealt with in parts II and III. In this way we may look at any party groups and coalitions likely to be formed in Europe after the first direct elections in 1979.

Part V: This section contains in full the most important and relevant documents of political and international law, declarations of the European Parliament, and manifestos and charters of the various European parties. They constitute the primary source material for the discussion and understanding of the elections. The election results are set out in full in Appendix 1.

Part I
Countries, Parties, European Consciousness

I. Government Motivations

This historical introduction to the problem focuses on two aspects of contemporary history of importance to the subject.

(1) The first question to be asked is why it is that only very recently the political leaders of the EC countries were able to decide to hold direct elections to the European Parliament, for it was these very same Governments which had attached little or no importance to the subject over so many years.

Which new motives, objectives or circumstances led to such a decision at this particular point in European development? **Questions and problems**

(2) The second question is how this decision influenced the manner in which the direct elections were held. In other words: how is the process of democratic political thinking conceived of on the transnational European level?

Apart from these two main issues, a number of other considerations need to be raised.

(3) How important are the direct European elections to the overall conception of the future constitutional organization of the European Community as a transnational political system? Does such a concept exist at all? If so, what are its outlines? It will soon become evident that these questions are important because they have a bearing on whether future direct elections will have practical value and meaning. Ultimately, their importance depends on whether they form an integral part of a well-balanced picture of a future European political system ("political union") or whether they merely represent an isolated political initiative born of current political considerations.

(4) Lastly, what is the role of the political parties in the process of the development of the European Community and which specific role do they play in direct elections? The answer to this question will lead into the latter considerations of this book. **Role of the parties**

II. The Historical Significance of Direct Elections

An explanation is needed for the fact that the decision of the summer of 1976 to hold the European direct elections in 1978 according to article 138 of the EEC treaty matured only relatively recently.

Various factors have to be considered: **Causes and reasons**

— First, one has to bear in mind the original conception of Europe that formed the basis of the foundation of the EEC.

— Furthermore, one has to take into account the real development of Western

11

European integration with its various developments, crises and setbacks.
— Finally, one has to examine the present state of the European Community and, taking this as starting point, the necessary steps for its further development.
It is helpful to start with a brief outline of the most important steps which led to the resolution.

III. Stages of Decision-Making

Contractual foundations

Those treaties which form the foundations of the European Communities (EEC; Euratom; ECSC = European Coal and Steel Community) all contain an identical clause which states that the common European Parliament, called "Assembly", consists "of representatives of the peoples of the States brought together in the Community" (Art. 137, 107 and 20 of the Treaties mentioned above). They state that the Assembly consists of delegates "who shall be designated by the respective Parliaments from among their members in accordance with the procedure laid down by each Member State" (Art. 138, 108 and 21 of the Treaties mentioned).
Finally it is mentioned in this context that "the *Assembly*" has the task of drawing up "proposals for elections by direct universal suffrage in accordance with a uniform procedure in all Member States", and that "the Council shall, acting unanimously, lay down the appropriate provisions, which it shall recommend to Member States for adoption in accordance with their respective constitutional requirements".
Even though they were not put into practice straightaway, these clauses contained from the start a democratic legitimisation of the European Parliament by means of direct elections. This fact is of great importance with regard to the further development of the European communities.

1. First Initiatives as far back as 1958

Dehousse report (1960)

The Assembly, that is, the common Parliament of the three European Communities, immediately began working on a plan for the introduction of direct elections, as stipulated in the Rome Treaties. As early as 1958 a team was formed which was part of the Political Committee and led by Fernand *Dehousse*. They drafted a "Convention on the election of members of the European Parliament by universal suffrage" (cf. *Europe-Archive*, 1960 part 2, D 164-169). The European Parliament had passed their plan in May 1960 and submitted it to the Council of Ministers in June 1960.
This plan assumed that each European Parliament would be elected for a period of five years; the number of delegates would be raised to 426; France, Italy and Germany were to send 108 delegates each, Belgium and the Netherlands 42 each, and Luxembourg 18. Direct elections of delegates would be held uniformly and according to the same electoral process; everybody belonging to a member country would be able to stand for Parliament in any other of the member countries; substitute delegates would not exist; no delegate would be able to cast a personal vote if bound by instructions. Lastly, a seat in the European Parliament would be

12

incompatible with a seat in one of the national Parliaments — a certain transitory period excluded.

2. No Progress in the Sixties

At the conference of EEC foreign ministers on July 10, 1961 in Bonn, the French Government made it quite clear that it was not in favour of introducing direct elections in Europe at this time. The issue was not put to the vote, as the French attitude made a unanimous decision impossible. Instead, the problem of direct elections was adjourned for several years. **France blocks the way**

The Council of Ministers' obstruction of direct elections at European level resulted in a whole series of initiatives by the various countries, "in order to achieve direct elections to the European Parliament at least in the individual member countries". (H. Knuth) *Direkte Walen zum Europ. Parliament* (in "Zeitschr. f. Parlamentsfragen", 1969, p. 50).

On June 10, 1964, the West German SPD — then an opposition party — submitted a draft for a "law on the election of Members of the European Parliament from the Federal Republic of Germany". This bill envisaged holding a direct election of the German members of the European Parliament at the same time as electing the Bundestag (every German voter was to have *three* votes instead of *two*). The governing parties rejected the bill because they saw a contradiction between "the exact terms and meaning of the Treaties" and the limitation of the bill to only one country. It was furthermore argued that direct elections in Europe could only have a democratizing effect if the European Parliament were to receive genuine power (cf. H. Knuth, ibid., p. 51/2). **Parliamentary initiatives**

In the 1960's the other EC counties — usually the opposition parties — launched similar initiatives which aimed at a direct election of the members of the European Parliament on an individual country basis. On the whole, all such attempts met with resistance and rejection by the Government and majority parties in the national Parliaments. This resistance was based on practical realities for it was generally accepted that de Gaulle's rigid attitude towards Europe obstructed any progress towards European integration and the extension of the Community at that time. In view of the French attitude it seemed then advisable "to hope for a time after de Gaulle" and "to avoid everything that would lead (de Gaulle) to steps that might irrevocably damage the federative process after his time". (Knuth, ibid, p. 55). **Governmental resistance**

3. New Activities after de Gaulle

Consequently, it was only in 1968/69 — after de Gaulle had left the political scene — that new initiatives began in the individual European countries as well as in the European Parliament itself. Pointing out that their failure to act could result in an action before the European Court of Justice (cf. Art. 1 and 2, 1957|EEC treaty), the European Parliament reminded the Council of Ministers of the need for a settlement **New initiatives after 1968**

13

of the election problem.

The legal committee of the European Parliament saw it as "the Council of Ministers' obligation to pass a resolution on direct elections, as an increasing number of responsibilities are passing from the national Parliaments to the Community. The basic treaties envisage a democratic structure of the Community. However, this is no longer guaranteed as the extensive legislative power of the Council of Ministers is beyond the control of Parliament". (H. Knuth., ibid, p. 50).

The European Parliament's activities were parelleled by new initiatives in various national Parliaments, also aiming at the introduction of direct elections. (cf. B. Kohler: Direkte Wahlen zum europaeischen Parlament, in: *Europe-Archive*, 20, 1971, p. 729 ff.). As a result of these various initiatives, the European summit conference in the Hague in December 1969 took up some of the demands for a further development of European institutions, using as key-words "completion", "intensification", and "extension". The conference agreed *inter alia* on the following points: —

Summit conference in The Hague (1969)

— to regard the transitory period of the European Community as completed and start the final phase on January 1st, 1970 ("Completion"),

— to continue the process of European integration towards an economic and monetary union, and also to strive for progress in political integration ("Intensification"),

— to start negotiations with Great Britain, Ireland, Denmark and Norway as potential members of the Community ("Extension").

The final communiqué of this conference states that "the question of direct elections was still being considered by the Council of Ministers" and that it was intended "to extend the budgetary powers of the European Parliament".

4. European Summit Conference 1974

Further delays

Soon afterwards negotiations started with the four countries mentioned, and Great Britain, Ireland and Denmark finally joined the Community (Norway did not join because of the negative results of an EC referendum). This once more delayed any serious consideration of the direct elections topic up to 1974. It was only at the important European summit conference in Paris in December 1974 that the political leaders again dealt extensively with the objectives of a political union of Europe. They took up the issues of the extension of responsibilities and of the democratization of European institutions, with specific regard to the European Parliament. The final communiqué of this conference comments as follows: "The responsibilities of the European Parliament are to be extended, particularly by giving it certain legislative powers within the Community." As far as the "direct elections" were concerned, the various Governments agreed "that the aim of holding general elections to the European Parliament, as stated in the treaty, should be attained as soon as possible. They (the Governments) look forward with interest to any suggestions Parliament might have and would like the Council to consider them in 1976. The general direct elections should then be held from 1978

Paris summit conference (1974)

14

onwards". (Quoted from: Chr. Sasse: *Regierungen, Parlamente, Ministerrat*, 1975, p. 254).

5. "Direct Elections" Remain a Topical Issue

The European Parliament at once (January 1975) started debating a (new) proposal on direct elections. This was called the "Patijn-report"; and although the number of delegates and the dual mandate were still controversial issues, 107 delegates of the European Parliament voted in favour, only 2 were against and 17 abstained. On the basis of the proposal, the European Council delegated (on July 16, 1975) to the conference of Foreign Ministers of the EC countries the task of drawing up a report on the problems of direct elections and their possible solution by the end of October 1975. (The term "European Council" had been coined to designate the European summit conferences of political leaders since 1975). However, at various European conferences in the autumn and winter of 1975/76 a final settlement of the problems raised by the question of direct elections could not be achieved. During the session of the European Council on December 1/2, 1975, agreement was reached about the date of the elections, namely to hold "the elections of the members of the European Parliament during the period from May to June 1978". However, the distribution of seats (the proportionate representation of nations by delegates) still remained a controversial point.

6. Agreement on Distribution of Seats (1976)

It was only during the session of the European Council in Brussels on June 12/13, 1976, that a final agreement was reached on this issue and that a resolution was passed concerning the direct elections to the European Parliament. The Council's decision on the distribution was definite and final. As far as the elections were concerned, the decision on the actual electoral system was left to the individual member countries.

Final agreement (1976)

On September 22, 1976, at the conference of Foreign Ministers of the EC countries, these agreements were included in a formal treaty which consists of:—
(1) a Decision which specifies how to settle the various details pertaining to the general direct elections of the European Parliament, and which fixed May/June 1978 as the election date; (2) an Act "concerning the election of the representatives of the Assembly by direct universal suffrage"; this document settles the questions of the distribution of seats, the length of the legislative period of the European Parliament (5 years), the status of the delegates and the possibility of a dual mandate. The document further states the task of the European Parliament to elaborate a plan for a uniform electoral system. In the meantime, each member country should decide internally on the mode of election. In addition, the document contains further details regarding the holding and ensuing evaluation of the elections.

Formal treaty (1976)

7. Risks, Reservations, Opposition

This resolution of the EC Foreign Ministers was still subject to ratification by the individual countries and furthermore needed supplementary bills and decrees to guarantee its execution on a national level. Yet it represented a milestone in the development of the direct election issue. *Now the realization of such an election appeared imminent (May/June 1978).* However, at that time (1976) it was already obvious that not all the countries concerned were equally determined to see the elections held at the appointed time. Great Britain and Denmark in particular raised objections against an election in the spring of 1978 for reasons of home affairs. The objections in France, particularly those of the Gaullists, were of a more fundamental nature, as it was feared that direct elections to the European Parliament would naturally create an increase in the long-term importance of the European Parliament. When the subject of European elections was dealt with in the individual countries through ratification of the Act of 1976 and the passing of corresponding electoral laws, two facts emerged in the course of the late summer and autumn of 1977.

Objections in Great Britain, Denmark and France

Situation in autumn 1977

(1) Each parliament of the individual countries was principally in favour of European direct elections and ratified the Act with a majority vote; it then started work on the relevant electoral legislation.

(2) By the autumn of 1977 it had become clear that the spring of 1978 was an unrealistic date for the elections and finally, at the EC summit meeting at the beginning of December 1977, Great Britain declared that it would not be able to observe the proposed timing. Until the beginning of April 1977 uncertainty reigned; various possibilities were considered and rejected. According to one of them, eight of the nine EC countries should stick to the fixed date of election, and Great Britain should hold her election in the following year. This suggestion was obviously undesirable as it would have lessened the full political impact of the direct elections. In this situation, a postponement of the election date for all EC countries seemed to be the lesser evil.

Consequently, at their summit meeting in Copenhagen at the beginning of April 1978, the EC political leaders agreed on a new date for the first direct elections: from June 7 – June 10, 1979. This resolution of the political leaders met with unanimous approval from the leaders of the parliamentary groups in the European Parliament. In this way the time-table for the first European direct elections, which was disturbed in the autumn of 1977, has been brought back to normal with a time lapse of exactly one year and the preparations could start again. In the meantime the national Parliaments of the nine EC countries passed those bills which were necessary for the holding of the elections. As a consequence, the actual organisational preparations of the elections in the various EC countries – for example, the nomination of candidates and the drawing-up of lists – could begin. In practice the choice of the early summer of 1979 as election date was based on a much more realistic evaluation of the overall situation than the resolution of 1976. Looking back, however, one has to bear in mind that only the initiatives of 1976 opened the way for direct elections to the European Parliament – so often delayed – before

New election date

Going into committee over electoral bills

16

the end of the seventies.

IV. Background to the Decision on Direct Elections

1. Introduction

The previous sections outlined the string of events which after many delays culminated in the decision to hold European direct elections. However, such an outline does not explain the motives of the parties concerned or the principal factors which led to this decision.
The following sections will deal with these matters.

2. Early conceptions

The motives and objectives are undoubtedly of a *political* nature: from the famous Zurich speech of Winston Churchill in 1946 which presented one of the very first conceptions of the "United States of Europe"; and, a little later, the Schumann plan; and also the "Europe Movement", which influenced Europeans of all levels and age-groups — particularly the student milieu. Following the 2nd World War and its consequences for all European countries, a *United States of Europe* seemed to many a logical, meaningful and worthwhile aim, if — as it appeared — countries in seeking political and economic security were required to become a member of some international political association.

The Union Européenne des Fédéralistes (UEF), for example, united all supporters of a confederate Europe. Their European conception initially embraced the *whole* of Europe, that is, it comprised all those Eastern European countries which after the end of the 2nd World War were under Soviet control (the UEF wanted to be the "bridge between East and West" and to prevent the division of Europe into two hostile sections). Soon the UEF had to accept far-reaching modifications of its political ideals during the first phase of the Cold War. On the one hand, the Soviet Union under Stalin brought the Communist regimes of Eastern Europe under its control; it prevented their participation in any wider European union and in the economic development programme of the Marshall plan; furthermore it defined an extremely nationalistic and anti-European course for the Communist parties of Western Europe. On the other hand, the United States pleaded for the creation of a united Europe and tried to exercise influence towards this end by means of the Marshall plan. In this way, the European movement soon became entangled in the East-West conflict. Short of abandoning it altogether, the logical consequence of this situation meant confining the plans of integration and federation to *Western* Europe. "In view of the present serious situation in Europe it is imperative to start realising a federal structure wherever an attempt can be made, where nations still enjoy a certain freedom of movement and decision . . . It would be tantamount to a crime not to seize the opportunities offered by the political tide, and not to start building a federal Europe wherever this is possible today". (Quotation from

17

from W. Lipgens, Europaeische Integration, *in*: Loewenthal/Schwarz (Eds): *Die zweite Republik*, 1974, p. 522). All those who — for reasons of the political situation in the world — favoured a restriction of European integration to Western Europe, had a sobering surprise in store. For soon it became evident "that Great Britain (and the Scandinavian countries as well) was not prepared to follow the concept of a European union in the sense of jointly handling responsibilities which up to that time had been in the hands of the individual countries. Instead, it insisted on institutionalised co-operation of autonomous governments as the only acceptable initial step towards a Western European Union". (*Handbuch der deutschen Aussenpolitik*, 1975, p. 682). Thus, the issue of political integration encompassing supranational organisations and structures reduced the remainder of Western Europe to those six countries which later founded the EC.

The countries held largely similar views, such as the one expressed in a basic resolution on European politics by the first German Bundestag on July 26th, 1950. "The Bundestag of the Federal Republic of Germany, which is chosen through free elections, supports the idea of a European federal pact, as it is convinced that the present division of Europe into sovereign states will lead these nations increasingly into misery and bondage". This pact "has first to create a supranational federal body by general, direct and free elections which has legislative, executive and judicial powers; and second to endow this body with all the powers that are necessary in order to *a)* bring about the economic unity of Europe on the basis of social justice, and *b)* make possible a common European foreign policy". (Quoted from: *Handbuch der deutschen Aussenpolitik*, p. 683).

On similar lines, the "Treaty of the Foundation of the European Community for Coal and Steel" was signed in 1951, following a French initiative (Schumann plan). It was the intention of the Schumann plan that the institutions of this first European Community were to be regarded as prototypes and as the "first foundation stones of a federal Europe". As far as the further development of European integration was concerned, military affairs were the next to be considered. This proved an unlucky choice and did not further the cause; it was a result of pressure brought about by the political situation at that time (Korean War). The "European Defense Community" (EDC) was founded in 1952, but in 1954 was rejected by the French National Assembly. Later it was superseded by a development which led to the foundation of NATO. The EDC treaty had envisaged in Article 38 a "Political Community" as the final product of European integration. In this way, the failure of the EDG meant at the same time "the end of an attempt to arrive at a European federal state via a *European Political Community*". (*Handbuch der deutschen Aussenpolitik*, p. 684). However, the process of unification did not come to an end. Amazingly enough, the "supranational functionalism", which already was a basic principle of the Schumann plan and which — through economic constraints, for example — was intended to achieve a staged integration in the political sphere as well, led as early as 1955 to the Messina resolution. This resolution envisaged the extension of the economic integration of the six countries, which had begun in the coal and steel sector, to all aspects of their economy. This then formed the basis for

18

Great Britain stands aside

Foundation of the European Community

Political aims

European Coal and Steel Community (1951)

Failure of the EDC (1954)

EEC and Euratom

the Rome treaties of 1957: the EEC treaty and the Euratom treaty. It was of political importance that these two newly created European Communities had the same organisational and institutional structure as the already existing European Coal and Steel Community: a Commission performed the executive role and a Council of Ministers the legislative; furthermore a Parliament ("Assembly", which was now responsible for all three Communities) and a Court of Justice existed. All these institutions can be regarded as prototypes of a federal political system.

3. Development of the European Economic Community

As far as its practical importance is concerned, the European Economic Community (EEC) was always the most important of the three Communities. Three phases were envisaged for the realization of a common European market (with a common customs system, uniform rules for free competition, no restrictions on capital and labour; but at first without a uniform economic policy or currency). It is interesting to note with regard to the further history of European integration that Great Britain — which did not want to have any part in such a supranational union — tried to counteract the European Economic Community by founding the European Free Trade Association (1960). Apart from Great Britain, the other members of EFTA were the Scandinavian countries, Austria, Portugal and Switzerland. After only a few years the economic success of the EEC became quite obvious; for example, industrial production in the EEC increased by 37% between 1958 and 1962 compared with 14% in Great Britain and 28% in the United States. Great Britain was forced to re-consider its attitude towards the EEC and the concept of European integration. In 1961 Great Britain, together with Ireland, Norway and Denmark, applied for membership of the EEC.

Following the apparent economic success, an advance in the *political* integration of Western Europe also seemed possible after 1961, as a logical consequence of the "supranational functionalism". However, towards the end of the Algeria crisis, which took a heavy toll on French home and foreign affairs, President de Gaulle took a firm stand against the realisation of a political union of Europe. The French veto in 1963 stopped all negotiations over membership with the countries concerned, in particular Great Britain. The fact that France clung so rigidly to traditional and nationalistic ways of thinking was the reason for a halt in further development from 1963 up to de Gaulle's retirement from active politics (1969). This stagnation had far-reaching and serious consequences in general, but affected political integration in particular. The period saw neither a consolidation nor an extension of the Community and its institutions of any significance; but above all there was a failure to achieve the democratisation of the Community through direct elections and an expansion of the responsibilities of the European Parliament. In 1965, France insisted on retaining the unanimous vote on "very important interests". It was only in 1967 that de Gaulle approved the merging of the three Councils of the three Communities into one, and similarly of forming one common Commission responsible for the three Communities. In return, he demanded and was granted the

EEC

Success of the EEC

Application for membership (GB, Ireland, Norway, Denmark)

French veto

resignation of Walter Hallstein, whose political activities aimed at strengthening the Communities had made him an unwelcome opponent of the General.

In the wake of the "Treaty of German-French Cooperation" concluded by Konrad Adenauer in 1963, the connections between the Federal Republic of Germany and France within the Community were of a special nature. The Federal Republic tried to prevent de Gaulle from ultimately jeopardizing the project of European unification, and was partly successful. In permanent German-French consultations, the French were made aware of what they could gain from European integration, particularly in the economic sector.

4. New Approaches after de Gaulle

Yet it was only when de Gaulle retired in 1969 and Georges Pompidou succeeded him as President that genuinely new possibilities arose for an active continuation of a European policy of integration. The European summit conference in The Hague in December 1969 put it like this: "the belief in the political objectives which make the Community meaningful and relevant" had been renewed. The political leaders — including France — finally removed all obstacles to the long-delayed negotiations of entry with Great Britain, Ireland, Norway and Denmark. The negotiations began in June 1970 and were successfully concluded only one

year later. In January 1972 these countries signed the treaty of accession which, after ratification, became operative on January 1, 1973. (Only in Norway were the majority of the people against joining the EC.) Also, the conference in The Hague attempted to start new initiatives towards a complete economic and monetary

union. To this end a plan had been worked out (in 1970) under Werner, the Prime Minister of Luxembourg, envisaging the following: over a period of ten years "the parities will be irrevocably fixed and movement of capital will be absolutely free"; a common European currency with a common central banking system will be introduced; national economic politics will develop in the direction of a uniform European economic policy so that "the restrictions in economic autonomy of the member countries will be paralleled by corresponding authorities on the level of the Community". These far-reaching plans were aimed at restarting movement towards European integration; but failed to achieve this in the following years for a variety of reasons. Firstly, it was soon clear that France under Pompidou was still not interested in effectively strengthening the Community and its institutions. Secondly, from 1970 on all economic and political aims were overshadowed by a worldwide economic and financial crisis which produced rising inflation, unemployment and declining production. Mainly as a consequence of the last war in the Middle East and the oil embargo imposed on the Western world by the Arabs in the autumn of 1973, the intended economic and monetary union of the European countries did not materialise. Instead, a general crisis developed. In this situation, the tools that were available to deal with the problems on the transnational level of the European Community proved distinctively ineffective; and the difficulties served to strengthen the general tendency to deal with economic difficulties — such as the energy crisis — on a national level.

5. Final Decisions

The crisis revealed how exposed and susceptible Western Europe is to developments in the world economy. After the election of Giscard d'Estaing as President of the French Republic (1974), there was a critical evaluation within the European Community of what had been achieved and what was sought for the future. At the summit conference in Paris in 1974 the political leaders passed a series of resolutions, related particularly to the further expansion of the European communities. Many an item that had long been ignored by the Council of Ministers was set in motion. For example, the final communique contains the following passage: "In view of a smoother functioning of the Council, the Community deems it necessary to abolish the practice of making a decision subject to unanimous approval by the member countries". At the same time, the political leaders all agreed on the need "to strengthen the solidarity of the Nine. This was to be achieved by improving common procedures; developing new common policies in sectors still to be decided; and by endowing the relevant bodies with the appropriate power to act".

Critical evaluation of the situation (1974)

This meant that the permanent representatives of the EC countries in Brussels, for example, should "have more scope for action and decision-making, so that the Council only has to deal with the most important political questions". It was also decided that the Commission should be granted more power; it was to be responsible for "the executive and administrative regulation of Community resolutions".

Expansion of institutions

A final remark emphasised "the importance of letting the European Parliament participate more closely in political matters. This political cooperation is growing in importance and is one of the foundations of a united Europe".

In this context, it seems particularly interesting that a committee is to be formed to examine "under which conditions and within which period the citizens of the nine member countries can be given special rights as members of the Community". Furthermore, it is important to mention "that the aim of holding general elections to the European Parliament" which the Council of Ministers in particular had neglected and postponed for so long, was now "to be attained as soon as possible". In a move towards this aim, the political leaders "look forward with interest to any suggestions Parliament might have and would like the Council to consider them in 1976. The general direct elections should then be held from 1978 onwards".

The reason for these suggestions was the fact that "the European Parliament consists of representatives of countries united by the Community, and therefore every country has to be appropriately represented."

Finally, the political leaders touched on the question of further powers for the European Parliament and remarked: "The European Parliament contributes to the shaping of Europe. The political leaders will take into account the opinions of the European Parliament which they had requested in October 1972". They said further: "The responsibilities of the European Parliament are to be extended, in particular by endowing it with certain legislative powers within the Communities".

Further Parliamentary powers

(All quotations taken from: Chr. Sass: *Regierungen, Parlamente, Ministerrat*, 1975, p.253/4).

Reading between the lines of these texts gives some insight into the true motives for the political leaders' sudden positive change of attitude towards Parliament and direct elections. It is presumably safe to assume that this change did not result from any sense of achievement after the successful development of the European Community over the preceding years. The more likely cause was its generally critical situation, particularly in the economic sector where the consequences of worldwide economic and monetary problems were being felt. Confidence in the economic strength of the European Community and the efficiency of its institutions was slowly dwindling and political leaders realised that they had to find new justification for the development of the Community, if the whole concept of European unification was not to be endangered. An expansion of the democratic foundations of the European Parliament and its institutions offered just such a means. Consequently, the subject of European direct elections — which had for so long been repressed — and with it the extension of powers for the European Parliament suddenly became attractive to the various Governments.

Importance and risks of direct elections

If this analysis is correct, then one has to realise that the holding of the first direct elections in 1979 was a considerable risk. If they were held mainly for the purpose of restoring lost credibility in the concept of the Community, then they have to show immediate results as far as the speedy democratization of the European Parliament is concerned. If the elections are considered a failure (for whatever reasons), then this will have dire consequences for the future of the European Community. In any case the outcome will be far less favourable now than it would have been in the years of continuous economic success and growth. In retrospect, one thing is quite clear: from a political point of view, it was a disadvantage and dangerous to hold back the *political* development of the European Community for so long. The democratization of its institutions, and direct elections to the Parliament in particular, should have been dealt with in the economically prosperous years.

It is true that the lack of democracy was not quite so noticeable in those years of constant growth; but it is undeniable that a democratization then would have been far less risky than in today's time of economic stagnation and difficulties.

Various recent studies of the state of the European Community corroborate this view. Ralf Dahrendorf's "Plea for a European Union" (1973) is one of them; the

Tindemans report (1975)

so-called "Tindemans report" of December 1975 is particularly impressive and has attracted a good deal of attention.

In his report to the European Council, the Belgian head of state arrived at a generally pessimistic evaluation of the current situation in the European Community. The study came to the conclusion: "Everything that has been achieved so far within the Community is at stake today". Tindemans stated that the European countries are as eager as ever to draw closer together, and appeals that they should be given (again) "that *political* dimension which alone makes it possible to act". In this spirit, the report tried to renew the idea of a "European Union" as *political* union and to make it "the instrument of European unification at the present stage". For such a conception of a European union, the following element is essential: "In order to achieve these tasks European Union is given institutions with the necessary powers to determine a common, coherent and all-inclusive political view, the efficiency needed for action, the legitimacy needed for democratic control". The fifth chapter of this report describes in detail the "strengthening of the institutions" which are imperative for the European Union. For it seems obvious that "a return to methods of cooperation between Governments . . . does not solve the problems of Europe". This applies in particular to future difficulties which will increasingly relate to the integration of individual national policies. For this reason, the institutions of the European Community have to be strengthened in the following way:

Strengthening of the institutions

"The realisation of a European Union presupposes that the European bodies already contain the *authority* necessary for the definition of a policy; that they contain a *potential of efficiency* needed for joint action; and that they contain the *legitimacy* required for democratic control. It presupposes furthermore that these bodies show *coherence* with regard to their ideals and actions, for it is this coherence that makes it possible to define and realise a certain policy. These four criteria *authority, efficiency, legitimacy* and *coherence* determine what has to be changed in the European bodies".

Criteria: authority, efficiency, legitimacy, coherence

In this line of argument, the European direct elections occupy a key position in more than one way: "Through the general direct elections of the Parliament the Assembly gains *new political authority*. At the same time, they strengthen the *democratic legitimacy* of the general European institutional framework".

Similar arguments apply to the increase in the powers of the European Parliament. "One of the consequences of the new authority of Parliament (stemming from the direct elections — T.St.) will be an increase of its powers. This will take place in step with the development of the European Union and will mainly lead to an increase in its *legislative* function". As a first step in this direction, the Tindemans report envisages an "initiating right" for the European Parliament. This means that the European Council (of the political leaders) is obliged to consider bills submitted by the Parliament. In this way "the Assembly can contribute effectively to the definition of the common policies." (Quotations from the Tindemans report taken from: Juettner/Liese: *Taschenbuch der Europaeischen Parteien und Wahlen,* 1977, p. 227 ff.).

Further powers for the Parliament

The detailed and critical argument advanced in the Tindemans report elucidates among other things the motives and objectives of the European Council of political leaders when in 1976 it finally called for the first direct elections. The question that was asked in the beginning, namely why a positive decision for direct elections could only recently be taken, can now be answered. In a phase of stagnation, crisis and disintegration, those political leaders who bear responsibility in Europe wanted to give a fresh impetus to the European Community by means of new political initiatives compelled by the overwhelming need to co-ordinate economic and monetary policies. It is, if you like, a 'leap in the dark' which created a new and critical situation in which the individual citizen plays a more important part. To date the ordinary European has been able to profit personally in many ways from

Motives and objectives of the European Council

'Leap in the dark'

European economic integration. Now his active co-operation is called for to ensure that the Community does not falter.

V. The Problems of Direct Elections

1. Introduction

The next important question to be asked deals with the content of the political leaders' decision: what are the precise regulations for the holding of the direct elections? In order to answer this question one has to refer to the 'Decision' and the ''Act' which were signed by the EC Foreign Ministers in Brussels on September 20, 1976. At the same time one has to take into consideration the various preliminary stages that led to this decision and that were debated in the European committees. Particularly important in this respect is the draft convention of the European Parliament dated January 14, 1975. In the following discussion, only the most important aspects and problems receive consideration.

2. Stages in the Development of 'Direct Elections'

Stages of discussion

The decisive stages in the debate about direct elections can be summarised briefly. The revival of the discussion at the summit conference in Paris in December 1974 was a direct consequence of the following events: de Gaulle's retirement from politics which made it possible to overcome the slowing of European development; and the extension of the European Community when three more countries joined in 1973.

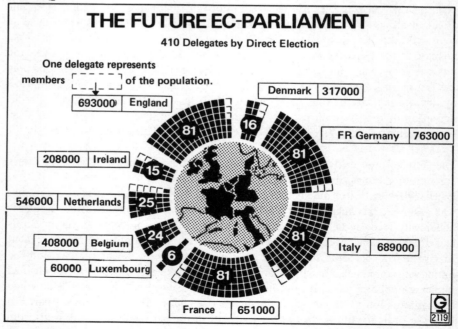

THE FUTURE EC-PARLIAMENT

410 Delegates by Direct Election

One delegate represents members [ ] of the population.

693000 | England
Denmark | 317000
FR Germany | 763000
208000 | Ireland
546000 | Netherlands
408000 | Belgium
60000 | Luxembourg
Italy | 689000
France | 651000

As early as January 1975 the European Parliament passed a new draft convention on the introduction of direct elections with a large majority. This text, which is sometimes called 'Patijn Report', received consideration from the European Council (of the political leaders) and the conference of EC Foreign Ministers at various meetings in 1975. Some essential points (still) remained unresolved — most importantly, the number of seats to be allocated to the national delegates. In July 1976 the European Council came to a final agreement which led to the resolution of the Foreign Ministers in September 1976. **Draft convention of the European Parliament**

It is interesting to compare the texts and documents brought out during this period with those issued by the European Parliament in 1960 on the same matter. As far as the content is concerned, a 'shrinking process' can be noticed: the documents become increasingly less voluminous.

This may be looked at from different points of view. On the one hand, it mirrors the natural process of elimination of alternatives in the course of decision-making. On the other hand, it shows that problems are continually 'set aside', namely those that fail to lead to agreement at a particular point in time. Such action seems necessary and acceptable in order not to jeopardise the fundamental conceptual issues.

Compared with the 'Dehousse Report', the Patijn Report appears remarkably short — only 17 articles are needed to formulate a convention on direct elections and to suggest its acceptance. **Patijn Report**

Chapter I (under the heading 'General Provisions') fixes among other things the number of delegates to be elected in each member country in accordance with a form of proportional representation; it also fixes the parliamentary term of the European Parliament (five years) and the status of its delegates. Chapter II deals with the electoral system. By 1980 the European Parliament has to decide on a uniform system; in the meantime, the choice of electoral system was left to the individual countries.

Chapter III fixed the election date as "the first Sunday of May, 1978". The number of delegates of the future European Parliament — elected in direct elections — represents the most fundamental problem. This becomes clear in the arguments of the Dutch delegate Schelto Patijn at the Political Committee of the European Parliament. There are two difficulties: a) fixing the *total* of seats, and b) *distributing* the mandates among the individual member countries. The solution of this double problem had to attempt "an optimal compromise", ensuring that the Parliament was *able to function properly* and at the time achieving an absolute degree of *representativeness*. **Total and distribution of seats**

The Patijn report argued that, as far as these two aspects are concerned, reform is needed: the initial size of 198 delegates in the European Parliament was too small and their distribution thought unfair. However, it was generally accepted that experience on a national level has shown that the upper limit for the size of a parliament is around 600 - 700; beyond that number, it is doubtful whether such a body can function properly.

The Patijn report did not argue in favour of the largest number of delegates as possible, as it was thought that the powers of the European Parliament were too limited. The report suggests a total of 355 delegates. As far as the *distribution* of seats among the individual EC countries is concerned, the following criteria had to be taken into account:

a) the total population of the individual countries and the number of its delegates should be proportionate;

b) each pertinent political movement in a given country ought to be represented in the European Parliament;

c) the number of delegates of a given country should not be less than the present total after the redistribution.

The Patijn report suggested a phased procedure which would lead to a graded representation and distribution of mandates, incorporating the factors above (cf. Art. 2 of the draft convention).

Electoral System

Before considering the reaction to this suggestion, consideration is given to the question of the *electoral system*. The European Parliament has laid down in its draft that by 1980 at the latest the European Parliament has to work out a uniform electoral system. "Pending the entry into force of this uniform electoral system ... the electoral system shall fall within the competence of each Member State" (Article 7 of the convention). This clause set aside a difficult problem. Each country of the Community has quite different traditions of electoral laws and systems. In view of this, a ruling acceptable to all parties would have been beyond the power of the European Parliament, as well as (subsequently) the European Council and the conference of EC Foreign Ministers.

As far as the electoral system was concerned, the European Council concurred with the European Parliament. Consequently, the question of the *distribution of mandates* began to dominate the discussion. The course of negotiations during the conferences in 1975 and 1976 makes it evident that this question remained controversial until the end (July, 1976). However, the question could not be ignored without endangering the direct elections; it had to be solved one way or the other.

Suggestions of the European Parliament

In the first phase of debate (up to the beginning of April, 1976), various alternative models emerged. They all tried to solve in different ways the problem of proportionally adjusting the number of mandates to the population of a member country, and at the same time of adequately representing the smaller countries. The ultimate effect of the draft convention suggested by the European Parliament was to increase the importance of those countries with a large population (see Table 1). Naturally this increase was at the expense of the smaller countries (Luxembourg, Ireland, Denmark, Belgium and the Netherlands) and they rejected this suggestion from the start. Instead they supported an Irish alternative proposal with also envisaged a general increase in the number of mandates, but at the same time gave more weight to the smaller nations. France soon opposed this idea with a model which was even more favourable to the larger countries. Italy and Germany contributed further proposals in an endeavour to find a compromise (see Table 1).

France, Italy Fed. Rep. of Germany

No decision

The matter could not be solved through discussion, and during its meeting of April 1st/2nd, 1976, the European Council was unable to decide on any of the suggestions. In view of this dilemma, the French President suggested that the

26

Models for the Distribution of Seats in the European Parliament

Table 1

	Population in millions	Percentage	Mandates at present	Percentage	EP model	Percentage	Irish model	Percentage	French model	Percentage	Italian model	Percentage	German model	Percentage
Luxembourg	0,357	0,138	6	3,0	6	1,7	9	2,3	3	1,0	6	1,6	6	1,54
Ireland	3,086	1,196	10	5,0	13	3,6	18	4,7	6	2,1	16	4,4	20	5,12
Denmark	5,045	1,956	10	5,0	17	4,8	20	5,2	8	2,8	18	5,0	20	5,12
Belgium	9,772	3,790	14	7,1	23	6,5	26	6,8	13	4,6	22	6,1	28	7,19
Netherlands	13,545	5,253	14	7,1	27	7,6	30	7,8	17	6,0	26	7,2	28	7,19
Total of the smaller countries	31,805	12,335	54	27,2	86	25,2	103	26,8	47	16,5	88	24,3	102	26,16
France	52,507	20,364	36	18,2	65	18,3	68	17,7	55	19,4	64	17,7	72	18,46
Italy	55,413	21,491	36	18,2	66	18,6	69	18,0	58	20,4	67	18,6	72	18,46
Great Britain	56,056	21,741	36	18,2	67	18,9	70	18,2	59	20,8	68	18,8	72	18,46
Federal Republic of Germany	62,054	24,067	36	18,2	71	20,0	74	19,3	65	22,9	74	20,5	72	18,46
Total of the larger countries	226,030	87,664	144	72,8	269	74,8	281	73,2	237	83,5	273	75,6	288	73,84
Total of all countries	257,835	100,000	198	100,0	355	100,0	384	100,0	284	100,0	361	100,0	390	100,00

27

Table 2

Models Discussed by the Council

Member countries	Population in % of total population	EP suggestion (14.1.1975) a)		Irish suggestion (22.11.1975) b)		French suggestion (4.12.1975) c)		Italian suggestion (9.2.1976) d)		2nd French suggestion (1.4.1976) e)	
		Seats	Total of seats in %	Seats	Total of seats in %	Seats	Total of seats in %	Seats	Total of seats in %	Seats	Total of seats in %
Belgium	3,78	23	6,48	26	6,77	13	4,6	22	6,09	14	7,07
Denmark	1,95	17	4,79	20	5,21	8	2,8	18	4,99	10	5,05
Germany	24,18	71	20,0	74	19,28	65	22,9	74	20,50	36	18,18
France	20,31	65	18,31	68	17,7	55	19,36	64	17,73	36	18,18
Ireland	1,17	13	3,66	18	4,68	6	2,11	16	4,46	10	5,05
Italy	21,41	66	18,59	69	17,97	58	20,4	67	18,56	36	18,18
Luxembourg	0,14	6	1,69	9	2,34	3	1,05	6	1,6	6	3,03
Netherlands	5,22	27	7,61	30	7,81	17	5,98	26	7,20	14	7,07
United Kingdom	21,84	67	18,87	70	18,23	59	20,77	68	18,84	36	18,18
Total	100%	355	100%	384	100%	284	100%	361	100%	198	100%

Member countries	German suggestion (9.4.1976) f)		Belgian suggestion (3.5.1976) g)		Luxembourg suggestion (30.5.1976) h)		British suggestion (5.7.1976) i)		Resolution of July 12th 1976 k)	
	Seats	Total of seats in %	Seats	Total of seats in %	Seats	Total of seats in %	Seats	Total of seats in %	Seats	Total of seats in %
Belgium	28	7,18	22	5,49	22	6,01	22	5,64	24	5,85
Denmark	20	5,12	14	3,49	14	3,83	14	3,59	16	3,90
Germany	72	18,46	84	20,95	72	19,67	78	20,00	81	19,76
France	72	18,46	78	19,45	72	19,67	78	20,00	81	19,76
Ireland	20	5,12	13	3,24	14	3,83	14	3,59	15	3,65
Italy	72	18,46	79	19,70	72	19,67	78	20,00	81	19,76
Luxembourg	6	1,53	7	1,75	6	1,64	6	1,54	6	1,46
Netherlands	28	7,18	25	6,23	22	6,01	22	5,64	25	6,10
United Kingdom	72	18,46	79	19,70	72	19,67	78	20,00	81	19,76
Total	390	100%	401	100%	366	100%	390	100%	410	100%

number and distribution be left unaltered. In this way he meant to eliminate a controversial issue which had begun to seriously endanger the elections and their timing. It was then that "everyone finally realised that Parliament's suggestion of adjusting the population/mandate proportion had no hope of finding the approval of all countries concerned". (Bangemann/Bieber, *Direktwahl*, p. 42). As a result, the subsequent models proposed did not aim for proportional distribution; they were more or less based on given distribution ratios. This meant that the so-called four 'large' countries (Italy, France, Great Britain and Federal Republic of Germany) were always allowed the same number of seats — ignoring the significant differences in the total number of their population (see Table 2).

New distribution models

On July 13, 1976, the European Council finally reached agreement on this controversial matter. The agreement is based on the following seat distribution:

Decision of the European Council (July 1976) and of the Foreign Ministers (Sept. 1976)

Belgium	= 24	Italy	= 81
Denmark	= 16	Luxembourg	= 6
Germany	= 81	Netherlands	= 25
France	= 81	United Kingdom	= 81
Ireland	= 15		

This division was then incorporated into the "Act concerning the election of the representatives of the Assembly by direct universal suffrage" of September 20, 1976.

The distribution of seats proved an immensely controversial issue and dominated most discussions. Consequently other important questions — such as the dual mandate, date of the elections, incompatibility, scrutiny, immunity, and so on — received less attention. The following paragraphs deal with the most salient points which were laid down in the September 1976 Act.

3. Dual Mandate

Before the elections the holder of a seat in the European Parliament has to hold a mandate in a national Parliament. There are two reasons for this arrangement. Each national Parliament had selected a certain number of delegates from among its members to be sent to the European Parliament (This became void after the introduction of direct elections). In this way — and that is the second reason — the two parliamentary levels (national and European) were closely connected. Article 5 of the Act of September 1976 contains the following clause: "The office of representative in the Assembly shall be *compatible* with membership of the Parliament of a Member State". This meant that in future, the dual mandate would be neither compulsory or forbidden. The wording in Article 5 represented a compromise between two contrasting demands put forward in the course of discussion. One side wanted a joint national and European mandate declared incompatible; and the two parliamentary levels to be completely independent — analogous to the levels of federal and *Laender* affairs in the Federal Republic of Germany. The other side

Present arrangement

Article 5 — the problem of compatibility

29

(represented mainly by Denmark) demanded that such a dual mandate be strictly compulsory in order to ensure a close connection between the two parliamentary levels and to avoid conflicts between them. At times, the Danish Government even wanted to make its approval of the introduction of direct elections dependent on whether the dual mandate in its old form was to be compulsory in future as well.

The first demand has already been rejected by the European Parliament. As far as the second is concerned, practical as well as legal reasons demonstrate the problems of such rigid regulations on the dual mandate. The compromise formula of the Act can be regarded as a sensible settlement, if one is to adhere to the principle: "the delegates of the European Parliament are elected by direct universal suffrage".

Cooperation between national Parliaments and European Parliament Today one might be well advised to try and achieve cooperation between the European and the various national parliamentary levels in a different way. In West Germany some people hold the view that the directly elected delegates of the European Parliament should have the status of observers in the Bundestag — analogous to the status of the members of the Bundesrat in the Bundestag. This would, at least, create proper communication in one direction. However, one should not stop at that: "the right of presence and speech should not be restricted only to European delegates in the national Parliaments ... the directly elected (European) Parliament should also give representatives of national Parliaments the right to observe and speak". (Bangemann/Bieber, *Direktwahlen*, p. 60).

4. Parliamentary Term

Five-year term The draft convention of the European Parliament and the Act of the Foreign Ministers both mention (in Article 3) that the "representatives shall be elected for a term of five years". Compared with most national four-year systems (with the exception of Great Britain) this parliamentary term seems rather long.

Reasons However, in many cases national parliamentary experience has shown four years to be too short; a longer period would seem more appropriate for a modern parliament. Once the five-year period is introduced on a European level, it is perfectly possible that the national Parliaments will follow suit. In West Germany, for example, this idea has frequently been put forward.

5. Electoral System

As already stated, the draft convention of the European Parliament as well as the Act of the Foreign Ministers had set aside the difficult issue of the electoral system. A satisfactory solution on a European level could not be achieved — particularly in such a short space of time. Therefore the Act lays down the following conditions for the first direct elections: "Pending the entry into force of a uniform electoral procedure (for which, according to Article 7, Paragraph 1, the Assembly has to draw up a proposal — Th.St) and subject to the other provisions of this Act, the electoral procedure shall be governed in each Member State by its national provisions". Insofar, the Act of 1976 deviated considerably from Article 138 of the EEC treaty, which read: "The Assembly shall draw up proposals for elections by direct universal suffrage in accordance with a uniform procedure in all Member States". It has already been mentioned that at present an agreement on a uniform electoral system for the first direct elections could not be achieved. Therefore national electoral laws had to be adopted; but arguably the first directly elected European Parliament will, by its democratic nature, create and put into force a uniform electoral law for the Community.

National provisions

What does this entail for the individual member countries? Two things have to be mentioned: first, the Parliaments of the individual countries have to approve the "Act" which is jointly resolved; second, the various countries have to pass national legislation relating to the actual holding of the elections. These executive laws must focus on two points in particular: the national electoral systems for the direct elections; and the legal status of the delegates in the European Parliament (this point is not comprehensively dealt with in the "Act"). As far as this book is concerned, the first point is both important and interesting; consequently it will be dealt with in some detail. It is safe to assume that the national laws which are to be created for the holding of the first direct elections are largely a copy of the electoral system and traditional electoral customs of each individual EC country. It has to be noted that there is a significant variance in this respect. On the one hand, there are a number of countries which traditionally use *proportional representation:* for example, in Italy, the Netherlands, Belgium, Luxembourg and Denmark. On the other hand, there are two countries which use different forms of *majority government:* France uses the absolute or *Romance* form, Great Britain uses the *relative* form. Finally, West Germany uses a peculiar *mixed system* which combines elements of proportional representation with those of majority representation; the system also includes a "minimum level" of 5%.

National electoral systems of the EC countries

The electoral laws for the first European elections can be summarised as follows:

National electoral laws for the European elections

(1) *Belgium:* The electoral law for the European direct elections was passed on October 4, 1977. Of the 24 Belgian delegates in the European Parliament, 13 are to represent the Flemish population and 11 the Walloon. For the purpose of the elections, Belgium was split in three constituencies: Flanders, Walloony and Brussels (bilingual). The parties, which are also divided by language, draw up their lists for each constituency.

(2) *Denmark:* The European electoral law was passed on December 2, 1977. The 16 Danish delegates (one of whom will represent Greenland) were elected by proportionate vote on the basis of national lists.

(3) *France:* The French National Assembly passed the electoral law in June 1977. The French electoral system is absolute majority vote. However, for the purpose of the European elections, a proportional system with national lists was chosen. Those lists which receive less than 5% of the votes cast will not be taken into account.

(4) *Ireland:* Ireland adopted the proportional system with the electorate divided into four constituencies.

(5) *Italy:* In Italy a system of proportional representation was used.

(6) *Luxembourg:* Similarly Luxembourg, as in national parliamentary elections,

31

adopted a proportional system to elect the 6 delegates. It represented one constituency in the European Parliament.

(7) *The Netherlands:* The Government crisis of 1977 delayed the passing of an electoral law for the European elections in the Netherlands. However, the parliamentary parties had no fundamental disagreements on the mode of the election of the 25 Dutch delegates: they were elected according to the proportional system from national lists.

(8) *United Kingdom:* The electoral system proved a particularly controversial point in the United Kingdom. The Liberals and the Labour Government, for example, favoured the proportional system (which is unknown in the United Kingdom except in Northern Ireland); they submitted a corresponding bill. Other groups – which finally gained the majority – supported the traditional relative majority vote. Early in 1978, the decision was taken in favour of the latter method. This solution is complicated and time-consuming as Great Britain, which is normally divided into 630 constituencies, had to be split into 81 constituencies for the European elections (the number of seats allocated to Great Britain in the European Parliament). This was one of the reasons why Britain asked for a one-year postponement in the elections.

**Federal Republic
of Germany**
(9) *Federal Republic of Germany:* The Bundestag passed the electoral law for the European elections in April 1978. For a long time, two different bills had been considered. That of the Federal Government (that is, the Government coalition) envisaged a new proportional system from *federal lists* with only one vote per voter. The opposition parties envisaged a system analogous to the federal electoral system; this means half of the delegates to the European Parliament are to be elected directly in constituencies, the other half from lists in the various "Laender". The law which was finally passed is a compromise, Article 2, paragraph 1 reads: "The election shall follow the principles of proportional representation with election proposals based on lists of candidates. Such lists may be drawn up for one *Land* or there may be a common list of all the *Laender*. Each voter shall have one vote". In choosing this system the Federal Republic, too, had decided on a system of pure proportional representation. However, the fact that *federal lists* as well as *"Laender" lists* were permitted seemed strange and gave rise to objections. Berlin had to be covered by special provisions. Article 29 of the electoral law states that "with regard to the existing rights and responsibilities of France, the United Kingdom of Great Britain and Northern Ireland and the United States of America, provisions shall apply to Berlin until further notice: Three Members out of the total number of Members allotted to the Federal Republic of Germany shall be elected in the Land of Berlin, subject to the following provisions: 1. The Berlin Chamber of Deputies shall elect the Members and a sufficient number of substitutes on the basis of the composition of the Chamber of Deputies at the time of the election to the European Parliament. The political groups represented in the Chamber of Deputies at this time shall draw up corresponding lists of candidates".

Summary
This summary of electoral legislation in the nine EC countries confirms the earlier assumption that as a rule the traditionally established electoral systems were

32

maintained, with minor modifications. Only France and the Federal Republic of Germany introduced significant changes.

The predominance of the proportional system is clear, and this will undoubtedly influence the European Parliament's choice of uniform electoral system. Thus, one may assume that Great Britain will adopt the system of proportional representation; but, perhaps, only for elections to the European Parliament.

6. Separation of Powers

Article 6 of the draft convention of the European Parliament as well as of the Act of the Foreign Ministers deals with the question of incompatibility of a mandate in the European Parliament and certain other political offices. The relevant regulations have two objectives. First, they try to avoid a nexus of national Governments and the European Parliament by declaring membership in the European Parliament incompatible with membership of the Government of a member country. Second, they try to prevent connections between the European Parliament and other institutions of the European Community (Commission, Court of Justice, Court of Audit, etc.). Under Article 5, membership of the European Parliament and membership of a national Parliament remain acceptable. These regulations on incompatibility are not mere technicalities; they relate ultimately to the form of the *political system*. This question which is emerging in the Community is considered in the following section.

Article 6

Repercussions on the political system

VI. Idea of a European Political System

1. Introduction

It is interesting to pose the question of whether the introduction of direct elections to the European Parliament forms an integral part of an understandable conception of a European political system; or whether it is no more than a "red herring" (as it has been called). What is meant by the latter suggestion? Perhaps, in the sense of the "Ten sceptical theses" by M. Pöhle which allege among other things that the direct elections distract from "the call for genuine, if only partial legislative powers for the European Parliament"; "from the continual slippage in time-schedules within the Community; and further "from the increasing degeneration of the Commission into the main secretariate of the Council". Finally the elections distract "from the continuing lack of any supervision of the main legislative body of the Community, the Council". The writer of these theses furthermore points out that the direct elections were used by some Governments "as a weapon in the interstate political debate". (In: *Zeitschrift fur Parlamentsfragen*, 1976, p. 222 ff). Against this one might point out that political actions are only very rarely to be explained by a single motive. Furthermore – and this is even more important – one has to differentiate between trigger motives and final objectives. The same aim may stem from widely differing causes; but this need not have any detrimental effect.

General objections

Secondly, even if different motivations led the various EC countries to agree to the direct elections, this does not prevent the elections from forming part of a proper evolution of a new political order. In any case, one cannot isolate the election issue from its structural and historic context, if one is to adequately consider and understand it.

I suggest the question is best answered in two ways. First, by outlining the structural ideas which have been inherent in the concept of the European Community and its institutions from the outset. Second, by considering the conceptions of a European political order which have been most predominant in this recent phase of European integration.

2. Initial Ideas of a European Political System

It is not by chance that the institutional framework has been maintained since the foundation of the first European Community — the European Coal and Steel Community, and which culminated in the creation of the EEC and Euratom.

This model contains the same political institutions in an identical arrangement and distribution of power. Consequently, it was not difficult to merge the Communities into a single political system in 1967. This system consists of the Commission, the Council, the Assembly of the Court of Justice. The Commission forms the body of communal interests. The Council has two functions: it is a federal body which establishes a balance between the individual interests of the member countries and common interests; it is also the major legislative body of the Community. The Assembly represents all nations that are united by the Community. The Court of Justice ensures that newly-created European law is interpreted in a uniform way.

If one takes a closer look at the original arrangement and distribution of responsibilities and powers, one realises that the European system was not initially a parliamentary system as we know it. The Assembly in particular is still too weak; it lacks a genuinely democratic foundation, and consequently authority, with regard to the other insitutions of the Community, and the Council of Ministers in particular.

However, the original model has undergone a certain evolution in the course of the first years of European communal development; and this is true also of individuals' self-awareness. In the early sixties, the Commission and (following its initiative) the Assembly made great efforts to create a federal parliamentary system of government. In such a system, the Commission — at that time under the dynamic leadership of W. Hallstein — sought recognition as the "European Government". The Assembly, which at a very early stage saw itself as a "European Parliament", modelled itself on the national Parliaments of parliamentary government systems. On the basis of the Rome treaties, the Assembly aimed as early as 1960 at a democratization by means of direct elections and an extension of its limited powers to the rights of a "classic" Parliament. The efforts of the Commission and Assembly were inevitably at the expense of the Council of Ministers. A systematic transformation of the system into a genuine parliamentary system would necessarily have reduced the functions of the Council to those of a federal body like the West German "Bundesrat". It is well known that this development towards a federal parliamentary system was halted in the mid-sixties by the intervention of General de Gaulle. The important Luxembourg resolutions (January 1966) caused a severe setback by abandoning the (already established) majority principle and returning to the principle of unanimity. At the same time, they represented a clean break with the previously dominant structural conception – affecting the Commission more severely than the Parliament. W. Hallstein was forced to resign; and after him "the Commission reverted to a glorified secretariate of the Council" (Neunreither). The ideal of a European parliamentary government system became an illusion. The return to the principle of unanimity in the Council resulted in another backward move: the federal body of the Community which had sought a balance between the national interest and the communal interest became a conference of Governments where the individual interests of member countries dominated. The era after de Gaulle did not immediately bring about a significant change in favour of earlier attitudes. It was only the profound experiences of the crises in the early seventies which made the leading politicians of the Community alter their opinions on political conceptions.

Intervention of de Gaulle

Return to the unanimity principle

3. Recent Ideas of a European Political System

The crisis, stagnation and disintegration of the European Community in the early seventies, which was brought about by problems of world economy and monetary policies, have shown that the European Community – in its present state and with its present institutions – was structurally unable to withstand extensive economic and political stress.

New approaches after the crisis

Experiences of this kind soon made it obvious that new political initiatives were necessary to rectify the defects in the conception of European political structure. In 1973 Ralf Dahrendorf submitted a "diagnosis and treatment" for the present European situation in his "Plea for a European Union". He arrived at the conclusion: "Europe needs a constitution for democrats". (p. 209 ff).

Recent initiatives for the European direct elections have to be viewed in this light. I suggest it is dangerous, therefore, to write-off the elections as a "red herring" or even as a diversion; they can be interpreted as a significant element in a comprehensive strategy to eliminate the structural defects and retrogressive steps taken in the European Community in recent years. In comparison with the earlier model of a European political framework, these conceptions contain a stronger emphasis on the Parliament and the democratic dimensions of the Community. The "first Europe" – as R. Dahrendorf calls it – was essentially based on the interplay of Commission and Council; with a distinct lack of democracy. Events have shown that the European Community and its further development cannot be left to the technocrats and the Government representatives in the Commission and the Council of Ministers alone.

Necessity for democratic reform

A democratization process must include direct elections and an extension of the powers of the European Parliament.

The term "European Union" represents this new or renewed conception of a European political structure. The European summit conferences in 1972 and 1974 made this once more the guiding principle of European politics. In his (already quoted) "Report to the European Council" (Dec. 1976), the Belgian Minister President Leo Tindemans tried to define the various components of this conception:

1. European Union implies that we present a united front to the outside world. We must tend to act in common in all the main fields of our external relations whether in foreign policy, security, economic relations or development aid. Our action is aimed at defending our interests but also at using our collective strength in support of law and justice in world discussions.

2. European Union recognises the interdependence of the economic prosperity of our States and accepts the consequences of this: a common economic and monetary policy to manage this prosperity, common policies in the industrial and agricultural sectors and on energy and research to safeguard the future.

3. European Union requires the solidarity of our peoples to be effective and adequate. Regional policy will correct inequalities in development and counteract the centralising effects of industrial societies. Social action will mitigate inequalities of income and encourage society to organise itself in a fairer and more humane fashion.

4. European Union makes itself felt in people's daily lives. It helps to protect their rights and to improve their life style.

5. In order to achieve these tasks European Union is given institutions with the necessary powers to determine a common, coherent and all-inclusive political view, the efficiency needed for action, the legitimacy needed for democratic control. The principle of the equality of all our States continues to be respected within the Union by each State's right to participate in political decision making.

6. Like the Community whose objectives it pursues and whose attainments it protects, European Union will be built gradually. So as to restart the construction of Europe straight away and increase its credibility, its initial basis is the political commitment of the States to carry out in different fields specific actions selected according to their importance and the chances of success.

Tindemans states: "This implies that the transfer of powers to common bodies is unavoidable". Not least for this reason must the European institutions be strengthened and expanded, as described in Chapter V of the Tindemans report. Tindemans, as well as Hallstein and Dahrendorf, firmly believes that the European Union can and must be formed on the institutional basis which has already been accepted by the member countries through existing treaties. A strengthening of the institutional mechanism will become all the more important as the tasks the institutions have to deal with become more complex. "The European Community integrated the markets. The European Union has to integrate the policies of the member countries. The qualitative change necessitated by this development is closely connected with the decision process, that is with the institutions". The direct elections (aimed at creating a democratization of the Union) as well as the extension of the powers of the European Parliament have to be viewed in this context.

VII. The Role of the Political Parties

1. Introduction

The main purpose of this book is to analyse the state of national party systems and the existing transnational party connections in the context of the European direct elections. National experience shows that in today's complex societies the democratic process of political thought and education is inconceivable without the contribution of political parties. This holds true on a transnational level as well (Europe).

The following two parts of the book deal with the national party systems and with the existing party connections in Europe. First, however, one has to arrive at a conclusive answer to the question as to the status and functions which the political parties have so far been "officially" allocated on a European level. *Two levels* are distinguishable and dealt with separately: the *European Parliament* and the *European direct elections.*

Status and functions of the parties in Europe

2. The Parties in the European Parliament

The third part of this book will be devoted to a detailed examination of the roles which the political parties play in the European Parliament. First, one has to recognise that the delegates to the European Parliament prior to direct elections were sent by the national Parliaments on a proportional basis. Therefore the members of the European Parliament belonged to national parties. These delegates, however, did not form national delegations. Parliamentary groups encompassing identical or similar political parties of different countries were formed. The European Parliament developed six such groups. The rules of procedure of the European Parliament contained legal regulations on the formation, status and rights of these parliamentary groups. One has to realise that these parliamentary groups (and through them the national parties involved) make an essential contribution to the functioning of the European Parliament; so that the political parties in the form of transnational parliamentary groups in the European Parliament were legally recognised, and of practical importance prior to direct elections.

a) In the European Parliament

Political parliamentary groups

3. The Parties and the European Direct Elections

In contrast to the legal determination of status of the political parties in the transnational parliamentary groups of the European Parliament, the parties were not specifically mentioned in the legislation regulating the European direct elections. For example, neither the term "political party" nor the concept is contained in the "Act" which was signed by the Foreign Ministers in September 1976. This may be partly due to the fact that the actual electoral procedure — as explained above — has not yet been uniformly determined for the European Community as a whole, but was decided by member countries statutes.

b) With regard to the European direct elections

In one important passage on the distribution of seats, the Patijn report refers indirectly to the political parties by stating: "All essential *political forces* of a country have to be represented in the European Parliament". The term "political forces" must be understood as including political parties.

Recognition of the parties

A passage like this makes it clear that the European Parliament and also the European Council (of the heads of state and Government leaders), which largely accepted the wording of the Parliament's draft convention, accept the reality of political parties and their decisive importance for a transnational development of political thinking.

It is probable that the significant role of the political parties in Europe will have consequences for the future. Following the direct elections to the European Parliament the role of the parties will become more firmly defined; and tendencies towards the creation of genuine European parties may become stronger and better established (this will be discussed in detail), while norms of constitutional law for parties, their organisation and activity may be issued as a kind of "European party law", valid in the European Community. As regards the European Parliament, the parliamentary and legal institutionalisation of political parties in the form of transnational parliamentary groups has already occurred. This could serve as a model after the direct elections; and the emerging European parties could become constitutionalised.

Situation at present

At present, the political parties are neither *legally* nor *practically* fully established on the European level. It is of supreme importance for the successful outcome of the European direct elections and for the intended democratisation of the European Parliament — and with it the European Community as a whole — that the political parties in Europe develop into genuine functional *European* parties (within as well as outside Parliament). The two following chapters will examine what stage this development has reached today and the extent to which the realisation of a political "European Union" may be expected.

Part II
Analysis of National Party Systems

I. Introduction

It has already been argued earlier that so far no genuine European parties, and consequently no functioning European party system exists. The European elections really required such a system; but the fact is that at present there are only national parties and party systems in Europe, and that only small steps towards transnational party connections can be detected.

Consequently, a study of the European party situation at this time must necessarily deal with the *national* sector; that is existing national parties and party systems. First, their idiosyncratic structures have to be examined; it will then be possible to arrive at a realistic evaluation of the chances of development into integrated European parties — such parties as are necessary for the proper expression of political opinion in direct European elections. The questions asked and considered in this second part concentrate on this theme. **National parties and party systems**

(1) Firstly, *the national party systems* in Western Europe are considered. For reasons still to be discussed, not only the EC countries, but also a number of the other Western (that is, non-Socialist) countries of Europe will be examined.

(2) Apart from this empirical consideration *the European party systems will be compared structurally*. The intention is to find similarities and conformities, but also differences, in the structure of national party systems. This sytematic comparison yields important insights into possible transnational co-operation between the national parties and into the probable outlines and structure of a future European party system.

(3) Both procedures — the consideration of empirical facts as well as the systematic comparison of structures — require a *theoretical framework*. Thus the second part of the book is divided as follows:

> II.   Theoretical framework
> III. Consideration of national party systems
> IV.   Structural comparison of national party systems
>   in Europe.

II. Theoretical Framework

1. The Study of Political Parties

In political science and sociology, along with historical science, the phenomenon of   **Modern research**

39

political parties has always been of keen interest. Since M. Ostrogorski, M. Weber and R. Michels, this area has become one of the focal points of research in these studies. As a consequence, the concept of "party" — despite its extensive empirical diversity and historical changes — is one of the most thoroughly analysed of fields. However, studies have not been exhaustive. Particularly recently, certain moves have been made towards a new orientation in research which Klaus von Beyme sums up as follows: "Recent party research increasingly turns away from the analysis of individual parties and their organisational structure in order to explore instead the interdependencies of individual parties in the context of a *party system*[1]". This change in perspective is mainly based on the following premise. While it is true that the individual political party is a more or less independent agent in the political process of its country, it also interacts with all the other parties in the same political system in an interdependent way. This is true of its actions, its organisational structure and its declared objectives. The way it interacts is, of course, largely dependent on the social, economic and political conditions in the society of the given country. The complexity of the situation suggests that it is inadequate to

study an individual party in isolation, that is, without considering its position and role within this framework. It is necessary to regard the various parties as a complex *unit* and to treat them as such, taking into account the social, economic and political conditions. This unit has to be considered as a frame of reference, even if only a single party or specific structural feature of a party system is to be examined. The term "party system" is used to designate the unit. "Party system" means more than just a quantitative statement on the number of parties that are active in a political system, as the current terms of "one-party system", "two-party system", and "multi-party system" may suggest.

The term denotes "the whole of all regular interaction between parties in a political system[2]". For such a definition to be used as a basis for practical research, its most important elements have to be made clear. In the following paragraphs I attempt to do this briefly; they deal with the following: 2) The party as a concept; 3) The framework of conditions in the political and social system; and 4) Party interactions.

2. The Party as a Concept

a) Definitions

The definition of the term "party system" makes it clear that the political parties are the decisive subjects or agents within party systems. They effect the various interactions, the whole of which constitutes the party system: a party system is not possible without parties.

However, what does the term "party" mean? Contemporary social science offers a multitude of definitions, which often refer to the "classic" definition by Max Weber, one of the important founder-fathers of political sociology, who defined the political phenomenon of the "party" as follows: "Societies which are based on (formally) free canvassing and which have the objective of bestowing power within

40

the association on their leaders and thereby giving their active members the opportunity of attaining material or idealistic goals or personal advantages (or both) are to be called parties[3]".

This statement has influenced many subsequent definitions — for example, O.K. Flechtheim's: "A party is a well-knit campaigning organisation, based on more or less free canvassing. Within a political body (state, community, and so on) it possesses or seeks to possess sufficient power by occupying positions in the governing body in order to realise its idealistic and/or material aims[4]".

O.K. Flechtheim

As far as the functions and structural features of political parties are concerned, the following basic differences to other political organisations or associations may be found:

Party functions

— "Readiness to occupy a leading position in the governing body (in contrast to representative groups),

— striving for the realisation of self-set, general political objectives which are not shared by all and are canvassed among the population (in contrast to the governing body itself),

— a permanent organisation (in contrast to temporary political movements or loose ad hoc groupings of politicians[5])"

b) Typologies

The criteria mentioned in the definitions above make it easy to distinguish political parties from other social configurations (social organisations in particular). This does not mean to say that empirically one party always looks exactly like another. In reality, a whole number of different forms exist. Political study has tried from the start to order and systematically classify them. This is usually done by grouping similar forms together and developing corresponding typologies or classifications. However, one has to be aware of the basic fact that the resulting individual types or classes only represent abstract (ancillary) constructions. They facilitate recognition by grouping a variety of types; but they do not occur in practice.

Empirical variety

Since Max Weber, party research has employed two different kinds of typologies which ultimately complement each other in the research process: *typologies of development* and *typologies of structure*. This duality corresponds to the study of (diachronic) historic processes of development and of (synchronic) present and contemporary structures in scientific research.

(1) Typologies of development

Typologies of development interpret forms in which political parties have presented themselves in the course of historical development as a *sequence* or *series* of different types. M. Weber, for example, set up such a typology of development on the basis of historical facts on the party up to the 1st World War which were available to him. It contains three types of parties: (1) parties with a charismatic leader, (2) parties of the upper and professional classes, (3) (bureaucratised and organised)

M. Weber

S. Neumann

mass parties. M. Weber's typology of development was later continued by other party researchers on the basis of new empirical evidence from 1914 onwards. S. Neumann, for example, copied Weber's typology in his book "The Parties of the Weimar Republic" (1932)[6] which is still of importance for general party research. Neumann redefined and extended the typology, because at that time the social structure and the intellectual/political nature of the parties had been severely affected by the political and social consequences of the 1st World War. In particular

"Representation party"

the older type of liberal "representation party" was being replaced by the new type of "integration party" which can be regarded as a further development of the bureaucratised mass party already recognised by Weber. Neumann uses the term "integration party" because of the demand that this type of party makes on human beings: "It (the integration party) fundamentally demands involvement of the person as a whole in the political organisation, not by means of permanent membership . . . but by affecting every sphere of that person's life[7]".

"Integration party"

It has proved especially important for the modern development of parties that Neumann distinguishes between two variants: the 'democratic' and the 'absolutist' integration party. While he considers the democratic variant as a kind of transitory type, he sees the absolutist variant of the integration party as having the most potential. At that time (1932!) Facism, Bolshevism and National Socialism were its most vigorous and effective representatives. These absolutist integration parties differ fundamentally from the democratic variant because of their "apparent personal leadership, hierarchical structure, rigid and comprehensive organisation in more or less military forms with a tendency towards exclusiveness and recruitment only from their own youth organisations". According to Neumann, they also show "a measure of democracy which is indispensable if one wants to politically mobilise the masses; but they have distinct dictatorial features". Acclamation became almost the only form of confirming personal decisions[8]. Later — particularly after the 2nd World War — this absolutist variant which has left its stamp on the history of the 20th century was also called 'totalitarian'.

O. Kirchheimer

After the 2nd World War, a further development of the parties took place in the Western countries. O. Kirchheimer has made this the subject of several comparative studies, among them in his essay on "The Change of the Western European Party Systems" (1965)[9]. Kirchheimer states that the old liberal or representation party is about to disappear — "the *bourgeois* party of the old style with its individual representation has now become the exception[10].". On critical examination, the mass integration party of the time between the wars achieved a *political mobilisation* of the masses rather than their political *integration*. ("But political mobilisation is not identical with political integration; integration presupposes that a given society is prepared to acknowledge fully and without reservation the political status of its citizens as partners. Whatever followed the integration into mass parties on a class level, depended on the attitude of the other powers in a given political system. In some cases this attitude proved so negative that it led to a delay of integration into the political system or to its dissolution[11]".) In the period since the end of the 2nd World War, Kirchheimer notices the *development* of the mass integration party,

42

"which was born at a time of acute class differences and obvious denominational structures, to a *catch-all party*, to a genuine *people's party*[12]". According to Kirchheimer, this new and soon widespread party type is distinguished from the traditional class party by the following characteristics: "It (the people's party) no longer attempts to incorporate the masses intellectually and morally, but concentrates to a greater extent on the voters. It gives up a deep ideological entrenchment in return for a broader appeal and quicker success in an election. This perspective of a more limited political task and immediate electoral success differs fundamentally from the earlier comprehensive objectives. Nowadays one considers the earlier aims as obstructive to success, as they deter potential voters[13]".

People's party

According to Kirchheimer, this development has occurred in different phases. The present (final) stage is one "in which the parties try to reach all parts of the population[14]." It may be noted that the transformation to "catch-all" parties is a "phenomenon resulting from *competition*. A party tends to copy the successful style of its opponents, because it hopes to do well in the elections or because it is afraid of losing votes.[15]"

Present situation

(2) Typologies of Structure

The static typologies of structure try to establish a logical order in the present multitude of political parties. They do this means of classification. However, as already pointed out, these typologies always represent *abstract constructions* which do not correspond directly to a single real phenomenon and which were created by researchers for purposes of systematisation. Consequently, various typologies are possible, in each case dependent on the principles that dominated their creation. *Three* points of view are predominant in relevant literature on political science; they can be combined with each other to form complex models. They are: (a) the *objectives* of the parties, (b) the *organisational structure* and (c) the *functions* of parties in the political and social system; these are the most important criteria of differentiation for the composition of a party typology.

(a) Objectives

The objectives of political parties are usually expressed in manifestos or programme declarations. Contemporary parties can be grouped into those which attach considerable importance to their programme (often ideological, but also pragmatic/political) objectives (such as the Continental European parties), and those that attach little or no importance to them (such as the parties in the USA). The first group can in turn be subdivided according to the quality of their programme or ideological objectives. One way of doing this is by using the well-known "right-left scheme" of political ideologies which contains two extremes: progressive or revolutionary positions which transcend the system on the one hand; reactionary or fascist positions which are equally destructive on the other. In between these extremes there is room for a whole range of different Socialist, Social-Democrat,

Manifesto

Ideological spectrum

43

Liberal, Christian-Democrat and Conservative positions which fundamentally conform with the system.

(b) Organisational Structures

Member party or voter party

The organisational structures of parties offer another important area of differentiation. Parties are clearly different in their number of members; some parties are more of a member party than a voter party; parties have a greater or lesser hold on their members (cf. the integration party in the sense of S. Neumann); the organisation of a party may be more centralised or more federal; the members may have little or considerable say within the party; the party body may be more or less bureaucratic. As far as the characterisation of political parties as a whole is concerned, these various aspects of organisational structure have to be combined to form an overall picture which will then determine to which organisational type a given party belongs.

(c) Functions

Class parties and representative parties

State parties and Government parties

Finally, political parties can be grouped according to the different functions they perform in their social and political system. As regards the relationship of party to social system (society), one can distinguish between *representative parties* (which mainly seek to represent *one* particular group interest), *class parties* (which represent the interests of a certain social class), and *interest integration parties* (which as people's parties seek to integrate as many "currents" of interest as possible). The parties' different attitudes towards the political system (state) also provides criteria for their classification. For example, one can distinguish between: "unity parties" — such as the Soviet Communist Party — which alone represent and control, embracing state and society; "state parties"; permanent "Government parties"; parties which consistently support the Government on the basis of a favourable key position in the party system; (usually smaller) parties which are continuously or frequently needed to form a Government; permanent or temporary system opposition parties; opposition parties which are fundamentally critical of the system; and smaller outsider parties at the edges of the party-political spectrum[16]

3. The Framework of Social and Political Conditions

The framework of social and political conditions forms the second of the two elements that constitute a party system, and need to be closely examined. The nature of these conditions determines the scope of activity and development of the political parties, and ultimately the form in which they present themselves.

a) Social Conditions

Let us first consider briefly the social conditions of a party system: we can distinguish between *socio-structural, economic* and *cultural conditions.*

(1) Socio-Structural Conditions

It is generally accepted that the structure of a given society (for example that of West Germany), its social differentiation and strata, and the existence of social classes and groups (as well as their social interactions) exercises lasting influence on the way in which political parties present themselves and act. The party system will, of necessity, mirror the class structure of a society if it has a pronounced class nature. This was, for example, typical of the Western European countries towards the end of the 19th century. Class parties with relatively unbridgeable class differences will be opposed in a more or less hostile way; the forms of interaction between parties will be strongly determined by the socio-structural conditions. The situation is different in a so-called egalitarian industrial or mass society of the 20th century with its "smoothed away" class differences and high (vertical and horizontal) mobility. In such a society the political parties will lose their rigid class attachment and come closer in form to a people's party.

In so-called segmented societies, the political parties will often only be able to represent certain parts of the population and not the society as a whole. This is typical of most of the developing countries of today which comprise loosely integrated groupings of regional, ethnic, linguistic and religious entities (tribes, etc.).

Social structures:

Classes

Strata

Ethinic aspects

(2) Economic Conditions

Similarly, economic structures affect the social and, consequently, the party-political differentiation of a country. The emergence of specific Labour parties as the political representation of the working class is a characteristic feature of almost all Western industrial societies (with the important exception of the USA). This development started in the third part of the 19th century and has markedly influenced political activity in these countries (for example, the development of German social democracy before the 1st World War and parallel to that the development of the British Labour Party). Conditions in the economic sector may vary considerably according to the state of development or the structure of an economic system: it may be more industrial, more agrarian, more capitalist or more socialist. The influence of these economic interest groupings will have differing consequences for the party system, its form and its practical political role.

Industry and workers

(3) Cultural Conditions

The cultural differentiation of a society also affects the party system and its inner structure. In societies with marked denominational contrasts, for example, this will often result in the emergence of specific denominational parties (as in the Netherlands). For many societies — in particular Southern Europe and Latin America — the contrast between Liberal/laicist/anti-clerical on the one hand, and Conservative/

Denominations

45

Christian/Catholic on the other, has become one of the decisive reasons for party-political differentiation since the early 19th century. This contrast is also responsible for the strong ideological orientation of the corresponding parties in these countries. In other countries — such as the USA — religious differentiation has not resulted in the formation of denominational parties. The reason for this is that an early public

Political ideologies

separation between state and church was achieved. Since the French Revolution (1789), the ideological contrasts between Liberalism and Conservatism have played a decisive part in the formation of parties in all Western societies. Later they were joined by other, often extreme ideological positions (such as radicalism, socialism, communism) and the well-known right-left concept of ideologically based party differentiation came into being. In the 19th century, the question of nationalism versus internationalism frequently influenced the formation and objectives of parties. These few examples sugguest that in the cultural sector there have been varied and mostly historical influences on party forms. By cultural sector we understand in particular the whole of the ideological systems (ideologies), attitudes and values that are represented in a given society. This sector clearly reveals most parties' commitment to tradition, as it is still mirrored today in party ideologies and manifestos.

b) Political Conditions

The political conditions of a party system are no less important than the social, economic and cultural ones. One can distinguish between factual and normative conditions on the one hand, and general and specific conditions on the other.

(1) Factual Political Conditions

Historical facts

The political structures that have developed through history have to be considered as factual political conditions. In each country, they assume an individual form. Their idiosyncracies have a lasting effect on the formation of the relevant party system: consequences which are still noticeable today. A comparison between political development in Great Britain and Germany may corroborate this point. A central political system with strong people's participation in Parliament developed relatively early in Great Britain; consequently, signs of the formation of a two-party system already appeared in the 17th and 18th centuries. By contrast, corresponding developments in Germany took place towards the end of the 19th century, that is about 200 years later. The formation of a national, central political system had been delayed that long, for political rule in the individual German territorial states had been of an autocratic or absolutist nature and largely prevented popular involvement in political decisions and the formation of political parties.

Apart from these historical facts, the contemporary political situations and structures — particularly in domestic matters — form a set of factual conditions which affect the party system through the distribution of power.

46

(2) Normative Political Conditions

Normative political conditions have an equal effect on parties and their systems of interaction; these conditions may be of a general or of a specific kind.

Among the *general* normative conditions of a political system the constitution is most important: it comprises the constitutional norms and regulations which define the political basic rights (freedom of association, coalition, assembly, opinion, and so on) on the one hand, and the structure of the political system (for example, parliamentary or presidential) on the other. By so doing, it at the same time largely determines the political parties' scope of activity and interaction. Together with these general normative determinants of the constitutional code, there are frequently additional *specific* norms which directly or indirectly influence the party system. For example, specific articles of the West German constitution define the status of political parties (Articles 21 and 38). Such articles, which are also to be found in valid Italian and French constitutional law under similar wording, contain obvious *privileges* for political parties as opposed to other political associations (interest groups) or groups (civil initiatives). On the other hand, the articles also contain special *conditions* which can be enforced by means of sanctions (or by prohibition if the worst comes to the worst). They can also be complemented by special party laws — such as the German federal party law of 1967 which contains further directives on parties (for example, their financing).

Constitution

Party law

Finally, the electoral system can be considered as a specific normative condition which indirectly, but lastingly, affects the party system in every political facet. It influences political thinking in all democracies, and it is a well-known fact that the different electoral systems — proportional representation, and the various majority vote configurations — have quantitative as well as qualitative effects on party systems.

Electoral system

4. Party Interactions

The social and political conditions outlined above form the framework for the interactions of parties in a given political environment which then constitute a party system. Conversely, the interactions in turn modify the conditions. It is in such a context that the parties can carry out their basic functions which were mentioned earlier: striving for a position of power in the Government body and the realisation of ideological and pragmatic objectives. In the pursuit of these aims, the political parties become entangled with each other and with the social and political system. They find themselves caught in a web of interrelations which may be determined by fundamentally different principles. The structural principles that are most important for party interactions are the following: (1) *the principle of competition*, (2) *the principle of concordance* and (3) *the principle of monopoly*. In considering these factors, it is necessary to distinguish between *horizontal* (that is, between parties) and *vertical* (that is, between parties and the social/political system) party interactions.

Principles of interaction

47

a) Horizontal Interactions

Configurations

According to the structural principles mentioned above, fundamentally different *configurations* between the parties of a political system may arise in individual party systems. Three main patterns of party configurations in a party system can be distinguished:

- *a system of competition*
- *a system of concordance*
- *a system of monopoly*

It is evident that these categories are merely *general terms*, and that in political reality each of these three types has its different variants.

Competition

Competition, for example, can occur in a party system in its pure form: all parties compete with each other. Competition may also only be partial: several parties may form a coalition which — for a certain period at least — puts an end to the rivalry among these groups; this is usually replaced by more intense competition with other parties which may possibly have formed a coalition as well. The degree of competition may be quite varied: it may go to the roots of the way parties see themselves as political bodies (cf. the slogan "Freedom or Socialism") so that parties are opposed in a "hostile" way. The competition may equally well be based on a fundamental consensus, and only relate to certain controversial political areas.

Pluralism

In other words, the political and social *pluralism*, which lies at the base of such a competitive system between political parties, may take an *extreme* or a *moderate* form and determine party interactions accordingly.

It is an important and typical feature of all systems of competition that decisions are made according to the *majority principle*. For example, one would decide on the formation of a Government and subsequently on Government and legislative programmes, on the basis of the distribution of seats in Parliament.

Concordance

By contrast, it is characteristic of the rate *system of concordance* that decisions are made not according to the majority principle, but according to the principle of "amicable agreement" (*amicabilis compositio*[19]). This procedure was traditionally used in Switzerland due to particular socio-cultural and ethnic-linguistic factors.

In other European (Austria, Netherland, Belgium) and non-European (Lebanon until recently) countries, too, it has often proved the only practicable way of decision-making. It has also contributed to the so-called "cooperative settlement of conflicts" which has particularly lasting consequences for the interactions in a party system.

Monopoly

Apart from the principles of competition and concordance, *the principle of monopoly* may dominate the structure of a given party system. In the course of the 20th century two main variants have emerged. Firstly, there is the *one-party system* which eliminates any competition by suppressing all other parties, such as the Fascist systems of Italy and Germany, and the Bolshevist system of the Soviet

48

Union. On the other hand, there is the *block system* which is typical of most of the socialist people's democracies (as in the German Democratic Republic). This system allows more than one party (and mass organisation), but all parties are subjected to the absolute and unimpeachable supremacy of a single party (like the SED in the German Democratic Republic). This *sub*ordination of the other parties curbs the competition andcreates a hierarchical party relationship. In accordance with the predominating structural principle, different forms of horizontal interaction occur which may vary considerably as to their quality. As a result, the specific configurations of parties (forms of coalition, forms of opposition, forms and frequence of change of power, etc.) correspond to fundamentally different patterns.

b) Vertical Interactions

Vertical interactions of parties with the social and political system also have to be considered; they, too, determine the particular character of an individual party system. A number of vertical interactions of the parties with the social system (the **Social system** society and its groups) have evolved through competition to capture votes. They are quite variable: they differ from country to country depending on the sectors in which, and the intensity with which parties involve themselves with society. This is closely related to the fact that the roles which parties play in the articulation and aggregation of interests, as well as the settlement of social conflicts, varies from society to society in its efficiency and scale. Of course, these differences are ultimately dependent on the respective variations in the socio-structural and cultural conditions of the societies concerned.

As regards vertical interactions with the political system considerable country **Political system** differences can again be noticed. On the one hand they refer to the penetration of the political system by parties, and on the other hand to the range and forms of party competition within that system. For example, party penetration of political systems (Parliament, Government, administration and justice) has steadily increased everywhere, so that today one often critically speaks of the "party state". However, **"Party state"** the actual penetration of political systems varies markedly from country to country. In some cases only Parliament and Government are affected; in others, full or partial penetration has already spread to administration and justice. In particular the problem of forming a Government sheds light on the range and forms of party competition in political systems: are we dealing with a purely dual system of competition, as we know it from pure two-party systems (such as in Great Britain and the USA), or are we dealing with different forms of coalition systems (small coalition, great coalition, all-party Government, and so on)?

The preceding remarks may suffice to explain the concept "party system" as a theoretical framework for the following empirical studies of the individual national European party systems and the subsequent systematic structural comparison.

Notes

1 Beyme, Kl.v. — article "Politische Parteien" in: | *Sowjetsystem und Demokratische Gesell-schaft*, vol. IV, col. 150

2 Lehmbruch, G. — article "Parteiensysteme" in: *Staatslexikon der Görresgesellschaft*, vol. 10, col. 864

3 Weber, M. — *Wirtschaft und Gesellschaft* (study edition 1964), p. 211

4 Fischer-Lexikon "Staat und Politik" (new edition) 1964, p. 226

5 Zeuner, B. — article "Parteien" in: H.H. Röhring/K. Sontheimer (eds.): *Handbuch des deutschen Parlamentarismus*, 1976, p. 366

6 Neumann, S. — *Die Parteien der Weimarer Republik* (new edition) 1973

7 Ibid, p. 105

8 Ibid, p. 107

9 Kirchheimer, O. — *Der Wandel des Westeuropäischen Parteiensystems* (1965), in: Ziebura, G. (ed.) — Beiträge zur allgemeinen Parteienlehre, 1969, p. 341 ff.

10 Ibid, p. 352

11 Ibid, p. 349

12 Ibid, p. 352

13 Ibid, p. 352

14 Ibid, p. 352

15 Ibid, p. 357

16 Cf. Zeuner, B.: article "Parteien", p. 168/9

17 Cf. Berg-Schlosser, D. (ed.) — *Die politischen Probleme der Dritten Welt*, 1972

18 Cf. Lehmbruch, G. — article "Parteiensysteme" (cf note 2)

19 Literature on this subject: Nassmacher, K.H. — *Politische Systeme und politische Soziologie* (— Politology I), 1973, p. 67 ff; Lehmbruch, G. — Proporzdemokratie, 1967 (mentions further literature)

III. Consideration of the National Party Systems in Europe

1. Introduction

On the basis of the theoretical framework outlined in the previous paragraphs we can now approach the real task set for this part of the book: a detailed empirical consideration of the national party systems in Europe.

To this purpose, a section will be devoted to each individual European country and **Historical** its party system; the analysis will follow the structure of the theoretical frame of **Conditions** reference which has to be supplemented in one respect: as the national party systems are to be portrayed individually, it is necessary to look at them also from an historical point of view. As a rule, the individuality of a system can only be explained in historical terms. Thus each section begins with a brief outline of the historical background. As this study is orientated towards the first European direct elections, the 9 EC countries are the focal point of attention. They will be dealt with first in the following order: the 6 founder members of the EC (France, Italy, Netherlands, Belgium, Luxembourg and Germany), followed by the 3 members which joined later (Great Britain, Ireland and Denmark).

In view of the fact that the 6 original members have been joined by new members, **The EC as an** one can assume with regard to the future that the European Community is an **open system** *open system*, that is, a transnational system that is open to expansion by accepting further countries as members. It is known that Greece has been negotiating its entry for a long time, and more recently Portugal as well as Spain have expressed serious interest in membership. It therefore seems advisable not to restrict this examination to the 9 EC countries, but to incorporate other European nations. This makes particular sense if one takes into account that the already existing transnational party connections in Europe go beyond the framework of the EC. Our main concern with the rudimentary stages and outlines of a European party system can only be dealt with comprehensively if the non-EC countries are also incorporated into the investigation.

Consequently, the second part of the following section will describe the party **Organisation** systems of the other 8 European countries. Only the socialist countries of Europe have been excluded. The examination is thus subdivided as follows:

— Consideration of the party systems of the EC countries (France, Italy, Netherlands, Belgium, Luxembourg, Germany, Great Britain, Ireland and Denmark).
— Consideration of the party systems of the non-EC countries (Norway, Sweden, Finland, Austria, Switzerland, Spain, Portugal, Greece).

51

2. The Party Systems of the EC Countries

Ireland

Denmark

Great Britain

Netherlands

Belgium

Federal Republic of Germany

Luxembourg

France

Italy

France

RAINER KUNZ

The French parties are part of a long political tradition. In the course of its development, the social and political determinants have constantly changed. The present French party system therefore contains traditional elements which date from the III and IV Republic, as well as relatively new elements which are the creation of the V Republic; that is, the form of Government established in 1958. It is this 1958 constitution which fundamentally changed the role that the French parties play in the process of political decision-making. Most of the developments which have taken place in the French party system over the last two decades resulted from the necessity to adapt to the changed situation. In order to understand the present structure, it is necessary to consider the party history of at least the IV Republic, and also the organisation of the government system of the V Republic.

Shaping of the French party|system

The Party System of the IV Republic

The party system of the IV French Republic, as it evolved between 1944 and 1946, differed very little from that of the preceding III Republic. Again it adopted a "multi-party system", the structure of which was to lastingly influence the political development of the IV Republic. The heterogeneous composition of the National Assemblies[1], which was due to the great number of parties, had one important consequence — government majorities could only be achieved on the basis of party coalitions. These coalitions were neither durable nor stable — during the twelve years of the IV Republic, 20 cabinets followed each other. The instability of the French party system is usually explained by pointing out the strongly differentiated political and social situation in France at that time. If one supports the theory that the exact nature of the party system is dependent on social interests, then the IV Republic was compelled to have a "multi-party system". France was confronted with many problems for which optimal solutions seemed impossible, that is, solutions which would satisfy the French voting population as a whole — domestic political appeasement after the occupation and Vichy-regime; settlement of colonial issues and a new re-interpretation of France's position in the framework of European and world politics; overcoming economic difficulties, many of which had been caused by the war; and far-reaching social changes[2]. Therefore, the French parties purposely represented specific social groups which were clearly distinct from each other and which all had their own ideological, social, economic and regional interests[3]. This had two consequences: the parties were not suited to form strong government majorities, nor could they develop into people's parties with a strong following and with the ability to govern on their own.[4]

Structure of the party system of the IV Republic

53

Cohesion of party organisations	The pluralism of interests was also evident within the party. Various Government majorities came to nothing. This was not due to the disintegration of the coalition, but to the heterogeneous character of the parliamentary groups which their leaders could not bring to vote collectively. For reasons of ideological conflict, two relatively large political groups which were represented in Parliament did not take part in the Cabinets. This of course presented additional difficulties: after 1947, the Communist Party was considered unfit to form a coalition by the other parties; because of its basic rejection of the existing party system, the Gaullist party of the IV Republic refused to participate in the Government.
Willingness to form coalitions	
Electoral system as determining factor	The effect of the electoral system also has to be mentioned. The electoral system did not directly cause the development of the party system in the IV republic[5]. However, the proportional system used from 1945 until 1958 contributed to the conservation of the multi-party system. Even small political groupings had a genuine chance of winning a mandate; thus accentuating the fact that the parties' policies were not really geared to the interests of the country as a whole.
Political power	In spite of the small degree of cohesion in the party system, the parties were undoubtedly the dominant political forces in the IV Republic. The Government's position was not strong enough to oppose them successfully. Its position was basically weakened by a belief that is rooted in French political tradition — the belief "in the principle of representation adopted from the Revolution and in the supremacy of the representative assembly[6]."
Overthrow of Government	This ideology resulted in a peculiarity of the parliamentary government system of the III and IV Republics which was advantageous to the Parliament. Parliament's right to bring down the Government by a no-confidence vote remained; but the Government's authority to dissolve Parliament, which was contained in the French constitution, was discredited politically to such an extent that it was hardly made use of[7]. In this way, the deputies could be sure of their mandate for the duration of the parliamentary term; the Government leaders, however, had lost the most efficient means of influencing Parliament which Governments in parliamentary systems can command.
Dissolution of Parliament	
End of IV Republic	Successive and frequent Government crises and changes did not enhance the reputation of the Republic, particularly as all Governments were equally unsuccessful. Proposals for parliamentary and constitutional reform which were submitted by various parties were not brought about, although they were favourably received by the public. In 1958, the rebellion of the French settlers in North Africa, which was supported by parts of the army and which at first was primarily directed against the Government's colonial policy, led to the major governmental crisis of the IV Republic. This crisis demonstrated that the French people had lost confidence, not only in the Pflimlin Cabinet which was in power at the time, but also in the political institutions of the Republic. The Governmental parties of the IV Republic had thus themselves paved the way for de Gaulle's takeover; the transfer of power was supported by the majority of the population.

54

The Political System of the V Republic

In 1958 Gaullism was firmly determined to prevent a repetition of the difficulties experienced during the IV Republic. The influence that the heterogeneous French party system exercised on the process of governing was seen as the primary cause of the difficulty. To change this the electoral system was altered. Furthermore, the constitution of 1958 legalised the reorganisation of the relationship between legislature and executive: Parliament, Government and the office of the President of State remained the formal sources of power, but their interrelation and political status were fundamentally changed. Whilst the President's office and the Government were vested with extraordinary powers, the authority of Parliament was drastically reduced. In the elections to the National Assembly, the proportional system of the IV Republic was replaced by majority system with two ballots. To win at the first ballot, a candidate is required to obtain an absolute majority of votes cast in the constituency. Where a first ballot results in no absolute majority a second ballot is held a week later, at which the candidate with a relative majority of votes is elected. Only those candidates who receive 10% at least of the total number of votes possible (that is, of the votes actually cast) can participate in a second ballot.

Reorganisation of the political system

Electoral system of V Republic

The latter condition tries to make it more difficult for splinter parties and small groups, which were numerous and active at the time of the IV Republic, to enter Parliament. In general, it was hoped that the majority electoral system would gradually concentrate votes on only a few big parties[9].

The Gaullist belief was that the constitutional system had become a tool of the political parties and consequently, the influence and control it gave — which were really those of the politcal parties — had to be reduced. This was achieved by generally curbing parliamentary rights as laid down in the constitution, as well as the rules of procedure of the National Assembly. So the right to set up the order of the day passed from Parliament to the Government; the session of the National Assembly, which in the IV Republic lasted almost throughout the year, was reduced to 170 days; the convening of special sessions by deputies was made considerably more difficult by introducing a number of organisational conditions and being made dependent on the approval of the President of State[10]. The parliamentary procedure for a motion of no-confidence in the Government contained several obstacles to its use. At least a tenth of the deputies were needed to submit a written request, and at least 48 hours had to elapse between putting a motion before the house and voting on it, which left the Government sufficient time to strengthen its position. In the calculation of whether a majority has been obtained abstentions were to be ignored; and if a motion is not supported by a majority, there could not be another motion placed before the Assembly in the same parliamentary term.

Restriction of parliamentary rights and control

The executive was also equipped with various prerogative rights vis-a-vis Parliament. Above all, these rights belong to the office of the President of State. In order to attend to the extensive tasks given him in the constitution, he can make use of comprehensive powers in the executive as well as in the legislative sector[11]. The President presides over the Council of Ministers and promulgates laws once they

Strengthening of the President of State

have been passed. Before the end of the expiry period fixed for the promulgation, he can demand that Parliament once more go into committee on a bill or on a particular article contained in it. Parliament cannot refuse; thus the President possesses the right of veto in the legislative process. Furthermore he can act upon the Government's suggestion – he can himself largely determine the Government's composition – and hold a referendum on each bill that he considers important for the continuation of the Republic, thus taking the matter out of Parliament's hands. Finally, the President is authorised to dissolve the National Assembly after consultations with the Prime Minister and the presidents of the two chambers.

The electoral system also strengthens the position of the President of State: he is directly elected by the people[12] and cannot be expelled by Parliament during his seven-year term of office.

Status of the Prime Minister

The Prime Minister is also responsible for a wide range of tasks. His parliamentary rights are accordingly extensive. Like the deputies, he has the right of initiative; he can convene special sessions of the National Assembly; he has the right of appointing an arbitration committee should differences arise between the two chambers of Parliament; and he consults the President on the dissolution of Parliament. With the exception of Chirac, all holders of this office have regarded themselves as loyal aides of the President who in this way could extend his influence into Cabinet and Parliament.

The Party System of the V Republic

The remarkably uneven distribution of political power between President of State, Government and Parliament is an intentional feature of the 1958 constitution. In view of the development of the French party system up to 1958 and the political and social structure of the country, the fathers of the constitution feared that in spite of change in the electoral system another multi-party system might establish itself. Such a system would again be incapable of forming a clear-cut parliamentary majority; to ensure the functioning of the state, the system would have to be balanced by a President of State endowed with extraordinary powers and a

Development of the party system in V Republic

Government which should be, as much as possible, independent of Parliament. The characteristic features of the French party system are partly due to the discrepancy between what the fathers of the constitution expected to happen politically and what actually happened. The system assumed its present shape mainly during four phases of development. These are:

– the dissolution of traditional parties and the emergence of new parties immediately after the beginning of the V Republic;
– the electorate's support of the large parties after 1958;
– the formation of coalitions between middle-class and left-wing parties which resulted in a political polarisation;
– efforts to create a new political centre which so far has not had any tangible success.

The most significant change in the party-political scene has been the disintegration of the "Mouvement Republicain Populaire" (MRP) which took place upon the collapse of the IV Republic. This predominantly Catholic-orientated collective movement had been the dominating middle-class party during the IV Republic. It was replaced by a party founded in 1958: the strictly National Conservative Gaullist Party which today is called "Rassemblement pour la Republique" (RPR). The left wing of the French party system kept its traditional structure: it consists of the Parti Socialiste (PS) and the Parti Communiste Francais (PCF). In the elections of the V Republic, voters increasingly concentrated on the large parties of the right or the left[13]. This development was mainly the result of the introduction of the majority vote system and the restructuring of constituences; however, it reflected as well, changes in voter behaviour. The Gaullist Party in particular benefited from the change: after the first elections in 1958 it assumed the leading role in the Government. The fact that it was a National Conservative party, together with the total decline of the MRP and the election defeats of the various small Liberal parties[14] led to a phase of right-left party political polarisation in the French party system. Its previous division into four sectors, namely a right and a left wing, and a right and left centre, ceased to exist. After 1958 the RPR and the Parti Republicain (the former "Federation Nationale des Republicains Independents" (FNRI)) formed a Government coalition as the two strongest middle class parties; the Socialist and the Communist Party regularly met before elections to discuss arrangements. As a consequence of the rigid polarisation, there are at present tendencies towards forming a political centre. The existing small non-socialist parties made a first move in this direction and found increasing support from Giscard d'Estaing, the President in office. The strengthening of the parties is a possible long-term solution to the political polarisation. The fact that these parties fought the election campaign in 1978 together and did well has already increased their weight on the political scale. The gap between the large parties of the two camps is filled by a number of small parties and political clubs which for the most part stem from the IV Republic. As their political influence is only marginal, they will not be examined in detail. For a better understanding of their nature it is necessary, however, to have a closer look at the organisational structure of the French parties.

Up to the first years of the V Republic, all parties — with the exception of the PCF — were characterised by a very loose organisational structure: they were "rather tendencies than parties"[15]. It is only during the past decade that the large parties have successfully attempted to consolidate their organisation. However, they are still a long way from the organisational unity of the German or British parties. The small extreme parties still fully adhere to the principle of political individualism. They have virtually no party machine; their parliamentary groups do not follow a uniform mode of voting; their deputies frequently change parliamentary groups; and they are involved in continuous processes of fusion and division. The small parties usually win their mandates by joining the large parties between the first and the second ballot. For the purposes of an election campaign, they sometimes form action groups. An example of this was the co-operation of the non-socialist parties in the "Union for French Democracy" (UDF) during the election campaign of 1978.

Re-structuring of the party system after 1958

Polarisation and political centre

Organisational structure of the parties

In the left camp, the small party of the Radical Socialists (MRG) joined the already existing Socialist-Communist alliance. Action groups of this kind are sometimes supported by joint political manifestos; they may well be the first step to a lasting parliamentary co-operation.

Before we deal with the major parties in greater detail, the following table gives an outline of the composition of the National Assembly elected in 1978 and of the ratios of power in the French party system.

The Non-socialist Parties

RPR

The RPR which was originally called "Union pour la Nouvelle Republique" (UNR) was founded in 1958 after de Gaulle's return to politics[16]. Between 1967 and 1977 it was called "Union de Democrates pour la Republique" (UDR). From its early days, it was gravely affected by de Gaulle's deep suspicion of the parliamentary system. He categorically refused to accept an office in the party and did not want his name to be used in connection with it. However, he had to realise that he needed the party as an instrument which formed part of the political system in order to "support his decisions and policies and to carry them through in a legal and democratic way"[17]. Leading Gaullist politicians (including Chirac) had repeatedly pointed out that the RPR was not a party in the traditional sense, but a 'movement' (mouvement)[18]. The party existed to fulfill the aims of this movement. It is led by a Secretary General; however, he did not possess the usual powers of a party chairman but received his instructions from the President of State. Any democractic political process was virtually non-existent within the party; and it was exactly this undemocratic element which, together with de Gaulle's prestige, contributed to the

Charisma and stability of the system

extraordinary success of the RPR[19] with the French voters who were tired of the continuous party bickering. The loyalty of the party (which expressed itself in a lack of individual initiative) was a major factor in the functioning and stabilisation of the constitutional system of the V Republic: it helped to avoid conflict between Parliament and the Gaullist President of State in the early stages[20].

De Gaulle's retirement, Pompidou's death and Giscard d'Estaing's election as the first non-Gaullist President represented moments of crisis and also a turning point in the development of the RPR. The retirement and death of de Gaulle resulted within the party in immediate battles of succession which Pompidou had difficulty in controlling. His unexpected death brought on a severe crisis in the party, but it also marked the beginning of a process of renewal and reorganisation which was long overdue. This was characterised by the systematic enlargement of the party organisation down to a local level, to a total membership of 200,000. Some members of leading committees were quickly replaced by younger ones and a democratisation of the party — if only a cautious one — was attempted[21].

Position of the RPR in contemporary politics

The resignation of the Secretary General Chirac is a clear sign of the RPR's intention to become a more individual political force independent of the President of State. The RPR held to this line during the elction campaign of 1978; it repeatedly distanced itself from the left-wing parties as well as from the non-socialist coalition

58

partners. Its reservation's towards the liberal tendencies of the President turned the party into the right wing of the party system; the voters, however, did not support their move to the extent that had been expected. In the elections to the National Assembly in 1978 the RPR remained the strongest party with 22.6 of the votes cast and 148 seats (a loss of 36 seats on the 1973 results). Chirac has successfully slowed up the decline of Gaullism but he has not been able to halt it or reverse the trend. In spite of this, a non-socialist Government without the RPR is inconceivable. Compared with its rival the UDF, the RPR is more united, and this will be an additional advantage in a coalition.

The "Parti Republicain" (PR) with its 69 parliamentary seats is the second largest **PR** party. Non-socialist since its foundation, it has shared the Government coalition with the Gaullists. The party came into existence in 1962 when a group of deputies left the "Centre National des Independants" (CNIP); it was first of all called "Federation Nationale des Republicains Independents" (FNRI). Like its mother **Development** party the PR was initially considered a party for the upper and professional classes. The gradual expansion of its party organisation and particularly its successful policies within the Government coalition resulted in a considerable gain of votes and seats. The PR managed to preserve its political independence and to force the RPR into significant compromises in election alliances and Cabinet formation. The **Policies in the** party's most obvious success was the election of its chairman Giscard for President. **Government** However, his election weakened rather than strengthened the PR's position within **coalition** the Government coalition by destroying the previous political independence from the Gaullist Presidents of State. The PR, which today more than ever is considered the party of the President, strengthened its position in the Government coalition by uniting all non-Gaullist non-socialist parties under its leadership in the action group "Union for French Democracy" (UDF). The united parties at present possess **More strength by** 137 seats in the National Assembly and are almost as strong as the Gaullist **forming the** parliamentary group. This of course presupposes that their political co-operation **UDF** will extend beyond the parliamentary term. In the past Government coalitions, conflicts between the RPR and PR could always be solved. As there is little hope at the moment for a coalition between parties from the left and right camps, the PR will remain the Gaullists' partner. The common desire of both parties to stay in power should increase their willingness to co-operate and compromise. The "Union for **UDF** French Democracy" is at present the third political force in the non-socialist party alliance. Apart from the "Parti Republicain", it consists of various other small parties and political groups with a very loose organisational structure. The parties contained in the Union are either former members of the Government coalition, or else they belonged to the Liberal "Mouvement Reformateur" founded in 1971. The **Composition of** "Centre Democratic et Progres" (CDP), which Jacques Duhamel led until his death in **CDP** 1977, merged with the Union. The CDP was founded in 1969 by deputies who left the "Centre Democrate Social"[22] led by Jean Lecanuet when it refused to co- **CDP** operate with the Government majority and de Gaulle. Thus the CDP consisted of deputies who were in favour of a presidential majority[23], and under Pompidou's influence a binding coalition agreement was reached. The CDP was a party for the upper and professional classes it had neither a party organisation, nor a party manifesto — nor even committed members. Its organisational structure was weak, consisting only of links among the candidates and deputies[24]. Before it joined the Union, its existence had already often been endangered by merging with the RPR and PR. In 1971 the " Parti Radical", the "Parti Democrate Socialiste", the "Centre Democrate" and the "Centre Republicain" united to form the "Mouvement Reformateur" which so far has tried to remain an independent force in the non-socialist group. The most distinguished leaders were Jean-Jacques Servain-Schreiber and Jean Lecanuet, chairmen of the "Parti Radicale" and the "Centre Democrate" respectively. Before the elections in 1973, the "Mouvement Reformateur" appealed to middle-class voters who disapproved of Government policies with their obvious Gaullist stamp and who at the same time did not consider the left-wing parties as a possible alternative. The parties of the "Mouvement Reformateur" refused a closer parliamentary co-operation with the Goverment coalition during de Gaulle's and Pompidou's terms of office. Various advances have been made since Giscard d'Estaing started to influence the policies of the presidential majority[25]. In the years following Giscard d'Estaing's succession to office, the fundamental differences between the concepts of the parties of the "Mouvement Reformateur" and those of the presidential majority no longer pertained to the socio-political sector. Rather, they concerned home affairs, as the "Mouvement Reformateur" demanded more citizen involvement and a greater transparency of the government process, together with regional decentralisation. As far as foreign affairs were concerned, the Mouvement wanted increased French co-operation in supranational bodies such as the EC and NATO. The final objective of the Mouvement, namely to create an independent force of the political centre between the Government coalition and the left wing, was not achieved in the elections of 1973. Continuous clashes between the RPR and PR led the latter also to believe that its policies could only be successfully realised if Gaullist influence were controlled by a strong new central group. In

Anti-Gaullist attitudes

this way, the ideological gap narrowed and led to the foundation of the "Union for French Democracy". At the present moment it is impossible to predict the ultimate parliamentary efficiency of the UDF which is composed of quite different elements. It is faced with the difficult task of adjusting the following levels of organisation and interest: the party organisations remain independent within the Union; four parties have a history of long-standing co-operation in the "Mouvement Reformateur" which now becomes a sub-group of the UDF, the PR clearly dominates in the new party alliance because of its numerical strength, and its close

Right-wing radicalism

ties with the President. In the IV Republic right-wing radicalism was quite strong, but has lost in importance since the disintegration of the Poujadists. When the colonial question was solved, it was robbed of its favourite platform. The RPR also integrated many right-wing groups, although it never accepted the ideas of the extreme right. The last large group, the "Alliance Republicaine pour les Libertes et le Progres", was dissolved when its candidate Tixier-Vignancour failed in the presidential elections in 1965. Those groups that still exist — among them the French monarchists — are politically without any influence.

The Parties of the Left Camp

The "Parti Socialiste" (PS) is one of the two large parties of the Left. It was formed in 1971 when the "Section Francaise l'Internationale d'Ouvriere" (SFIO) founded in 1905 — merged with a number of small left-wing groups. In 1972 it also incorporated the "Mouvement des Radicaux de Gauche", a group which had left Servan-Schreiber's "Parti Radicale", and called itself "Union de la Gauche Socialiste et Democrate" (UGSD). However, the alliance did not extend beyond the common nomination of candidates and election agreements; and the PS with its 75,000 members still has to be considered as the leading socialist party. The socialist party leaders have realised that only a solid union can successfully counteract the stable non-socialist party block; this accounts for the merging of various socialist parties that has already occurred and that is expected to occur. Since 1971 Francois Mitterand has been chairman of the PS. The integration of all the heterogenous party represents a difficult task for him. The PS is faced with similar problems with regard to their declared programmes. The party could only expect to win votes in the marginal groups of the non-socialist camp; in view of the polarised party system, it would only be possible to gain a Government majority by forming a coalition with the Communist Party. In the last elections[26], the PS managed to gain votes outside its traditional area of the working classes; it also issued joint election programmes and government manifestos with the Communist Party[27]. This seems largely due to Mitterand's reputation and clever tactics. In the elections of 1978, however, he could not achieve his goal. The PS had committed itself at an early stage to a coalition with the Communist Party. The non-socialist parties had emphatically pointed out the risks in foreign and economic affairs which would arise if a popular front Government came to power. During his election campaign Mitterand therefore tried to convince his voters that the PS would, without any doubt, be the dominating force in a left-wing coalition. Mitterand failed because the Communist Party was not prepared to accept this subordinate role during the election campaign. After the defeat in the elections and the dissolution of the left-wing alliance, the differences between right-wing Social-Democrat and left-wing socialist groups within the PS have flared up again. In view of the present state of the party, it is to be expected that the PS needs a long phase of consolidation before once more playing an active role in French home affairs.

Integration policies

Difficulties of PS in the left-wing coalition

The second large party of the Left is the "Parti Communiste Francais" (PCF) which can boast a party tradition that has never been interrupted since its foundation in 1920. Furthermore, it is the only French party with a rigid party organisation; it is divided into small units[28], sections and departmental federations. It has about 450,000[29] members who belong mainly to the working class or who are small farmers and agricultural labourers; but it attracts support also from the lower-middle classes and the intelligentsia[30]. The party obtains most of its votes in the big cities and the industrial areas; it's support is thus restricted to relatively few constituencies and, in accordance with the electoral system, is not allocated many seats[31]. The

PCF

Organisation and membership

PCF's influence in the political system depends very much on the degree to which it is active. The PCF can count on a loyal core of voters which enabled it to participate in every Parliament of the III and IV Republics; it was sometimes even the strongest party. Yet only twice it shared Government responsibility in 1935/1936 in Leon Blum's popular front Government (together with the Socialists) and in 1946/1947 in various short-lived Cabinets of the IV Republic[32]. By comparison the party is traditionally very active on the local and "Departement" level, with extraordinary success. It produces a large number of mayors and municpal and general councillors; and it co-operates widely and enters into coalitions with other parties.

Ideology

The PCF's dogmatism has always caused problems in its internal structure as well as in its attitude towards general political questions. Together with a hierarchical organisational structure that is unusual in the French party system, this was obviously responsible for a marked lack of democracy within the party. It was thus more difficult to integrate new members; at least it is alleged that the PCF's fluctuation of members is extraordinarily high. Politically, the PCF was considered to be the most faithful to Moscow of all the large Western European Communist parties. This reputation created the impression that it was not the master of its own decisions, and so diminished the party's chances of being elected or chosen as a coalition partner. Because of the number of its mandates, participation in the

Ideological felxibility

Government is only possible in coalition; and in order to realise this the PCF's attitude in questions of social, economic and security policies has become more flexibile over the past years. This has, above all, prepared the ground for a rapproachement with the Socialists. The party convention in 1976 can be regarded as the climax of this ideological change. Its party chairman Georges Marchais publicly acknowledged fundamental differences between the Soviet Communist Party's and the PCF's conception of social democracy[33]. The new manifesto of the PCF abandoned the demand for a "dictatorship of the proletariate" which Marchais explained by saying that the term did not cover "the realities of the policies and proposals that we have to make for our country today"[34].

PSU

One would have to discard traditional dogmas and properly consider the political and social situation in France. The two large wage-earning groups of the population, the industrial workers and the office workers, represent three-quarters of the active population of France. As their interests are basically identical, it would seem possible that the majority of the French population will decide in favour of a move towards a socialist society that is, the "greatest possible democratisation of the entire encomic, social and political life of the country"[35]. In view of this majority situation, the PCF might agree to continue to use democratic elections for determining the Government[36]. Apart from pledging itself to a pluralistic democracy, the PCF also abandoned the idea of Marxist internationalism by pointing out the specifically French element of its policies which would lead to a "socialism in the colours of France".[37] If the results of the 1978 election are anything to go by, the French voters were not convinced by these proclamations of ideological change. It is true that the PCF won votes and mandates, but the political landslide that had been expected did not happen. Following this defeat, which was corroborated quite clearly at the second ballot, Government participation seems to be beyond the PCF's grasp.

The two small groups of the "Parti Socialiste Unifie" (PSU) and of the left-wing Radical Socialists are of some importance to the left. The PSU came into existence in 1960 when the three groups "Parti Socialiste Autonome", the "Union de la Gauche Socialiste" and the "Tribune du Communisme" merged. There is no party organisation to speak of; the PSU's membership of 20,000 is only an estimated figure. From the beginning, the PSU's supporters — which for the most part belong to left-wing student and trades union milieux — have held extremely varied political views; a consequence of this were the numerous internal struggles and divisions. The fluctuation of the marginal groups of the PS and PCF between the PSU and their respective mother parties became particularly complex. The PSU occupies a position which is politically left of the PS and PCF, and therefore forms a "transition from the non-parliamentary new radical Left to the traditional parties of the Left"[38]. In 1972, the left-wing Radical Socialists — "Mouvement des Radicaux de Gauche" (MRG) — left the Parti Radical after the latter had, under its leader Servan-Schreiber, joined the Mouvement Reformateur. Similar to the PSU, the left-wing Radical Socialists have neither an established party organisation, nor a homogeneous following. They send a small number of deputies to Parliament by means of election agreements. In 1978 the Radical Socialists joined the alliance of PS and PCF. However, after the election defeat they were the first party to publicly break with the alliance and blamed the failure of the left-wing coalition on the tactics of the PCF. The MRG is politically closest to the PS, and a merging of the two has often been considered. The PSU and the left-wing Radical Socialists are essentially participants in a continuous process of political discussion. They integrate minorities into the political system, yet they do not represent active forces in a parliamentary sense. After the riots in May 1968 which marked the peak of their influence, these groups of the extreme Left have increasingly lost importance. Various factors have contributed to this: the Government's interdiction of the leading extreme left organisation "Gauche Proletarienne"; the aggressive policies of the large left-wing parties which were anxious to keep their ideological lead; and discord and the inability to organise within the groups themselves. The successor to the "Gauche Proletarienne" split into a Trotskyist and a Maoist camp, following the overall ideological trend. "L'Organisation Communiste Internationaliste" (OCI), "Lutte Ouvriere" (LO) and "Front Communiste Revolutionnaire" are leading Trotskyist groups which also nominate candidates for the National Assembly. The most important Maoist groups, "Humanite Rouge", "Union des Communistes de France" and "Partie Communiste Revolutionnaire" have so far refused to participate in the elections.

Left-wing radicalism

Outlook

Structure of the
party system

The concentration of votes obtained by a few large parties, as was the case during the V Republic, and the formation of the non-socialist and the left-wing party block should not obscure the fact that the French party system has essentially remained a multi-party structure. The results of the election for the National Assembly in 1978 emphasise this. The number of the parties represented in Parliament did not increase; however, because of the formation of the UDF, more parties participated in Government. The three large parties and the group of the UDF all achieved well-balanced election results; this may lead to increased autonomy of the parties and difficulties in further co-operation. Whether coalitions will remain, and which of those coalitions the French parties will form is all-important. This was the novelty which the V Republic introduced into French party history: the parties' willingness to enter into coalitions or co-operative forms over a period of time, either sharing Government responsibility or representing the Opposition. The majority electoral system which was introduced in 1958 has had a considerable influence. The stipulation that there should be two ballots held at different times virtually challenges the parties to agree on mutual support, at least at the first ballot. Such agreements have frequently proved a sound basis for extended co-operation after the elections. There has been a similar development regarding the election of the President which is conducted according to the same system: experience has taught that only those candidates who are supported by more than one party win the necessary high percentage of votes[39]. The introduction of the majority system has changed little of the parties' diversity and their individual organisational structure; but it has introduced a new form of interaction into the party system which has expressed itself in the parties' coalition behaviour since 1958, and which is bound to affect the structure of the party system.

Coalition
behaviour

Electoral system
and election
campaign tactics

Although the French parties now show greater willingness to form coalitions, agreements can seldom be reached without creating and solving problems and conflicts. This applies to the non-socialist camp as well as to the left-wing camp. However, the specific composition of the former proved advantageous for a considerable period of time: it included the Gaullist party. Because of its large number of members and its close attachment to the Gaullist Presidents de Gaulle and Pompidou, who during their term of office strongly influenced the process of political decision-making, this party played a leading role. The PRI, however, maintained its participative rights as it was the only non-socialist party that was prepared to give the Gaullists those votes which they needed for an absolute majority. The two parties' attitudes towards socio-political, social and foreign affairs problems were finely differentiated[40], yet the parties' basic ideologies did not clash and this allowed sufficient room for compromise. Giscard d'Estaing's election as President of State brought about an obvious change in the relationship of the two coalition partners. Previously the RPR had needed the PR in order to carry through the Gaullist President's ideas in the National Assembly; now the RPR was the only party which could provide Giscard d'Estaing with the necessary parliamentary majorities. Thus the RPR was

Reaching an
agreement in the
coalition

64

able to exercise a strong influence on presidential policies; this was exemplified in the numerous modificiations of the original government programme as well as in the composition of his cabinets[41]. When the Secretary General of the RPR, Chirac, resigned from the office of Prime Minister, the Gaullists' critical view of the policies of the President was made clear. As the election date in 1978 drew nearer, the relationship between the two coalition partners grew more and more tense. It became evident that the Gaullists' election campaign would also be directed against their coalition partner in order to increase the number of their seats and, by so doing, regain their leading position in the non-socialist camp which had been weakened by Giscard d'Estaing's election. The PR counteracted by forming the UDF which comprised all non-Gaullist non-socialist parties. The Gaullists[42] dominated the initial debate within the group, but, during the decisive months preceding the election, the UDF made an increasing impact on public opinion. Raymond Barre, whom Giscard d'Estaing had appointed as Chirac's successor, developed into the UDF's most distinguished representative. His economic success – a stimulation of trade and sinking inflation – probably improved the UDF's chances significantly in the election. In the "Blois Manifesto" Barre presented to the public the economic and political ideas of the President and the UDF. The manifesto was at first criticised for its step-by-step procedure, but in the course of the election campaign it proved the most substantial government manifesto[43]. Without doubt Barre also contributed to the success of the UDF by well-founded criticism of the common manifesto of the left-wing parties. The outcome of the elections was an unexpectedly clear victory for the non-socialist camp. However, neither of the two groups were satisfied with the distribution of seats. The UDF's success was considerable, but not sufficient for the party to establish itself as an independent force of the political centre. It is furthermore uncertain how the co-operation of the individual parties will develop. The RPR only just remained the strongest party, but suffered losses and failed in its declared goal of a clear majority. After the elections, both groups emphasised their independence within the framework of the coalition. However, they are forced to co-operate if they want to stay in power: a situation that will not be without conflict. For example, the Gaullists refused to approve a suggestion by Giscard d'Estaing that politicians of the socialist opposition should preside in two parliamentary committees. The UDF took its revenge by preventing the election of Edgar Faure who had been nominated by the Gaullist party for the office of parliamentary President[44].

Similar developments can be observed in the group of the left-wing parties. Their long-range planning of the election campaign was supposed to be based on the joint political manifestos of the PS and PCF in 1972. However, the attempt to bring this manifesto up-to-date led to controversies on fundamental issues; and as these lasted up to the elections, it was not possible to present a common manifesto for a potential government takeover. Members of the Government examined the social reforms as suggested by the Socialists (raising the wage minimum, a minimal age pension, lowering of the pension age, longer holidays) together with the compensation arrangements which a Socialist Government would award to employers. The

Distribution of power in the coalition

Election campaign of the left-wing parties

65

result of the study was that the suggested reforms and schemes could not be financed unless taxation were to be drastically increased. The two parties were also unable to reach agreement on the tactics of the election campaign. Both intended to assume an uncompromising attitude and thereby demonstrate the leading role that they hoped to play in the future left-wing Government. As the PCF wanted to prevent a numerical majority of the PS, it was not even prepared to agree in good time on the nomination of candidates for the second ballot. This fact undoubtedly contributed to the huge victory of the Government parties which was only secured at the second ballot. The debate between the leading politicians was heated, including personal defamation and reproaches of political unreliability[45]. This style of confrontation certainly lessened the left-wing parties' chances of success, and this is particularly true if we can believe the opinion polls which claim that more than 20% of the voters were undecided up to the last moment. A successful outcome to the elections would most certainly have forced the parties to compromise; instead, the defeat increased the political tensions. At present, the left-wing party camp, which it has taken years to unite, is in a state of disharmony which cannot be overcome in the foreseeable future.

Search for a
political centre

In both large French party camps, the divisive elements dominate. The Government coalition has a safe majority, but the coalition partners' differences in attitudes and ideas will certainly affect its efficiency. One can therefore understand the call for a new political centre of moderate parties from between the two extreme wings of the Gaullists and Communists. These parties should be able to form coalitions and majorities. Giscard d'Estaing seems to share the desire for such a development but cannot contribute very much to it. The UDF which is close to him is by itself weak and not sufficiently organised; Giscard cannot do without the RPR. At present, a coalition between the UDF and PS is not feasible: this would almost certainly mean the end of the PS. Mitterand has furthermore opposed such a possibility for ideological reasons. Yet in spite of this, the President seems to favour a long-term rapprochement with the moderate Social Democrat groups in the PS [46]. In the near future, the structure of the French party system — four almost equally strong parties grouped in two party blocks — can be expected to alter little. A change of a different kind is, however, possible: the increased political influence which the French parties have gained since the Liberal Giscard d'Estaing came into office may possibly revert to the President in view of the present party structure.

Influence of the
parties

Notes

1 On average, 10 parties were represented in the National Assemblies. In addition to that, the Assemblies contained representatives of so-called political clubs and other small groups, as well as a comparatively high number of independent deputies. The three large parties (Socialists, Communists and MRP) together only took about 60% of the votes.
2 In particular: an increase in the birth rate; support of the growing number of people who are no longer involved in production processes; high immigration from overseas colonies; industrialisation and formation of new densely populated areas; a rural exodus as a consequence of recession and agricultural mechanisation; and a levelling of the inequalities in education and distribution of income.

3 See also MacRae, Duncan: *Parliament, Parties and Society in France 1946–1958*, p. 15 ff.

4 See also Ehrmann, Henry W.: *Das politische System Frankreichs*, p. 11 ff, 48 ff, 142 ff.

5 Fenske's comment on the III Republic undoubtedly also applies to the IV Republic: "In the complex of determining factors for the shaping of the party system in France, the electoral system, so it seems, did not play a particularly important part . . . One can assume that even the relative majority system would not have overcome the multitude of parliamentary groups and the coexistence of various parties, each with its own subtle variations." Fenske, H.: *Wahlrecht und Parteiensystem*, p. 204.

6 Loewenstein, Karl: *Verfassungslehre, p. 87.*

7 The National Assembly was dissolved only once, by President Coty in 1955 following a motion by Prime Minister Faure.

8 It would not be correct to assume that the Governments always wish to continue. Only a few Governments have fought for their survival; in some cases there was a tendency to self-dissolution. The very limited movement of personnel was certainly of importance: the members of an overthrown Government could expect to be responsible for a department in the next government.

9 Due to the distribution of the voting population, the Gaullists expected the Socialists and Communists to get less votes when the majority electoral system was introduced. The latter could only be certain of receiving an absolute majority in the large cities. Relevant statistics are to be found in Kempf, Udo: *Das politische System Frankreichs*, p. 127 ff.

10 This is based on Article 30 of the constitution; it allows different interpretations. The parliamentary forces held the view that the President of State had to comply if the majority of deputies proposed a motion for a special session. However, in 1960 in a situation approaching a constitutional conflict, de Gaulle enforced his interpretation that the President is free to decide on the motion; this meant the loss of a further parliamentary power.

11 Definition of the tasks of the President are in Article 5 of the constitution.

12 The weakness of the Presidents of the IV Republic was partly caused by their election by the two chambers of Parliament on which they then depended. The 1958 constitution therefore envisaged the election committee as consisting of Members of Parliament, of the general councils, of assemblies from overseas territories, as well as of mayors and municipal councillors. The local representatives were in the majority. In the 1962 referendum, the population approved a change in the constitution which introduced the direct election of the President by the people. De Gaulle had worked particularly hard towards this goal.

13 A comparison of the percentage of votes won by the three strongest parties at the time (MRP, SFIO, PCF in the IV Republic, RPR, PS and PCF in the V Republic) shows that the percentage of these groups had increased from 50% to 80% in 1946.

14 The RP has to be excluded. As the coalition partner of the RPR it had gained more influence than it deserved on the basis of its number of seats.

15 Fensk, Hans: *Die europaeischen Parteiensysteme: Jahrbuch des oeffentlichen Rechts*, NF 22, p. 288.

16 The first Gaullist parliamentary party, the "Rassemblement de Peuple Francais" (RPF) which was founded in 1945, could only boast a short-term success in the mid-fifties. After that, it split up into various unimportant groups and then vanished completely from the political scene.

17 Neurohr, Jean: *Was ist Gaullismus?* ZS für Politik, NF 16, 1969, p. 19.

18 On the Gaullist movement, see also Mohler, Armin: *Die Französiche Rechte heute*, ZS für Politik, NF 16, 1969, p. 40 ff.

19 Only two months after its foundation and without a comprehensive party machine, the RPR won 40% of the seats in the National Assembly in the parliamentary elections of 1958. In the parliamentary elections of 1969, it attained a percentage of 46 of all votes coast: this is the best election result ever achieved in French party history.

20 This political constellation contributed significantly to the stabilisation of the V Republic. The constitutional system of the Republic will undergo its ultimate test when the president

and the parliamentary majority do not belong to the same party block. See also: Sommer, Theo: "Das bittere Erbe des Generals de Gaulle" *Die Zeit*, 15/1977, p. 3.

[21] At present one can only speculate as to whether Chirac will become the new leader in the Gaullist movement, and whether the RPR will maintain its traditional character of a party with charismatic leaders.

[22] The Centre Democrate is one of the various successors of the MRP. It has lost many voters to the RPR and the FNRI.

[23] The deputies of the CDP in the National Assembly call themselves "Union Centriste".

[24] This process is difficult to understand. Deputies of other national parliaments under these conditions would be called "not belonging to a parlimanetary group" or "independent".

[25] Lecanuer was Minister of regional planning until the transformation of the first government under Barre in the spring of 1977.

[26] In the parliamentary elections of 1973, the PS won 20.65% of votes cast (compared with 16.53% in 1968).

[27] The PS and PCF have so far co-operated in three ways: election agreements concerning mutual support of candidates at the second ballot; nomination of a common candidate (Mitterand) in the presidential elections of 1965 and 1974; issuing a common government manifesto in preparation for the parliamentary elections of 1973.

[28] Most of the total number of the 19,500 small units are groups in factories.

[29] Number of members in 1972 taken from sources of the PCF. Other sources quote lower figures; the Munzinger archive says between 275,000 and 350,000.

[30] From the lowest level upwards, members of the intelligentsia are over-represented in the PCF in all bodies of the party leadership.

[31] One of the aims behind the change of the electoral system in 1958 and the division into new constituencies (all inspired by the Gaullists) was to weaken the influence of Socialists and Communists.

[32] For example in the Bidault Cabinet (19 June – 10 November, 1946) and the Ramadier Cabinet (23 January – 6 May, 1947). In both Cabinets, the Communists did not occupy any key ministerial posts.

[33] Georges Marchais in a television interview. Printed in: Etienne Balibar: *Über die Diktatur des Proletariats*, p. 146.

[34] G. Marchais at the 22nd party convention. Ibid, p. 166.

[35] G. Marchais in a newspaper interview of 19.1.76. Ibid, p. 150.

[36] G. Marchais at the 22nd party convention: "This force (which will effect the socialist transformation of society) will originate and operate on the basis of decisions made in general free elections . . . " Ibid, p. 168.

[37] G. Marchais in an interview. Ibid, p. 148.

[38] Kempf, Udo: *Das politische System Frankreichs, p. 175.*

[39] As there are usually more than two candidates in a presidential election, it is difficult to get the absolute majority required at the first ballot. Before the second ballot, some candidates usually withdraw from their candidature, so that even a relative victory requires quite a high percentage of votes.

[40] The PR has always been more pro-European than the RPR.

[41] The formation of a new Cabinet (2nd Barre Cabinet) after the failure in the 1977 local elections led to a swing to the Right in the Government; for under Gaullist pressure the two centre-ministers Lecanuet and Poniatowski had to resign. This swing was of course contrary to Giscard's declared intentions.

[42] This applies in particular to the Secretary General of the RPR, Chirac.

[43] The Blois manifesto comprises 30 "action objectives for freedom and rights" which are supplemented by 110 suggestions for their realisation. The action objectives were divided into four categories: 1) Free and protected citizens; 2) Economic progress to support employment; 3) Social justice; 4) Raising the standard of living in France.

44 Chaban-Delmas, who was elected instead, is also a member of the Gaullist parliamentary group. However, he is considered to be a supporter of the President and an opponent of Chirac; this is why the Gaullist parliamentary group rejected him. In order to make sure that he was elected, Giscard d'Estaing obviously even delayed the formation of a Government. Deputies who have been appointed minister have no vote in the National Assembly.

45 Mitterand accused the PCF of demagogy and neo-Stalinism. Marchais in turn reproached the PS for not defending the interests of the workers, but rather those of the capitalist; he also thought that Mitterand was losing control (from: Die Zeit, 16.12.77). The following accusations were rather common: the PS wanted to form a pact with the non-socialist parties, and the PCF was striving for an alliance with the Gaullists, thus copying the Italian model.

46 This might, in the long-term, create the political centre. The more the co-operation is extended, the less dependent will Giscard become on the Gaullists.

Italy

HERBERT MAIER

Social and Economic Conditions

Social structure

The social structure of Italy conforms to a clear dualistic pattern. This is illustrated in the marked separation of social strata and by the economic division of the country into the highly industrialised north and into the underdeveloped regions of the Mezzogiorno which extends to Sicily. This situation is further aggravated by a high susceptibility to conflicts which has to be interpreted as a consequence of quick economic changes.

In the years between 1958 and 1968, Italy's gross national product, for example, increased by 70%, industrial production by 100%, income per person by 60% and exports by 170%[1]. A comparison of the employment structure over a period of about 50 years may help to explain this. In 1914, 55% of the whole working population were agriculturally employed (in Germany 35%) and 28% worked in industry (in Germany 40%)[2]. In 1973, only 17.4% are still agriculturally employed (in Germany 7.5%) and 44% work now in industry (in Germany 49%)[3]. These processes of transformation occurred with immense speed in the fifties. Between 1951 and 1961, for example, about 8 million Italians left their original place of residence either temporarily or permanently[4]. This was accompanied by a process of urbanisation — above all due to emigration from the south to the north, and also from the Mezzogiornointerno to the regions of the Esterno[5] — and the creation of slums at the periphery of urban developments.

Differences in income

The 5 poorest Italian regions (Apulia, Campania, Molise, Basilicata and Calabria) have an income of about £725 per head per year. In comparison, the regions of the north (Lombardy, Liguria, Piemont, Emilia-Romagna and Latium) have an income of £1,300 per head per year[6]. After the end of the 1st World War the north in particular had experienced industrial expansion which became relatively stagnant during the fascist era (1922-1944) and which only recovered because of massive American help (Marshall plan) after 1948.

Unemployment

Today, Italy is still characterised by the low percentage of its working population (about 35%). It is a striking fact that only 25% of the female population go to work; most of these women are employed in the agricultural sector which aggravates the situation still further. There is also the institution of "secondo lavoro" (secondary labour) which affects about one million jobs. They do not form part of the controllable job market and thus reinforce and stabilise the social rule of the "padrone". In the north, secondary labour tends to take the form of out-work; in the south, tertiary services which are accordingly badly paid[7].

70

Apart from its economic crises, Italy is confronted with problems of social structure. In the north, one finds the following social classes: an upper class of industrialists and landowners — for example, the family businesses, Fiat and Pirelli; a middle class which is relatively broad; a lower class consisting of industrial workers, travelling salesmen, agricultural helpers, (braccianti) builders and workers employed in the service industries. The lower class is still considerably larger than the two others put together. In the south, the social stratum differs: there is a small upper class consisting of owners of latifundia and local people of political rank; a relatively small middle class consisting of employees, teachers and self-employed; a very large lower class consisting of labourers, tenant farmers, constantly unemployed people and a marginal industrial proletariat. It is noticeable that the various social classes can be distinguished in the south by characteristics of appearance and language; the middle classes often expect to be addressed with a title, such as "commendatore, don, cavaliere, maestro" etc. The population of the "Mezzogiorno" futhermore consists to a great extent of illiterate and uneducated people. All these phenomena reveal a passive and depressing profile of the largest part of the population; they result in a political culture that is limited to the parish[8] and create a stagnant traditional society. Parallel with this development, the north has seen the creation of a dynamic industrial society which demands its own say in political matters. However, these demands are hampered by the relative isolation of the large cities and industrial regions.

Social strata

The Political System

Apart from the socio-economic factors referred to earlier, the political system of Italy is largely determined by ideological and religious differences which have their effects on the structure of the party system. On the one hand, this is a direct outcome of historical development: Italy's unity and the foundation of the Republic could only be achieved by destroying the papal state. This in turn resulted in the second half of the 19th century in two directly opposed fronts: republican laicism and catholic clericalism which today remain important. On the other hand, party-political developments, which by and large were aimed at certain social classes, led to a relatively extreme ideological difference which expresses itself through open hostility towards the opposing political party and its supporters. The overall result is a fragmented political culture split into at least three categories: laicist, catholic and socialist[9].

Ideological and religious discrepancy

The origins of Italian constitutionalism were from abroad. When — in the wake of the French Revolution — the French invaded Italian territory, the satellite states were given constitutions based on the French pattern. After the Restoration and various minor revolutions during the first half of the 19th century, King Albert of Piemont appointed a constitutional commission in 1848. The work of this commission, the "statuto" lasted until the end of the 2nd World War. The 1947 constitution of the Republic of Italy was the first to be legitimised by a constituent

Historical summary

71

assembly of the whole of Italy. After the Italian unification of 1861, the "statuto" of the Piemont kingdom had simply been imposed on the remainder of Italy. It is true that since Cavour the political system had been basically parliamentary; but from the 1st World War on it suffered a growing crisis and was finally exposed by Mussolini's sham parliamentarianism which destroyed its credibility.

Consitution of 1947

The destruction of the constitution by the fascists forced Italy – similarly to the Federal Republic of Germany, France and Austria – to work out a new constitution after 1945. This was done in 1947 with a large majority in the Assembly. Its main features are: Italy's form of government as a republic; an enumeration of the rights and duties of the citizens (similar to the American bill of human rights); and the introduction of a parliamentary political system with two chambers.

Party norms

For the first time, the constitution contains a passage on parties. The relevant Article 49 reads: "Every citizen has the right to form parties with other citizens, in order to participate in a democratic way in the process of national politics". Up to the present day, there has been no further legislation on party matters. However, since 1974, the parties have been financed on a general basis during elections.

The unrestricted proportional electoral system allows a wide party spectrum. The "free mandate" principle (Article 67) is considerably limited by strict discipline within the parliamentary group – illustrating the power of the parties. As is common in parliamentary systems, the Prime Minister can be suspended by a vote of no-confidence; his office is not protected by special regulations, such as a "constructive no-confidence vote", and its absence allows the parliamentary parties considerable room for action. The problems created for Governments by the constant loss of a parliamentary majority has not been the responsibility of the parliamentary parties in themselves: approximately every fifth Government overthrown has been caused by Parliamentary upheaval. The constant collapse of Governments, (the average duration of a Government in recent times being less than a year) results from many causes: with changing supporting majorities, crises within the Democrazia Christiana, or the collapse of a formal coalition being the main reasons for a change in the ruling party.

The Parties

Modern Italy is characterised by a multi-party system. The DC (Democrazia Christiana) occupies a position of political predominance; the DC together with the PSDI (Partito Socialdemocratio Italiano), the PLI (Partito Liberale Italiano), the PRI (Partito Republicano Italiano) and the PSI (Partito Socialista Italiano) – though at times not so closely connected – form the so-called "system parties". That is, they are the parties which recognise the existing republic and democracy and wish to retain them. Since about 1966, the greatest rival to the DC, the PCI (Partito Communista Italiano), has also claimed to be one of the "system parties"; one can presumably accept this claim on the basis of the PCI's permanent support of a DC minority Government since 1976. The Monarchists (PNM = Partito Nazionale Monarchico) and the Neo-Fascists (MSI = Movimento Sociale Italiano) do not belong to the group of "system parties".

The origins of the DC can be traced back to the Partito Populare Italiano (PPI) **DC** which was founded in 1919 by the Sicilian priest Luigi Sturzo. After the 1st World War, this party strove for and successfully achieved the return of a Catholic force in Italy's political life. After the founding of the Italian kingdom, the catholics acted on the following principle until 1900: no cooperation with the new regime; no candidates; and consequently no voters. With the foundation of the PPI, they fulfilled their political potential and once more became involved in political activities; together with the Socialists, they had the absolute majority in the chamber of deputies. After Mussolini's march on Rome and after the general prohibition of parties in 1926, the PPI's structure survived under the guise of the "Movimento Guelfo" and "Catholic Action". This is why as early as 25th July 1943, (after the deposition of Mussolini and the take-over by Marshal Badoglio) the DC could issue its first manifesto in Milan. Since the foundation of the Republic, the DC has always led the Government. In spite of all its weaknesses, three important elements ensure its efficiency: 1) its anti-fascist tradition, 2) Catholicism and 3) its "mass party" nature. Today, the party has about 1.85 million members. The social **Membership** division of its members does not support a current view that the DC is the party of **structure** the rural population. It has successfully attracted civil servants, the self-employed and students (about 20% of the total membership) who one would normally expect to support liberal parties. The industrial workers make up about 18% of its members, and the agricultural workers about 16%. Like its largest and strongest rival, the PCI, the party is highly organised. About 13,000 groups are to be found in more than 8,000 districts. After the war these small units mainly relied on the clergy and the catholic lay organisations, particularly the "Azione Cattolica". Since then, a more varied structure has developed. On the one hand — this applies in particular to the rural areas of the Mezzogiorno — the party still retains its close ties with local dignitaries and the professional classes; on the other hand, it contains features of a bureaucratic "mass" party as is the case in the industrial triangle in the north and in Rome, its headquarters. On the whole, its structure is federal and in clear contrast to the centralised organisation of the PCI.

The DC is connected with the catholic church through social groups, such as **DC and the** "Catholic Action" which at present has almost 2.8 million members, is subordinate **Vatican** to the Curia, and follows the directives of the Vatican. Further important groups are: the "Association of Catholic Teachers" comprising about 60,000 people; the "Centre for Women" which consists of catholic women's associations with more than 2 million members; the farmers' association "Coltivatori dirette" which incorporates about 1.75 million families; and the catholic workers' organisation "Associazione christiana dei lavoratori italiani" with 1.5 million members[10]. These groupings suggest a merging of the clerical hierarchy, other catholic associations and the DC, and could lead to the conclusion that the Vatican continues to exert a decisive influence on Italian politics.

In fact, different ideologies have been able to evolve within the DC after 1945. They do not always fully correspond to the ideas of the church; and indeed the Vatican has gradually been distancing itself from Italian domestic politics. These differing elements of thought find expression in the "correnti" — the various infra-party and parliamentary groups — and results from both ideological convictions and a desire for political power. They may be listed (from right to left) as follows: 1) the Nuove Chronache under A. Fanfani which thinks along the lines of a corporate state; 2) the Iniziativa Popolare which is a more locally orientated group containing a variety of ideologies; 3) the Impegno Democratico which is relatively technocratic; and 4) the left-wing group of the Base, Force Nuovo and Nuovo Sinistra which represent about 20% of the leading party figures. However, none of these elements has enough power to enforce its ideas; the votes of the various groups are rather used to prevent any attempt at reform by a Christian Democrat Government in Italy.

The scope of the DC on a governmental level appears even more restricted, if one considers the DC's involvement with political and economic bodies below this level (sottogoverno). Almost two thirds of all mayors and over 50% of local councillors are members of the DC; and the national average vote is some 39%. Public banking is almost entirely in the hands of DC members. Furthermore, 90% of all key positions in the various state-owned or semi-state-owned societies (ENTI) — there are an estimated 60,000 of these societies — are occupied by the DC[11]. The state holdings which 10 years ago were considered as driving forces in the development of the Italian economy are today merely "agencies for the benefit of bankrupt firms; agencies which are ruined themselves by office patronage"[12]. As a consequence of this development, free enterprise has increasingly assumed an attitude of "wait and see" towards the DC. This development increases the distrust that large parts of the population have towards state-owned institutions; for all too often those accused of bribery and their investigators are to be found in the same political camp. However, the DC's position with the media is relatively strong. Radio and television are state-controlled and are thus subject to considerable influence by Government groups. Daily papers and magazines which are close to the DC cover between 60 and 75% of total circulation; compared with the electoral support of under 40%.

It is difficult to outline the programme of the DC. Like all parties which aim at integrating a variety of interests and which claim to be a people's party, the DC lacks a real programme: its policies are essentially pragmatic. During the first years after the war, the DC's policy was directed towards rebuilding Italy economically as well as constitutionally. Virtually all parties were united in their anti-fascist attitude. But the DC was divided on the question of form of government. The north called for a republic, the south was more in favour of retaining the monarchy. From 1948 on, after the popular front Governments of Czechoslovakia, Hungary and Poland had become dependent on the Soviet Union, the DC presented itself as an anti-communist stronghold. The 4th Cabinet of Gaspari (31/5/47 — 23/5/48) acted along the following principles: 1) a Western-orientated foreign policy; 2) economic development with American support; 3) public order and 4) cooperation with non-socialist and moderate socialist parties. After its success in the elections between 1948 and 1953, the guiding principles of centrism dominated home affairs: political objectives were to be achieved without the help of other parties, and only in special cases should a coalition of the centre and right be formed (DC, PSDI, PLI). As a result, Italy experienced from 1953 to 1962 a policy of unrestricted economic growth with all its negative side-effects, accompanied by a relative neglect of social problems.

Choosing the "centro-sinistra" (middle-left) formula was supposed to put a stop to the social problems of this industrial expansion. However, no reforms of note were introduced, apart from the laws on divorce in 1969. The debate on the abolition of these new divorce laws once again showed the contrasts in the "correnti": its right wing under Lombardi and Gedda was determined to have a referendum on the re-introduction of the indissolubility of marriage principle. This referendum was lost in May 1974 with 19 million votes against 13 million. With it failed the Vatican's last attempt to exercise influence on Italian politics. From 1970 on, the Italian economic miracle showed signs of crumbling; the "centro-sinistra" Government tried to counteract this by printing more currency and taking international loans, instead of introducing genuine reforms. This situation proved to be a time of stress for the DC, as well as its other coalition partners. **"Centro-sinistra" policies**

A clear sign of this crisis was the steady growth of support for the Communists. The PCI was founded after the 1st World War when the new mass parties, the PPI (predecessor of the DC) and the Socialist Party began to take over from the old parties of the laicist "risorgimento". In the wake of Lenin's revolution in the Soviet Union, the Socialists in Italy — as in the whole of Europe — were split into reformist and radical wings. In 1921, the radical wing under its leader Antonio Gramsci founded the PCI in Livorno. Gramsci's personality left its mark on the party, distinguishing the PCI today from its sister parties in the Eastern bloc. "His emphasis on the role of the intellectual, his dynamism — ... — his concentration on Italy's special situation, his historic commitment and will-power which made him revolt against the easy and mechanical opportunism of the II International: all this contained some of the force of spirit which makes the PCI of influence today in international communism"[13]. In the short time before the Fascist take-over, the PCI did not achieve political success abroad, but it managed to spread its political cells all over Italy. Gramsci had to suffer 10 years of fascist imprisonment; other leading members went into exile. However, the party *cadres* of the underground combined the class war with the struggle for national freedom; non-socialist classes also participated in this movement. Only a group of exiles involved themselves in world communism. Consequently, the mass of the party was spared any inner conflicts resulting from the sudden change from popular front policies to the pact between Hitler and Stalin. **PCI**

A. Gramsci died in 1937. In 1944, Palmiro Togliatti returned from his Moscow exile and became the leader of the Italian PCI. In accordance with the guidelines of Stalin's foreign policy, he immediately pledged the PCI to national reconstruction **Policies after the war** and cooperation with all socialist and catholic forces, and he gave the order to hand over all weapons used in the partisan battles[14]. This was the origin of "the Italian way to socialism" — a concept since developed. It tries to overcome the system by means of reforms; it acknowledges *bourgeois* rights and liberties (basic and human rights) as fundamental values, and does not merely set them up as a tactical framework to be used solely if the party's activities can profit from them. The existing body of the state is not to be destroyed, but is to be gradually adjusted to the socialist model through the PCI's participation in the power structure. The first expression of these ideas is to be found in Togliatti's will which was published, in a shortened version, in the communist paper "Rinascita" on September 5, 1964.

Programme

The PCI currently advocates an austerity programme: stimulation of production; a fight against absenteeism (assenteismo); firm guidelines on wages; state intervention and subvention for the developing regions in Italy; creation of an efficient financial administration; restoration of public finances, and the maintenance of market forces instead of the introduction of a planned economy. Other items are: a limited commitment to the European Community; support of the call for European elections and for a strengthening of the parliamentary level of the EC; no further rejection of NATO (the demand for its dissolution parallels that of reduction of the Warsaw pact)[15]. The "Centro Studi i per la Riforma dello Stato", a study centre of the PCI, calls for greater accountability in ministerial and parliamentary affairs; control of government funds (pensions and health insurance, etc) and of the Banca d'Italia (central bank); separation of the two chambers' functions: chamber of deputies as the legislative, senate as the control instrument; installation of permanent commissions consisting of parliamentary members and trade union representatives; the creation of a policy co-ordinating body for the Prime Minister; and a reduction and concentration of government departments. All these policy objectives could be subscribed to by a *bourgeois* party[16].

Historical compromise

The PCI does not want to fulfil this programme by emulating a left-wing popular front Government such as that of Allende in Chile. Instead, it favours the "historical compromise" (compromesso historico): that is, a government coalition between the DC and the PCI. This coalition is intended to represent and cover both socialist and catholic classes of the population. From a historical point of view, this coalition would continue in the tradition of Gramsci and Togliatti; however, the direct cause for a definite commitment to the policy may have been the failure of the Chilean popular front Government.

Membership structure

This programme, which is rather unusual for a Communist party, corresponds with the variety of membership and the structure and behaviour of individual sections and members of the party. In 1947, the percentage of workers in the PCI was 62% of total membership. By 1972, the percentage had fallen by a third to 41%. Craftsmen and self-employed now account for 7.7%, and pensioners and housewives make up 27.5%. The disintegration of *cadre* structures is illustrated by the fall in industrial party groups which between 1950 and 1971 shrank from about 11,300 to about 3,000. Only 20-25% of the members regularly attend section meetings. At the same time, more and more positions of the higher party officials are occupied

76

by well-educated people with GCE A-level equivalent or a university degree. Only about 30% of provincial secretaries come from the working classes; and a little more than half of all deputies at the party convention have A-levels or a university degree[17]. The total membership fluctuates between 1.8 and 2 millions. One can draw parallels between the social composition of the PCI and its voters. Only about 40% of the working classes vote for the PCI, which is why it has to canvass support from other social classes. In its stronghold, the so-called "red belt" (comprising the provinces Manuta, Brescia, Rovigo, Viterbo, Emilia, Toscana and the Marches), the PCI gets about 43% of the working class votes and, significantly high for a "pure" class party, about 22% of the votes from the middle and upper classes[18].

The relatively free strategy of the PCI is possible because of its financial independence from the Eastern bloc. This results from an efficient membership subscription system, and also from the economic activities of the PCI. It owns publishing houses and bookshops, agricultural cooperatives and firms trading with Eastern Europe. The daily paper "Unita" (circulation 600,000), the members' paper "Rinascita" and the magazine "Critica Marxists" are its media. The PCI receives **Public** particular support from the following associations: the trade union CGIL **relations** (Confederazione generale italiana del lavoro), the women's association Unione Donne Italiana and the sports union Unione Italiana Sport Popolare.

Finally, it has to be pointed out that the PCI's movement away from the class party **Final** (Duverger) and from Moscow's influence was on the whole a successful step, for **evaluation** between 1953 and 1976, the percentage of votes gained by the party in elections increased by 11.8%. This means that 50% more people voted for the PCI.

Two other left-wing parties are the PSI and the PSDI. Both are characterised by **Socialist** their heterogeneous nature. The PSI likes using Marxist terms, but its programme is **parties** one of reform. Its main opponent is the DC, although the PSI participated for 12 years in DC cabinets.

Traditionally, the PSI is one of Italy's oldest parties. It was founded in 1891 as **Historical** "Partito dei Lavoratori Italiani", and from 1892 on it called itself PSI. At the time **background** of the First International, it stood for the anarchism of Bakunin and glorified violence as a means in the coming revolution. From 1900 on the party underwent an internal struggle between reformists and syndicalists. In 1912, the Partito Socialista Riformista Italiano (PSRI) became an independent group; in 1921, the Communists followed; in 1922 the PSU (Partito Socialista Unitario) was founded after some so-called right extremists had been excluded; in 1925 the Fascists banned all parties, and forced underground the Socialists again took their old name PSLI. At the end of the war, the various socialist groups made up the PSIUP (Partito Socialista Italiano di Unita Proletaria). In the Republic, this configuration split up once more in 1947. The right-wing reformist group under G. Sarragat favoured cooperation with the non-socialist parties and in 1952 adopted the name of PSDI (Partito Socialdemocratico Italiano). The other group were the Nenni Socialists; they fell back on the name PSI and at the time called for a left-wing popular front. In the years between 1966 and 1969, these two groups again united to form the PSI. However, the party remained heterogeneous and three sections of it developed:

a left-wing radical group under Celio Basso, the old Nenni Socialists, and the social democrat wing. Since then, only the PSI and the PSDI have been able to exercise political influence on the parliamentary political system. The left-wing radical PDUP (founded in 1964, Partito di Unita Proletaria per il Communismo) today has to be considered as an extra-parliamentary opposition. Its characteristic features are the formation of small groups of strong student *cadres* and concentration on regional activities. At present, the phenomenon of "correnti" has developed to such an extent in the socialist camp that the PSI has at least 5 and the PSDI at least 3. When the "Constituent Assembly" was elected in 1946, the socialists received only 20.7% of the total votes (PCI 18.9%); in the parliamentary elections in June 1976, the PSI and PSDI together polled only 13%. Today, more than 50% of the socialist parties' members belong to the middle classes (ceto medio), and a third of the members are workers and farmers. Participation in the government has had negative rather than positive effects, for the PSI as well as the PSDI had their full share of the DC's sinecures and the protectionist network and thus helped to give rise to the system of "sotto governo".

Non-socialist parties

Two parties are to be found in the non-socialist camp: the "Republicans" (PRI) who go back to Mazzini, and the "Liberals" (PLI) of whom the historian and philosopher B. Croce was once a member. The latter party can today be regarded as a small, rather conservative intellectual party. Its economic concepts correspond to the liberal ideas of the 19th century. Einaudi, who was many times minister of economics and finance, was the party's most prominent member. With its 18,000 members, it is among the small Italian parties and is in itself divided into at least 4 "correnti". The members live predominantly in the big cities of the north. In the 1976 elections, the party polled 1.3% of the votes; but by 1963, the percentage had increased to 7% falling back slightly in 1968 to 5.8%.

In comparison, the PRI is slightly more successful. Its political objective of enlightened capitalism permitted the party to participate in the "centro-sinistra" coalitions. The PRI's leader, Ugo de la Malfa, repeatedly managed to ensure that competent men of his party participated in coalitions, and they made constructive contributions towards the reform of the Italian political and administrative system. Overall, the PRI is less ideological and more technocratic in its outlook.

To sum up, while the two parties PRI and PLI poll only 20% of the Italian vote, they have managed to obtain a disproportionately large share of top government positions. However, they have not succeeded in developing into a non-socialist "mass" party — as, for example, the Conservative Party in England. They have failed also to prevent the polarisation of two dominant sub-cultures (the one influenced by Marxism and the other Catholic) and, therefore, have been unable to occupy the political centre as an independent "mass" party. As the two major political camps adopt many liberal and republican ideas and thus consistently attract particular groups of voters, the PRI's and PLI's already low vote potential, mainly to be found in the large cities of the north-west, has diminished.

Right wing

In the political spectrum, the Monarchists and Neo-Fascists lie to the right of all other parties. Despite the official anti-fascist attitude, the Neo-Fascists have succeeded in playing a not unimportant role in Italian politics, albeit a negative one. As early as the summer of 1945, the Neo-Fascists were organised in the form of the "Fronte dell'Uomo Qualunque" (Everyman Movement). Its leading ideologist, Guglielmo Gionannini attacked party rule, bureaucracy, the Allies' Italian policies and punishment of Fascists. In the election for the Constitutent Assembly, the Neo-Fascists polled 5.3% of all votes cast; in the south they even reached 9.7%. A little later, the Everyman Movement split into Monarchists (Partito Democratico di Unita Monarchico, later called Partito Nazionale Monarchico, since 1954 Partito Populare Monarchico, and in 1959 once more PDIUM) and Neo-Fascists (Movimento Sociale Italiano, MSI). Giorgio Almirante, former Under-Secretary of State in the republic of Salo (a city on lake Garda, where from September 1943 to April 1945 the expelled Mussolini Government had its headquarters), became the Neo-Fascists' first party secretary. He steered the party on a course of flexibility and adjustment to the existing parliamentary system; while arguing for the tactic of street canvassing and debate. The party soon achieved some weight, particularly at a regional level. In 1947, the election of the Christian Democrat mayor of Rome depended on the votes of neo-fascist town councillors, in Naples, the Neo-Fascists supported the Monarchist Lauro until the late sixties — later they supported the Gava group in the communal Government.

The further south one goes, the more people vote neo-fascist. There are two main reasons for this: 1) In 1943, a change of power occurred in the south when the monarchy, the army and the allies formed an alliance. This did not bring about persecution of Fascists who had held an office, nor did Fascists lose their positions to any notable extent. 2) In the north, the democratic resistance movements were relatively successful in their fight against the republic of Salo; later they started an anti-fascist campaign.

The followers of the MSI are mainly to be found in the middle classes of the bureaucracy, the services, the nationalised industries, as well as among the owners of small businesses, and also among the poor social classes of the south which are dependent on a patron. In Parliament, the leaders of the MSI stood for a policy which was nationalistic, pro-employer, anti-communist and ready to fight the alleged red terror. As the DC Governments find themselves in a situation of crisis, the MSI's parliamentary activities are orchestrated by a strategy of well-planned terror in the streets. Fights, bomb outrages, arson and gun-battles are staged in order to create a climate of social unrest where the Neo-Fascists aim to appear as the final upholders of law and order, and in a position to effect a coup d'etat together with other right-wing forces[19]. Although the Italian constitution prohibits the reorganisation of the dissolved Fascist Party in any form (transitory and final regulations, paragraph XII (1)), this regulation has not so far been applied nor has it led to any legal investigation of the MSI. Since 1971, the MSI has joined forces with the Monarchists: the MSI-DN (MSI-Destra Nazionale) obtained 8.7% of the votes in 1972; in 1976, the percentage was still 6.1%.

The MSI-DN split up on December 22, 1976. Leading party members without a

Fascist past (the Monarchist Covelli, the shipowner Achille Lauro, the national conservative secretary general of the CISNAL union (Confederazione Italiana Sindicaty Nazionali dei Lavoratori) and the previous leader of the parliamentary group, de Marizon) all accused Almirante, the secretary general of the Neo-Fascists, of lacking a political programme and of blindly glorifying pre-war fascism. Following a motion by Almirante, 9 out of 15 senators and 16 out of 36 deputies were excluded. These formed a new party: the "Constituant of the Right/National Democracy".

The South Tyrolese People's Party (SVP) occupies a special place within the Italian party system. The party considers itself a Christian movement which aims to unite the German-speaking minority of Italy in the Trentino region. It was founded in 1945 in order to succeed the "German Association" which had attended to the interests of the Tyrolese People's Party and the Liberal German Party after South Tyrol had become Italian in 1919. Originally, it was a party of the professional classes. But since 1957, it has been modernised by the party chairman, Dr Silvius Magnago, and at present it influences almost all public life in the province of Bozen. The party achieves this by an extensive nexus with societies and social organisations, via the German-speaking daily "Dolomites" (25,000) and through good relations with the Catholic church of South Tyrol. Today about 260,000 German-speaking people live in South Tyrol. In 1976, the SVP got 184,286 votes; one may assume that the whole of the German-speaking population that was able and willing to vote chose the SVP. As regards home affairs, the SVP clearly rejects the "historic compromise" between the DCI and the PCI.

Overall Picture

In the first elections to the chamber of deputies in 1948, eight parties were represented. From political right to left, these parties were: (1) extreme right: Monarchists (PNM) and Neo-Fascists (MSI); (2) right: Christian Democrats (DC) and Liberals (PLI); (3) centre-left: Republicans (PRI) and Social-Democrats (PSLI); (4) left: Socialists (PSI) and Communists (PCI). From the beginning, votes were concentrated on the DC and the PCI. In 1948, the parties to the right of the DC got 4.8% of the votes, and can therefore be considered as splinter groups; as, similarly, can be the Liberals with 3.8% and the Republicans with 2.5%. The socialist non-Communists accounted for about half of the communist votes. They found themselves in a 'socialist diaspora' where there was little else apart from the PCI.

On the governmental level, the decision about possible coalitions has been almost exclusively the responsibility of the DC; the intentions of the potential coalition party were of minor importance. Until 1953, de Gasperi (DC) governed with PSLI, PRI and PLI alternating as coalition partners. During the centralist phase, the DC tried to govern on its own whenever possible, and during the years 1953-1962 it spent only 2½ years in coalition with the PSDI (formerly PSLI) and the PLI. After the "opening towards the left" (apertura a sinistra), the PSI was also considered a possible coalition partner. However, not all coalitions that are logically possible can in practice be brought into being.

All the parties considered the extremists of the right (MSI and PRI) as unworthy coalition partners. Up to the present day, the DC has officially refused to share government with the Communists; the PSDI and the PLI adopt a similar attitude. The PRI does not want to commit itself, and the PSI is divided on the subject. The Communists, whose percentage of votes has come close to that of the DC, are guided by fundamental considerations in rejecting a left-wing popular front coalition and striving of the "historic compromise".

It is questionable whether such a difficult and complex situation can be characterised as "bipartismo imperfetto".[21] The electoral system in Italy has been a concentration of voting for the DC and PCI less pronounced than, for example, in West Germany with the CDU/CSU and SPD. G. Sartori[22] regards the Italian party system as an example of an extreme, multi-polar pluralism which functions as a political mirror of contrasts and conflicts in Italian society which have not yet been overcome. These are its essential features:

— The ideological content is high and contrasts with limited flexibility and inclination towards pragmatic political activities. **Critical points**
— Parties which are close to each other follow a strategy of 'going one better than the other party'.
— Any form of centralisation is missing; 'spin-off' tendencies predominate.
— Instead of a democratic change of power by means of alternative Governments, a 'peripheral' rotation occurs.
— For the extreme parties it is worth while being irresponsible in opposition; because of a lack of integration, parties which are against the system have a good chance of establishing themselves step by step.

It seems inconceivable that any change can be achieved without taking the PCI into account. At first glance, the executive appears relatively unstable: as is shown in the high number of changes in Government. Yet appearances are deceptive: in practice little genuine political change takes place, as the same politicians always occupy the leading positions[23].

After the elections in June 1976, a so-called "Constitutional Circle" came into being **Constitutional circle** which consisted of Christian Democrats, Communists, Social Democrats, Socialists, Republicans and Liberals. An agreement was reached that the PCI should preside in the chamber of deputies, and the Christian Democrats in the senate. The new Government under Andreotti (39th Government after the war, 3rd Andreotti cabinet) consisted only of DC members (monocolore). The former prime ministers, Moro, Rumor and Colombo, who were regarded as "pillars of the Christian Democrat establishment", no longer formed part of the Government. The Government could only function provided the previous partners of the DC and the Communists abstained from voting in the confidence vote. A year later, on July 12, the spokesmen of the parliamentary groups in the Constitutional Circle submitted a common declaration intended to restore the situation. However, as early as autumn

81

1977, this agreement began to crumble, and on January 16, 1978 received its final blow when the Andreotti Government resigned. Fresh negotiations with five parties of the Constitutional Circle (the Liberals were missing) resulted in a second party agreement, enabling another "monocolore" Government under Andreotti to be formed in March. This was the third "small compromise" with the Communists since 1976.

It seems questionable whether a DC/PCI coalition would be politically successful: it could prosper only in an atmostphere of permanent international detente. At the same time, the leaders of the PCI would have to be able to counteract and assuage all the conflicts of interests which would result from the ideology of class struggle. The PCI would also have to refrain from entanglement in the system of existing patronage and corruption. At this point in time, it is impossible to make good predictions about the development of the Italian party system over the next few years.[24]

Notes

[1] See Bibes, Genevieve: *Le Systeme Politique Italien* Vendome 1974, p. 63.

[2] See Chabod, Federico: *Die Entshehung des neuen Italien* rde 237, 1974, p. 17 f.

[3] See Commision of the European Communities (Ed.): *The Economic Situation of the Community*, No. 2, 1975, p. 27.

[4] See Sophie, G., Alf: *Leitfaden Italien*, Berlin 1977, p. 192.

[5] Mezzogiorno interno: regions in the south, upcountry, mostly consisting of bare rock, little fertile, remote from economic centres. — Mezzogiorno esterno: coastal regions of the south with flourishing agriculture and an infrastructure that is in the process of developing.

[6] Mean value of data in Rosenbaum, Petra: *Italien 1976 — Christdemokraten mit Kommunisten?* rororo aktuell 1944, Hamburg 1976, p. 23.

[7] Cf for the system of 'secondo lavoro' Rosenbaum, ibid., p. 18 ff.

[8] Parish: all activities are geared to the concerns of one's own village and go on further.

[9] CF Beyme, Klaus v.: *Das politische System Italiens*, Stuttgart 1970, p. 126 and Bibes, Genevieve, ibid., p. 15.

[10] Cf Frölich, Roland: *Die Democracia Christiana nach dreissig Jahren Machtausübung.* In: Der Bürger im Staat, No. 3, 1976, p. 163.

[11] This subject is treated in detail in: *L'iceberg demochristiano* by G. Tamburrano, Milano 1974.

[12] Quotation by the former president of the Italian central bank, Guido Carli.

[13] See Beyme, Klaus v., ibid., p. 90.

[14] Cf Buck, Karl-Hermann: *Wie glaubwürdig ist die italienische KP?* In: Der Bürger im Staat, No. 3, 1976, p. 167.

[15] On the programmes of the PCI see Barca, Luciano e.a.: *I communisti e l'economia italiana 1944—1974.* Bari 1975, and C. Galluzi: *Crisi e perspettive dell'Europa* In: Critica Marxista No. 6, 1972.

[16] Cf Rosenbaum, Petra, ibid., p. 64 f.

[17] Taken from Buck, Karl-Herman, ibid., p. 169

[18] Cf Sani, G: *La Strategia del PCI e l'elettorato italiano* In: Rivista Italiana di Scienza Politica 1973, p. 551—579.

[19] Just think of the affairs of the chief of the secret police, de Lorenzo, in 1963/4, and the arrest of the chief of the secret service, Miceli, in 1974. Both generals secretly trained troups for a putsch; Miceli ordered the occupation of ministeries and public institutions in Rome.

[20] See G. Galli: *Il difficile governo*, Bologna 1972, p. 84.

[21] Bipartismo imperfetto: imperfect two-party system, cf G. Sartori: European Political Parties: The Case of Polarised Pluralism. In: Palombara J. la and Weiner, M. (Ed.): *Political Parties and Political Development*, Princeton 1966, p. 137 ff.

[22] See G. Sartori: *European Political Parties and Political Development*, Princeton 1966, p. 137 ff.

[23] The Sueddeutsche Zeitung wrote on 7.12.1974: "This team of skip-jacks which is still so agile despite countless falls is without parallel throughout the world".

[24] The 1979 national election results are given in Appendix I.

Netherlands

THEO STAMMEN

The Netherlands and European integration

The Netherlands, which form the BENELUX economic union together with Belgium and Luxembourg, is one of the "three small democracies" among the founder states of the European Community. Like Belgium and Luxembourg, the Netherlands committed itself with particular dedication to the cause of European integration after the 2nd World War; mainly as a result of the German occupation. The Netherlands never gave up hope of realising the European cause, even at times when French resistance under de Gaulle seemed to block the process of European unification for the foreseeable future; leading Dutch politicians and parties made repeated initiatives towards a strengthening and expansion of the Community. It was the Dutch parties in particular which constantly called for direct elections to the European Parliament.

Historical Background

Origins

According to the resolution of the congress in Vienna (1815), the northern and southern Netherlands were to be united to form a state, the "Kingdom of the Netherlands". Despite the traditional historical connections between the two regions, the formation of this state was not successful. The denominational contrasts between the predominantly Protestant north and the Catholic south immediately led to severe conflicts in constitutional and home affairs; in 1830 the southern provinces declared their independence and called themselves Belgium, forcing the northern provinces to form a state of their own.

Constitution (1815)

The 1815 consitution envisaged a constitutional monarchy with a distribution of power between King and Government on the one hand and Parliament (2 chambers) on the other. The revisions of the constitution in 1840 and 1848 specified that the Government should be answerable in parliamentary terms to the second chamber (the representation of the people). This change still did not give the Netherlands a full parliamentary system. Finally, in a constitutional conflict during the 1860s, the King's political influence was curbed to such a degree that the Government was bound by the prevailing majority in Parliament.

Electoral reform

The last third of the 19th century as well as the time up to the end of the 1st World War was dominated by discussion about electoral reform. The right to vote was only gradually granted to new groups of voters; it was only in 1917 that all men received equal franchise and 1919, when the same right was introduced for women.

Development of the parties

From a party-political point of view, constitutional development in the 19th century was above all influenced by the Liberals. Apart from them, the Catholics — although a minority in this predominantly protestant state — formed their political organisation early on. The Conservative Party felt it had to defend royal prerogatives; as a consequence, it rapidly lost its political importance after the

84

constitutional conflict of the sixties. There also existed a party of (protestant) anti-revolutionaries who — on the basis of the strict religious convictions — set themselves firmly against the revolutionary ideal of the sovereignty of the people.

At first, these parties were essentially parliamentary groups. The census system of voting in the 19th century favoured in particular the urban bourgeoisie which voted mainly Liberal. Party-political organisations were not yet needed. Matters changed when various electoral reforms were introduced towards the end of the 19th century. Now extra-parliamentary party organisations were needed in order to organise the growing number of voters; furthermore, new small parties gained seats in Parliament. The Liberals as well as the Protestants split into various groups and thereby lost in strength and political influence. This was paralleled by the political rise of the Dutch workers and the formation of a Social-Democrat Worker's Party. **Worker's party** The expansion and simultaneous division in the party field made it particularly difficult to form coalitions and Governments during this period.

The Social Democrats and Catholics benefited above all from the introduction of **Proportional** the system of proportional representation in 1917. Other than that, it did not **representation** result in any cohesiveness in the party system, despite its effects on tiny splinter **since 1917** parties. The reverse was true: in the period between the wars, the Dutch party system was characterised by the absence of clear-cut majorities. A multitude of parties, sometimes as many as 40, fought in the elections. As a rule, 10-12 parties won seats in Parliament; the Communists were among these parties after 1919. The formation of a coalition was necessarily a complicated and tedious matter as there were not established connections between the parties. The number of Government **Coalition** and coalition crises and changes is therefore not surprising: 9 between 1919 and **problems** 1940. Circumstances were further aggravated by the fact that the Netherlands did not have a close relationship between Government and Parliament; as , for example, in the United Kingdom. The doctrine of separation of powers was formally incorporated into the constitution in 1938, but had already been practised before that time.

The Present Party System

The 2nd World War, the invasion and occupation by the Germans, have left deep **New start after** marks in the national history of the Netherlands; but the continuity of the political **1945** order and of the party system was not destroyed. The Monarch and the Government went into exile in London, and from there they kept Dutch democracy alive. After 1945, there was a relatively quick return to normal political life.

Social Conditions

The social conditions which determine the Dutch party system have deep historical roots. There are two main social divisions which are politically relevant.

First, the country is divided according to religious denomination, an outcome of historical development, but which continues to exercise a strong influence on the party-political structure. About 40% of the population are Catholics; 28% members of the Dutch Reformed Church; while 9% belong to other protestant groups and the remainder consists of non-religious social groups.

Denominationally, Dutch society up to the present day has consisted of three groups: (1) Catholics, (2) Calvinists and (3) the non-denominational. These three sectors each have their own geographical stronghold. Catholics live mainly in the south (where they represent more than 90% of the population), Calvinists live in the south-west and in central Holland, and the non-denominational in the west and the north.

Apart from this religious division, Dutch society has its own (horizontal) class structure which is similar to those of other modern industrial societies. However, for historical reasons, the differences between the middle and working classes is of particular importance in the Netherlands; these differences strongly influence social attitudes. Compared with most European countries, the *bourgeoisie* of Dutch society achieved power and influence very early. The social inequality between the two classes is also greater in the Netherlands than, for example, in Scandinavia, and corresponds to a strong feeling of attachment to social class. This horizontal class structure naturally cuts across the (vertical) religious division of society. As far as the Catholic and Calvinist groups are concerned, horizontal divisions do not result in a further fundamental distinction, as both groups are united by the Christian faith. However, in the non-denominational groups, the social class division is between the middle and working classes.

On the basis of these distinctions, one can talk of a fourfold social division: Catholics, Protestants, Liberal *bourgeoisie* and socialist workers. This social structure determines the character of the Dutch party system.

Political Conditions

After 1945, the political system of the Netherlands was renewed on the basis of the former constitutional law. Thus the 'Basic Law of the Kingdom of the Netherlands of 1815' is still valid, although some constitutional changes have occured. As a result, the Netherlands has a constitutional monarchy with a parliamentary political system which has become more democratic with the reform of the electoral laws.

Parliament consists of two chambers: the *first* chamber which is elected indirectly (and which has less political influence); and the *second* chamber which is elected directly by the people for a term of five years. Both chambers have the same position and powers in relation to the Government: that is, the Government needs the support of *both* chambers. In practice, however, only the second chamber needs to support the Government, as the political process is largely an interplay between the two.

In the Netherlands, it is not possible to hold Government office and a seat in Parliament. The interrelationship is, therefore, indirect through the parties. Consequently, Parliament enjoys more independence and greater political freedom from the Government than, for example, the British House of Commons. This is one of the reasons why the Dutch Parliament is relatively strong; despite the fact that today almost all political initiatives come from the Government.

The multitude of political parties in Parliament (usually more than 10) does not make government an easy matter. It is interesting to note that even the smallest splinter groups can freely go about their political and parliamentary activities. They also take part in parliamentary committees which in other countries (for example the German Parliament) are reserved for large parliamentary groups.

Multi-party system

Governments are invariably formed by coalition because of the large number of parties represented in Parliament. Generally, this process is tedious and difficult, even more so than in Belgium. Once a Government coalition has been achieved (which may take months) is does not need the express confidence of the second chamber. Confidence is assumed as long as it is not explicitly withdrawn by a vote of Parliament. Basically, it is only possible to suspend a Government by dissolving the coalition. However, this would not automatically lead to the dissolution of Parliament and to new elections, but to the formation of a new coalition (with the exclusion of the party which brought about the dissolution of the previous coalition). For this reason all coalition partners are usually interested in keeping alive the alliance they have entered and the Government's position is strong, even when formed from multi-party coalition.

Coalition problems

The position of the Dutch Prime Minister in relation to his Government is not quite as strong as that of the British Prime Minister or the German Chancellor; it is rather a position of "primus inter pares" (first among equals). Consequently, the Netherlands does not have a "prime minister" or "chancellor" democracy. The Prime Minister is not able to force the Queen to dissolve Parliament on his own; he needs the agreement of the Government. Thus he lacks the means of pressuring Government as well as Parliament.

Position of the Prime Minister in the Government

The Prime Minister is not the only mediator between the Crown and the Government, for the Queen has the right (and makes use of it) to receive each minister for information and advice.

It has already been hinted at that the electoral system of the Netherlands functions as an important and specific political determinant of the party system. The Netherlands votes according to a system of proportional representation which is combined with a particular mechanism of seat distribution: votes cast for all parties in the whole of the country are at first added up, and then divided by the number of available parliamentary seats (150). The resultant quotient determines the distribution of seats. More precisely: the number of seats that a party is allocated depends on how often the quotient divides into the total of votes cast for that particular party. This system is of political significance, because even the smallest parties polling fewer than 1% of the votes can expect to have a seat in Parliament.

Electoral system

Distribution of seats

The Contemporary Party System

As we have seen, the Dutch electoral system favours small and even tiny party groups. This is one of the reasons why, during the time after the war, the spectrum of the Dutch party system has constantly changed. Sometimes up to 20 parties or more contest elections; more than 10 to 12 have had regular seats in Parliament.

For some time after 1945 it seemed as if the party system might be reduced to the following five parties: (1) the Catholic People's Party which usually emerged from the elections as the strongest party; (2) the "Anti-Revolutionary Party" and (3) the "Christian Historic Union" on the protestant side. The remaining two parties were non-denominational: (4) the liberal "People's Party for Freedom and Democracy" and (5) the social democratic "Labour Party". Apart from these larger parties, some

small splinter groups existed such as the "Farmer's Party", the "Communist Party" and the "Pacifist-Socialist Party" but none of these could expect more than a few parliamentary seats.

The growing discontent among the voters with the governing larger parties became evident in the election of 1967. The results produced significant changes in the structure of the Dutch party system, and ultimately led to its disintegration. The number of parties contesting the election had increased to 24; of these, 11 gained seats in Parliament. The Catholic People's Party and the Social Democrats suffered considerable losses; the number of seats for the splinter parties increased from 15 to 27. The newly founded party called "Democrats '66" won 7 seats straight away; it had been founded mainly by intellectuals with the intention of reforming Dutch democracy. The right-extremist Farmers' Party won an identical number of seats.

The "Democrats '66" aimed at breaking down the rigid structures of Dutch parliamentarism and reforming them. So far, this movement does not seem to have been successful: the diversity of the party structure became more pronounced in the early seventies. In the 1972 elections, 14 parties won seats in Parliament. The Catholic People's Party and the traditional Protestant parties lost their votes and seats to newly created Catholic and Calvinist splinter groups. The "Democratic Socialists '70" which competed with the Workers' Party, won 6 seats immediately.

Such a strong differentiation between parties was unusual even by Dutch standards; as a result the party system itself began to collapse. In such circumstances it was difficult to form a Government: it took 164 days! The Government finally comprised a complicated five-party coalition consisting of the Workers' Party, the Radical People's Party, the Democrats '66, the Catholic People's Party and the Anti-Revolutionary Party under the leadership of the socialist den Uyl.

Since 1945, there had usually been four-party (at the most) or three-party coalition Governments. The five traditional parties have participated in various combinations. The Catholic People's Party, as the largest party, had until the elections in 1967 and 1972 always played the major role. These elections put an end to this tradition and gave rise to untried party alliances.

It now seems that this trend (which resulted in a gradual disintegration of the Dutch party system) has been reversed by the election in May, 1977: all is set for a concentration of party-political forces and the party system. The fact that in the autumn of 1976 the various traditional denominational parties finally united to

88

form a 'Christian Democrat' party is indicative of this desire since denominational and ideological differences had long been in the way of such a union.

The May elections brought clear gains for the large parties at the expense of the The end to differentiation? small groups. One could deduce from this that the Dutch electorate had realised the dangers of a disintegration of the party system. It was true that 11 parties won seats in Parliament; but the number of seats won by the small splinter parties was greatly reduced: 4 out of the 11 parties are represented by only one deputy, one party (the Communist Party) by two, and two other parties by three deputies each. The greater part of the 150 parliamentary seats was won by large parties: in particular by the Social Democrats (53), and the Christian Democrats (49) and by the Liberals (28). The Democrats '66 still have 8 seats. The exact distribution of seats in the Dutch Parliament after the election in March 1977 is as follows:

Social Democrats	(PVDA)	53	(43)
Christian Democrats	(CDA)	49	(48)
Liberals	(VVD)	28	(22)
Democrats '66	(D'66)	8	(5)
Radicals	(PPR)	3	(7)
Communist Party	(KPN)	2	(7)
Democratic Socialists	(DS'70)	1	(6)
Reform Party	(SGP)	3	(3)
Farmers' Party	(BP)	1	(3)
Politically Reformed League	(GPV)	1	(2)
Pacifist Socialists	(PSP)	1	(2)
Roman-Catholic Party	(RKPN)	0	(1)

At first it had been suspected that the previous head of Government of the Netherlands might become the leader of a new coalition which (only) consisted of two parties: his own Social Democrats and the Christian Democrats.

Finally, after the longest process of Government formation in Dutch history, and after the two parties had already reached agreement on all factual matters of their government programme, the coalition collapsed because of disagreement on the distribution of ministerial posts. Relatively soon after the failure of this coalition, the Christian Democrats and Liberals, who had a very slight majority in Parliament, formed a small coalition. The Social Democrats had to go into opposition. In this way, the political opportunities open to a coalition between the Social Democrats and the Christian Democrats through their two-thirds majority in Parliament were wasted. Such a coalition might have introduced a reform of the electoral system and thus helped to further stabilise the party system.

Belgium

THEO STAMMEN

Belgium and European integration

Together with the Netherlands and Luxembourg, with which Belgium has been closely connected since 1947 in the BENELUX economic union, Belgium is one of the so-called "small democracies" of Western Europe. Following its bitter experiences in the 2nd World War, Belgium was always intensely dedicated to the cause of European integration and the formation of a political union in Europe. Belgian politicians such as the Socialist Spaak and the Christian Democrat Tindemans count among the most distinguished "Europeans" of our time. The Belgian political parties are particularly receptive to the idea of forming European parties and of holding European direct elections.

Historical Background

Foundation of the Belgian state (1830)

The beginnings of the Belgian party system coincide with the foundation of the Belgian state, and are closely connected with the foundation movement. At the Congress of Vienna in 1815, the southern Belgian provinces were united with the northern Netherlands to form the "Kingdom of the Netherlands". Since that day, the southern, mainly Catholic, provinces opposed Dutch (and this meant Protestant) rule. They rejected, for example, the Dutch constitution of 1814. This conflict culminated in a unilateral declaration of independence in 1830 and the foundation of an independent Belgian state. In 1931, a formal written constitution was adopted which was based on liberal prinicples and which was to have great influence on European consitutionalism in general and German consitutionalism in particular.

Alliance of Liberals and Catholics

The Catholic and Liberal French-speaking citizens of the large cities who were receptive to the ideas of the French Revolution formed the basis of the independence movement which led to the foundation of the Belgian state. Up to the middle of the century, these two groups were politically united by their rejection of the Netherlands and by their endeavour to secure Belgian independence. After that time, their ideological differences became more obvious: a radical and basically anti-clerical liberalism contrasted with a strong political catholicism. These

Conflicts

differences were epitomised in the schools conflict which was treated in the style of a "Kulturkampf" (struggle between the state and the Roman Catholic church). Although the Liberals were in power up to 1880, they were not able to improve their ideal of a completely secularised state, for they met with the opposition of the predominantly catholic population which proved very strong in the rural areas. In 1884, the Liberals lost their dominance and the Catholics, who stayed in power until 1914, succeeded in removing the "Kulturkampf" fronts to a large extent.

The secular role of the state was not the only source of party difference during that

90

time. The social problems arising from industrialisation that had emerged, created tensions and differences in domestic and party politics, and these led to the foundation of the Belgian Socialist Party (from 1885 called the "Belgian Workers' Party) in 1879. This working class movement, together with the Pope's social encyclical "Rerum Novarum", had strong repercussions on Belgian political catholicism and resulted in the Belgian Christian Democrats placing great emphasis on social reform.

Closely connected with the resolution of social questions was that of the reform of the electoral system which was of importance to the emergent working classes. The 1831 consitution envisaged an exclusive electoral system by property census which limited the franchise to the property-owning class. In the last third of the 19th century, the growing social movement together with progressive Liberal groups demanded, with increasing determination, the introduction of a general right to vote. As a result of demonstrations and strikes in 1892/3, the electoral system was finally reformed; a universal franchise of election by majority vote was introduced. Although expected to favour the Socialists, the Catholics profited from it, and gained a Parliamentary majority. **Social questions**

The 19th century also saw the origins of the Flemish movement. This upsurge of interest in Flemish culture tended to exaggerate the conflicts of language and culture, which remains a major problem in Belgian politics. As already mentioned, the foundation of the Belgian state had been supported mainly by the French-speaking urban *bourgeoisie*, guided by the ideas of the French Revolution. They had created a unity state, following the French model, but had not taken into account the ethnic and linguistic differences of the country. By contrast, the "Vlaamse Beweging" (Flemish movement), which was influenced by the nationalist ideas of the romantic period, strove for equal rights for the Flemish language and culture within the Belgian state. From 1877 this movement gradually succeeded in emancipating the Flemish part of the population. As a consequence of this, all political parties in Belgium have since had to make concessions to the Flemish demand for equal linguistic and cultural attention. **Electoral system**

The Belgian party structure developed into a three-party system in the course of the 19th century: it consisted of Catholics, Socialists and Liberals. The existing electoral system of majority vote worked increasingly in favour of the Catholics and Socialists who had real strongholds in Flanders and Walloon respectively. The Liberals, however, who were scattered all over the country, experienced a crisis that threatened their very existence. The introduction of proportional representation in 1899 and combined lists in 1919 prevented the development of a two-party system. The change of the electoral system saved the Liberals from extinction and in the years up to the 1st World War they had time to re-establish their influence. **Flemish movement**

The new electoral system also had another significant effect: it created the necessity for extra-parliamentary party organisations. Close connections developed between the parties, in particular between the Socialists and non-parliamentary pressure groups.

Although the system of proportional representation basically furthers the formation of smaller parties, this did not occur in Belgium. The three larger parties remained dominant in the period between the two wars.

The Catholic Party was not totally unified. Within the party, tensions existed between Flemish and Walloon and conservative and democratic elements. During this period, several groups left the party. It was only when the party was re-founded after 1945 as the "Christian Social Party" ("Parti Social Chretien") that it achieved greater unity.

The Socialists, too, had their problems: in 1920, a left-wing radical group intent on class warfare left the party; and in the thirties, the party experienced various internal crises. Finally, it adopted a more pragmatic attitude changing its name to "Parti Socialiste Belge" (PSB) in 1945.

The Liberals as the third strongest party followed a course of pragmatic change in the time between the wars: they rejected classic liberalism and called for a policy of social reform. This brought them close to the Belgian Socialists, with whom they occasionally worked.

The time between the wars

The narrowing of the gap between the large Belgian parties became clear in the coalitions which formed from 1919 to 1940. Governments in this period consisted of two or three of the large parties: always including the Catholics. In the event of the new formation of a Government or a coalition, it often occurred that not only did the coalition partners change, but also different groups from within the parties were given a share in Government. Language differences between the Flemish and Walloon population began to affect the structure of such coalitions at this time.

The Contemporary Party System

Coalitions

Following the 2nd World War and the German occupation, new political order was restored. The party-political developments followed traditional lines: the three large parties — the Catholic Party, the Socialist Party and the Liberal Party — took over the leading roles, sometimes under new names.

Since the war, however, the party system has noticeably changed: mainly because an increasing proportion of the Flemish and Walloon people speak French.

Social Conditions

Renewal based on tradition

However unlikely it may sound, the class or denominational structure of the country is *not* the decisive social determinant of the contemporary Belgian party system. The present party structure clearly shows that these historically significant factors have been over-shadowed by linguistic differences: 56.3% of the population speak Flemish, and 32.1% speak Walloon; 11% are bilingual (Brussels), while 0.6% speak German. In the fifties and particularly in the sixties, the language and culture conflicts were severe and occasionally (for example, during the controversy in the university city of Lowen) came close to destroying the unity of the Belgian state.

Linguistic dualism

Even consitutional reforms (as in 1971) have not yet succeeded in "defusing" the situation. The only solution that might prove satisfactory in the long term would be

92

a change in the Belgian political structure: from a unitary to a federal state (as for example in Switzerland which is also multi-lingual). So far, there has been some hesitation over taking such a radical step and in its absence it seems, from the evidence of the last elections in April 1977, that the language controversy will remain a major problem of Belgian politics. However, there are indications of serious endeavours to find a fundamental solution to the problem.

All party-political re-groupings, divisions and changes, with the exception of the Communist Party's split into a Moscow — and a Peking — orientated group, are a direct result of the language controversy. The unity of the three large parties has also been deeply affected, with the formation of internal factions.

Necessary federalisation

By comparison, all other social problems and tensions which are unavoidable by — products of modern Western industrial societies are of secondary importance. Belgium has an established trade union system, with three main unions: the (Socialist) "General Belgian Workers' Union" which consists of 15 individual trade unions and about 700,000 members; the "Association of Christian Trade Unions" with its 900,000 members; and the (Liberal) "General Association of Free Trade Unions" with about 100,000 me·nbers.

Political Conditions

The constitution of 1831 remains, although it has undergone a series of changes. According to this constitution, Belgium is a unitary state with a constitutional monarchy. Originally, political power was shared by the King and the Government on the one hand, and Parliament on the other. This dualistic system has long since developed into a parliamentary system and has been democratised by various reforms to the electoral system. Women in Belgium received the right to vote comparatively late — in 1948.

Consequences of the language controversy

There is a close political relationship between Parliament and Government. According to the constitution, the King still has a number of rights which are politically relevant (for example, he can veto certain bills); but in practice no longer makes use of them.

The Belgian Parliament consists of two chambers: a chamber of deputies and a senate. The chamber of deputies is the representative house; it has 212 members who are elected for a term of 4 years on a proportional representation system. In Belgium, it is compulsory to vote. The choice of senators is complicated: they are partly elected directly by the people (106, that is half of the members of the chamber of deputies) for a term of 4 years; 48 senators are elected by councillors of the provinces, and a further 24 are chosen by the senators already elected ("co-opted").

Constitutional monarchy

The Prime Minister and ministers are appointed by the King, their choice must be supported by the majority of the two chambers. The King has the right to dissolve Parliament: he can dissolve both chambers at the same time or individually.

93

The Party System at Present

Parliamentary
system

As already pointed out, deeply rooted linguistic dualism has led to a considerable differentiation in the spectrum of the Belgian party system since the fifties. Apart from the four traditional parties, namely the Christian Social Party, the Socialists, the Liberals and the Communists, there are now various other nationalist parties; first, the Flemish People's Union was founded, later the French-Speaking Democratic Front (which was mainly active in Brussels) and the Walloon Collective Movement.

Differentiations
of the party
system

The language differences have also affected the inner unity of the four traditional parties. In each one, strong Flemish and Walloon groups have developed; they have become largely independent, compete with each other and fight for the interests of the various language groups. This naturally has a detrimental effect on the larger parties' cohesive strength.

Christian
Social Party

The Christian Social Party, founded in 1945 as successor of the Catholic Party, is still the strongest force in the country. The party has about 200,000 members. Traditionally, it is strongest in Flanders but today it also has a considerable following in the Walloon part of the country. The party has always been influenced by the social reformism of Belgian Catholicism, and had adopted a positive attitude to social reform. Language differences have disrupted the party badly.

Socialist Party

It has split into two virtually independent factions each of which has its leader: the (Flemish) Christian People's Party and the (Walloon) Christian Social Party. The Socialist Party has always been stronger in the Walloon region, because originally Belgian industry was concentrated in this area. More recently, and this is a direct consequence of the European Economic Community, the Flemish part of the country has been greatly industrialised, so that today the Socialist Party is active here too. The party's organisation is split into two in order to take account of the language differences.

Liberals

The Liberals, who played a dominant role in the 19th century, are at present the third force in the party system. Since 1961, their party has been called "Party for Freedom and Progress". The party is traditionally anti-clerical. It represents the interests of the (non-Catholic) middle class, the self-employed and employers. Given the interests that it represents, it is progressive in favouring social reform. The party does not possess any particular geographical stronghold; it has a following throughout the country. Consequently, because of the language problem, its unity is in even greater danger than that of the other parties. Three Liberal party groups fought in the last election (April 1977): a Flemish, a Walloon and a bilingual group (for Brussels).

Communists

The Communist Party has existed in Belgium since 1921. Its electoral programme is Moscow-orientated. However, in 1963 a Peking-orientated faction left the party to form an independent group; and in 1968 a further split occurred and a Maoist group emerged. Partly due to its patriotic cooperation in the resistance against the German occupation forces, the Belgian CP played an important role for a short period immediately after the war. Between 1944 and 1946, it participated in three Governments. However, since the beginning of the Cold War, it has been permanently in opposition. Recently, the Belgian CP has split into a Flemish and a Walloon group, each with its own leader.

With the foundation of the Flemish People's Union in 1953, a Flemish national party came into existence. It followed in the steps of similar parties during the twenties and thirties. At times this party had a considerable following in the Flanders region of the country, but so far has not participated in a Government. It is the party's declared objective to federalise the country, granting as much autonomy as possible, in the belief that this will solve the language conflict. In this context, it seeks greater economic development, particularly in the Flanders area. **Flemish People's Union**

In response to the activities of the Flemish People's Union, two Walloon groups have evolved: the French-Speaking Democratic Front (focussed on Brussels) and the Walloon Collective Movement. **Walloon groups**

Finally, the small and politically irrelevant Party of German-Speaking Belgians should be mentioned. Founded in 1972, it represents the cultural and educational interests of a German-speaking minority in Eastern Belgium (about 25 communities). **German representation**

The post-war Belgium political structure has necessitated Government by coalition. These coalitions have become more difficult to form. Since 1945, the Christian Social Party has only once been able to win an absolute majority and govern on its own (1950 to 1954). All other Governments have consisted of coalitions in which the three large parties participated alternatively. The Christian Social Party, however, together with the Liberals or the Socialists, has shared political power most frequently and produced most of the political leaders. **Coalition politics**

Negotiations on coalitions invariably take a considerable time and have almost developed into a ritual. First, the King appoints a politician as an "informateur", it is his task to assess the situation. At an appropriate stage (when the framework of a possible coalition has been worked out) a "formateur" is appointed who is responsible for the formation of the coalition and the Government, and who then becomes the political leader.

The effect that the language problems have had on the inner structure of the three large Belgian parties has naturally increased the difficulties in forming coalition Governments. The constitutional reform of 1971 sought to alleviate language and cultural conflicts by granting greater autonomy to the various parts of the country and since that time, it has been imperative to let all groups and sub-groups take part in the formation of Governments according to a finely balanced proportional representation procedure. The most recent Government formed following the elections of April 18th, 1977, illustrates the difficulties perfectly. It was only on June 2nd that the Christian Democrat Tindemans could present a new coalition Government to the King. His Government consists of 4 parties which together hold 172 of the 212 parliamentary seats (that is, they have more than a two-thirds majority). The parties involved are: the Flemish and Walloon Christian Democrats, the Socialists with their two wings, (for the first time) the Flemish People's Union and the (Brussels) French-Speaking Democratic Front. The Liberals, the Walloon Collective Movement and the Communists together form the opposition. **Proportional participation**

This enumeration does not, however, convey the "microstructure" of the coalition

95

which ultimately consists of a fine quantitative group division. The new Government has 30 members (23 ministers and 7 secretaries of state). They are recruited from the various parties as follows: Flemish Christian People's Party: the Prime Minister and 7 ministers/secretaries of state; French-Speaking Christian Social Party: 4; Walloon Socialists: 7; Flemish Socialists: 5; Flemish People's Union: 3; French-Speaking Democratic Front: 3. Even before it was sworn in, this Government faced a crisis because the French-Speaking Christian Socialists were not content with their ministerial allotment. This shows only too clearly how much patience and skill is needed to establish a balance which can serve as a proper basis for a functioning Government. The astonishingly broad foundation of this new coalition (two-thirds majority in Parliament) indicates that the new Government regards the federalisation of the country as the consitutional solution of Belgium's permanent political crisis. Establishing regional political units whose parameters coincide with the language frontiers, and introducing a federal political structure may be the only way to put an end to the continuing crisis in the Belgian state and in the Belgian party system.

Following the elections of April 1977, the Belgian Parliament is composed as follows:

CVP (Flemish Christian Democrats)	56 (+6)
PSC (French-Speaking Christian Democrats)	24 (+2)
PSB-BSP (Socialist Party)	62 (+3)
PVV (Flemish Liberals)	17 (−4)
PRLW (Walloon Liberals)	14 (+5)
PL (Brussels Liberals)	2 (−1)
FDF (French-Speaking Democratic Front)	11 (+2)
VU (Flemish People's Union)	20 (−2)
RW (Walloon Collective Movement	(4) (−9)
PC-KP (Communists)	(2) (−2)

96

Luxembourg

THEO STAMMEN

Among the countries of the European Community, the Grand Duchy of Luxembourg is by far the smallest: it covers an area of about 2,500km² and has 360,000 inhabitants. Following its bitter experiences under German occupation, Luxembourg gave up its neutrality (1945) and committed itself to a policy of European integration. This occurred initially in the framework of the BENELUX economic union (1947), and later in the EEC (1957) of which Luxembourg is one of the founder members.

Historical Background

Luxembourg's present configuration and constitutional position was determined by the restructuring of Europe after the Vienna Congress. Luxembourg was made a Grand Duchy within the German Confederation, and at the same time it was attached to the Kingdom of the Netherlands. When in 1830 Belgium separated itself from the Netherlands, Luxembourg followed its example and joined Belgium. However, in 1839 Luxembourg was divided: the Walloon part became Belgian, the remaining area as a member of the German Confederation came once more under the sovereignty of the Dutch King. In 1841, Luxembourg received its first constitution which was still very monarchical. Following the 1848 revolution, the constitution was revised, copying the Belgian model. It is true that this revision did not yet entail an acknowledgement of the principle of sovereignty of the people, but the Government was responsible to Parliament. In the first elections under this constitution, the most important political groups emerged as parliamentary groups: Radical-Liberals, Conservative-Liberals and Political Catholicism.

In the second half of the 19th century the restoration policies of the Dutch King curtailed the development of the constitution and the parties. After the dissolution of the German Confederation (1866), Luxembourg finally became independent. It was only then that a constitutional reform was initiated (1867) which realised the concept of a parliamentary political system. The rights of the monarch were curbed; the Privy Council appointed by him could only advise or put a suspending veto on legislation. The Government needed the support of a majority in Parliament; the Parliament itself was elected according to the majority vote system.

On the face of it Governments and parties remained fairly stable up to the 1st World War. The Radical-Liberals dominated and formed the Governments. The Conservative-Liberals joined the Catholics. The parties still consisted mainly of parliamentary groups; they did not yet possess a permanent organisation throughout the country. Things changed when a socialist movement was formed towards

Origins of the state

First constitution (1841)

Independence (1866)

Parties

97

the end of the century; in 1896, its first deputy entered Parliament, and in 1902, this movement established itself nationwide as the "Socialist Party". This in turn stimulated the other parties to improve their organisational structure. The Liberals soon lost their dominant role to the Catholic Right-Wing Party, and at times they formed a block together with the Socialists.

Democratisation

The end of the 1st World War also saw a completion of the process of democratisation in Luxembourg. The principle of the sovereignty of the people was incorporated into the constitution; universal suffrage for men and women was introduced. The system of proportional representation was chosen as the electoral method and voting became compulsory.

These developments led to a situation between the wars when no party had the absolute majority, and consequently no party could form a Government on its own.

2nd World War

Thus, most Governments consisted of coalitions led by the Catholic Right-Wing Party. The democratic development of Luxembourg came to an abrupt halt when German troups invaded and occupied the country in 1940. Monarch and Government went into exile in London. After the end of the 2nd World War, democracy and the parties were quickly re-established.

Political Conditions

Parlimentary democracy

The previous constitution was re-introduced after 1945, but was revised in 1956. Luxembourg was now declared a 'parliamentary democracy' (Art. 51). This meant that a phenomenon which had for some time been developing was incorporated in the constitution. According to the rules of a parliamentary political system, the political process consists mainly of an interplay between Government and Parliament. The Grand Duke's duties as head of state are predominantly representative. Based on the election results, he appoints the Prime Minister ('minister of state') who in turn forms the Cabinet. The members of the Government generally have more than one department; they have a collective and individual political responsibility to Parliament. Following a directive of the Prime Minister, the Grand Duke can dissolve Parliament. However, due to the very stable parliamentary and party situation, this has seldom happened in the past.

Luxembourg makes one exception to the rules of the parliamentary system: a Government office and a seat in Parliament are incompatible. A parliamentarian who wants to accept an office in Government has to give up his seat.

Parliament

The (one-chamber) Parliament, the "Chambre des Deputes", is elected by proportional representation for a term of five years (since 1956), and at present has 56 members. It can exercise comparatively strict control over the Government, and possesses a well-established network of committees in which the parties are represented in proportion to their parliamentary strength.

There is also a Privy Council, a "Conseil d'Etat", which is appointed by the Grand Duke and takes part in the legislative process in an advisory capacity.

98

Social Conditions

In contrast to other Western European countries, the social structure of Luxembourg Social structure is relatively homogeneous. The main reason for this lies in the size of the country. The population as a whole can be compared in number to that of a medium-sized city; it is comparatively uniform, and there are no sharp social conflicts or tensions.

Nevertheless, a fully fledged system of representation of interests exists: for example, Groups of interests the Farmers' Central Organisation for Agriculture. There is a free trade union with about 30,000 members and a Christian one with about 10,000. The Association of Industrialists of Luxembourg represents the interests of the employers. The Catholic church has traditionally played an important public role as the country is mainly Catholic.

Luxembourg is characterised by a broad social consensus on fundamental issues; this is mirrored in the political parties and their attitudes. Only the Communist Party is somewhat of an exception.

The Contemporary Party System

The rebuilding of a democracy after 1945 on the basis of the former constitution Traditional party constellations made it possible to simultaneously renew the traditional party system. Apart from the fact that some parties changed their names (the Catholic Right-Wing Party became the Christian Social Party; the Liberals call themselves the Democratic Party), the same party structure emerged as that which had dominated political life in Luxembourg between the wars.

The first Government coalition, formed after the first elections in 1945, was an all-party coalition of 'National Unity': the Christian Social Party was involved, the Democrats, the Socialists and the Communists. After economic and political life had returned to normal, traditional forms of coalitions and party alliances again prevailed. Up to 1974, the Christian Social Party was always dominant. It can be seen that the system of proportional representation with its constituencies of varying size and different numbers of votes works slightly in favour of this party. Together with the Democrats or the Socialists, it has formed every Government, and all Prime Ministers have been chosen from its ranks since 1945.

The following coalitions were formed between 1945 and 1974: Coalitions

1945–47: Coalition of 'National Unity'
1947–51: Christian Social Party/Democrats
1951–59: Christian Social Party/Socialists
1959–64: Christian Social Party/Democrats
1964–69: Christian Social Party/Socialists
1969–74: Christian Social Party/Democrats

The continuity of these coalition forms ended in 1974: in these elections the Christian Social Party lost more than 7% of votes and 3 seats in Parliament. It remained the strongest parliamentary group, but for the first time since 1945 it did not participate in the Government, as a coalition of Democrats and Socialists forced it into the role of the opposition. Since that day, Luxembourg has been governed by a Social-Liberal coalition — as in the Federal Republic of Germany — under the leadership of the Liberal Gaston Thorn, who is both leader of the Government and minister for foreign affairs.

Traditionally, the Christian Social Party follows a conservative line. They are in favour of a free economy, and are middle-class and agriculturally-orientated. Under their dynamic leader Gaston Thorn, the Liberal Democrats have developed into a progressive party committed to social reform.

The Socialists follow a pragmatic social-democratic course, similar to that of the West German Social Democrats with whom they cooperate in the European Parliament in the same parliamentary group.

The question of local cooperation with Communists led to a division in the Socialist Party and the establishment of a separate Social Democrat Party in 1971.

Luxembourg's Communist Party is characterised by its orthodoxy. It was among the few communist parties of the West which defended Soviet intervention in the CSSR in 1968.

Following the parliamentary elections in 1979, the seats in Parliament were distributed as follows:

Christian Social Party	=	24 seats
Socialists	=	15 seats
Democrats	=	14 seats
Social Democrats	=	2 seats
Communists	=	2 seats
Others	=	2 seats

Federal Republic of Germany

THEO STAMMEN

Due to its size, economic strength and political stability, West Germany is an important part of the community of Western European states. All previous Governments of the Federal Republic have committed themselves to the economic and political integration of Western Europe, although with varying intensity and success.

Political importance

The German party system, as it developed after the 2nd World War, was characterised by the following factors: a moderate pluralism; a freedom of coalition structure; and a lack of politically significant splinter or radical parties. These features were and still are essential prerequisites for the political stability of the Federal Republic. Within the European framework, the German parties (the CDU/CSU, SPD and FDP) are the driving forces in the respective European party camps, together with the parties of the BENELUX countries. They are in favour of the formation of European parties and direct elections to the European Parliament.

Historical Background

Even the briefest outline of the *contemporary* West German party system needs to look back at the *historical* foundations of the German parties. For our purposes it may suffice to distinguish *four periods* in the history of the German parties: (1) the 19th century, (2) the Weimar Republic, (3) the Third Reich, and (4) the years immediately after the war (1945–1949).

Four periods of German party history

(1) The *first period*, the 19th century, is important for two reasons: the birth of political parties in Germany on the one hand, and the transformation of the constitutional monarchy of the Bismarck era into a parliamentary political system on the other. The latter change met with many difficulties and interruptions and was effected comparatively late.

First period: the 19th century

It is true that as early as the revolutionary period of 1848/49 the basic pattern of the German party system had emerged in the political ideology of the "Vormaerz" era (the period previous to the March revolution of 1848). This pattern remained much the same until the Weimar Republic: Conservatism, Liberalism, political Catholicism, political Radicalism and Socialism. During the 19th century, there was a further structured development. However, it was a significant fact that the unfolding party system was unable to exercise any real influence on political decision-making, above all on the appointment and recall of the Government. This was due to the constitutional framework in the Bismarck Reich. This lack of political power had far-reaching consequences for the German parties, not only during the Bismarck era, but also later during the Weimar Republic. The parties

Genesis of political parties

101

were not made to take a pragmatic attitude towards party-political adjustment and compromise; instead they adopted an ideological and dogmatic stand, which of course had negative effects on party interactions.

Second period:
Weimar period
(1919-1933)

'Party State'

(2) In the *second period*, during the Weimar Republic (1919–1933), the parties in a competitive party system were now given complete access to power on all levels of the political system. The Weimar Republic was already a "party state" (not in a legal constitutional sense, but in a political sense). However, following their experiences in the Bismarck era, none of the parties managed to cope with the new political reality of a democratic state and a parliamentary system as well as their own role in such a framework. In view of the considerable number of groups, it was of particular importance to come to party-political compromises and coalitions with other parties; on the whole, there was little readiness to do so. The parties remained largely in a state of ideological isolation and only seldom was there any interaction between them. The situation was further complicated by the fact that most of the parties of the Weimar period did not fully support the republican State that they themselves had shaped. Early on, politically extreme parties were formed on the left and right wing with the declared intention of destroying the first German Republic. So it is not surprising that the Weimar parliamentary system gradually moved towards a crisis. In the final phase, the parliamentary system was replaced by presidential Governments which were no longer based on the unstable majorities of the Reichstag, but on the emerging powers of the Reich president. All this contributed to a further undermining of the Weimar system. The situation was made even worse by the fact that the party State was not recognised by large parts of the German population.

Crisis of the
Weimar State

Attitude of the
population

Political culture in Germany was still entrenched in the traditions and values of the authoritarian State: that is, the State as a superior neutral power had to care for the common good by establishing a balance between social groups and parties; the political parties on the other hand, which represent the various social groups and interests, could not make the State their target.

We can see, therefore, that in the first German democracy, the Weimar Republic, considerable pressures in home and foreign affairs combined with the above factors prevented the formation of a fully functioning party system. An essential democratic element was lacking.

Third period:
Hitler's Reich
(1933-1945)

(3) Everything that had been achieved so far was completely suppressed and destroyed in the following *third period* which heralded the advent of National Socialism in Germany (1933–1945). The National Socialists, following their ideal of a totalitarian mass integration party, had already been active towards the end of the Weimar Republic, often cooperating with the extreme left-wing Communists. They had proved themselves to be totally opposed to the existing political system, and had disapproved of the party State and above all of the plurality and competition of the various political groups. Immediately after coming to power, they brought about (by means of suppression and terror as well as "equalization") the "end of the parties" (this is the title of a relevant study on the dissolution of the Weimar party system). This move was an important part in the National Socialists' takeover;

End of the
parties

it was completed as early as July 1933 by the "Law against the new formation of parties". After that date, only a single party existed in Germany: the NSDAP.

(4) in the *fourth period* of party history (1945–1949), German politics was faced with the task of completely rebuilding the democratic parties and the party system. The first steps were made immediately after the end of the war under the Allied occupation Government. The occupying powers permitted the formation of new political parties on the basis of a licensing procedure which they themselves controlled. As early as June and July 1945, *before* the Potsdam Conference, the first German parties of the post-war period were formed in the Soviet Sector: the KPD, the SPD, the CDU and the CDPD. During the months following the Potsdam Conference, similar party structures were created in the three Western Sectors under the supervision of the occupying forces. However, before the various developments could be co-ordinated, the growing controversy between the Western powers and the Soviet Union led to the division of Germany. This naturally meant a division of the newly-created German parties. The parties in the sector under Soviet occupation followed a separate course of development under strict supervision. They quickly developed into the anti-fascist democratic block which preceded the present block party system in the GDR.

Fourth period: time after the war (1945-1949)

New formation of political parties

Division of Germany

For our purposes, we shall concentrate on the development in the three Western Sectors. It was to be expected that the newly formed parties would continue the traditions of the German parties in the Weimar Republic. This applied particularly to the SPD (Social Democrat Party of Germany), but also to the Liberal parties and the Catholic Centre. Only the CDU/CSU (Christian Democrat Union/Christian Social Union) deliberately severed all direct ties with the Weimar period, and arrived at a fundamental party-political re-orientation, based on the experiences of the rule of the National Socialists. The common experience of the NS-dictatorship, the resistance against it and the persecutions resulting from it, united Catholic and Protestant politicians and led them to form a Christian Democrat and a Christian Socialist Party.

Development in the Western Sectors

The formation of these parties after 1945 originated in various centres. Due to the sector borders and the occupation regime, there were many obstacles to the creation of uniform parties for all three Western Sectors. In the beginning, standardisation could only be achieved within a given sector; contracts that went beyond this could only be of an informal nature. This explains why the German parties of the post-war period only established themselves much later as general or federal parties: namely during the Parliamentary Council's deliberations and even after the foundation of the Federal Republic.

Regional centres

The German parties were re-established as "licensed parties". Directly after the war, while still under the Allied occupation Government, these parties began to have a decisive influence on the renewal and stabilisation of political order. It was in particular the democratic renewal of the German "Laender" (after the beginning of 1946) to which the new German political parties gave considerable support. On the level of the "Land", the parties could accept greater political responsibility. They exercised considerable political influence in the constituent assemblies of the

Licensed parties

The parties' contribution

"Land" (which worked out the new constitutions of the "Laender") as well as later in the democratically elected first German Diet (Landtag), and they took over the Government. Also as far as the institutions within and beyond the sectors were concerned (for example, bi-sectoral economic administration; institutions of the tri-sectoral United Economic Zone) which were formed a little later, the political parties participated in them. As a representative of the German side, they shared the responsibility for any decisions taken. These were mainly important economic decisions; for example, currency reform. The parties helped to shape the political face of Germany even before the West German state was founded in 1948/49 (following the initiative of the Western Allies) and before the legal-constitutional foundation of the Federal Republic was deliberated upon.

Participation in the Parliamentary Council

From September 1948 until May 1949, the Parliamentary Council was in session in Bonn to work out the constitutional law. The new political parties were represented in the Council. These were: the CDU/CSU and SPD, the leading parties at that time, the Liberals (FDP/DVP), the Centre (Z), the Communists (KPD) and the German Party (DP). The contours of the new German party system were already emerging. As a consequence of work in the Parliamentary Council, forms of inter-party cooperation and interaction developed on a federal level. This is why one can justifiably say that the outlines of the party system of the Federal Republic were already in existence when the second German democracy was constituted; and, as the first federal diet (Bundestag) was to show, the system functioned.

Party democracy

It is almost self-evident that these new political parties, which had such a large share in the foundation of the democracy in Western Germany, conceived it essentially as of a *party* democracy and structured it as such. They certainly gave more weight to the representative component than to the plebiscite area. Furthermore, they gave the political parties a prominent constitutional position (Article 21 of the "Grundgesetz").

Outline of the new party system

In the short time from 1945 until 1949, the political parties developed into genuine agents of political opinion. Their necessary cooperation on various levels had already shaped the outlines of the new party system. While the "Grundgesetz" was being worked out in the Parliamentary Council in 1948/49, these first contours took on a more concrete shape. It is true that the period 1945—1949 was of prime importance for the reconstruction of the German party system. However, one should point out that the German federal party system has undergone considerable and continuous change since 1949. This was effected by general economic, social and political conditions and structural changes in the Federal Republic. It is therefore necessary to deal at least briefly with these factors which determined the contemporary German party system.

Change of the party system after 1949

Social and Economic Conditions

Consequences of the war

In contrast to the Soviet-occupied Sector and the later GDR, no fundamental social and economic changes occurred in the Western Sectors. However, old structures were not simply restored. Apart from the elimination of the elite of National-

Socialist leaders, the consequences of the war brought about a considerable change in West German society. The internal migration of refugees and exiles, the resettlement of people who had suffered from air-raids, all this brought social repercussions, particularly in regional distribution. Furthermore, the so-called economic miracle occurred: after the currency reform (1948) West Germany experienced rapid economic progress and rose to an important position in the world economy. This had marked effects on social structures. Increasing economic success and growing prosperity among the West German population led to a levelling of class differences. It also proved relatively easy to integrate the great number of refugees and exiles into the economic process and into society, and this was done quite quickly. The new West German society and the dynamics of its social changes are characterised by a high horizontal movement (internal migration) and by corresponding vertical movement (social rise and fall). *Economic miracle*

Integration of exiles

The economic as well as the general social development in the fifties and early sixties had negative effects on the parties and the party system of the young Federal Republic. As social differences were destroyed, so the party-political polarisation and ideological contrasts in politics lost their importance. The political parties increasingly developed from class parties to "people's" parties. *Consequences of the party system*

Political Conditions

The political conditions, as specified in the "Grundgesetz", were of particular importance for the development of the new German party system after 1949.

In clear contrast to the constitution of the Weimar Reich, the "Grundgesetz" is the foundation of a purely parliamentary political system which can only function properly if the party system succeeds. In this respect, Article 21 is significant. For the first time in the history of German constitutional law (excluding some earlier regulations in the constitutions of individual German "Laender" after 1945), the parties were incorporated into the inner sphere of the political system. This article also lays down the parties' role in creating and influencing political opinion, and it puts certain conditions on their possible aims (they must not abolish the constitution) and on the order within the party (which must correspond to democratic principles). The Party Law of 1967 specifies still further the constitutional and legal status of the political parties in West Germany. For example, the definition of the term "political party" reads as follows: *Constitutional structure*

"Parties are associations of citizens which permanently or over a period of time want to influence political opinion on a federal or "Laender" level, and which wish to represent parts of the population in the German Bundestag or a "Landtag". The earnestness of their objectives will be indicated by the overall picture they present, particularly the scope and soundness of their organisation, the number of members and their public appearances. Only natural persons can be members of a party." *Definition of "party" (Party Law)*

Parties which correspond to this definition have — according to the Party Law — the following constitutional status and task: "From the viewpoint of constitutional law, the parties form a necessary part of a free democratic structure. Constantly *The parties' tasks (Party Law)*

105

involved in the formation of political opinion, they fulfil a public task which is allocated to them and guaranteed by the "Grundgesetz". The parties are active in all sectors of public life. In particular, they influence public opinion; they stimulate and deepen political education; they encourage the citizens' active participation in political life; they prepare citizens for the assumption of public responsibility; they take part in the elections on a federal, "Land" and communal level by nominating candidates; they exercise influence on political development in Parliament and Government; they introduce their objectives into the political arena; and they ensure that the connection between the people and the organs of state is kept alive. The parties shall declare their intentions in political manifestos." (Article 1 of the 1967 Party Law).

Limits to the activities of political parties

The parties' comprehensive incorporation into the constitution forms a distinctive framework from their political function. It is such a clear-cut framework that any violation can result in the prohibition of a political party. Only the Federal Constitutional Court can issue such a prohibition order. Compare Article 21 of the "Grundgesetz":

Prohibition of a party possible

"Those parties which, according to their objectives of the behaviour of their supporters, aim at the infringement or abolition of the free democratic structure or put the existence of the Federal Republic of Germany in danger, are unconstitutional. The Federal Constitutional Court decides whether a party is unconstitutional or not." In the history of the Federal Republic, the Federal Constitutional Court has so far — following a motion by the federal Government — started proceedings against two political parties: in 1952, the Socialist Reichs Party (SRP) was declared unconstitutional; and in 1956, the Communist Party of Germany (KPD).

Electoral system

Another very important aspect of the political system which affects the party system is the method of election. The German federal electoral system makes use of a so-called "5% clause" (according to which a political party can only enter the Bundestag or a "Laender" parliament if it polls at least 5% of the votes cast or three seats). As a consequence of this clause, the initial large number of political parties in the German Bundestag has decreased to the present level. We will see that this resulted in a quantitative as well as in a qualitative change of the party system.

Development of the Parties and the Party System

The development of the federal republican party system from 1949 begins with the second German Bundestag and quickly transforms the Weimar *multi-party system* into a *three-party system*. 11 parties were represented in the first German Bundestag: CDU/CSU, SPD, FDP, KDP, BP (Bavaria Party), DP (German Party), Z (Centre), WAV (Association for Economic Development), DRP/DKP (German Reichs Party/German Conservative Party), NG (Emergency Association), and SSW (South-Silesian Voters' Association). In the elections to the second German Bundestag (1953), the 5% clause was introduced and used for the first time on a federal level. This had the effect of reducing the number of parties represented in

Reduction of the number of parties

the Bundestag by almost half, to six: CDU/CSU, SPD, FDP, GB/BHE (All-German Block/Association of Expatriates and Disenfranchised), DP and Z. After the election to the third Bundestag (1957), the number of parties had shrunk to four: CDU/CSU, SPD, FDP and DP. Since the fourth Bundestag (1961), only three parties have been able to get in: CDU/CSU, SPD and FDP. Since that time, they have been the only political competitors on the federal level. The FDP (by far the smallest party of the three) has become a decisive factor in the balance of power; in this capacity it has participated in most of the Government coalitions.

This reduction of party numbers, which occurred in the early stages of the Federal Republic's history, must not be analysed from a *quantitative* point of view only. The development from a multi-party to a three-party system is also a *qualitative* process which can be best defined as passing from an "extreme pluralism" to a "moderate pluralism". Compared with a system of extreme pluralism, the latter is characterised by far less *polarisation*.

From extreme to moderate pluralism

This political concentration becomes even more evident if one compares the reduction in the number of parties with the increase in votes for the remaining three political parties in the Bundestag. In 1949, the CDU/CSU, SPD and FDP together polled 72% of all votes cast; in 1953, 83%; in 1957, 89%; in 1961, 91%; in 1965, 96%; in 1969. 95%; in 1972, 99% and in 1976 again 99%. This means that in 1972 and 1976 only 1% of votes cast were polled by splinter parties, and of course they were unable to overcome the 5% barrier. A possible reason for this is that when casting their votes, the West German electorate assesses the effectiveness of each vote and votes only to a small extent for parties whose prospect of entering the Bundestag are low.

Parties and elections

The move to a three-party system necessarily affected the parties themselves: it changed the dominating type of political party. Towards the beginning of the Federal Republic's history, most parties were more less modelled on older typologies, mainly on those from the Weimar period. The workers' parties SPD and KPD at that time corresponded largely to the type S. Neumann called "integration party"; the middle class parties fell into the category of the representation party. Apart from these, there were also a number of smaller parties representing particular ideologies or the special interests of social groups (for example, expatriates and refugees). Then the dominating type of party underwent a marked change.

Dominating type of party: people's party

O. Kirchheimer coined the term "catch-all party"; this category is most suitable to describe the new type of party that evolved in the German party system. In the meantime, the term "people's party" which designates the same thing, has become more common. One can argue that the present political parties in the Federal Republic are all to a greater or lesser degree realisations of this type. According to O. Kirchheimer, it is typical of this "catch-all" or people's party that it has stopped trying "to get a spiritual and moral hold on the masses"; instead it concentrates on the voter and sacrifices "a deeper ideological penetration (of society) in favour of a wider appeal and more rapid success in elections".

The term "people's party"

The following definition by Kirchheimer exactly fits the development of the federal

German parties: "The transformation into a "catch-all" party is basically a phenomenon of competition. A party tends to emulate the successful style of its competitors in the hope of doing well in the elections or of retaining its voters". This applies to the development of the federal German parties in as much as the CDU/CSU under the leadership of Konrad Adenauer followed the line of a people's party soon after the foundation of the Federal Republic. After some hesitation, the SPD also chose to become a people's party; the change occurred after the death of its first chairman Kurt Schumacher and was based on discussions about reform within the party and above all on the Godesberg Programme (1959). Previously a class-orientated mass-integration party (mainly for the workers), the SPD now became a modern people's party. The SPD was proved right in its decision, as its percentage of votes increased steadily with every election; in 1972, it became the strongest party in the Federal Republic for the first time. However, in the last election to the Bundestag, the CDU/CSU again won slightly more votes.

The FDP has experienced a similar development; although, as the smallest party of the three, it has to cope with special problems. Over the past years, the FDP has tried, with varying success, to establish itself as a liberal left-wing people's party.

The "people's party" also finds its expression in the internal organisational structure of these parties and in the number of their members. The relatively low organisation density of the federal German parties is evidence of this: out of every 100 voters in West Germany, only three are actually members of a particular party. In neighbouring countries such as Austria and Switzerland, the figure in the non-socialist parties is as high as 50%. In the FDP and the CDU particularly, the bureaucracy of the party is relatively undeveloped; this is also typical of the people's party which is essentially a *voters'* party rather than a *members'* party. In this respect, the SPD still differs from a pure people's party; this is due to its long tradition as an organised mass-integration party. In recent years, the CSU had developed a rigid and comprehensive organisational structure, in contrast to its sister party the CDU.

Party Interactions

Let us finally briefly consider the forms of interaction among the various parties. The first thing to note is that in West Germany such interaction takes the form of a *competitive system*. This is neither characterised by a pronounced dualism (as in the British two-party system) nor by an extreme pluralism (as is to be found in many European countries, particularly in Italy); instead, it is typified by a moderate pluralism consisting of the three parties mentioned.

As already indicated, this has only gradually evolved in the course of the Federal Republic's history. At the same time the *configurations* of political parties which are typical of this type of system developed. In this respect, the German party

108

Development of
CDU/CSU

SPD

FDP

Organisation

Competitive
system

Party
configurations

structure has changed remarkably. In the beginning, the typical configuration was: a non-socialist Government coalition against the workers' parties SPD and KPD. This constellation of parties and coalitions (non-socialist governing parties and a Social Democrat opposition) remained more or less the same until the mid-sixties. The non-socialist parties, under the leadership of the CDU/CSU, formed every Government, and the Chancellor was always chosen from their ranks.

It was only in 1969 that a fundamentally new party structure came into effect. This **Coalitions** was a result of years of crisis, partially the result of previous Government coalitions. The Great Coalition was formed; for the first time in the history of the Federal Republic a Social Democrat Party came into Government. If only for this reason, the Great Coalition between CDU/CSU and SPD from 1966 until 1969 was an important step in the development not only of the SPD, but also of the German party and political system. However, this coalition has been (rightly) criticised as too problematic and undesirable.

The next significant phase began with the elections to the Bundestag in 1969. The "small" Social-Liberal coalition between SPD and FDP was formed, as it is now. The formation of this coalition signified a point in the development of the German party system at which all parties had become eligible for coalition.

During the first decade and a half in federal republican history, the *frequency of a* **Frequency of** *change in the ruling parties* was dangerously low. From 1949 to 1969, the CDU/ **change of** CSU ruled with varying partners and coalitions (finally with the SPD), and **Government** produced all the federal Chancellors. This fact might have led these parties to believe that they were the sole pillars of the state and that a victory by the SPD would — as Adenauer once provocatively put it — mean the fall of the Federal Republic. So it was not at all a bad thing when, after twenty years in government, the CDU/CSU had to take on the role of opposition. **Opposition role**

Conversely, it was equally important for the political system that the SPD had the opportunity to share government responsibility. The Social-Liberal coalition has now ruled for quite a few years, and certain signs of "wear" can be detected. However, despite great efforts in the 1976 elections, the CDU/CSU was unable to bring down the coalition.

The party-political *polarisation* of the German parties decreased from the beginn- **Party-political** ings of the Federal Republic to the end of the fifties/beginning of the sixties, at **polarisation** which time the phrase "end of the ideologies" came into being. The German parties' development to people's parties, as described above, levelled out or at least reduced ideological differences. If one looks at the first decade and a half of federal republican history, one realises that during this time ideological principles were not the prime concern in German politics. The main issues were the consider- able political differences regarding, for example, Adenauer's concentration of foreign policy on the West, the question of re-armament and European politics. **Return of** This has changed greatly since the early seventies. As already mentioned, the interest **ideology in** in theoretical and programmatic discussions within and among the parties has been **the parties** rekindled. The German parties have issued new programmes, and are consequently more polarised in relation to each other than before. In the election campaign of the

1976 elections to the Bundestag, the CDU/CSU used the slogan "Freedom or Socialism". This was one of the reasons for a discussion on "basic values" throughout the Federal Republic, which was at times very heated but on the whole not very productive. At the same time it became apparent that considerable ideological tension and theoretical difference of opinion existed *within* the parties, particularly in the SPD. This has also contributed to a return to an ideological emphasis in the political field. Yet it is very questionable whether this shift in thought had or still has a positive influence on the working out and execution of given Government programmes. As all political parties in the Federal Republic have been or still are in power, the integration of German political parties is distinctively high, particularly if one compares it with the Weimar Republic. One has to remember, however, that all modern parties are firmly bound by the parliamentary system as laid down in the "Grundgesetz". The political parties have penetrated the political system on a federal level as well as in the "Laender" and, increasingly, on a regional level. One may therefore justifiably call the Federal Republic a "party State". In clear contrast to the Weimar Republic, it is acknowledged as such by the population. This is true despite occasional protest movements, such as the citizen initiative groups, which are clearly directed against the established parties.

In the elections to the last Bundestag (October 3, 1976), the Social-Liberal coalition, which in 1972 won with 54.2% of the secondary votes, only had a very close victory — with just 50.5% of the votes. The extraction distribution of votes polled and seats won in the German Bundestag is as follows:

	Parties	Percentage of Votes	Seats
1972	CDU/CSU	44.9	225
	SPD	45.8	230
	FDP	4.4	41
1976:	CDU/CSU	48.0	243
	SPD	42.6	214
	FDP	6.9	39

110

Great Britain

DIRK BERG-SCHLOSSER

Historical/Political, Economic and Social Conditions

Historical/Political Background

The political and social development of the United Kingdom over the past 300 years shows, at least at first glance, a rare continuity. Since the "Glorious Revolution" of 1688, political life has remained within the boundaries of the constitution (which is unwritten, but with a clearly-defined substance). The institutions of the Crown, the Cabinet and the two Houses of Parliament (House of Commons, House of Lords) have survived until the present day. These institutions have never experienced a violent or abrupt change which was not sanctioned by constitutional law. However, their nature and interrelationship underwent decisive changes during that same period.

An almost absolutist monarchy became a constitutional political system in which the Monarch only has a representative and symbolic function.

The House of Lords which was formerly the most important representative organ (it consisted only of members of the aristocracy, peers and the high clergy) was reduced to a chamber which can only impose a delaying veto. (However, as the supreme court, part of the House of Lords still enjoys special status.)

Conversely, the House of Commons has gained in importance; it became the decisive parliamentary body. The role of the Cabinet and above all that of the Prime Minister changed, too. Today, the latter decides his political programme independently of the Monarch's directives and supported by a parliamentary majority.

Historical development

Economic Background

The economic development during this period was even more far-reaching. From a largely feudal agrarian State, the United Kingdom developed into the world's first highly industrialised country. Technological developments were made (the steam-engine, railway and so on); productivity was increased to a previously unimaginable level. The resultant accumulation of capital led to an expansion of commerce and industry to all internationally important markets. Finally, in the 'imperialist' phase during the second half of the 19th century, Great Britain built the most important world-wide colonial empire in history. Since the end of the 2nd World War, this empire has disintegrated; and today it has been replaced by the very loosely connected "Commonwealth of Nations". The decline of the colonial empire and the falling importance of the Commonwealth has been paralleled by a more open

Economic development

111

approach towards Europe. After many delays, this finally culminated in 1972 in Great Britain joining the European Community.

Social Background

The social structure of Great Britain changed fundamentally in the time since the Revolution. The development of a market-orientated agriculture and industrialisation, together with the system of 'enclosures' led to a high degree of urbanisation (today more than 70% of the population live in big cities). As the population grew very quickly in the early phase of industrialisation, an urban proletariat emerged with its own employment problems.

State institutions and trade union organisations, protecting the individual from exploitation, were unknown. The misery among great parts of the population was indescribable. Karl Marx used it as an empirical basis for his scientific analyses. The situation improved only gradually: through the formation of the working class movement and through reforms initiated by the State (starting under Prime Minister

Disraeli in 1867). However, the privileges of the aristocracy and the economic upper classes and a social class-orientated educational system have survived. To an outside observer there are greater differences in social class (and a greater awareness of this fact) than in most of the other European countries.

Apart from these tensions in the vertical structure of society, there are further regional contrasts which still create political conflict, particularly between England, Scotland and Wales. There is also a new element in English social structure: coloured immigrants from the Commonwealth countries. Over the last two decades the influx and growth of the immigrant population has created some 2 million coloured citizens: a growth which at times was the cause of racial conflict.

Conditions Imposed by the Political System

General Conditions

The mainly unwritten law which is based on precedent and historic development ('common law') is a British tradition. Similarly, the political framework has been shaped by tradition and historic development rather than by constitution. In a very general sense, the guarantee of the 'rule of law' and of general 'civil rights' determines the scope of any kind of social or political organisation. The "Magna Charta Libertatum" (1215), the "Petition of Rights" (1628), the "Habeas Corpus Act" (1679) and the "Bill of Rights" (1689) were national milestones and equally important for the development of constitutions in other parts of the world. In 1945, the "Charter of the United Nations" was signed, and the British Parliament accepted that all the social and political rights deriving from the charter were in a sense a separate element of the British constitution.

The rule of law and the guarantee of basic rights, which include the general freedom of organisation, assembly and the Press, are an inalienable part of the

112

British constitution. However, there is no specific mention of political parties in the Status of parties 'constitution'; neither does it make provision for the express prohibition of a party. A given political system determines the political parties' scope of action. In the United Kingdom the constitutional monarchy functions as a framework within which the political system has developed into *the* parliamentary system *par excellence*. Based on the principle of sovereignity of the people, Parliament today is the most important formal power in the State — deciding the composition of the Government and its term of office. On the other hand, a Prime Minister, once Prime Minister democracy he is elected, can dissolve Parliament at any time during its normal parliamentary term of five years, and can thus choose a date for new elections which seems most convenient to him. Each leader of the British Government is also the leader of his party. As a rule, he is supported by an absolute majority in Parliament. Thus during his term of office he holds powers which (at least in a formal sense) are far more comprehensive than those of, say, the American President. For this reason, this form of Government is usually called a "Prime Ministerial democracy".

Specific Conditions

The specific determinants in the development of the British party system have to be seen against this political background. Such factors are the gradual increase in the number of people who are entitled to vote, and the electoral system. As the Right to vote importance of Parliament grew vis a vis the Crown, so the number of people entitled to vote increased. This was an expression of the changed social circumstances and the growing demands for 'democracy'; culminating in the introduction of universal suffrage for all adult citizens. The following table illustrates the development:

Year	Number of people entitled to vote (as percent of adult population)
Before 1832	5%
1832	7%
1867	16%
1884	20%
1918	74% (Women over 30 entitled to vote)
1928	97% (Universal suffrage for all people over 21)
1948	% (Abolition of the right to more than one vote)
1969	% (Reduction of the voting age to 18)

The electoral system, too, underwent a series of changes over the centuries. Today, the United Kingdom uses the system of the relative majority vote in one-man Majority vote constituencies; that is, irrespective of the number of candidates and the absolute percentage of votes received, the constituency is won by the candidate with the (relatively) greatest number of votes at one ballot. A 'majority' of votes (sometimes

113

only just a majority) is enough to elect the only MP for that constituency; all other votes count for nothing. In extreme cases this system can lead to the situation that, with narrow victories in a large number of constituencies and very high wins by the opposing parties in other areas, one party can gain a majority of seats, although it has a smaller absolute proportion of votes (this happened, for example, in 1951). The system fails to achieve a 'fair' representation of all political groups in Parliament; but it usually produces clear-cut parliamentary majorities and thus the basis for a 'stable' Government.

There are altogether 634 constituencies which should, in principle, each represent the same number of people. About every six or seven years, an independent commission examines and re-adjusts the number of constituencies and their boundaries according to any demographic changes that may have occurred. Every citizen who has the passive right to vote (everybody who is 21 years old and has full civil rights) can in theory run as candidate in his constituency, even if he is not supported by a party. Only members of the aristocracy who might be called to the House of Lords, clergymen and certain higher Civil Servants (for example, the inspectors in the elections) are ineligible.

Election campaign

Each candidate has to deposit a sum of £150. If he wins at least an eighth of the votes cast, he will be refunded. The sums that a candidate can spend on the election campaign are closely restricted by law; (since 1969) they must not amount to more than £750 plus 2 pence for each person that has the right to vote in the candidate's constituency. The parties, however, are not restricted in this way. The duration of the election campaign, that is, the period between the dissolution of Parliament and the new elections, is also laid down by law and rarely exceeds four weeks.

The Parties

Origins and Development

The first parties were loosely formed parliamentary groups (that is, of "endogenous" origin, Duverger). After the end of the 17th century (and the controversial accession to the throne by Charles II which later led to his overthrow in the "Glorious Revolution" of 1688), two larger groups evolved which became known as the "Whigs" (probably derived from "whiggamores", a group of Scottish presbyterians) and "Tories" (initially a term designating Catholic-Irish partisans). The former were the predecessors of the "Liberals"; from the latter the "Conservative" Party of today was

Tories

born. The Tories were predominantly representatives of the rural landowners; whereas the Whigs stood for capitalism and, later, industry. The Tories upheld the monarchy and its rights (compare Hooker and Filmer) on a religious basis; the Whigs

Whigs

claimed that a 'political contract' between individuals possessing natural rights had been concluded (compare the different versions in Hobbes and Locke).

At first, both groups had a very lax organisational structure. They tried to gain influence by means of patronage, corruption and the buying of votes. The clubs frequented by these groups (Tories: Carlton Club, Liberals: Reform Club) became

114

the nuclei of parliamentary organisation. "Registering associations" intended to make contact with the voters (whose number was initially very restricted by the census method) were the first genuine party organisations outside Parliament.

In the wake of the Industrial Revolution, the working class developed during the 19th century, bringing its own political demands. Together with a gradual extension of the right to vote, this led to the call for a separate party to represent the workers. In 1900, the "Labour Representation Committee" (later changed to "Labour Party") was founded. Initially, "Labour" was merely a union of already existing collective associations, such as trade unions, co-operative societies, the "Fabian Society" and the "Independent Labour Party" which had existed since 1894. It was only in 1918 that individuals could join the party as members. Today, the Labour Party still relies primarily on organised workers. However, it should be noted that a considerable proportion of working class people and trade unionists vote Conservative. In its programme, the Labour Party has always steered a course of 'social reform', as was advocated from the start by leading theoreticians of the Fabian Society such as Harold Laski and Stafford Cripps. **Labour Party**

The emergence of the Labour Party had a radical effect on the British party system. Up to this time, the system had been characterised by a largely uncontested dualism of the two large traditional parties. The Whigs, and later the Liberals, had dominated over long periods (for example, until Disraeli came into office in 1868, and again later under Gladstone and Lloyd George). Suddenly, within a few years, they not only lost this dominancy, but were pushed back by Labour into third place. Since then (partly because of the system of majority vote) they have been relegated to almost total political insignificance. **Change of the party system**

Labour not only managed to replace the Liberals. In 1925 it formed its first Government under Ramsay MacDonald. However, its initial term of office was short-lived. From 1931 to 1935, MacDonald again presided over a coalition Cabinet that had been formed in the world economic crisis. From 1935 to 1945, the Conservatives dominated once more. After the fall of the Liberals, the Conservatives became a 'catchment area' for almost the entire middle class and the agrarian and industrial upper classes.

After the end of the war, the Labour leader Clement Attlee won a clear majority in the House of Commons. Since that time, the party system in Great Britain has consisted of two alternating parties which are both supported by an almost identical number of voters (the Conservatives won in 1955, 1959 and 1970; the Labour party in 1964, 1966 and 1974). Only recently have the separatist movements of the Scottish and Welsh nationalists again come to the fore. As regional parties, they are less endangered by the 'guillotine' of the system of the relative majority vote than the Liberals, who poll a higher percentage of votes but are evenly spread over the country. In the case of small seat majorities in Parliament, these splinter groups have shown that their role can be decisive in holding the balance of power. **The situation today**

115

Present Forms of Organisation

The following section will deal exclusively with the two large parties, which are modern "mass" organisations. Compared with most parties in Europe, their membership numbers are very high. The Conservative Party has claimed a membership of up to 2.4 million members; Labour claims about 800,000 individual and 6 million corporate members. Both parties possess a comprehensive and complex party organisation; each party's structure contains a number of parallels, but also some historical peculiarities. At the lowest level (of each constituency), there are so-called "constituency parties". Formally, they are largely independent of party headquarters; but as a rule a candidate standing for Parliament has to be vetted by them. The constituency parties consist of individual members sometimes further divided into "wards". In the case of the Labour Party, one has to include the corporate members (local trade union organisations, consumers' associations, and so on) at this level. Each constituency party is headed by an elected committee (central committee) which in turn is presided over by an executive committee.

Regions

Between the constituency and the central organisation, there are certain "regions". The Conservatives have 12 and Labour 11. As there is no corresponding division in the structure of the State's political institutions, they are only of minor importance — mainly for the regional co-ordination of the constituency parties.

Annual congress

The Annual Congress is, at least formally, the supreme decision-making organ of both parties. It is held every year in the autumn, and attended by thousands of delegates from the various parts of the party (in the case of Labour, this includes the corporate members). The Conservatives' Annual Congress in particular is usually only a form of acclamation; the leaders of the party, especially if in power, do not as a rule feel bound by any resolutions taken. Labour Governments, too, often fail to adhere to Annual Congress decisions. Apart from the Congress, the Conservative Party has a Central Council which has almost as many members and which convenes every year in the spring. All extra-parliamentary organisations of the Conservatives are comprised in the "National Union" on which the "Executive Committee" is based. This has about 150 members, and fulfils regular and important political functions.

Labour's corresponding body is the "National Executive Committee" which consists of 28 members.

Parliamentary party

The most important bodies of both parties are their parliamentary parties. The Conservatives' parliamentary party is also known as the "1922 Committee". When the Conservatives are in power, the "front benchers" (that is, the members of the Government) are excluded from this committee. The parliamentary parties elect the leader of their party whose power and personal weight is far greater than of any of his counterparts in Western Europe. In the Conservative Party, the decisions of the party leader are, as a rule, uncontested. He or she is measured more or less by success or failure in the parliamentary elections. The Labour Party leader is more answerable to the parliamentary party, and has to give more consideration to wing groups.

116

Apart from the dominating Conservative and Labour Parties and the much depleted Liberals, there are other national parties which are not represented in Parliament. **Small parties** The most important of these is the Russian influenced "Communist Party of Great Britain". At present, it has about 30,000 members, but its percentage of votes in the parliamentary elections has remained negligible. The "Co-operative Party" which tries to promote the idea of co-operatives deserves particular mention. In many ways, it is closely related to Labour, and, a specified number of Labour and Co-operative candidates stand in every election.

The "Scottish National Party" and the "Plaid Cymru" (Welsh National Party) are of regional importance. Both call for more autonomy and independence of the central Government in their respective areas. As already indicated, these parties do not suffer as much as the other smaller parties from the electoral system of majority vote as their supporters are concentrated in certain areas. They both won parliamentary seats in the last elections.

The distribution of votes and seats in Parliament following the 1974[1] elections was as follows:

Parties	% of votes	Seats	
Labour Party	39.3	319	**Distribution of mandates**
Conservative Party	35.8	276	
Liberal Party	18.3	13	
Scottish Nationalists	(30.4 in their area) ⎱ 3.4	11	
Welsh Nationalists	(10.8 in their area) ⎰	3	
Parties in Northern Ireland	together about 3.5	12	
	Total	634	

[1] The dramatic effects of the relatively small percentage swing were illustrated in the 1979 elections:

	% of Votes	Seats
Conservative	43.9	339
Labour	36.9	268
Liberal	13.8	11

Party Interaction
Horizontal Interactions
Historical development, combined with the relative majority electoral system, has resulted in a two-party system, at least on the parliamentary level. Accordingly, the majority party has only rarely been forced to find a coalition partner to form the **Coalitions** Government. Only at times of crises, for example during the 1st and 2nd World War and in the wake of the world economic crisis (1931—1935), were coalitions formed.

117

It is only a recent development that the superiority of the two large parties has suffered from the increase in regional voters' associations in Scotland and Wales. In spring 1977, the nationalist parties threatened the majority of the governing Labour Party. As a result, a rare "tacit" coalition between Labour and the Liberals was formed.

Change of Government

In the majority vote system, a relatively small swing from one party to another can lead to considerable changes in the distribution of seats. The party in government has consequently changed fairly frequently. The Conservatives were in power from 1951 to 1964 (at first under Churchill, then under Eden, Macmillan and Douglas-Home): this was the only time since the reform bill of 1832 that a Government had ruled for more than 10 years in peace-time.

Ideological polarisation

The two-party character of the British system also resulted in a relatively strong ideological polarisation between the two major opponents. Political argument, at least verbally, is often quite forceful. However, the long established status of the opposition ("Her Majesty's loyal opposition") ensures that in practice tolerance is observed. Furthermore, most Governments, once they had come to power, proved themselves more pragmatic than ideological; thus easing the tensions of debate.

It has happened that major decisions made by a previous Government (for example on the nationalisation of important industrial sectors, the health and education system and the tax system) were reversed by their successors. The discontinuity in these areas is therefore much greater than in most other parliamentary systems in Western Europe.

Integration of parties

The two-party system has made the question of party integration in the political process largely irrelevant; the same is true of parties' mutual acceptance as coalition partners. In this respect, the Communist Party is the only party which occupies a marginal position in the party spectrum. Its dogmatic policies which are largely orientated towards Soviet attitudes are responsible for the fact that so far the party has not imposed itself on the political arena.

Vertical Interactions

The vertical interactions of the parties are those "downwards" in the direction of society, and "upwards" in the direction of the political system as such. They have also been shaped by a long and relatively continuous historical development, and have characteristic features. The Conservatives as well as Labour have deep roots among the voters of certain social groups and strata (the latter particularly among the trade unions); and the "core" of their respective supporters remained over many elections at more than 80% of those who voted for the party. This applies to most of the local elections as well as for the General Elections.

Core of voters

118

In spite of all this, the parties' scope of action in the British social system is considerably limited. There is a tight network of groups which have developed over the years; interest groups, organisations, religious societies, and so on. They have remained relatively free of party influence. This also holds true for central parts of the "inner political system": for example, the judiciary, the Civil Service and the armed forces; and also for public broadcasting corporations and the media. In this sense, Great Britain is less a "party state" than some other European countries.

Ireland

DIRK BERG-SCHLOSSER

Conditions

Historical Background

Geographical situation

Much in the historical development of Ireland can be attributed to its geographical situation. Situated on the periphery of the European hemisphere, this island was spared most of the continental political and military conflicts. At the same time it was somewhat isolated from the important spiritual and social movements that affected Europe. However, Ireland was very much influenced by her immediate neighbour, Great Britain. Since the beginning of the 19th century, Ireland's geographical situation was used as a gateway to the "New World" on the other side of the ocean; today, about 16 million people of Irish extraction live in America.

The Irish island was among the first regions in Europe which became totally Christian (through St. Patrick in the 5th century), and which played an important role in converting other countries to the Christian faith. The Irish feudal lords long fought against each other, the Danes, Vikings and other invaders, without being able to establish a common lasting rule over the whole of the territory. In

Conquest

the 12th century Henry II subjected them to English rule. In the 16th century Henry VIII and Elizabeth I invested Irish and English lords with direct fiefs, thus making Ireland a part of their realm.

Religious conflict

Since that time, the religious conflict between the Catholic church and Irish population on the one hand and the Protestant "Church of Ireland", which had severed all ties with Rome, on the other has remained virulent. The settlement of Protestant immigrants, particularly in the north of the island, further aggravated the problem. Various attempts at rebellion, as in 1641, 1690 and 1798, were bloodily suppressed. In 1800, Ireland finally became an integral part of the "United Kingdom of Great Britain and Ireland" by statute.

Nevertheless, a subservient relationship remained between the two. The Irish farmers still had to pay tribute to their lords of the manor who for the most part resided in England. Irish exports were only allowed if they supplemented British

Dependent economy

production. If they were in competition with British products (as in the case of wool and some other agricultural products), they were prohibited or excluded by means of customs regulations. Industrialisation was limited to a few sectors only (for example, the production of linen which did not represent a threat to any English factories); and capital was mostly in English hands.

In the middle of the last century, Ireland (which is basically a fertile and not very densely populated country) suffered severe famines. They had been triggered off

120

by some poor potato harvests; traditionally potatoes were the most important basic food in Ireland. Within a few years, the island's population sank from about 8.5 to less than 5 million. At that time, emigration to America was the only hope for many of the jobless and starving population. Ireland's population has remained at the same low level, in relation to most other European and non-European countries. It is only since the beginning of the 1960's that there has been a slight increase (up to about 3 million in the south, where the population density is 44 persons/square km; and 1.5 million in the northern part of the island, where the figure is 109 persons/square km). About 50% of the southern population is today concentrated in cities with more than 1,500 inhabitants; nearly a quarter of the entire population lives in the greater Dublin area. Around 95% of people in the south, and a third in the north, are Catholic. A quarter of the population speaks Gaelic as well as English; Gaelic being the second official language in the south.

Development of the population

As in other parts of Europe, nationalist tendencies in Ireland have increased since the early 19th century. The strongest force initially was the "Irish Nationalist Party", which consisted of a group of Irish parliamentarians in the British House of Commons. They were particularly committed to the cause of a limited "home rule" for Ireland. After various unsuccessful attempts, a corresponding Bill was finally passed in 1914; but it never came into effect because the 1st World War broke out in the same year. In the meantime other groups had formed whose aims were more far-reaching. The following were the most important: the middle-class "Sinn Fein" ("We ourselves") movement, founded in 1905, which initially called for a double monarchy such as in Austria and Hungary; the "Irish Trade Union Congress and Labour Party", founded in 1912, which strove for a republic; and some smaller separatist groups, some of which resembled "secret societies" (like the "Irish Republican Brotherhood" IRB). The armed rebellion of Easter 1916 which had been organised by the latter groups was bloodily suppressed by Great Britain. It was this brutality which made previously moderate political circles harden their attitudes towards a final separation from England. The Irish delegates who had been elected to the British Parliament in 1918 made little or no use of their seats; instead, they formed their own Irish constituent assembly, the "Dail Eireann", in January 1919.

Struggle for independence

After further reprisals had proved ineffective (at one time more than half of the delegates had been arrested), England tried to solve the conflict on a constitutional basis. In 1920, the British Government suggested dividing Ireland into two states, each having its own Parliament and limited Government according to the terms of the "home rule" status which had been granted earlier. The 6 counties of the northern province Ulster, where the Protestants were in the majority, approved this concept (today it still forms the essential basis for governing Northern Ireland); however, the Irish nationalists in the south were not satisfied.

Division of Ireland

In 1921, the British Government offered to conclude a treaty which contained the foundation of an "Irish Free State" in the south; this state would have the status of a dominion within the British Commonwealth (roughly similar to the position of Canada or Australia at that time). The question whether this treaty should be

121

accepted or not led to a rift in the Sinn Fein movement. It split into supporters of the treaty who formed an organisation called "Cumman nan Gaedheal" (League of the Gaelic people) which later merged with the "Fine Gael" Party (Tribe of the Gaelic people); and into opponents of the treaty who were organised in the "Fianna Fail" Party (Soldiers of fate). Under its leader Eamon de Valera, who later became President for many years, the latter wanted a complete separation from England. Both groups created at times a situation of open civil war. On the side of those opposing the treaty, the militant wing of the "Irish Republican Army" (IRA), founded in 1919 to fight British rule, was particularly active (since 1969 its successor, and various other republican "off-shoots", have been active in the conflict in Northern Ireland).

Republic

In 1923 the pro-treaty group under the leadership of William Cosgrave finally prevailed, and the first Government of the Free State was formed. In 1937 Ireland became the sovereign state Eire and was given a new constitution. In 1949 it left the Commonwealth and has since then been a Republic. However, the effects of the historical division of the Irish party system into the two large groups — the Fianna Fail and the Fine Gael Party — are still felt today.

Member of the EC

In 1973 Ireland became a member of the European Community. From an economic point of view, Ireland is the weakest member, even weaker than Italy: the income per head in Ireland is only about half as much as in West Germany. The degree of the country's industrialisation is still relatively low. About a third of the working population is still employed in farming, and the methods of production are all too often inefficient. The world economic crisis of the past years has had particularly serious consequences: in 1976, unemployment stood at 12% and the inflation rate was at 20%. In spite of all this, Ireland's prospects in the EC appear good. Increased industrialisation and an intensification of the agricultural programme seem possible in view of the high level of qualified workers, relatively low wages and favourable investment conditions. Much depends, of course, on a well-balanced structural and social policy in the EC.

Political Conditions

President

The Irish Republic of today has a parliamentary political system; it is headed by a President who is directly elected by the people for a term of seven years. His functions are not merely of a representative nature; for example, he can dissolve Parliament at any time and call new elections.

Government

However, the proper reins of government are in the hands of the Minister President who is elected by the house of representatives ("Dail Eireann"). At his own responsibility he appoints the members of his Cabinet, and generally lays down the political guidelines. The house of representatives at present has 148 members; it is directly elected by the people for a maximum of 5 years. There is also a second chamber, the senate ("Seanad Eireann"), consisting of 60 prominent public people. They are partly elected according to professional principles by important organisations and associations, and about a fifth of the members are directly appointed by the

Parliament

122

leader of the Government. As far as the process of legislation is concerned, the senate has a limited right to advise and hear which could delay the passing of a bill for 3 months at the most.

A "Supreme Court", consisting of 6 members, is the highest court of appeal of a largely independent legal body. If a corresponding motion is passed, the Supreme Court has to decide whether certain laws passed by Parliament are constitutional or not. As for the rest, the British principle of "common law" prevails. **Law**

From the point of view of administration, Ireland is divided into the four historic provinces Leinster, Munster, Connaught and Ulster. They in turn are divided into 32 counties. Six of the nine counties in the province Ulster today form the autonomous Northern Ireland which is part of the United Kingdom. **Administration**

The delegates of the Lower House ("Dail") are elected according to the system of proportional representation. However, and this is an Irish idiosyncracy, they are not chosen from uniform national lists, but in each constituency the voter has the choice between 3 to 5 candidates. This means that more than one candidate can be elected in each constituency on the basis of their relative majority. Furthermore, the voters can indicate on their ballot paper the order in which they elect the candidates; that is, the electorate can weight their votes for as many candidates as there are delegates in a given constituency. This of course complicates the ensuing evaluation of election results, but the democratic principle is applied more "directly". The system also attaches more importance to individual personalities who are well-known in a constituency. On the whole, it has a limited "majority-forming" effect: it tends to favour larger parties and to prevent extreme party divisions. In this respect, the Irish system can be regarded as a compromise between the exclusive majority system in one-candidate constituencies and the pure system of proportional representation. Every citizen over 21 who is registered in his particular constituency has the active and passive right to vote. Candidates who stand for President have to be at least 35 years old. **Electoral system**

The Parties

The political parties which exist in Ireland today may be characterised in two ways: on the one hand, they express a certain attitude of the population with regard to the "national question" (this was particularly true during the critical phase of separation from the United Kingdom), and on the other hand, they represent different social groups and interests. This duality which is most evident in the two largest parties, Fianna Fail and Fine Gael, makes it very difficult to classify the parties.

Fianna Fail

The Fianna Fail (FF) is the largest party and has been in power for the greatest length of time. It emerged from the "anti-treaty" group of the divided Sinn Fein movement, and after an extra-parliamentary phase from 1922 to 1927, it once **History**

123

more took part in the parliamentary elections. Except for brief periods in the years 1948–51, 1954–57, 1973–77, it has been the sole governing party. Its supporters are to be found mainly among the small farmers, particularly in the western provinces; on their behalf, the Fianna Fail called for the abolition of ground rent to British landowners. The party is also supported by a proportion of the working class, and today even by some groups of the urban *nouveaux riches*. In the course of its long term of office and because of the lessening importance of the national question, the party has changed from a radical nationalist to a moderate party with Liberal-Conservative features. Nevertheless, the party's attitude towards Northern Ireland and the now active IRA is determined to a great extent by "national" considerations, which seek an eventual re-unification of Ireland.

Fianna Fail may be termed a modern "mass" party with a membership of about 40,000 and a developed organisational structure. It is active and permanently represented at all levels of political life: with about 2,000 regularly meeting local groups; district committees (in local constituencies); county committees (in parliamentary constituencies); and the national committee, the "National Executive".

Organisation

The annual party conference ("Ard-Fheis") is the supreme decision-making body, which also elects the 10-strong party executive. However, resolutions passed by the party conference are often only of a declamatory nature, and the parliamentary group and the Government are not bound by them. The party conference also elects 15 delegates ("Committee of the Fifteen") – who must not be parliamentary members – to the National Executive. The other members of the National Executive are: 1 from each of the 52 constituencies, and 8 parliamentary members (3 of them being members of the Government, or, if the party is in opposition, of the "shadow cabinet"). The National Executive is the highest executive body of the party and is coupled with the party's central secretariat ("Central Office, Headquarters") which employs some salaried staff. The parliamentary group ("Party in the Dail") is largely independent of the other party bodies, but it is bound by the party's constitution. The party is run on general democratic principles, although some oligarchic tendencies are apparent at its top level.

Fine Gael

In comparison with the FF, the Fine Gael (FG), which is today the second-largest party of the country, has remained more of a loosely-structured party for the professional and upper classes. Like the FF, the Fine Gael originated from the Sinn Fein movement before and during the 1st World War, but its supporters agreed to the constitutional treaty concluded with Great Britain in December 1921. At first called "Cumman nan Gaedheal", the party formed the first Governments (up to 1932) after Ireland become independent. Later on, the "Farmers' Party" and the relatively small "National League", founded in 1927, merged with the Fine Gael.

History

It has been called by this name, "Fine Gael – The United Ireland Party", since 1933. Apart from short coalition Governments during the years 1948–53, 1954–57 and 1973–77, the party has always been in opposition. Its supporters come from among the larger farmers, businessmen and the urban upper-middle classes. The party does not have regional centres. Apart from its slightly more conciliatory position on the "national question" which is still reflected in its attitude towards Northern Ireland, there are no major ideological differences between the FF and the FG. Only its more pronounced following among the middle and upper social strata and the nature of its organisational structure make it more of a *bourgeois* Conservative party.

At present the FG has about 15,000 registered members and about 1,500 local **Organisation** groups. On the district and county level, its organisation is similar to that of the FF. However, the party only becomes really active before elections. For the pre-election period, the party headquarters appoint organisers who are responsible for conducting the election campaign on the various levels. As in the FF, the FG's annual party conference is the most important occasion for forming and voicing party opinion. The conference elects the executive. Because of the relatively undeveloped party structure and the fact that the middle levels of the party only function at certain times, the FG's annual conference is slightly more important than that of the FF. On a national level, the FG also has a permanent "Constituency Council" in which the committee leaders are represented. Finally, the "National Executive" consists of 10 Dail deputies, 5 senators, 15 members of the Constituency Council, 5 party members appointed by the party leader and executive. A "Standing Committee" is drawn from the members of the National Executive. Today it is the most important body in decision-making and administration. It is coupled with a permanent party secretariat. The parliamentary group ("Party in the Dail"), however, is relatively independent. The principle of incompatibility of certain party offices with a parliamentary seat (as it is to be found in the FF) does not exist. The party organisation is in general strongly hierarchical; policy-forming and decision-making are in many respects a "downward" process from the top echelons. The party leaders have a very dominant position, which results in very few changes in their composition.

Labour Party

In contrast to the other large parties, the Labour Party (LP) can be called a "class" party rather than a "people's" party. It has its followers mainly among the urban working class. As far as its programme is concerned, it has largely remained faithful to socialist ideals and the idea of a "workers' republic" which it wants to create constitutionally. The LP has only verbally committed itself to national unity. Today the LP has about 5,000 individual members and (with one exception) the country's largest trade unions which in turn represent 150,000 members. At present, the 700 local groups ("branches") and the national bodies are most important for **Organisation** the party's organisation. As in the FG, the intermediate district and constituency levels are of relatively little importance. The annual party conference ("National Conference") has even more significance than in the other parties. This conference elects the 3-strong executive, as well as 17 members of the national "Administrative

Council"; and its resolutions on party politics can be binding on the executive and the parliamentary group. Delegates sent by the local branches and corporate members are entitled to vote on these issues according to a certain code. The Administrative Council, whose other members are the leader of the parliamentary group, his deputy and 6 further delegates elected by the parliamentary group, is the most important executive body. On the whole, the LP's organisation seems to come closest to the ideal of party democracy; the authority of the party conference and the direct election of all delegates and important officials are evidence of this. On the other hand, the corporate membership of the trade unions can bring considerable influence from these organisations.

Party Interaction

Vertical Interactions

Today the Irish parties have become an integral part of society and play by far the most important role in influencing political opinion. Yet in view of the continuing .gnificance of personalities, Ireland cannot be called a genuine "party State" as in countries already discussed. The parties' position vis-a-vis the various professional and other associations is partly determined by the social background of their

Associations   supporters and partly by their political programmes. For example, the LP has particularly close relations with the major trade union association, the Irish Trade Union Congress; this fact is reflected in the corporate membership of the main trade unions and the personnel network. The "National Farmers' Association", on the other hand, is closer to the Fine Gael. The employers' unions, which together form the "Federated Union of Employers", also regard the FG as their most important partner. After Ireland had become independent, the Catholic church was at first on the side of the pro-treaty group (the FG); its relationship with the FF remained tense over some time. Today the Catholic church is accepted by all large parties as a partner in public discussions, and it exercises considerable influence on issues within its own sphere of interest (for example, social legislation, birth control, and so on).

Media   The Irish daily newspaper with the largest edition, the "Irish Independent", and the regional "Cork Examiner" are both close to the FG. The FF can rely on the voice of the second-largest daily paper, the "Irish Press", which was originally a purely party publication. As a rule, all these papers adopt a moderate Catholic-Conservative tone. By contrast, the party-independent "Irish Times", originally Protestant-Unionist, is now basically Liberal. Up to 1960, the broadcasting company was entirely an organ of the state. In the meantime, both radio and television have been given the status of public institutions pledged to political neutrality ("Radio Telefis Eirean"). Private broadcasting and television companies do not exist (although British television programmes can be received in most parts of the island, particularly in the north and east).

126

Horizontal Interactions

Since the day that Ireland became independent, the Irish party system has developed **Party system** from a multi-party system, in which up to 7 parties were at times represented in Parliament, into a relatively stable three-party system. The following proportion of votes remained almost unchanged for a long time: 3 (FF): 2 (FG): 1 (LP). After the 1977 elections, the seat distributions was as follows (the results of the 1973 and 1969 elections are given in brackets): FF 84 (69; 75); FG 43 (54; 50); LP 17 (19; 18).

As the electoral system is more personality-orientated, independent MPs have always played a significant role; on occasions such delegates have won 10 or more seats in the house of representatives. The proportion of "floating voters" is an estimated 10% of the entire voting population. The distribution of votes enables **Close** the FF to stay in power for relatively long periods of time, but its majority was **Government** always very close, and frequently elections had to be called earlier than expected. **majorities** Small splinter parties and independents were often the decisive weight in the balance of powers on such occasions. So far, the second- and third-largest parties have formed three coalition Governments; each time, their term of office was short, only three to four years. Both coalition partners had in common an anti-FF attitude and a slightly more moderate attitude on the national question, but with regard to their voters' background and their social and economic objectives domestically they were far apart.

From a socio-economic point of view, the largest party in the Irish party system **Outlook** occupies a central position, flanked by its far smaller political opponents on the "right" and "left". Consequently, no major transformation of the party system can be expected in the near future, despite steady industrialisation and urbanisation. The FG might lose some votes and LP might make gains, but this will have a self-cancelling effect on their chances of forming a coalition. Only the Ulster problem and the uncertain role that the Protestants would play in re-unified Ireland might have any fundamental effect in the long-term.

Denmark

RAINER KUNZ

The Political Development of Denmark

The Danish parties evolved in a community with a political development relatively typical of Western European countries. The continuity of development, however, has been above-average, mainly because of Denmark's neutrality in the 1st World War. The modern development of the Danish state began with the French Revolution in 1848; the Danish King was forced by the country's Liberal forces to renounce his claim to supreme rule and to agree to the election of a constituent assembly.[1] In 1849, the King signed the first Danish Constitution, thus making the country a constitutional monarchy. The constitution envisaged a division of legislative power between the King and a Parliament consisting of two chambers.[2] The Parliament was given all rights concerning the budget and taxes; the King was head of the executive and appointed the Government. The members of the first parliamentary chamber were elected indirectly by delegate; while members of the second chamber were directly elected according to the relative majority system in one-member constituencies.[3]

Development of the constitution

As in other European countries, the further development of political parties in Denmark was significantly influenced by the existence of a freely elected Parliament which was endowed with full political powers. For their work in Parliament, the parties had to form parliamentary groups; the fighting of elections forced the parties to expand their organisation. Consequently, as early as the mid-19th century the basic features of the Danish party system were formed, some of which are still noticeable today.

Factors determining the party development

Around 1860, three main groups emerged from the party spectrum:

Early party groups

— The "Venstre" Party was, on membership, the largest political group. Based on farming groups, such as the "Society of Farmers' Friends", this party was committed to liberal ideas. Its supporters were mainly to be found among the small and medium-sized farmers.

— It was opposed by various Conservative groups which were Monarchist and anti-parliament. They had followers among the large landowners and upper middle classes.

— Between these two large groups which held politically contrasting views, there was a smaller group called "National Liberal" or "Free Conservative". This group was mainly supported by the middle classes, civil servants and parts of the urban intelligentsia.

At that time, the Venstre Party proved to be the most active political force: it was the first Danish party to set up political clubs in order to influence the electorate,

128

and to form a parliamentary group for parliamentary work. The National Liberals showed less organisational development: their position in the political centre led to the formation of wings and splinter groups; and by the turn of the century, the party was to be completely absorbed by the Liberal and Conservative camps. The Conservatives did not possess any real political organisation; yet they exercised extraordinary political influence throughout the whole of the 19th century, as the Danish monarchs continually formed Conservative cabinets.

In 1884, Social Democrat delegates entered the "Folketing" for the first time as representatives of the still small number of industrial workers and the larger section of agricultural workers. However, the Social Democrat Party was only to achieve genuine political importance when the constitutional development of Denmark was almost complete. Until that time, the party could only try to realize its aims in alliance with other parties; and its preferred partners were left-wing groups of the Venstre Party.

Social Democrats

In its fight for a modern democratic revision of the Danish constitution, frequently against the opposition of the Conservatives, the Venstre Party emphasised three points:

Introduction of the parliamentary system

— The political rights of the first[4] chamber (which was dominated by the Conservatives as a result of the electoral method) were to be curbed;
— The restrictions on the right to vote were to be abolished, enfranchising a much greater proportion of the population;
— The King was to be compelled to give due consideration to majority parties in the "Folketing" when appointing the Government.

These aims were realised in two phases. In 1901, the Liberal majority in the "Folketing", supported by some Conservative groups and Social Democrats, succeeded in making the King promise to appoint the cabinets according to the parliamentary majority.[5] Thus Denmark became a parliamentary monarchy. However, this decision had been preceded by a constitutional battle that had lasted over 30 years; for long periods, the Conservative cabinets appointed by the King had governed against the majority in the Folketing.[6] The issues of electoral reform and the status of the chambers towards each other remained unsettled until 1915.

1915 Constitution

In that year, the larger parties reached a compromise which resulted in the new constitution signed by the King in the same year.[7] This constitution contained the final implementation of the universal, equal and direct right to vote,[8] and also the changeover to a system of proportional representation which was to affect the further development of the modern Danish party system. As far as the political parties were concerned, the 1915 constitution had almost completed Denmark's political development. The constitution that is valid today, which came into effect in 1953, gave one further right to the parties: the referendum. If a minority of at least one third of the members in the "Folketing" vote against a bill, they can demand that a referendum be held on the bill in question.

1953 Constitution

The Danish Parties

Today Denmark has a multi-party system. The following table gives a breakdown of the existing parties; only the five strongest parties in the "Folketing" are to be discussed in more detail.

Party	Percentage of votes			Seats		
	1977	1975	1973	1977	1975	1973
Social Democrats	37.1	30.0	25.7	65	53	46
People's Socialists	3.9	4.9	6.0	7	9	11
Socialists of the Left	2.7	2.1	1.5	5	4	0
Communists	3.7	4.2	3.6	7	7	6
Liberals (Lib. Venstre)	12.0	23.3	12.3	21	42	20
Progress Party (Glistrup)	14.6	13.6	15.9	26	24	28
Social Liberals (Rad. Venstre)	3.6	7.1	11.2	6	13	20
Cons. People's Party	8.5	5.5	11.2	15	10	20
Christian People's Party	3.4	5.3	4.0	6	9	7
Centre — Democrats (Jacobsen)	6.4	2.2	7.8	11	4	14
Party of the Lawful State	3.3	1.8	2.9	6	0	5
				175	175	175

The Social Democrat Party (Socialdemocratiet)

Position in the party system

For more than 50 years, the Social Democrat Party has been the strongest party in the Danish Parliament. It was founded in 1871; in 1884, the first Social Democrat members sat in the national Parliament. Its political breakthrough came in the 1920 elections when the party won 29% of all votes. In the following elections, the party's percentage of votes went as high as 46% and rarely fell below 40%. Since the Social Democrat Party formed its first Government in 1924, it has been the most frequent governing party, either on its own or in coalition.

Social structure

The traditional supporters of the Danish Social Democrats are to be found among the industrial workers, the lower-paid and the small farmers. However, in the elections after 1945 the party made some impact on other sections. The party

Party organisation

possesses a relatively tight organisational network. There are 1,300 local groups[10] which, apart from their political activities, play a part in cultural and social life. The highest body is the party congress which meets at least once every four years; it consists of elected district delegates, representatives of all party sub-groups and organisations closely related to the party.[11] The congress decides on procedural matters, elects the party chairman (at present Anker Joergensen[12]) and members of the party's executive committee.

Party membership is restricted to individuals, but the party is closely connected with a number of organisations. The most important ones are the associated youth, student and womens' organisations; by agreement they are obliged to support the Social Democrat Party's political activities and in return receive mainly financial help. The party is also closely linked with the trade unions, which send their own "guest" delegates to the party's conferences. The Social Democrat press is of particular importance for the party's public relations work; furthermore, the party has very close links with certain community organisations.

At the time of its foundation, the Danish Social Democrat Party was committed to orthodox Marxist thought. However, long before it first came to power it emphasised that it did not want to achieve its aims through revolution, but through constitutional reform. It increasingly turned its back on Marxist theories and concerned itself with the specific problems of Danish society. The party's chief objective became the social integration of the working class on equal terms. In 1945, the party swung once more to the left, for it believed that European communism would increase in the post-war era. Through this move, with its comprehensive plans for nationalisation,[13] the party hoped to put itself into a more favourable position. In fact, it found itself worse placed than before. The Communist movement in Western Europe was weaker than expected; emphasising the Socialist element in politics resulted in difficulties with the Social Liberal coalition partner and made the party a target for Liberal and Conservative attacks. Following defeats in the elections, the party returned to a more moderate course. The "Basic Programme" of 1961 lays down a programme of democratic socialism which is characterised by the endeavour to harmonise individual well-being and social security with the interests of society as a whole. The population's discontent, particularly with economic development, led in 1973 to a bleak period for the Social Democrat Party; its results improved, however, in the 1975 and 1977 elections.

Ideological development

Democratic socialism

The Liberal Party (Venstre)

The Liberal Party regards itself as part of the tradition of the international Liberal movement which in Denmark, too, was the force striving for democratisation and parliamentarianism. Initially split into various groups,[14] a uniform Liberal Party developed only towards the close of the 19th century. The Liberals were the strongest party in the "Folketing" until 1924; after that, they lost their dominating position to the Social Democrats. Despite continuous losses in the following elections, the Liberal Party has remained the country's second or third largest party[15] maintaining its political reputation. Large parts of the Danish population consider the Liberals as the only possible alternative to the Social Democrats; and the party's minority Government from 1973 until 1975 proved this assessment correct.

The Liberal Party's strongest supporters are anyway the rural population and the self-employed middle classes. The organisational structure of the party is not well developed. There is a high number (around 1,600) of local groups which for the

Origins

Position in the party system

Social structure

131

most part are used to making their own decisions. The annual party conference is the supreme party organ: it deals with procedural matters, decides on fundamental issues of policy, elects the party chairman – at present Knut Engard and Jens Foged – as well as some of the members of the party's national committee. The Liberal Party also has a number of affiliated organisations; the most important ones are youth, women's and press groups. The Liberal youth organisation (with more than 50,000 members) is the largest political group of its kind in the whole country; together with the women's organisation, it fulfils political, cultural and social functions, particularly in non-urban areas.

Programme

The party has two main objectives in its programme. On the one hand, it tries to re-model the image it still has as a party which is mainly concerned with the agrarian sector; on the other hand, it fights against its own tradition – the idea of the Liberal "laissez-faire" party of the 19th century. The former objective is not easy to realise. The party is compelled to represent the interests of the agrarian sector with considerable vigour, as this is expected by the majority of its voters; and as agriculture is an essential part of Denmark's economy.[16] Basically the Liberals attempt to combine traditional Liberal thinking with the modern concept of the welfare state. Particular emphasis is given to the need for private ownership and enterprise. The state should have certain rights and obligations; duties in the social sector for maintaining the Welfare State; rights to participation in social and economic planning, in the securing of full employment, in the comprehensive distribution of wealth and in the fight against economic monopolies. However, the party constantly points out the dangers of a bureaucratic State endowed with too many powers; for this leads to an encroachment on the personal and economic freedom of the individual.

Conservative People's Party (Det Konservative Folkepart)

History

Apart from the Liberals, the Conservatives were the other influencing factor on Danish politics in the 19th century. The modern Conservative Party was founded in 1916. Due to the democratisation of the electoral and the political system, the Conservatives' influence gradually decreased: judged by overall vote percentage[17] and participation in Government, the party now only plays a minor role.

Social structure

The Conservative Party is a distinctly urban party. The greater part of its supporters today come from the urban middle classes, particularly from among the higher-paid,

Organisation

employers and businessmen. The party's organisation is based on about 800 local groups. The annual party conference in the autumn is the most important body, deciding on the fundamental policy issues. There is also an annual party convention in the spring which is attended by 300 to 500 delegates from various party sections and by representatives of organisations which are close to the Conservative Party. The party's executive committee comprises about 65 members; they are recruited from among the party's sections, the associated organisations and the parliamentary group. The executive committee meets every other month to support and advise the party leaders. Apart from the party chairman, who is elected by the party

132

convention, the leader of the parliamentary group plays an important role.[18] As all other large Danish parties, the Conservatives have their own youth, women's and press organisations.

Ideology

Similar to the Venstre Party, the Conservatives have tried to bury their anti-democratic and anti-parliamentary past. They categorically reject the conservatism of the 19th century and modern socialism. They share the Liberal's fear that the socialist State's all-powerful bureaucracy endangers private ownership and enterprise. The Conservatives intend to continue the achievements of the Welfare State in the social sector; for this purpose, the State is given the right of planning and intervention. Conservative attitudes towards the distribution of wealth, worker participation and wages policies, however, differ radically from those of the Social Democrats and Liberals.

Social Liberal Party (Det Radikale Venstre)

Position in the party system

Social structure

Organisation

The Social Liberal Party was formed in 1905 as an independent party, mainly consisting of politicians who had previously belonged to one of the various "Venstre" groups. It achieved its best election results in 1918 when it polled more than 20% of the votes cast; since 1945 the percentage has sunk below 10%. The present supporters of this party have a mixed background: they are mainly members of the middle class, small farmers and the intelligentsia. The organisation of the party is relatively undeveloped, reflecting its size and financial constraints. The annual party conference has the most important function — debating and deciding on fundamental issues, passing the party's programmes and electing the party chairman and the executive committee. In the Social Liberal Party, too, the leader of the parliamentary group plays an important role. In spite of its generally small number of delegates, the party has considerable political stature; and because of its position in the left centre, Social Democrats as well as Conservatives and Liberals regarded it as a possible coalition partner. During the long coalition with the Social Democrat Party, the Social Liberals prevented a right/left polarisation of Danish politics.

Coalition politics

Progress Party (Fremskridtpartiet)

Programme

Election results

The Progress Party, under its chairman Mogens Glistrup, is one of the most amazing phenomena of the Danish party system. In 1972, it presented a programme which was generally regarded as unrealistic. Some of its more spectacular features were the demands for a reduction in state control in all public sectors, complete disarmament, abolition of the professional civil servant, abolition of taxes and a drastic reduction and re-organisation of the existing educational system. Strangely enough, the party won 15.9% of votes cast in 1972. After it had suffered some losses in the 1975 elections, it became the second largest party in the "Folketing" in 1977, polling 14.6%. As the Danish electorate has no doubt recognised the unreality of the party's programmes, the election results are generally interpreted as an act of protest against the established parties. So far, the other parties in the "Folketing" have refused to co-operate with the Progress Party.

The Small Parties

Characteristic features

Apart from the above four traditional parties and the Progress Party, there are a number of other small parties which owe their place in Parliament to the system of proportional representation. They frequently represent quite particular interests; they cannot form coalitions with each other and are not regarded as desirable coalition partners by the large parties. All in all, they are largely excluded from exercising any political influence.

The "Socialist People's Party" was founded by former communist parliamentary members; it is committed to a socialism on a democratic and parliamentary basis. The "Left-wing Socialist Party" emerged from the left-wing youth and student rebellion of the 1960's: it is against communism and social democracy; instead it strives for a humane socialism and direct democracy. The "Danish Communist Party" lost all its seats in 1960 and only returned to Parliament in 1973. "The Centre Democrats" left the Social Democrat Party when the latter swung to the left centre. The "Rights Association", a small party dating back to 1926, stands for economic liberalism and the greatest possible freedom of the individual. The "Independent Party" is also for economic liberalism, together with the call for a life style that is based on the Christian moral code. The "Christian People's Party" campaigns against pornography and abortion.

The Party System

Party systems

By the end of the constituting period of the political parties, Denmark had at the turn of the century (1900) a four-party system consisting of the Conservative, Liberal, Social Liberal and Social Democrat Parties. Judged by the number of votes

Consequences of the electoral system

polled, the parties' strength remained constant; but as a consequence of the existing majority system, shifts occurred within the party group of the 4. The Conservative Party in particular lost more and more seats. It was quite imaginable that the system might develop into a three-party system without the Conservative Party, possibly even a two-party system should the Social Democrats and Social Liberals merge. The introduction of the system of proportional representation put an end to this development. The new electoral system was initially disadvantageous for the Liberals and Social Liberals, but did not threaten their existence as such. The Social Democrat Party's growth into the strongest parliamentary group, which was mainly a result of the greatly increased number of people entitled to vote, completed the structural changes. The 4 large parties were joined by.a number of small groups with only a few seats; so creating a multi-party system.

Government formation

It seems amazing that up to the present day this multi-party system has always been capable of forming a Government. The following points may help to explain this:

– The 4 large Danish parties together have the absolute majority of votes. Even

134

after the appearance of the Progress Party they still had more than 61% of all votes cast.

— The system of 4 large parties contains sufficient scope for coalitions. The preferred combinations are: Social Democrats/Social Liberals, Liberals/Social Liberals, Liberals/Conservatives.

— Other parties which entered the "Folketing" were frequently unable to keep their seat in Parliament for any length of time.

— None of the parties that were new to Parliament succeeded in forming a coalition with one of the traditional parties.

— The multitude of small parties could not form coalitions with each other.

— The number of minority Cabinets in the political development of Denmark seems to lie well above average; each of these Cabinets was supported by one of the 4 large parties. Even if they rarely survived their full term, they showed remarkable stability and ability to govern, as they were usually supported by different groups of the other traditional parties in opposition. The stability of the Danish party system can be seen as a direct result of the 4 traditional parties' cooperation; they seem to form an integrated system of interaction and decision. This of course implies a restriction in political competition, and it is this fact which may have contributed to numerous voters' disillusionment from which the Progress Party benefits. The particular nature of the party system also makes coalitions possible such as the one formed in August 1978 between the Social Democrat and the Liberal Venstre Party. Although the new Government coalition with 88 out of a total of 179 parliamentary seats does not have the absolute majority in Parliament, it can expect to be tolerated by the left-wing as well as the *bourgeois* party camps.

Notes

[1] A quarter of the members of the assembly were appointed by the King; the rest were elected according to a system which was restricted to self-supporting male Danes over 30 who had legal indigenous status. This system corresponded to the liberal mode of election.

[2] First chamber = "Landsting"; second chamber = "Folketing".

[3] The right to vote was subject to similar restrictions as those concerning the election to the constituent assembly.

[4] 12 of the 66 members of the "Landsting" were appointed by the King as life members; the others were elected according to a census system which favoured the wealthier social classes.

[5] This promise was firmly embodied in the 1953 constitution. Between 1901 and 1953, the Danish monarchy only broke their promise on two occasions (which were both tolerated by Parliament).

[6] From 1875 until 1884, the Conservative Prime Minister Estrup governed against the parliamentary majority; he did this with the help of provisional budgets and under circumstances which resembled a constitutional conflict. His Government was only possible because the King supported him and because the various Liberal parties could not come to any agreement.

[7] Because of the 1st World War, it only came into effect in 1920.

[8] The introduction of the women's right to vote was particularly important in this respect.

[9] The Conservatives wanted the change-over to proportional representation, because they hoped to do better in the elections. As their approval of the new constitution was essential, the Venstre Party also agreed to the change in the electoral system.

135

10 The individual local groups vary very much with regard to their size and activities; their membership can be anything between 50 and 5000. This is indicative of the problems that the party, and most of the other parties too, faces in adjusting its organisational structure to the quickly changing social framework.

11 For every 1000 members, there is one delegate at the conference; only the elected party delegates have the right to vote, the representatives of the associated organisations do not.

12 The leadership of the party has been extremely stable. From 1882 up to the present day, the Social Democrat Party was led by only 7 chairmen.

13 The contacts with Great Britain, which were particularly strong during the German occupation, (and with the Labour Party in particular) have certainly played a part.

14 As early as 1870, the Liberal groups had united to form the "United Liberal Party"; it issued the first Danish party programme and immediately won the majority in the "Folketing". The union only lasted until 1878. Thereafter, the two most important Liberal groups were "Det forhandlende Venstre" and "Venstrereformpartiet".

15 In the 1935 and 1943 elections, they lost their position as the second-strongest party to the Conservatives; in 1973 and 1977 to the Progress Party.

16 The party is faced with a dilemma. The farming communities are steadily dying out; this no doubt contributes to the decrease in Liberal votes. The party consequently has to appeal to other voters. However, it cannot give up its commitment to agrarian problems (as demonstrated during the negotiations about Denmark's accession to the EC), because the farming population still forms the largest part of their voters.

17 The last time that it polled more than 20% of the votes was in the 1964 elections.

18 Leadership of the party and leadership of the parliamentary group are strictly separate. The weaker the party organisation, the stronger the influence of the parliamentary group.

3. The Party Systems of the Non-EC Countries

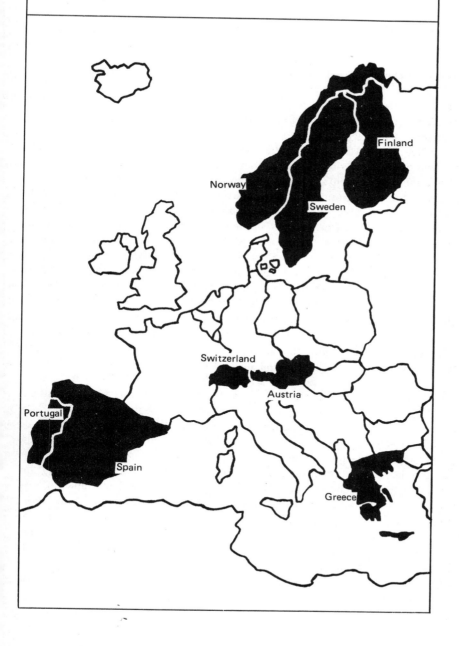

Norway

Finland

Sweden

Switzerland

Austria

Portugal

Spain

Greece

Austria

HERBERT MAIER

Social and Economic Conditions

Social structure

Modern Austria is characterised by a complex social structure of distinctive class levels. These differences have, however, been eroded (partly by legislation) creating a relatively open society.

The decline of the Hapsburg Empire towards the end of the 1st World War, the migration of large parts of the population and the economic rebuilding after 1945 brought about fundamental changes in the structure of Austrian society. There was an influx of refugees from the Sudetes, south-east Europe and southern Tyrol. The economic growth during the post-war period resulted in a considerable fall in the number of agricultural workers, and an increase in the urban working population. Over a period of 15 years, the percentage of working women increased by almost 90%.[1] Only 20% of the rural alpine region today work as farmers, compared with 40% before the war.[2] The old *grande bourgeoisie* (large industrialists, bankers) has lost in importance, replaced now by high civil servants, politicians and managers of nationalised industry. All in all, Austria's social structure corresponds to that of a rapidly developing Western industrial society.

Economic system

Two factors determine the economic system: the form of the so-called "free economy" on the one hand, and the high degree of nationalisation on the other. After 1945, the basic industries and major banks were nationalised in order to prevent the occupying powers from seizing German property.[3] Although there was little ideology behind this action, it proved very advantageous for the Austrian Socialists. It enabled them to get into industrial management, something they had never been able to do under the 1st Republic. The state institutions cooperate relatively closely and have links with the various representative organisations. The

Role of the representative organisations

union system has always been an integral part of Austria's constitution; in extreme cases, this has meant compulsory membership for certain groups. Consequently, the interplay between economy and politics is rather intense; and the representative organisations, such as the Chambers of Trade, the Austrian Industrialists' Association, the Austrian Trade Union, the Chamber for Workers and Employees and the Agricultural Chamber all interrelate relatively well. Compared with other European countries, Austria's overall economic situation is healthy. However, due to its reliance on exports, Austria has become heavily dependent on world trade; if the worldwide economic recession continues, Austria's aim of full employment will be unattainable.

138

The Political System

The political climate in Austria today is quite different from that of the period between the wars. In the First Republic (1918–1943), Austria appeared to concentrate more on the German Reich than on herself. All parties – except for the Communists – were in favour of Austria's union with Germany.[4] The most important political groups were divided into three irreconcilable "camps": the Christian Conservative, Socialist and National groups. The only thing they had in common was the rejection of an unrestricted liberalism; as far as their social background and their political ideas were concerned, they were diametrically opposed. The farmers and the *bourgeoisie* of the rural regions belonged to the Christian Conservative camp; the Viennese workers and those in the industrial areas formed part of the anti-clerical Socialist group which regarded itself as German-national and was therefore relatively easily integrated into the National Socialist German Reich in 1938. As the various parties represented quite particular interests, they were unable to put a stop to a growing radicalism during the economic crisis after the 1st World War. Parliamentary democracy began to crumble and the "National Front" under Dollfuss was able to come to power in 1933. By means of an authoritarian corporate State, he tried to bring political order back to Austria in this formative period. The similarities of the situation of the Weimar Republic are quite obvious. As in Germany, a change in these narrow and rigid political attitudes was only effected by the bitter experiences of the Third Reich.

After the 2nd World War, party coalitions comprising the majority of the various groups became possible because there was a genuine desire for political agreement. This was quite often less a compromise of party attitudes and more the result of the distribution of power (the proportional system). In any event this situation was a great improvement on the First Republic. The changes occurred on a party level – the greater part of the population have remained rather passive politically which may be partly explained by the predominant policy of "proportional thinking". The middle classes have manifested a stronger interest in politics, whereas the lower social classes appear prepared to blindly adopt the ideas and values of the highest social groups. The self-employed and higher-paid employees as well as the farming population tend towards a *status quo* attitude. It is true that the middle-class working population want reforms and wish to see their status improved, but they are not prepared to question the existing political system as a whole. Radical political behaviour is only to be found among a marginal group of extreme left-wing students or among ex-National Socialists. Such groups no longer play any significant role in Austria.

The constitutional framework of present-day Austria has a decisive influence on the parties. Its political system can generally be called "parliamentary"; it has additional federal, plebiscite and presidial components. The "National Council" and the "Federal President" are directly elected by the people. The Government, which is in effect the parliamentary majority, is the primary political organ. Since 1945 there have been 4 forms of Government:

(marginal notes:) Political climate / 1st Republic / 2nd Republic / Constitutional determinants

- All-party Government
- "Great Coalition"
- Sole Government
- Minority Government

Great Coalition

During the time of the Great Coalition (1945—66), the so-called coalition committee, a body not envisaged in the constitution, achieved considerable political influence. It took political decisions before or without consulting Parliament. Its "camp" attitude virtually guaranteed a high standard of discipline within the parliamentary groups; largely excluded the possibility of genuine political conflicts within a party; and at the same time proved itself relatively amenable to compromise at the highest level. In the economic and social-political sector, the "wages and price commission" was invested with considerable powers in the political process of decision-making, and was quite autonomous.

Party norms

The Austrian constitution presupposes the existence of parties. Art. 26 and 117 refer to "election parties"; that is, associations which are only formed for particular election purposes. The political parties obviously extend beyond this definition. Art. 35 (1), 55 (2) and 81a (1) are still limited in scope, for they conceive of parties as intraparliamentary groups. Austria does not possess comprehensive legislation on parties such as exists in West Germany. Professor Hans Kelsen, one of the fathers of the Austrian constitution, has always been aware of this fact and has called for corresponding amendments. However, on July 2nd, 1975, a federal law came into effect which specifies the purpose, financing and election campaign procedures of all political parties.

The Parties

Of the 80 existing parties, 23 have fought for a seat in the National Council at the beginning of the Second Austrian Republic. After the first elections, only 3 parties were represented on the National Council: the ÖVP (Austrian People's Party), the SPÖ (Socialist Party of Austria) and the KPÖ (Communist Party of Austria).

.OVP

The ÖVP can be regarded as a non-socialist collective party which represents the Christian Socialist group, basing its ideology on their political thinking and acknowledging the Austrian state as its native country. Its fundamental doctrine was that religion is vital for education as well as for human co-existence. Since 1965, presumably as a result of the Klagenfurt Manifesto, this view has increasingly been replaced by a non-ideologicical attitude, and the party now presents itself as a party of the political centre. Although many of its members belonged to the former Christian Socialist Party, the ÖVP does not regard itself as this party's immediate successor. In contrast to the CSP, the ÖVP has avoided forming definite ties with the Church, although one of the reasons for this may have been the prohibition of the Church's party-political activity issued by the Austrian bishops.

Party organisation

The ÖVP was formed by the union of three vocational groups: the Austrian Farmers' Association (ÖBB), the Austrian Economic Association (ÖWB) and the Austrian Association of Workers and Employees (ÖAAB). The Austrian Youth

Movement (ÖJB) and the Austrian Women's Movement (ÖFB) also form part of the ÖVP. The various associations are financially and economically independent and issue their own programmes. According to K.H. Nassmacher, the process of forming political opinion in the party as a whole is as follows: "First of all, the leading members of the associations have to define the interests of each particular association. These separate interests then have to be harmonised and integrated into the objectives of the party as a whole".[6]

The most important political decisions are pre-formulated by a "5-man team" consisting of the party's federal chairman (1st party chairman), the secretary-general and the three association leaders.

This integration of interests between the various associations is paralleled on a federal level by a nexus of the different states. The party's organisation is one of a modern "mass" party with its constant efforts to remain in contact with its supporters, and to recruit new voters from the electorate. The ÖVP is more of a member party than voter party, having a member/vote ratio of approximately 1/2.3. This is far greater than in, for example, the German or British Conservative parties. Its supporters and members come from the following groups: the self-employed; the higher-paid workers; civil servants and the farmers who live in rural or provincial areas, with a middle to high income. The party has about 4,000 offices and local branches.

The SPÖ was re-founded in 1945 and regards itself as the successor to the Social Democrats from the 1st Republic. It succeeded in uniting the previously separate wings of the Social Democrats and the revolutionary Socialists, at the same time rejecting the extreme socialist radicalism and its exponents. The SPÖ sets itself clearly apart from the Communists. This may be a consequence of various factors: the population's embitterment following the Soviet occupation, the Social Democrats' experiences during their exile in the Anglo-Saxon democracies, and the result of participation in Government. Until the late fifties, the party's programme was orientated towards orthodox Marxism. The turning point came with the party's 1958 programme. "Humanistic Socialism" became a key term: it stands for the free and unhampered development of the individual and seeks the necessary economic, political and social conditions through reform. The individual has freedom of religious choice — unheard of under the 1st Republic. The "Programme for Austria", resolved in 1966, was the final step in the development of the SPÖ from an ideological to a pragmatic left-wing liberal party.

Organisationally, the SPÖ is more centralised; it is supported by about as many local groups as the ÖVP and possesses a huge number of officials. The SPÖ, too, can fall back upon strong corporate organisations: the "Austrian Trade Union", the "Federal Chamber of Workers and Employees", the "Free Economy Association" and the "Austrian Labour Farmers' Association".[7] In comparison with the ÖVP, these organisations are not party organs and as such not essential elements, as membership of the SPÖ can only be on a personal level. In the individual local groups, a special type of official, the "confidant" is supposed to act as link between members and voters on the one hand and the party leaders on the other. Today

SPO

Programme

Party
organisation

141

there are about 70,000 of these "confidants" in the SPÖ, but only a third of them is fully active. The party headquarters give them their basic training; they make up about a tenth of the party's total membership.[8] The party's top officials are recruited from among this group; they are appointed on the basis of long service, achievement and political adaptability. However, over the past years qualified technocrats have increasingly been recruited for the upper ranks of the party. The SPÖ's supporters come chiefly from in and around large cities, they are largely working and middle-class, and their attitude towards the Catholic church ranges from indifference to rejection. With around 700,000 members, the party can on average expect to poll over 2 million votes.

FPO The FPÖ does not regard itself as a Liberal party, as might be expected from its name. It is supported by those groups of the population which were German-national during the first Republic, and which later supported National Socialism. Its predecessor was the "Association of Independents" which after 1949 attempted to get politicians into Parliament who either had a bad reputation as National Socialists or were members of the "National" camp. Its success in 1949 was considerable: it won 12% of the total vote and 16 seats. Due to internal disagreements, the party was dissolved in 1955. Its successor was the FPÖ which has always been in opposition on a federal level and has never participated in Government. It has, however, secured some influence among the Austrian member states. In its programme, the FPÖ distinguishes between the German nation and the Austrian State; the fact that it approves of the latter is presumably only the acknowledgement of an unalterable but not exactly desirable situation. Today the FPÖ is divided into two sections: on the one hand, the "Liberal Progressive" group which would rather join the SPÖ as a coalition partner; and on the other hand, the "National Conservative" group which is more interested in cooperating with the ÖVP. 10% of the FPÖ's voters are also members of the party: it can therefore be called a voter party. Liberal ideas seem to enjoy an increasing influence, so that the party is beginning to lose its underlying extreme nationalist character. This may be ascribed to changing generations in the party's top ranks, and also to the demands of certain groups of voters who no longer hold with traditional party values.

KPO The KPÖ was formed in 1819 as a "left-wing section" of the Austrian social democracy. Under the Dollfuss regime it was banned and had to go underground until 1945. After the 2nd World War, it gained a certain amount of importance as it was supported by the Soviet occupying force, and consequently received some key positions in the Renner Government. After the Austrian national treaty and the withdrawal of the Russians, it was unable to get another seat on the National Council. The invasion of Czechoslovakia was seen by the Austrian people as a threat to their own State, and this cost the KPÖ many votes. Furthermore, reaction within the party to the Russian intervention was so divisive that its existence was put in jeopardy.[9] What remained was a politically insignificant *cadre*. The well-known Austrian Marxist Ernst Fischer was thrown out of the party; his colleague F. Marek left of his own volition.

142

The Position of the Parties

Elections

If one looks at the 10 elections that have been held since 1945, one finds proof of the "camp" mentality of the Austrian electorate. In the percentage share of votes polled, the ÖVP showed variations of 55% and the SPÖ of 11% (compare West Germany: CDU/CSU 19%, SPD 17%). This is paralleled by the relatively low number of "floating voters" which until 1966 totalled 5% of the electorate and today stands at 10%. This continuity is indicative of a firmly established base of tradition and socialisation.[10] 40% of the voters are also members of a party; this figure is unusually high compared with other Western or Eastern European countries. However, this relatively high degree of organisation must not be equated with an extremely "democratised" political culture; wide-spread political apathy, a system of recruitment which is almost exclusively based on the principle of seniority, and the common belief that party membership entails personal advantages suggest that this is not the case.

The Austrian party system can almost be called a two-party system. The reason for this is that the two largest parties have polled about 90% of the total votes in 10 separate elections; furthermore, the small FPÖ (which polls on average 5.5% of the votes) was long regarded as incapable of governing, and today only holds some significance in the federal states of Austria and on a community level. Both of the large Austrian parties are now people's parties. They have the typical characteristics: neglect or rejection of fundamental programmatic principles in favour of class-orientated publicity strategies; strengthening of the party's top levels at the expense of its base; membership mainly by subscription which implies less scope for the activity and participation of the individual member. There is still a fairly pronounced polarisation of the parties at grass-root level. At a higher level, however, the long life of the Great Coalition and the relatively peaceful toleration of minority Governments has demonstrated a relatively high consensus. The Austrian system of proportional representation makes it difficult for the large parties to gain an absolute majority in the National Council; a smaller party needs less votes to get a seat. It is not clear whether this, together with the recently developed willingness to form a coalition with the FPÖ, may lead to a three-party system similar to that of West Germany, but it is now certainly a possibility.

The interactions among the parties represented in the National Council have followed various patterns since 1945. After the foundation of the 2nd Republic, the ÖVP, SPÖ and KPÖ formed an all-party Government until 1947. Without the Communists, neither of the two large parties had a sufficient majority to govern on its own. Consequently, a permanent Great Coalition was formed and lasted until 1966. After 1953, the leaders of the ÖVP toyed with the idea of having the VdU and later the FPÖ as coalition partners. However, the Socialist Federal Presidents in particular rejected this idea because of the parties' National Socialist past, and anyway the ÖVP would have had to modify the constitution to form such a coalition.

143

In the 1966 elections, the ÖVP gained an absolute majority in Parliament and formed its own Government under its party chairman Dr. Josef Klaus. This changed the usual party configuration: for the first time in Austrian history, there was a powerful opposition in the National Council. In 1970, a change in power occurred when the minority Government of Dr. Bruno Kreisky was unable to form a coalition with the FPÖ as the SPÖ had excluded this possibility durings its election campaign. When new elections were held in 1971, the SPÖ intimated that it might be willing to choose the FPÖ as a coalition partner; but after it had gained a close absolute majority and its negotiations with the FPÖ failed, the SPÖ formed its own Government. The FPÖ has thus become an acknowledged potential partner of the two large parties. Generally, then one can state that there has been a steady consolidation of the Austrian parliamentary democracy, for changes in the political power structure and a strong and efficient parliamentary opposition have replaced the former proportional democracy which was widely regarded as undemocratic. However, competition between the parties, at least during the election campaigns, has become harder and more vehement.

Notes

1 See März, Eduard: Die Klassenstruktur der Zweiten Österreichischen Republik. In: Kienzle, Heinz: Probleme der österreichischen Politik, Vol. 1, Wien 1968, p. 87.
2 Cf Knoll and Pelinka: L'evolution de la structure sociale en Autriche depuis 1945. In: Austriaca 3, 1976, p. 52.
3 Cf Fischer, Heinz (Ed.): Das politische System Österreichs. Wien 1974, p. 543.
4 Cf Skuhra, Anselm: Das politische System Österreichs. In: Zeitgeschichte No. 1, 1974, p. 278.
5 Cf Ritschel, Heinz (Ed.): Demokratiereform. Die Existenzfragen Österreichs. Wien and Hamburg 1969, p. 133.
6 See Nassmacher, Karl-Heinz: Das österreichische Regierungssystem. Köln 1968, p. 47.
7 The self-employed tradesmen are organised in the FWV; the ARB is the farmers' organisation with close links to the SPÖ.
8 Cf Fischer, ibid., p. 39.
9 Cf Pelinka, Anton and Welan, Manfred: Demokratie und Verfassung in Österreich. Wien 1971, p. 298 f.
10 Cf Skuhra, ibid., p. 277.

Switzerland

THEO STAMMEN

The "Schweizer Eidgenossenschaft" has a special status within the EC countries. **Switzerland's** This is due to its particular national development as well as to the highly differ- **special** entiated ethnic, cultural and linguistic structure of the country and specific **status** features of the traditional political system. All these factors make the Swiss party system particularly interesting.

Historical Background

The origins of the modern Swiss parties date back to the early 19th century when **Origins** far-reaching social and economic changes occurred in Switzerland, as throughout **of the** Europe. These changes had constitutional and political consequences for the whole **parties** of the country.

Under the protection of the "Holy Alliance" of the European powers, the old "Eidgenossenschaft" was restored by a federal treaty at the Vienna congress in 1815. This Swiss confederation, which had been fundamentally restructured in the wake of the French Revolution and the Napoleonic era, was a loose grouping of states based on old canton constitutions and only slightly modernised statutes of the "Tag" (assembly of delegates from the cantons). But as early as 1830, during **Regeneration** the so-called "Regeneration Period", it became absolutely clear (particularly in the **period** middle-class urban cantons) that these constitutions bore less and less relation to the social and economic environment; for it was during this period that industrialisation, particularly in textiles and clock manufacture, began to rapidly accelerate.

So the Liberal movement which had been silenced by the Restoration gathered new **Liberal** impetus, now supported by a growing feeling of Swiss national unity. A political **movement** reform movement began which (after 1830) spread to numerous cantons and introduced new constitutions based on the principles of sovereignty of the people and general franchise. However, Conservative opposition forces gathered in the old, mainly Catholic cantons. Opposition grew as the call for a centralised federal reform was raised. The tensions and conflicts between Conservative and Liberal forces dominated Swiss home affairs, and finally came to a head in a (very short) civil war, the so called "Separatist League War" (1847). The victory of the Liberal forces and cantons paved the way for a fundamental reform of the Swiss constitution. In 1848, Switzerland received its modern federal constitution which underwent a total revision in 1874, but whose basic features are still valid today. **Reform of** During this period of constitutional upheaval, the Swiss political parties emerged, **the constitution** at first mainly on a cantonal level. They were essentially the main groups that make up the Swiss party system of today: the Liberals ("Freisinnige") and the Catholic

145

Conservatives with their local variations.

Following their victory in the Separatist League War, the Liberals held the reins of Swiss federal politics over a period of several decades up until the 20th century. During this time, they appointed all members of the Federal Council (the Swiss Government), and they constantly had an absolute majority in the National Council. For most of the 19th century the Liberals were not a uniform party, but rather an association comprising a number of cantonal variations. They were a "Liberal family group" (E. Gruner) which only in 1878 became a unified parliamentary group in the National Council; in 1894 the Swiss "Liberal Democrat Party" was born. During this period, it favoured a strengthening of centralised political power.

The Catholic Conservatives, who had their roots in the old cantons of the separatist league, initially opposed the new Swiss federal state. They tried to make the Liberal Government take note of their views through referendum. It was only around the turn of the century (1900) that they gave up their opposition and accepted the new constitutional order. They delegated their first member of the Federal Council (the Swiss Government) in 1891. After several abortive attempts, a party active throughout Switzerland was finally formed in 1922: the "Swiss Conservative People's Party". In 1947 it changed its name to the "Conservative Christian Social People's Party of Switzerland".

In contrast to these the most important non-socialist groups of the 19th century, the Conservative Protestant Party, which existed in some cantons, did not succeed in establishing itself on a federal level. Later, it even lost its influence in the cantons, and its supporters swung to the Liberal Democrats and to the Farmers' Party. The

Liberal Democrats had emerged towards the end of the 19th century, supplanting another non-socialist group, the "Centre". Since 1961 they have called themselves the "Liberal Democrat Union of Switzerland", and have been able to maintain their position up to the present day.

Compared with these non-socialist parties, the Swiss Labour movement and the Social Democrats emerged quite late on a federal level. Although, as already mentioned, industrialisation began rather early in Switzerland and was naturally accompanied by the emergence of a class of industrial workers, the Social Democrats — orientated towards socialism and internationalism — were faced with a difficult task. The reason was that shortly after 1830 almost all cantons had introduced universal franchise, and since that date the working classes had either joined the existing non-socialist parties and remained faithful to them, or had become members of the workers' national educational society, the "Grütli Society", which joined the Social Democrat Party as late as 1901. It was only at that time (around 1900) that the Social Democrats in Switzerland developed a mass party on

a federal level. However, they did not participate in Government until they had abandoned their call for "dictatorship of the proletariat" and with it their rejection of the existing social and political order in Switzerland. When Switzerland was threatened by German National Socialism, the Swiss Social Democrats renounced their Marxist ideas and professed themselves loyal to the Swiss State and its active

This means that the Government is not elected on the basis of the majority principle, but formed according to the already mentioned doctrine of "amicable settlement". One could call it a kind of "Great Coalition", in which, however, the federal councillors are not closely bound to their parties or parliamentary groups. The reasons for this lie in the incompatibility rule and the technically orientated character of the federal councillors whose re-election usually proves straightforward.

Great Coalition

Plebiscite Component

The pronounced plebiscite character of Swiss democracy sets it apart from all other Western countries. Plebiscite elements are to be found on all levels: in the communes, in the cantons and in the confederation. Since the "Regeneration Period" (around 1830), Switzerland has greatly extended the rights of the people. For the Swiss citizen of today, this is more than one way of participating in the political process: by means of the usual (personal) elections; by means of an obligatory or optional referendum; or by means of a people's request (initiative). The citizen is the real sovereign, he can even contest resolutions passed by the Federal Assembly and the Federal Council. It has already been mentioned that the four large parties share the responsibility of Government, and that the other parties represented in Parliament are small and insignificant. Against this background, the Swiss people frequently assume the role of the opposition by making use of civil rights. This also gives the smaller parties and interest groups the opportunity of voicing their opposition to Government plans. The marked emphasis on civil rights necessarily affects interactions among the parties, and this will be discussed in greater detail in the following section.

Civil rights

Referendum and request

The Contemporary Party System

The contemporary Swiss party system has scarcely changed from the time between the wars. It may be characterised as a multi-party system (using the proportional representation system) which mirrors the socio-cultural variety of the country on a federal and cantonal level.

On the national level, the four large parties still dominate the scene. They are supplemented by a varying number of smaller parties which reflect the changing attitudes on the political system and particular national and regional problems.

Recently, some of the large parties altered their configuration: in 1970, the traditional Conservative Christian Social People's Party merged with the Democrat Party and is now called "Christian Democrat People's Party". The Farmers', Tradesmen's and Citizens' Party changed its name to "Swiss People's Party".

The parties' programmes, however, have not changed. The traditional Liberal Democrat Party still has all the features of a Liberal progressive party; in particular it is committed to the idea of economic and cultural freedom and calls for greater centralisation. By comparison, the Christian Democrat People's Party leans more towards federalism; although it represents mainly the Catholic part of the population,

The four large parties

151

it can no longer be called a purely denominational party. Having abandoned the Marxist idea of class warfare, the present Social Democrat Party follows a Western brand of democratic socialism and is decidedly anti-communist. The Swiss People's Party is (by origin too) clearly a middle-class party, representing the interests of the farming and trading middle classes.

The smaller parties

Of the smaller Swiss parties, only two have achieved a certain amount of influence: the National Union of Independents, founded in 1935 in the wake of the world-wide economic crisis, and the communist Labour Party, founded in 1918. The National Union sees itself less as a party than as a movement; up to the present it has remained the strongest of the smaller parties. Its economic policies are chiefly concerned with the consumer interest, and it functions as a kind of opposition to the non-socialist parties in Government and the Social Democrats.

The Labour Party, which has most of its supporters in the industrialised west of Switzerland, regards itself as a Marxist party. However, it has only had limited success in a Swiss society which is traditionally rather conservative.

Parties of the right

It is interesting to note that small parties are continually being formed on the right of the political spectrum. They usually concern themselves with topical issues giving rise to public concern. Two recent examples are the "National Action against the Alienation of Population and Country" and the "Swiss Republican Movement"; both groups emphatically reject the employment of foreign manpower in Switzerland.

The "Protestant People's Party" is also worth mentioning; although a greater part of the population is Protestant, this party has never been anything but a denominational splinter group.

The last parliamentary elections (1979) resulted in the following distribution of seats in the National Council and the Professions Council:

Parties	1975	1979
Social Democrat Party	55/5	51
Liberal Democrat Party	47/15	51
Christian Democrat People's Party	46/17	44
Swiss People's Party	21/5	23
National Union of Independents	11/1	8
Liberal Democrat Union	6/—	8
Workers' Party	4/—	3
Protestant People's Party	3/—	3
Swiss Republican Movement	4/—	1
National Action	2/—	2
Autonomous Socialist Party	1/—	— [others 6]

Let us now consider in more detail the forms of interaction between the political parties.

Principle of concord

Firstly, it should be noted that in Switzerland there is a general tendency to form the Government according to the principle of "amicable settlement" (principle of

152

concord), and to let all parties participate in Government in relation to their parliamentary strength. The application of the principle is only suspended in cases where a party does not acknowledge the constitutional system of Switzerland (as in the case of the communist Labour Party).

It is an interesting fact that this procedure for the formation of a Government is also used if one party gains the absolute majority and could theoretically govern on its own. Even in such an event, it is generally ensured that minority parties get a proportional share in the Government; a situation which often occurs in certain cantons.

This principle does not require the parties involved to form firm coalitions, with fixed agreements and Government programmes. Instead, the parties are only loosely connected by the fact of having sufficient parliamentary representation to claim a share of Government responsibility. They need not have any common programmatic views.
Loose coalitions

The 7 federal councillors are elected by the Federal Assembly in separate ballots. For this reason, it would be hardly feasible for them to draft a Government programme in advance; this has to be done *after* its election.
Government formation

The loose connections between the Government parties as well as the division of the Government into 7 departments enables the various groups to form a kind of "opposition within the Government". This means that departments which are led by federal councillors of differing parties can sometimes adopt an oppositional attitude towards each other's policies. Sometimes it seems to the public as though there were "seven Governments within the confederation, namely the seven departments; in each department, the Government is formed by the party of the departmental leader, and all other parties are in opposition". (J. Steiner, *Das politische System der Schweiz*, 1971, p.85).

This kind of opposition cannot lead to an overthrow of the Government; at the most, it might result in the resignation or non-re-election of individual federal councillors. But this is an exception.

Those parties which cannot participate in the Government because of their low number of seats still have several means of influencing Government policies. For example, if they possess a larger number of seats on the cantonal level, they can participate in the cantonal Governments. Even smaller parties can make use of the referendum and "initiative" already mentioned.
Forms of opposition

It should be said, however, that one of all the smaller parties not in the Government only two regard themselves as genuine opposition parties on a federal level: the National Union of Independents and, more fundamentally, the communist Labour Party. As these two parties are totally different in their origins and objectives, they have up to now never employed a joint strategy of opposition against Government policies.

The other traditional small parties (the Protestant People's Party and the Liberal Democrat Union) only occasionally oppose the Government; in general, they behave more like the Government parties themselves.

Looking at these forms of interaction, it is difficult to differentiate clearly between Government and opposition parties: a further demonstration of the special nature of the Swiss party system in comparison with its neighbouring countries.

153

Sweden

RAINER KUNZ

Political
system

Sweden is one of those European countries in which the hereditary monarchy has survived. The political rule of the Crown, however, has long since been replaced by the principle of sovereignty of the people. The Crown's remaining functions are merely of a representative or, at the most, an integrative nature; the governing process has now fully developed into a parliamentary democracy. Consequently, the political parties have come to play their full role. The parties' history is relatively short in comparison to Sweden's existence as a State; for a better understanding of the party system, it seems advisable to look back at Swedish constitutional history, particularly as various elements of the contemporary party system have been preformed by the development of Parliament and universal suffrage.

Development of Parliament and Universal Suffrage

The Swedish political system developed with extraordinary continuity, largely unaffected by all events outside Scandinavia. A marked feature of this development is the sustained balance between the concentration of political power and decentralisation. The State and the Crown have never been questioned as central political institutions; decentralisation, on the other hand, was expressed by the use made by individual groups of Swedish society of their traditional rights, independently of, and sometimes even against the King. The Crown, although acknowledged, was not omnipotent. Even the farmers and middle classes were never politically dependent to the same extent as their middle-European counterparts. Within this framework, various representative bodies with at first only regional powers began to develop from the 14th century onwards; these bodies gradually merged to form the first Swedish "Diets".[1] Initially, they only convened occasionally, mostly in situations of political crisis. From the 17th century on, they met more regularly and became the second political force in the country after the King. Since their early stages, the Diets have been divided into four chambers in which the four classes of Swedish society are represented: aristocracy, clergy, urban *bourgeoisie* and farmers. The individual chambers frequently have certain regional subdivisions.

Development
of the
"Diets"

Conflict:
Crown-
social classes

Sweden's development thereafter into a modern constitutional state was dominated by the clashes between the Crown and the social classes in the Diets. Weakness in the monarchy[2] was exploited to extend the Diet influence; strong monarchs delayed parliamentary development. This was not, however, solely an interplay between King and Diet, for the Crown often joined forces with the individual classes against the remainder of Parliament.[3] During the period of Absolutism, the Swedish Crown achieved a very strong position; but this lasted only for a short

154

period. After the death of King Charles XII in 1718, the concerted opposition in the Diet against the absolutist rule of the King forced through significant changes in the constitution. Between 1718 and 1789,[4] the Diet was able to extend its powers so that it could appoint and dismiss the Government. Partly due to disagreement and poor policies of the Diet, a phase of restoration of Absolutism began in 1789. It was at first successful, but ended with the overthrow of the King in an officers' revolt in 1809. In the same year, the new Bernadotte[5] dynasty was installed in Sweden, and the country received its first modern political constitution.

The fundamental principle of the new constitution was the clear separation of powers between King and Parliament. The traditional division of the Diet into four chambers, representing the four social classes, remained unchanged. In view of Parliament's growing responsibilities, efforts were made to increase its efficiency; for this reason, a complicated committee system was introduced distinct from the assemblies in the Diet. The Diet and the King had equal legislative rights; the former also had the right to initiate or veto. Parliament was solely responsible for legislation in tax and budgetary matters, and for constitutional control; the Crown had the right to pass administrative laws and appoint or dismiss ministers.[6] It was also laid down in the constitution[7] that the Diet had the right to convene without having been summoned by the King; this represented a decisive extension of parliamentary powers.

1809 Constitution

Although the 1809 Constitution undoubtedly strengthened Parliament, it was soon subject to growing criticism: in particular, the division of Parliament into four equal chambers and the electoral system to the Diet. In the four-chamber system, the aristocracy and the clergy enjoyed a disproportionate influence;[8] other relatively new but already strong groups of the population (such as the small farmers and agricultural workers, non-tradesmen, and above all the industrial workers) had no representatives in the Diet and were excluded from the elections.

Call for a constitutional reform

The Liberals' call for a fundamental parliamentary and electoral reform was not satisfied by such changes as a lengthening of the parliamentary sessions, enfranchisement of non-tradesmen, and the introduction of a graduated right to vote in provincial and communal elections. In 1866 a new Act was passed which brought significant changes for the structure of Parliament and the electoral system. The division of the Diet into social classes was abolished; the new Diet consisting of two chambers. The delegates of the first chamber were elected directly by the provincial diets and town councils.[9] The delegates of the second chamber were elected by a simple majority system in one-man constituencies; the active right to vote also depended on property ownership, which was graded so high that large parts of the population still remained excluded from the elections. In the years to follow, the electoral system followed the continued development of democracy in Sweden. The change in the electoral system in 1909 introduced the system of proportional representation in constituencies[10] and extended the right to vote to all men over 24 who had fulfilled their tax (a minimum rate was not fixed) and military obligations.

Act of the Diet (1866)

In 1922 general suffrage for men and women was finally introduced; the age limit

General suffrage

was lowered to 23 years, and all restrictive conditions removed. This also meant that the members of the first chamber were elected by the entire voting population.[11] The development of the Swedish constitution was completed between 1965 and 1975. The two-chamber system was then replaced by a Parliament consisting of one chamber with 350 delegates of which 310 were elected in the constituencies and 40 indirectly on a proportional basis on a national level. Parties had to achieve a 4% share of the vote nationally and 12% in the constituencies.

The role of the King was also modified by the final change in the constitution. He lost all executive powers which he had at least formally commanded. Thus the Government was no longer formally answerable to the King, but only to Parliament. From a constitutional point of view, Sweden then changed over to a parliamentary political system, although Government activities had already followed purely parliamentary and democratic rules for more than half a century.

The Swedish Parties

Party types

As in other multi-party systems, no distinct people's and "catch-all" parties have been able to establish themselves in Sweden. The democratic parties[12] represented in the present Swedish Parliament can most easily be classified as a type of "interest" party, and the middle-class parties perhaps correspond more closely to that definition than the Social Democrat Workers' Party. Apart from the given social stratification, the development of Parliament and the electoral system have made an essential contribution to the formation of these party features.

Forms of party development

For a better understanding of the parties' development it has to be mentioned that, in their early stages, none of the Swedish parties possessed the party and parliamentary organisation which is common today. The Swedish parties developed from two different starting points. The Liberal and Conservative Party only had groups in Parliament; the Social Democrats and the Farmers' Party[13] were only organised outside Parliament. The Conservatives and the Liberals could look back on a long tradition to the days of the four-chamber Diet, which helped them with the immediate formation of Conservative and Liberal parliamentary groups in the two-chamber Parliament. It was not necessary to establish an extra-parliamentary party organisation; there existed a strong sense of group identification in those sectors of society which traditionally held Conservative or Liberal views. The farmers' delegates, however, did not succeed in initiating a similar development. Having lost their chamber in the parliamentary reform of 1866, their parliamentary group was only temporarily represented in the second chambers of the new Diet.[14] The then valid electoral system did not include the small farmers; this also contributed to a

Electoral system as determining factor of party development

decrease in the number of delegates who were concerned with farming affairs. The Social Democrat Workers' Party could not boast of any parliamentary traditions. As a result of the country's industrialisation, support for this party was constantly growing, but the majority of its supporters were excluded from voting until the electoral reform of 1922. This meant that the number of Social Democrat delegates did not suffice to form a politically-efficient parliamentary group. Consequently, the party focussed on the extension of its extra-parliamentary national organisation in order to fight for more parliamentary and electoral reforms.

As an immediate result of the electoral reforms in 1909 and 1922, the existing parties developed into modern party organisations. The reform made all their potential voters available to the Social Democrats, and they became the strongest parliamentary group. The Farmers' Party, too, was able to improve its parliamentary position, but not quite to the same extent as the Social Democrats. The Liberal and Conservative Party were forced to set up extra-parliamentary party organisations. With the help of these organisations, the parties tried to win new supporters among the mass of new voters; but were only modestly successful because the Swedish electorate has continually shown little ideological flexibility. This political entrench- **Voters'** ment, which is correlated to social class, is the reason why the parties have retained **behaviour** the features of interest groups, and it is also responsible for the fact that the majorities in Parliament have never fundamentally changed since 1922.

The following section will deal briefly with each of the parties represented in the Swedish Diet.

Social Democrat Workers' Party

The Social Democrat Workers' Party was founded in 1889 as a party organisation. **Development** In 1896, the first Social Democrat delegate[15] was elected, with the support of the Liberals, to the second chamber of Parliament. Since the introduction of general suffrage, the Social Democrat Workers' Party has developed into the strongest Swedish party. It is supported throughout the country by a very comprehensive **Organisation** organisation which further benefits from the fact that the Social Democrats have frenquently been the governing party. Of the 885,000 party members, two-thirds are trade union members and as such collective members of the party, but they do not form separate groups. Olof Palme has been party Chairman since 1969; until the 1976 election defeat, he was also the Swedish Prime Minister. The party leadership can boast an extraordinary continuity and long periods of office. [16] The party cooperates very closely with the Swedish trade unions and has affiliated youth and women's organisations.[17] As far as the media are concerned, the party **Party** has its own comprehensive press, which is further supported by press units close **press** to the Social Democrats or owned by the trade unions.[18] The workers' votes make **Social** up an estimated 70% of the total of Social Democrat votes; the rest come mainly **structure** from the middle classes. The party was only able to gain absolute majorities after successfully capturing the middle-class vote; this was then reflected in its domestic policies. The party soon abandoned the orthodox Marxist theories that it had held **Ideology** during its first years. They were replaced by a moderate Socialist policy of reform whose objectives were greater social equality and a welfare state in which almost all sectors are state-controlled. With regard to foreign affairs, the party pursues a policy of neutrality (following Swedish tradition), non-intervention and freedom of alliance; while at the same time it is very active in almost all supra-national organisations.

157

Centre Party

Development

Social
structure

Party
organisation

Ideology

The Centre Party was founded in 1913 under the name of "Farmers' Party", representing the farming population. It was formed to counteract the ever-decreasing political influence held by farmers who were not, however, integrated into the party to the same extent as the workers were integrated into the Social Democrat Workers' Party. Only an estimated 50% of the rural electorate vote for the Centre Party. Nevertheless, the majority of voters is still to be found among the rural population. The party's change of name demonstrates that the party leaders have realised the need to make the party attractive to other groups of voters, as the farming part of the population is continually decreasing. The party organisation is well-established in the flat regions of the country. The party has about 115,000 members, excluding the women's and youth organisations. There is quite close cooperation with the various farming interest groups whose representatives are also to be found in the leading party committees. Economically and socially, the party's objectives do not differ fundamentally from those of the Social Democrats, but some measures, such as the extension of state administration and a number of social policies have been poorly received. Because of this ideological nexus, the Centre Party entered into various Government coalitions with the Social Democrat Workers' Party. The political influence that it thereby gained was used by the Centre Party predominantly in the agrarian sector. In the 1973 and 1976 elections, the party's gain in votes was significant. The party chairman Thorbjoern Fälldin has been Prime Minister of the ruling coalition Government since 1976.

Liberal People's Party

Development

Party
Organisations

Programme

The party came into being when various Liberal parliamentary groups merged in 1902. At the time of the party's foundation, the period of "laissez-faire" Liberalism was already over. The Liberals concerned themselves with social problems, and this led to close cooperation with the Social Democrats. The parties fought in conjunction against the attempts of the Swedish Crown to prevent the implementation of a parliamentary political system. The process of democratisation in Sweden was completed during the first Liberal/Social Democrat coalition in 1917/1920. After the introduction of universal suffrage, the party lost its dominating position; its influence was further diminished by various divisions that occured within the party and that only disappeared as late as 1934. Between 1948 and 1958 the party established itself as the leading opposition party to the Social Democrat Government.

The party has about 100,000 members but an organisation regarded as weak. Two-thirds of the voters come from the middle and upper-middle classes, one third from the working classes. Thus the Liberal Party is the second-largest Swedish workers' party. The party's domestic programme closely resembles that of the Centre Party with the exception of any agrarian commitment. The Liberals find strong support in the Swedish press, particularly with the large-circulation newspapers. The party has participated in the Government coalition under its Chairman Gunnar Helen since 1976.

Conservative Party

The Conservative Party has called itself a "moderate collective party" since 1968; it was formed in 1904 from a number of parliamentary Conservative groups. Until 1910, it exerted a decisive influence on Swedish politics, partly with the King's support; however, the introduction of universal suffrage, the drop in the farming population and the growth of the Centre Party meant a decline in their vote share. The party also held political views which were generally unpopular. They fought against electoral reform; they also opposed the policy of disarmament which was very popular in Sweden between the two world wars; and they pointed out the financial and social consequences of an extension of the Welfare State which they considered wholly undesirable. Since 1955, the criticism voiced by the Conservatives has found an increasing echo among the Swedish population; this is reflected in the slightly improving election results.

The party has about 260,000 members. An estimated 30% of its voters belong to the upper classes, 15% to the working classes, with the majority of votes coming from the middle classes. Under the leadership of its Chairman Gösta Bohmann, the party has been part of the Government coalition since 1976.

Development

Programme

Social structure

Organisation

Communist Party

The Communist Party has had the title "Left-Wing Party of the Communists" since 1967. It was founded in 1920, originating from a Social Democrat group which was not prepared to follow the Social Democrat Party's change of course to a moderate socialism. Although it rejects the Brezhnev doctrine, the party is considered fairly orthodox. It attracted considerable political attention when it supported the Social Democrat minority Cabinets led by Olof Palme. There are widely differing views as to how the Social Democrat election results were affected by this support. Following a slight gain in votes in the last two elections to the Diet, the party now has 19 seats.

Ideology

The Swedish Party System

Although there are 5 parties represented in Parliament, the Swedish party system appears very stable. Its course of development since the turn of the century may be divided into five periods.

Stability

1st Period 1900–1917: This phase marked the genesis of development of the present major parties. The Liberals became the dominating party, for the electoral reform in 1909 brought them a large number of new voters. The Crown's final attempts to exert political influence were now firmly rejected by the Liberals who committed themselves to a consistent policy of democratisation which leads at times to close co-operation with the Social Democrat Workers' Party.

Phase of development

2nd Period 1917–1939: In this period, the Swedish party system was at its most unstable. The 1917 Liberal/Social Democrat coalition ended in 1920, and was

Phase of instability

159

followed (until 1939) by 9 minority Governments alternately formed by the Social Democrats, the Farmers' Party, the Liberals and the Conservatives. The enormous problems created by the world-wide economic crisis made the parties less eager to accept Government responsibility; they feared reaction against the stringent policies they would be forced to adopt. The governing parties, however, could count on a tolerant opposition; this is why the minority Cabinets stayed in power for two years on average, and consequently guranteed a certain degree of political stability and continuity. It was only from 1936 to 1939, that a majority coalition was again formed, this time between the Social Democrats and the Farmers' Party.

National Government

3rd Period 1939–1945: During the 2nd World War, the four large parties (with the exception of the Communists) united to form the so-called "National Government". The political tasks confronting them in the immediate post-war era eventually led to the dissolution of this Government, although some form of continuation remained a possibility.

Social Democrat Government

4th Period 1946–1976: During this period the Social Democrat Workers' Party came to power. Following the break-up of the war-time coalition, it took over Government as the strongest party in Parliament. Up to 1951 it maintained a bare majority and was dependent on the Communists' support; between 1951 and 1957, it entered into coalitions with the Farmers' Party. The minority Government 1957/58 was followed by a phase of absolute Social Democrat majorities until 1970. In the 1970 and 1973 elections, the Social Democrats failed to gain an absolute majority; but, with the support of the Communist delegates, the party was able to create a situation of "stalemate" and stay in power.

Centre party coalition

5th Period 1976– : The 1976 elections to the Diet brought further losses for the Social Democrats. This may be explained by a general fear of too much power for one particular party; the party's involvement with the state bureaucracy; a fear of extensive social measures; doubts in the real value of a comprehensive Welfare State; and opposition to the energy policy of the Social Democral Government which included atomic power. All these factors resulted in a close victory of the three centre parties which then formed the Government under the Chairman of the Centre Party, Fälldin. It will largely depend on the performance of this coalition as to whether the exclusion of the Social Democrat Workers' Party, still by far the strongest parliamentary group, will initiate another phase of instability in the Swedish party system.

Notes

[1] This process was furthered by foreign policies which were of national importance.

[2] In particular: disputes of succession, regency, etc.

[3] Frequently occuring coalition patterns are: King and aristocracy against the rest of Parliament, or King and middle classes against the rest of Parliament.

[4] In Swedish history, this is often called the "Era of Freedom".

[5] Also called the "Bourgeois Dynasty"; its progenitor is the French Marshal Jean Baptiste Bernadotte who became King Charles XIV. John of Sweden at a time when it was still united with Norway.

6 The Diet social classes had the right to lay accusations against a minister and to demand his dismissal. Accusations against ministers were dealt with before a special court of justice.

7 Article 49.

8 The aristocracy and the clergy represented 1% of the entire population but constituted two of the four chambers. Figures taken from: Sternberger, D., Vogel, B. (Eds.): Die Wahl der Parlamente, p. 1084 ff.

9 This prevented the first chamber from simply becoming the successor to the chambers of the aristocracy and the clergy of the former Diet. Until the abolition of the property census, the wealthy *bourgeoisie* dominated the first chamber.

10 The method of d'Hondt was used.

11 Following the electoral reform of 1909, 19% of the entire Swedish population received the right to vote; the reform of 1922 extended this to 22%.

12 The Communist Party is not included, but this seems justifiable in view of its small vote percentage and its negligible political influence.

13 In 1957, the Farmers' Party changed its name to "Centre Party".

14 The group of the farmers' delegates in the second chamber was called "Farmers' Party" as early as 1867, and was repeatedly successful due to the discipline within their parliamentary group. However, the group did not achieve any permanency.

15 Hjalmar Branting; he was later elected party Chairman.

16 From 1896 until the present day, the Social Democrat Workers' Party has only had four Chairmen (Branting, Hansson, Erlander, Palme).

17 For information on the women's and youth organisations of the Scandinavian parties, see: Fusilier, Raymond: *Les Pays Nordiques*, p. 61 ff.

18 See also: Hadenius/Sveveborg/Weibull: *The Social Democratic Press and Newspaper Policy in Sweden*. Scandinavian Political Studies Vol. 3, 1968, p. 49–69.

Norway

RAINER KUNZ

Together with Sweden and Denmark, Norway has retained its monarchy to the present day; but here, too, the principle of sovereignty of the people has replaced monarchic rule. Norway has developed into a constitutional monarchy and the parliamentary political parties play their full role.

Development of the Constitution and of Universal Suffrage

History

The political development of Norway was closely connected with that of its neighbours Sweden and Denmark. Due to the laws of dynastic succession, the previously independent Norway became part of the Swedish Kingdom in 1319, and part of the Danish Kingdom in 1387. The year 1814 marked a turning-point in Norwegian history. The states of the anti-Napoleonic coalition laid down in the treaty of Kiel that Denmark, which had formed an alliance with France, was to cede its Norwegian province to Sweden.[1] This project met with opposition both in Denmark and Norway. The Danish Crown did not want to lose Norway; the Norwegian population wanted political autonomy, and therefore approved the separation from Denmark but rejected the union with Sweden. The Danish Crown Prince Christian Frederik, who held the office of Governor in Norway, attempted to reach a compromise between the Danish and Norwegian interests. At his initiative, representatives[2] of the Norwegian population formed a constituent assembly; this assembly declared Norway an independent constitutional monarchy under Christian Frederik, who had been elected King, and issued the first Norwegian constitution in the spring of 1814. But the country's independence did not last for long. In the same year Sweden used the threat of war to compel Norway to form a Swedish-Norwegian union. Norway kept its new constitution[3] and its national identity, but the rights that were envisaged in the constitution for the Norwegian Monarch were now transferred to the Swedish King as the new head of state. This configuration meant that the political development of Norway was not only influenced by the struggle between Parliament and King, which was a typical phenomenon of the 19th century, but also by the Norwegian-Swedish conflict which became more and more acute.

Swedish-Norwegian Union

Swedish-Norwegian conflict

1814 Constitution

The 1814 Constitution based on Montesquieu's ideas, attempted a division of political power into three equal sectors: the legislature, executive and judiciary.[4] Parliament ("Storting") held the legislative function; it was subdivided into the "Lagting" and the "Odelsting"[5] The "Storting" convened every third year and

162

could not be dissolved by the King. Apart from its general legislative functions, it had to deal with taxes, budget and customs duties. The constitution gave Parliament extensive rights; in reality, however, they were considerably restricted by the constitutional rights of the Monarch.[6] The Monarch was the head of the entire executive: he appointed the Government and Civil Servants, and was at the same time responsible for foreign affairs. As regards the legislature, he possessed the right of initiation and a suspending veto. In practice, this was equivalent to an absolute veto, as it could only be annulled by three consecutive resolutions passed in the "Storting".[7] The King's veto was absolute in the case of constitutional changes.[8] His position was further strengthened by the fact that he was above the common law. The Government members who had been appointed by the King were politically and legally responsible for his actions.[9]

It is not surprising that relations between King and Parliament continuously deteriorated. The "Storting", and in particular its Liberal delegates, fought for more parliamentary and democratic rights, and for greater and national independence from Sweden. Parliament made some progress in these areas through the 19th century. The first successful step was the introduction of regional self-administration in 1837. Urban and rural authorities were formed as counterpart to the central state administration controlled by the King. These bodies also furthered political interest and a new self-confidence among the Norwegian population. In 1869, the "Storting" passed a law making their own session annual as opposed to every third year. This severely limited the Monarch's right to make use of his right of "interim legislation". In 1884, after almost 10 years of conflict, the King was finally forced by Parliament and the Supreme Court to form Governments on a parliamentary majority basis. Norway thus acquired a modern parliamentary system under which the Government is responsible to Parliament and not to the King.[10] The Norwegian public regarded it as a further important step towards national independence when the Swedish Governor was recalled from Norway. The final break-up of the Union became imminent when in 1905 the Swedish King rejected the "Storting" call for a Norwegian consulate. The Norwegian Government resigned but was reinstated by the "Storting". Up to this point the King had had the right to appoint the Government and this encroachment upon his rights was generally interpreted as severance of the Union. The "Storting" quickly held a referendum in the autumn of 1905, Norway decided to retain its monarchy. A Danish prince was chosen as the new Norwegian King and founder of the still ruling dynasty.

The electoral system and the political involvement of the Norwegian people were important factors in the development of the political system and the party system in particular. After 1814, the delegates to the "Storting" were elected according to an indirect majority system with more than one candidate per party in each constituency. The number of people who were entitled to vote was small, as franchise conditions were typical of the early Liberal attitude to society and politics. Tenure of a public office or a minimum capital holding were basic requirements. Consequently, only about 12% of the entire population were eligible to vote. Further administrative conditions and technicalities reduced the actual voter

Conflict between Monarch and Parliament

Regional self-administration

Annual session of Parliament

Parliamentary system

Political independence

Electoral System

163

figure to less than 3%. The farmers in particular frequently failed to use their right to vote.[11] Because of relatively little political involvement of the population, the first change in the electoral system occurred as late as 1884. Franchise was then correlated with taxable income. The final steps towards a democratisation of the electoral system began in 1897 when Parliament enacted universal suffrage for men and later for women in 1913. The electoral method also underwent various changes. The original indirect majority system was replaced in 1905 by a majority system in "one-man" constituencies; the candidate with the absolute majority at the first ballot was elected. If no candidate obtains an abolsute majority, the relative majority at the second ballot decides the winner. However, this system sometimes caused extraordinary distortions in the election results.[12] This fact, together with the general desire for fairer and more general representation, brought about the introduction of the proportional system, with each party nominating more than one candidate in every constituency. The system of proportional representation has remained, although changes have occurred in constituency boundaries and in the distribution of parliamentary seats: the "d'Hondt" method that was originally used was replaced by the so-called "Balanced Method".[13]

Development of the Parties and the Party System

Development of parties

Role of the Civil Servants

Political organisation of the farmers

The 1814 Constitution did not envisage a subdivision of Parliament into rival factions; but social conflicts in Norwegian society soon led to the formation of various political representative groups. The most influential social group at the beginning of the 19th century were the Civil Servants. Their loyalty to the Danish Crown had gained them many privileges before 1814, and they occupied the key political positions.[14] At first, the Civil Servants were able to maintain their influence in the new parliamentary era: the first Norwegian "Stortings" almost exclusively consisted of Civil Servants. But it was the farmers[15] who represented the overwhelming majority of the entire Norwegian population as well as of all citizens entitled to vote. Naturally, the farmers felt that the Civil Servant Parliaments did not properly care for their interest; but they did not have sufficient experience or self-confidence to represent themselves politically. Their discontentment with the political situation after 1814 was initially expressed by an attempt to ignore Parliament;[16] but from 1830 on, under the leadership of Ole Gabriel Ueland, the farmers became organised and represented their ideas at a parliamentary level. The farmers' delegates obtained their first majority in the "Storting" in 1833.[17] Their political objectives were: local self-administration (realised after 1837); less privileges for the Civil Servants; cuts in public spending, and tax reductions for the agrarian sector. Until the political system became parliamentary, the King had refused to accept the farmers' representatives in Government. The latter's political attitude thus became more and more radical: they demanded a curb on the rights of the Monarch and more power for Parliament. The opposition against the Swedish King demonstrated a desire for political independence from Norway. The farmers' parliamentary demands found support among the urban middle class representatives whose number in Parliament had gradually increased since the middle of the century. The group of Civil Servants in the "Storting", together with the small group of representatives of the upper middle classes and the aristocracy, usually supported the Monarch.

With the emergence of the two large factions of the farmers and Civil Servants, a Liberal-Conservative dualism evolved in the "Storting". Such a structure was typical of many European Parliaments of the period; and in Norway it determined the party system until 1918. The initially sparse contact between the two groups gradually hardened in the course of joint political activity. When in 1884 the Liberals finally achieved the introduction of Government by parliamentary majority, the Liberal Venstre Party and the Conservative Höyre Party were officially founded in the same year. At first, the party organisation consisted only of the parliamentary groups.[18] It was only the major electoral reform in 1897 which led to an extra-parliamentary extension of party structure; for now a party's position in Parliament had become dependent on the votes of much greater parts of the population: it was essential to try and exert political influence throughout the electorate. Between 1884 and 1918, Norway basically had a two-party system: the Liberals and Conservatives were the strongest parliamentary groups and alternately formed the Government.[19] During this particular period, however, these two parties underwent considerable changes in size and composition, mainly because of the changing structure of Norwegian society. Following the era of industrialisation, which began in Norway in 1890, the working population grew rapidly. The electoral reform of 1884 had already lowered the required income minima to such a point that certain groups of workers were entitled to vote.[20] This change in the structure of the electorate brought initial disadvantages for the Conservatives who had to suffer parliamentary losses. The Liberal Venstre Party, on the other hand, managed to adjust successfully to the new situation. It found a good deal of support among the working classes because of its active social policy and its call for free universal suffrage. The national question was also of extreme importance for Liberal politics. The Liberals' consistent anti-Swedish policy, together with their call for the dissolution of the Union, reflected the wishes of the Norwegian people. In 1905, it became evident how much the national question had united the Liberal Party; after the separation with Sweden, social and economic interests immediately became of prime importance and led to divisions[21] and fierce conflict on the wings. After 1905, the workers began to turn to the Norwegian Workers' Party which, since its foundation in 1887, had been unable to properly establish itself.[22] In 1903 the Workers' Party entered the "Storting" for the first time and quickly gained a large following, although it was still at a disadvantage under the electoral system.[23] As a result of the 1918 elections, the Norwegian two-party system developed into a three-party system in which the Liberals, Conservatives and Workers' Party were for a short time almost on equal terms.[24] When the majority system was introduced in 1919, the present-day multi-party system finally came into being.

Parliamentary system

Two-party system

Factors determining the development of the parties

Development into a multi-party system

165

The Present Party System

If one takes party size as a classification criterion, the parties represented in the "Storting" can be divided into three categories. The Norwegian Workers' Party is the only large party; the Conservative Party, Centre Party and Christian People's Party form the group of medium-sized parties; while in the third category of small parties, we find traditional groups such as the Liberal Venstre Party as well as some *ad hoc* groups. The table below gives an idea of the parties' strength in the "Storting"[25] (for the term which began in 1977); the following section will then discuss the parties in greater detail.

Party	Votes		Percentage		Seats	
Workers' Party	962 728	(759 499)	42.4	(35.3)	76	(62)
Conservative Party	560 025	(370 370)	24.7	(17.5)	41	(29)
Christian People's Party	274 516	(255 456)	12.1	(12.2)	22	(20)
Centre	196 005	(146 312)	8.6	(11.0)	12	(21)
Soc. Party of the Left*	94 016	(241 851)	4.1	(11.2)	2	(16)
Communists	8 355		0.4		0	
Liberal Party	72 371	(49 668)	3.2	(3.5)	2	(2)
Progressive Party	42 862	(107 784)	1.9	(5.0)	0	(4)
New People's Party	38 061	(73 854)	1.7	(3.4)	0	(1)

*In 1973, the Communist Party joined other left-wing groups in the so-called "Socialist Election Alliance"; in March 1975, this became the "Socialist Party of the Left". The CP did not join this new party. Chairman of the Socialist Party of the Left: Berge Furre.

Norwegian Workers' Party (Det norske Arbeiderparti)

Since 1927, the Norwegian Workers' Party had been the strongest group in the "Storting". Unique in Norwegian parliamentary history, it had the absolute majority from 1945 until 1961. In the early twenties, the party closely followed the ideas of the 3rd Socialist International; however, it soon abandoned all such connections and today practises a modern democratic socialism. The Workers' Party's orientation to the West in foreign affairs was demonstrated by Norway's joining the Western

camp after 1945; the final step was Norway's accession to NATO. As far as the party's economic programme is concerned, plans for the nationalisation of major industries and public transport have been repeatedly drafted, but so far without any attempt to realise them. The Workers' Party has a times incurred strong criticism from left-wing groups for its cautious attitude. The party's main objective was the

realisation of social and educational projects. Considerable state control was exercised in the expansion of educational institutions, the health service and old age pension schemes; while a simultaneous effort was made to guarantee full employment and improve the infrastructure of the underdeveloped parts of the country.

Conservative Party (Höyre)

Apart from the Liberals, the Conservative Party is the oldest group in the Norwegian party system. Its policies were frequently regarded as a defense of the political, economic and social status quo. The Conservative Party's links with the social upper classes certainly affected its reactions to the major changes of the 20th century. The party remained pro-Monarchy, and its attitude to the extension of democratic rights, in particular universal suffrage, ranged from scepticism to rejection. Its economic policy was based on private ownership, unrestricted private enterprise and a free economy. The Conservatives initially rejected the extensive changes in the educational and social system which the Workers' Party Governments initiated after 1945. The party's attitude has since changed in many respects, partly for the simple reason that they have to compete for the electorate's favour. In particular, the party has abandoned its initial rejection of the Workers' Party's social policy. But the economic objectives have remained unchanged: rejection of nationalisation; furtherance of private enterprise; protection of private ownership; and a wage, tax and investment policy that favours the employer. The Conservatives also oppose the increasing influence of the State, fearing ultimately for basic democratic rights. On foreign policy, the Conservatives fully support Norway's connections with the West.

Social structure

Ideology

Centre Party (Senterpartiet)

The Centre Party originated from the Liberal Venstre Party from which it finally separated in 1920 taking the name of "Farmers' Party". In 1959, it changed its name to "Centre Party" in the hope of attracting more voters. In spite of the change of name, the Centre Party still almost exclusively represents agricultural interests. On the political spectrum, it lies between the Conservative and Liberal Party. So far the party has hardly developed any ideological conceptions of its own; furthermore, its programme on non-agricultural sectors leaves many areas untouched. If the farming population decreases further, the Centre Party will face difficulties in retaining their seats in the "Storting".

Social structure

Christian People's Party (Kristelig Folkeparti)

The party was founded in 1933 as a Conservative group. It was its objective to create a democratic State based on Christian ethics, and the party was particularly active in social and legal politics. Its stronghold is in the western part of Norway, and as the party's supporters are concentrated in only a few areas, the electoral system is to its disadvantage.

Programme

167

Liberal Party (Venstre)

Ideology

Apart from the Conservative Party, the Liberal Venstre Party has the longest tradition of the Norwegian parties. In its fight against the Swedish Monarchy it played an essential role in shaping the present democratic Norwegian state. The party's preoccupation with the national question and emerging social problems induced many Liberals in the 1920's to change over to the Workers' and Farmers' Parties whose programmes were geared to specific interests. In common with all other European Liberal parties, the Venstre Party had difficulty in adjusting its Liberal ideology to the social, economic and political conditions of the 20th century. It abandoned early on the concept of the classical Liberalism and handed social responsibility over to the State. Many social measures that were completed after 1945 by Governments of the Workers' Party had already been initiated by the Liberal Government around 1930. The party's social policies are similar to those of the Workers' Party, whereas in the economic sector it is closer to the Conservatives. Conservative and moderately Social Democrat wings exist within the party, a situation which has caused structural problems. A further difficulty has been the steady development into an urban party. An offshoot of the Liberal Party is the "New People's Party" which is in favour of Norway's accession to the European Community in contrast to the Liberal Party itself.

Socialist People's Party (Sosalistik Folkeparti)

In 1961 the Socialist People's Party separated from the Workers' Party,[26] accusing it of betraying the Socialist ideal. Extensive nationalisation, Norway's withdrawal from NATO and the renewal of the Norwegian pre-war policy of neutrality are among the most spectacular demands of this party. The Socialist People's Party has grown into a serious opponent to the Workers' Party, not so much through its parliamentary size but more because of its permanent attitude of ideological confrontation. In the 1973 elections to the "Folketing", the Socialist People's Party joined the Socialist Voters' Union and represents the latters' largest division in Parliament.

Communist Party of Norway (Norges Kommunistiske Parti)

The Communist Party was formed in 1923, originating from a former group of the Workers' Party which did not approve of the party's withdrawal from the Socialist International. Due to its size the Communist Party has never represented a threat to Norwegian democracy. Its main attack is on Norway's membership of NATO; its fundamental political objective is a parliamentary Socialist republic, although the exact structure is not described in the party programme.

Development of the Party System

The Norwegian party system, as it developed after 1919, went through an initial phase of political instability. No party succeeded between 1920 and 1935 in winning a parliamentary majority; nor was any party strong enough to be regarded as a sure part of the Government formation. In contrast to other multi-party systems, no coalition Governments were formed in Norway. The transitional state of all Norwegian parties, which also affected their internal structure,[27] did not allow the formation of coalitions that could have threatened the parties' very existence. Consequently, minority Cabinets were formed which could only survive through the toleration of those parties not involved in Government. After 1930 the party scene became gradually more stable; in the 1936 elections the Workers' Party polled 46.6% of the votes, and was able to set up a strong Government with the support of the Farmers' Party. Between 1920 and 1940 there were 12 different Cabinets.

The German occupation of Norway interrupted the development of the party system with the prohibition of all parties except the Norwegian National Socialist Party. The party organisations went underground or into exile in Britain. In the first elections after the war in autumn 1945, the Workers' Party gained the absolute majority, which it retained until 1961. It stayed in power during the following term with the support of the Socialist People's Party. This period of extraordinary stability left its mark on post-war Norway and although a new phase of multi-party coalitions[28] and minority Governments led by the Workers' Party began after 1965, the stability of the political system has remained. Even the minority Cabinets stayed in power longer than their equivalents before the war, a fact which is indicative of their more permanent support from the non-Government parties.[29]

The cause of this change in the parties' behaviour was thought to be the growing similarity of the Norwegian parties' programmes. Although the workers' and upper/ middle class parties are clearly separate, the two camps have not polarised. Both groups are largely in agreement on basic issues: no party has opposed a development of the existing Welfare State; compared with other European countries, income distribution is very well balanced; there are neither racial nor denominational conflicts; foreign policy is not a controversial issue among the large parties.[30] Economic policy is the only really sensitive theme, but all parties remain open to compromise. The mutual rapprochement between parties has developed particularly quickly and suggests that Norway is heading towards a two-party system as in Britain.[31] This system would consist of an extended Conservative and Workers' Party.

Notes

[1] Sweden had joined Napoleon's opponents; it received Norway as compensation for Finland which it had ceded to Russia in 1809.

[2] The delegates came from the cities, the rural communities, the army and the navy.

[3] The Norwegian "Storting" itself made all the changes in the Constitution that had become necessary because of the formation of the Norwegian-Swedish Union.

4 The Eidsvolt Constitution closely resembled the so-called "Batavian" Constitution which the Netherlands had received during the time of the French Revolution.

5 The smaller section, the "Lagting", comprised a quarter of the total seats. Despite its division, the "Storting" has to be regarded as a one-chamber Parliament. It is true that bills were separately debated and passed; but if the two sections arrived at different results during the debate and vote, the final vote was taken in the united Parliament where the stronger "Odelsting" usually won.

6 European literature usually classifies the extensive rights of the Norwegian Parliament as an exemplary early parliamentary development; Scandinavian scientific theory puts them into perspective by taking political practice into account.

7 As the "Storting" only met every third year, the introduction of a suspending veto meant delaying the passing of a bill for at least six years.

8 The exact extent of the royal veto was a controversial point between Crown and Parliament. According to Parliament's interpretation, the King could only veto legislative resolutions; the King, however, insisted until 1884 that his veto was valid for all resolutions of the "Storting".

9 It was their duty to appeal against those decrees of the Monarch which did not correspond to the Constitution or other valid laws. If they neglected their duty, the "Odelsting" could bring an action against them before the "Lagting" and the Supreme Court.

10 Up to the present day, the change-over to the parliamentary political system has never been incorporated in the Norwegian Constitution.

11 Tables on franchise and election turnout of the Norwegian population are to be found in the statistical records of the Norwegian Central Bureau for Statistics; extracts reprinted in: Sternberger/Vogel, *Die Wahl der Parlamente*, p. 898 f.

12 The Workers' Party in particular was for a long time at a disadvantage.

13 Also called the modified "Sainte-Lague" method. The divisors used in the "d'Hondt" method (1, 2, 3, 4, 5 etc.) are replaced by the divisors 1,4-3-5-7 etc.

14 The Norwegian Civil Service occupied an equal social position to that of the aristocracy in other European countries. In Norway, there were only few aristocrats, and they exerted little influence.

15 In 1820, 90% of the Norwegian population lived in rural communities; about 75–80% were employed in agriculture and forestry.

16 This explains the initially extremely low election turnout. Many farmers were entitled to vote according to the electoral requirements, but they refused to do so in protest at the existing political system. As the selection of candidates was largely in the hands of the Civil Service, it often occurred that no farmers were nominated.

17 45 farming delegates, 35 Civil Servants, 17 merchants.

18 Outside Parliament, so-called "election committees" existed (presided over by a parliamentary member), formed shortly before new elections were due, and again dissolved after the elections.

19 In the 34 years between 1884 and 1918, the Liberals governed for 21 years and the Conservatives for 13. Both parties at times entered into coalitions with splinter parties but without making any programmatic concessions to the latter.

20 In 1885, 15% of the electorate were working class; after the introduction of universal suffrage for men this rose to 37%. The election turnout of the workers was usually extremely high.

21 The most important break-away parties were: the "Free Liberal Party" which opposed the economic and social policies of the Venstre Party and finally merged with the Conservative Party; and the "Farmers' Union" from which the Farmers' Party originated.

22 The origins of the Norwegian workers' movement date back to the "Thranite" movement of the fifties which the Government broke up.

23 In the 1915 elections the Workers' Party obtained only 32.1% of the votes cast; that is it gained 15.4% of the seats in the "Storting".

24 A certain parallel to the development of the British parties is undeniable.

25 Figures taken from the Munziger archive's international handbook. The missing four delegates belong to the "Tax Party" which is not taken seriously politically.

26 Some extreme left-wing delegates had already left the party. The Norwegian Workers' Party only rarely made the attempt of holding such splinter groups.

27 Vehement discussions within the party to define the party's ideological position were quite normal at that time in the parties of the left and right.

28 In 1965, the Government consisted of the Conservatives, Centre Party, Venstre Party and Christian People's Party.

29 The usual term of "opposition party" cannot very well be applied to these parties that support the Government.

30 The Norwegian parties' reaction to the referendum on Europe reflected the mistrust that the population had shown towards the political leaders. European politics as such are not regarded as so important in Norway that they could cause serious conflicts.

31 See for example: Eckstein, Harry, *Division and Cohesion in Democracy,* and Valen/Katz *Political Parties in Norway.*

Finland

RAINER KUNZ

Historical development

Finland attained autonomy and political independence rather late compared with its Scandinavian neighbour countries. As first as a duchy and after 1581 as a grand duchy, Finland had been part of the territory of the Swedish Kingdom since the 13th century. The country came under Russian rule in 1809 and regained her freedom in 1917 after the Russian revolution. Until 1809, Finland's internal and political development largely corresponded to that of Sweden. Between 1809 and 1917 the influence of Russian politics was decisive; it was only after 1917 that Finland's political development could continue unimpeded by any foreign powers.

Development of the Constitution

Finland, a Russian province

When Finland became part of the Russian Empire in 1809, the country's constitution and political autonomy remained at first untouched. This served to demonstrate to Western Europe that the Russian Government was prepared to exercise a liberal policy; while at the same time the Russians hoped to prevent unrest among the Finnish population. Russia risked little by adopting this attitude, for the Swedish constitution which was still valid in Finland[1] had undergone a number of changes in 1789.[2] These changes had paved the way for the restoration of the absolutist Monarchy in Sweden and were therefore in accordance with the political intentions of the Russian Crown. The Czar assumed the rights of the Swedish King; his representative was the Russian Governor General in Finland. At his side was the Senate in which the country's highest administrative officers convened; the Senate itself consisted of a state and an administrative chamber.[3] The structure and method of appointment to the Finnish Parliament remained unchanged.

Finland was aware of the progressing political liberalisation in the West European and Scandinavian countries, but herself participated in this development to a much smaller extent. The struggle between Liberal Finnish forces and the Conservative czarist Russia was determined by an uneven power balance: only when the Russian Empire showed signs of weakness could the Finnish reformists hope for political change; and as soon as Russian political stability was restored, previously made promises were revoked. Consequently, Finnish conceptions of a constitution developed along the lines of those of West European countries. Constitutional practice, however, remained largely unchanged between 1809 and 1917. The conflicts between Finland and Russia were few and relatively insignificant up to 1917; this may partly be attributed to the discord between the various Liberal groups, but mainly to the wisdom of the country's politicians who knew exactly what the political situation was.

Development of the Constitution until 1917

172

The Russian attitude towards the Finnish Parliament gave increasing cause for concern. The Czar had the duty to convene Parliament, but did not exercise this power. The Finnish parliamentary parties wanted to avoid an open constitutional conflict as they feared they might lose the remaining vestiges of autonomy. It was only in 1863 when Russia had been weakened by the Polish uprising that the possibility arose of forcing the Czar to convene Parliament after 54 years. The most important result of this parliamentary term was a new parliamentary structure; in view of the Russian reaction, the innovations were kept relatively moderate. The electoral system was only slightly changed by the phased introduction of graded franchise. The representation of trades and professions in the social chambers was improved; not, however, to a sufficient extent to meet the changing social environment.[4] Only the demand for regular sessions of Parliament was at all controversial, as the Czar was to be obliged to convene Parliament at least once every five years. This parliamentary reform was passed in 1869 without Russian objections,[5] but it did not really make a difference to the existing political situation. During the following years, Russia's policy towards Finland hardened increasingly under the influence of the Pan-Slavistic movement. Particularly after the accession of Nicholas II greater efforts were made to shape Finland on the Soviet model, and Finnish autonomy was continually ignored.[6]

The Russian revolution of 1905 brought a repetition of the events of 1863. The Russian Government suffered military and political defeat at home;[7] by convening Parliament it hoped to contain the unrest among the Finnish population, which had already led in 1904 to the assassination of the Russian Governor General. Parliament immediately set about an electoral and parliamentary reform which envisaged far-reaching changes to the Finnish political system. The four-chamber Parliament made way for a one-chamber Parliament;[8] its 200 delegates were chosen in the constituencies by direct election according to the proportional representation system and using the "d'Hondt" method.[9] Active and passive franchise was extended to all male and female citizens over 24 years. Finland had thus given itself one of the most advanced constitutions in Europe. As in 1869, the realisation of all theoretical concepts was seriously endangered by Russian politics. The Czar still possessed an absolute veto on parliamentary resolutions and also had the power to dissolve Parliament; and he did not hesitate to make ample use of these rights.

The decisive turning-point for Finnish politics came with the great Russian revolution of 1917. The Czar was the legitimate ruler of Finland; after his deposition the Finnish Parliament considered Finland's union with Russia at an end. The Fins ultimately had to fight for their independence because the Kerenski Government as well as the ensuing Bolshevik Government were keen to retain their position of control in Finland. As the Finnish Marxists were actively involved in this struggle, the country was at times on the brink of civil war.[10] It was at this time, too, that the Monarchists and Republicans finally decided on the republican form of government.[11]

The new constitution, passed in 1919, divides political power between Parliament, the President of State and the Government formed by Parliament. The President of

Independence and republican form of Government

Separation of powers in the political system

173

State is elected indirectly (through an intermediate committee) by the people for a term of six years, and is independent of Parliament. The President has become the dominating political figure in the State, for he possesses extensive powers in the legislative process[12] and has the right to dissolve Parliament. Furthermore, the Finnish multi-party system with its inherent difficulties of forming a majority Government has enhanced the importance of the presidential role. The Government's role lies between the President, who delegates the task of forming the Government, and Parliament, to which it is responsible. The parliamentary electoral system as well as regulations on the formation of Parliament were copied from local Government statutes and the electoral system of 1905.

The 1919 Constitution has proved extremely stable. Apart from minor modifications, it is still the constitutional foundation of the present Finnish state, although between 1939 and 1948 Finland had to negotiate various crises.[13] There are two basic reasons for this unusual political stability: above all, the continuing overwhelming support of the Finnish people for the new foundation of the Finnish state in 1919,[14] and the country's social structure which is exceptionally well-balanced.

Party Development

The development of the Finnish multi-party system can be traced back to the early days of Finnish parliamentarianism. The wide party spectrum can first of all be attributed to the division of the Finnish Parliament into four class chambers which pursued different interests and frequently did not assemble collectively. In the 19th century, political groups emerged with widely differing views on the problematic issues of Finnish politics. Such issues included the struggle with Liberalism, the language barriers between the Finnish and the Swedish parts of the population, and the attitude towards Russia, the new dominating political power. A little later, the social effects of industrialisation became the major talking-point. This wide variety of problem areas led to strong differentiation of the Finnish party system in its early stages. As in most other European countries, one can distinguish in Finland between a Liberal and a Conservative grouping.[15]

The language controversy had lasting effects on the party system. Only 10% of the population used the Swedish language although this was the language that dominated the public sector. The efforts of the Finnish-speaking part of the population to achieve linguistic equality must, therefore, be seen as attempts to attain social equality. The "Svekomanes" and the "Fennomanes", emerged in this conflict as the two most important representative groups. The "Svekomanes" exerted particular influence in the aristocratic chamber, whereas the Fennomanes determined the policies of the farmers and the clergy, and later also that of the middle-class chamber.

In 1809 the attitude towards Russia was by no means a purely hostile one. It is true that the Liberal groups and the "Svekomanes" rejected all Russian influence, but the Finnish-speaking part of the population hoped for Russian support to fight the domination of Sweden. When Russia began to try to shape Finland on the

Russian model, however, the Finnish camp split up into the "Old-Finnish Party" which called for further cooperation with Russia, and the "Finnish Constitutional Party" which vigorously defended Finnish autonomy. All these early party groups were characterised by a loosely-structured organisation; in the course of the 19th century, similar party forms evolved in the class chambers of Parliament.

Social question and formation of the workers' party

The most significant changes in the Finnish party system were brought about by industrialisation. Towards the end of the century, the Social Democrat Party of Finland was founded as the political representative of the rapidly growing working population. The Social Democrats developed into a new type of party. It was at first excluded from Parliament,[16] because the social class division there did not make provision for the workers. Furthermore, the electoral system excluded most of the party's followers from voting, so an extra-parliamentary organisation was formed to campaign for their ideals. In the great parliamentary and electoral reform of 1906, the party's fundamental demands became reality. The 1907 elections, held according to the new electoral system, established the Finnish party system in its modern form. Although all parties had worked towards this reform, the Social Democrats benefited particularly from the increased electorate.[17] With 37% of all votes cast and 80 out of 200 parliamentary mandates, they entered Parliament as the strongest party. The remaining seats were distributed among the traditional parties of the Finnish Parliament: the Old-Finnish Party, the Finnish Constitutional Party, the Swedish Party, the Farmers' Union and the Christian Workers' Party.

Establishment of the modern party system

The relatively large number of parties in Parliament was a direct result of the proportional representation system, giving small groups the chance of winning seats.[18] During the following years, modifications occurred in the party system (the merging of the Old-Finnish with the Finnish Constitutional Party after the separation from Russia; various splits in the Social Democrat Party; the emergence of the Communists), but its basic structure remained the same.

The following table presents an overview of the composition of the present Finnish Parliament; the largest parliamentary parties will then be discussed in greater detail.

Party	Percentage	Seats
Social Democrat Party	25	54
Popular Democratic Party	19	41
Centre Party	17.7	39
National Party	18.4	34
Swedish People's Party	4.7	10
Liberal Party	4.4	9

Distribution of seats in the present Parliament

The remaining 13 seats belong to various splinter groups without any political influence.

Social Democrat Party

Social Democrat
Party

The Social Democrat Party was founded to represent the workers in the wake of industrialisation; it soon spread to rural areas as well. After considerable success between 1907 and 1917, the party suffered a number of set-backs. In the 1917/18 civil war, it was tested by internal conflicts when some parts of the party started to support the Bolsheviks who wanted Finland to remain part of a Marxist Russia. These tensions within the party were resolved in 1922 when the party's left wing formed the "Socialist Party", the first communist organisation in Finland.

Although the Social Democrats at times made up the largest group in Parliament, the Liberal and Conservative parties excluded them from Government from 1917/18 until 1927. It was only in 1927 that a Social Democrat minority Government was formed; it had only a brief life, however, and it was not before 1937 that the Social Democrat Party was accepted as coalition partner by the other centre parties.

After 1944, the party had to face another period of division: the Communist Party returned under Soviet pressure and parts of the Social Democrat Party, discontent with the party's wartime policy, joined the Communists. In 1958, the party was subject to heated intra-party discussions on economic issues. In order to be able to cope with the after-effects of the war,[19] the majority of party members called for an extensive stimulation and support of the economy. This meant that private business and the centre parties had to cooperate, and this in turn led to the formation of a group representing employees and small farmers. Despite these difficulties, the Social Democrat Party has developed into the major party of the Finnish party system and has participated in most of the post-war Governments.

Compared with the political development of Scandinavia in general, the Social Democrats abandoned their orthodox Marxist principles rather late; today, the party follows a moderate socialist line. The party's members are to be found among the workers and middle classes; the number is estimated at about 150,000.[20]

Finnish Popular Democratic Union

Finnish Popular
Democratic
Union

The Finnish Popular Democratic Union comprises various left-wing groups under the leadership of the Communist Party which has twice been banned in Finland. The Marxist wing of the Social Democrats became independent in 1919, and in 1922 called itself the "Socialist Party", as the first Finnish Communist party organisation it was banned in 1923. It was succeeded by the "Workers' and Farmers' Party" which was declared illegal in 1930.[21]

Communist parties were permitted again in 1944 following Soviet pressure. Thus the "Finnish Popular Democratic Union" was formed, a union of various left-wing groups (among them a group of Social Democrats).

For a short period the party participated in the Governments (1944—48), but was then excluded until 1966. It was during this period, however, that it developed into the leading opposition party. At times it benefited greatly from the Finnish voters' discontentment with the ruling Government parties: in 1958, although the strongest parliamentary group, it failed to form a government because the other parties were not prepared to enter into a coalition.

From 1966 until 1976, the party finally entered into Government coalition; it was then that it modified its previous Russian ideology to a more moderate national Communism. Even at the time of the coalition, the Union's attitude towards the Social Democrats was the cause of permanent confrontation. The Union has an estimated 15,000 members.

Centre Party

The party was founded in 1906 as the "Agrarian Union". At first, it represented in particular the interests of the small Finnish farmers, but it extended its influence to other groups of the rural population. Even after the party's change of name (intended to appeal to more voters) the emphasis on rural concerns and Finnish culture has remained. The party is strongly committed to supporting the numerous small Finnish farmers, and has thus become the greatest competitor of the Communist Popular Union in rural areas. The Centre Party was the strongest parliamentary party for a long period and held a leading position in many Government coalitions. The Soviets had good relations with this party, and sometimes even tried to support it in government; for they approved of the Centre Party's political position and of its absolute neutrality in foreign politics. Since the 1960's, the party has slowly lost in importance;[22] it has had to surrender its dominating role in government to the Social Democrats. With more than 270,000 members, the Centre Party enjoys the strongest party organisation.[23] The present President of State, Kekkonen, comes from its ranks and has been in office since 1956.

National Party

This party was formed to unite various Conservative/National groups. Their common ideological bond is opposition to Socialism. The party calls for unlimited national sovereignty and freedom of alliance. At the time of the five-party coalition, the National Party represented the largest opposition group.

Swedish People's Party

This party represents primarily the interests of the country's Swedish minority. It is really only a representative group, having a very mixed social structure, and no real ideological programme. The party can count on 80% of the votes of the Swedish part of the population. The relatively good election results of the Swedish People's Party are partly due to the fact that the election turn-out of its core of voters lies well above average.

Liberal Party

The Liberal Party came into existence as late as 1965 when the Finnish People's Party and the Liberal Union merged. By joining forces the two parties hoped to retain their parliamentary position. Their programme is particularly designed to appeal to the upper middle classes. In the present Parliament, the Liberal Party helps to support the ruling minority Cabinet. The party only has about 1,500 members and judging by previous election results, it is not certain whether the party will remain in Parliament.

The Party System

A characteristic feature of the Finnish party system is the large number of parties represented in Parliament. The formation of a majority or a Government presents considerable difficulties, and accounts for the low degree of stability. Between 1919 and 1977, Finland had 58 different Governments of which only 6 lasted longer than two years. On four occasions, the situation in Parliament was so hopeless that the President of State had to create Government teams of independent experts.[24] Two further factors complicate the formation of a Government. Firstly, the Finnish Parliament lacks a clearly dominating party which would, on the grounds of its strength, be responsible for forming a Government even if it did not gain an absolute majority. Apart from the numerous small groups, there are three or four large parties of similar size.[25]

The second complication results from the fact that over long periods of time certain parties were not regarded as possible coalition partners. Between the two World Wars this applied to the Social Democrat Party; and between 1948 and 1966 to the Popular Democratic Union. The great number of governmental crises and changing Cabinets has certainly had a detrimental effect on the quality of Finnish politics. Further damage was avoided by the fact that there were no radical parties which fundamentally rejected the existing form of Government; and because of the strong position of the President of State which is embodied in the Constitution and proven in political reality.[26]

The Finnish Government can be divided into four groups: one-party Governments, coalitions of the middle-class parties, coalitions between the middle-class parties and the Social Democrat Party, and popular front Governments. One-party Governments only occurred very seldom, and were always minority Governments[27] which were only able to survive through the partial support of other parliamentary parties. The political possibilities of such Governments were accordingly limited. Coalitions between the middle-class parties were formed mainly between the two World Wars; the election results of the past two decades have altered the parliamentary situation so strongly in favour of the left-wing parties that further such coalitions are at present inconceivable. The 1950's in particular witnessed coalitions between various middle-class parties and the Social Democrats. Popular Front Governments, with Social Democrats and Communists as the leading parties, occurred immediately after the war and in the years between 1966 and 1976.[28]

The variety of coalition types that occur in Finnish politics becomes evident in a survey of Finnish post-war politics. The first four Governments, from 1944 until 1948, consisted of various middle-class parties, the Social Democrat Party and the Popular Democratic Union. Because of the tensions between Finland and the Soviet Union, it seemed advisable to include the Communists in the Cabinets. After 1948, however, a systematic effort was made to exclude them from Government; the developments in Eastern Europe cast doubt on their attitude towards the existing political system.[29] A Social Democrat one-party minority Government from 1948 until 1950 was followed by a period of relative stability; during this time the Centre Party and the Social Democrat Party as the two strongest groups alternated in leading various coalitions, and even formed coalitions with each other. From 1956 on, the Social Democrat Party was confronted with problems within the party which caused it to retire from Government responsibilities; and as a result of this, three minority Governments were formed in 1957, all composed of various middle-class parties. In 1958, two Cabinets of independent ministers were installed. In 1958/59, the Social Democrat Party formed a short coalition which was followed from 1959 until 1962 by two minority Governments of the Centre Party. Between 1962 and 1966, the Cabinets were composed of middle-class parties and independents, as well as of independents alone. By 1966 the Social Democrat Party had found its shape and political (left-wing) position; and in view of the country's economic difficulties felt ready for a coalition with the Popular Democratic Union, in which the Centre Party also participated. When the Liberal Party and the Swedish People's Party also entered the Government coalition, they held a safe majority of 166 seats. As was to be expected, however, the political efficiency of this Government was damaged by argument between the partners. The coalition finally collapsed in September 1976, after numerous crises and Cabinet reshuffles. Finland then had a minority Government until 1977 consisting of the Centre Party, the Liberal People's Party and the Swedish People's Party; between them they had only 58 of the 200 parliamentary seats. It was replaced by a five-party Government composed of the Social Democrats, the Centre Party, the Communist Party, the Swedish People's Party and the Liberal People's Party. In March 1978 the Swedish People's Party resigned from the Government, but this did not alter the parliamentary majority.

Government formation since 1945

Notes

1 Sweden suspended the constitution in 1809.

2 This was the year in which parliamentary rule in Sweden was once more replaced by the absolutist restoration.

3 The Senate was a Finnish body, which had executive but no legislative functions.

4 One of the changes was that the universities and secondary schools were allowed to send their representatives to the clerical chamber.

5 Parliament had made a special effort to secure its new constitution by giving it the status of an "unchangeable basic law".

6 The Russian Government attached particular importance to the reduction of Finland's special military rights. After 1895, attempts were made to subjugate the Finnish population to Russian compulsory military service.

[7] This unrest was a consequence of the devastating defeats that Russia had suffered in East Asia in the war with Japan.

[8] This was one of the first ever one-chamber Parliaments. The second parliamentary chamber had only been created by demand of the Monarch during the constitutional monarchies; he meant to use it to counterbalance the first (usually Liberal) chamber.

[9] Until 1945, the North Finnish constituency was an exception because of its extremely low population. The delegate for this constituency was chosen according to a relative majority system. Today similar special regulations apply to the semi-autonomous Aland isles.

[10] The military intervention of the German Empire was a decisive factor in the outcome of the battles; Germany wanted to prevent another Russian occupation of Finland.

[11] In 1918, Parliament had initially decided on the introduction of a Finnish monarchy. The German prince Friedrich Karl von Hessen was chosen to be King of Finland, but he declined after the German surrender. In the newly elected Parliament of 1919, the supporters of the Republic gained the upper hand. The leaning towards a monarchy during the deliberation on the constitution is reflected in the extensive rights of the President of State.

[12] The President of State has the right of initiative in the legislative process (Art.18); his veto is nullified only if the Bill is approved a second time by a new Parliament.

[13] The wars with Russia in 1939/40 and 1941/44; the extensive surrender of territories after 1944; the refugee problem, and so on.

[14] Scandinavian political science offers different interpretations as to how Finnish politics have been influenced by the lateness of the state's foundation and by the long period of enforced non-application of democratic principles. See on this point: Andren, Nils = Government and Politics in the Nordic Countries, p. 63.

[15] Without monarchic rule, the Finnish Conservatives could not act as defendants of a particular dynasty, but instead had to develop a general Conservative ideology.

[16] The division of Parliament into social classes caused the Social Democral Party to refuse to get individual delegates into Parliament with the assistance of other parties, as was done in other Scandinavian countries.

[17] The new electoral system increased the number of voters from about 120,000 to about 1,200,000. The parties already represented in Parliament had assumed that they would appeal to a large percentage of new voters because of their support for reforms.

[18] Finland never considered abolishing the system of proportional representation. According to various studies, the introduction of the relative majority system would only negligibly reduce the number of parties in the Finnish Parliament. See also: Sternberger/Vogel = Die Wahl der Parlamente, Vol I, p. 427f.

[19] Surrender of territory, re-integration of refugees, and vast reparation to the Soviet Union.

[20] This figure, as all other following membership figures, refers to the years 1965-70.

[21] The prohibitions were basically the work of right-wing national groups which accused the Communist Party of treason. Finland's anti-Russian politics between the wars influenced the development of the Communist Party to the same extent as the present Finnish policy of neutrality.

[22] This is partly due to the decrease in the farming population.

[23] More than half of its voters are party members; suggesting this to be an interest group.

[24] For the last time in 1963/4 with the Lehto Cabinet.

[25] The strength of the Social Democral Party puts it at present in a dominating position.

[26] Finnish neutrality and the country's relative inactivity in the international sector allow extra scope for home affairs.

[27] This occurred for the last time in 1961/62, when the Centre Party formed a one-party minority Government.

[28] A survey of all Finnish Governments until 1968 is given by Tornudd, Klaus = Composition of Cabinets in Finland 1917-1968. Scandinavian Political Studies 4/69, p. 58 ff.

[29] The Czechoslovak Communist Party's attitude was of particular importance in this respect.

Greece

HERBERT MAIER

Historical Summary

It is true that modern Greece leans towards Western culture; but even so it is strikingly different from the highly developed societies of industrialised Middle and Western Europe. It was inevitable that basic structural peculiarities, such as the deep gulfs between social classes, would affect the political system.

Until 1830, Greece belonged to the Ottoman Turkish Empire; in the early days of the Greek State, therefore, a large proportion of the upper classes did not come from within the new nation, but from the economic metropoles of the Turkish Empire. Curiously enough these people were nevertheless of Greek nationality. Their political culture was largely determined by that of the Turkish Empire which was at that time in decline; as a result, corruption, nepotism and prejudice were rife in Greece. The majority of the rest of the population lived in rural areas, were poorly educated, and knew only their parish as a political centre. In this pre-industrial agrarian society, which was strongly religious, political freedom had not been regarded as a social revolution, but rather as a national fight for freedom from Turkish dominance. Those foreign powers which supported this struggle were also mainly interested in the destruction of the Ottoman Empire, and less interested in the creation of a constitutionally free Greek State.

Problems of becoming a nation

Political influence of the Balkan

Development of the State

The development of the Greek State can be divided into several distinct phases. The first phase was that of the national fight for freedom which lasted from 1821 until 1930.

Foundation of the state

On February 3rd 1830, Greece was acknowledged as a sovereign monarchic State in the London Press; its protecting powers (Great Britain, France and Russia) instated the Wittelsbach Crown Prince Otto as King in 1832. Until 1843 he was the ruler of an absolute monarchy, dominated by Bavarian military officers and Bavarian Civil Servants. It was only following a bloodless rebellion by the army and people that the Monarch was forced to constitute a National Assembly. But corruption, office patronage and "fixed" elections were typical of the ensuing period of constitutional monarchy. Property parties did not exist. Instead, politics were in the hands of some leading figures who had won themselves a reputation during the war against the Ottoman-Bavarian absolutism; at election times, these people used every method, legel and illegal, to win the necessary votes for re-election.

With English help, Otto was dethroned in 1862/63, and a more democratic and

Otto I abdicates

liberal constitution was developed. In the 1880's a kind of two-party system emerged. There was the Progressive party, supported by the Liberal upper middle-classes and the intellectuals; and also a Conservative/reactionary party which united all the old oligarichal elements. Both were parties of the upper professional classes. In 1911 another constitutional reform was introduced which was even more liberal and which extended the rights of the citizen within the State. A real differentiation now began to form between Liberal, Progressive and Republican party groups and strong monarchic elements. The Liberal wing was led by the political Veniselos. When King Constantine declined to enter the war on the side of the Entente powers, he lost all political influence through foreign pressure.

The 1st Republic

In 1924 Greece was finally declared a republic, which was then supported by the followers of Veniselos. The Conservative forces were reduced to political impotency for more than ten years, as the electoral system only allowed them very few seats despite a relatively high percentage of votes. "Fixed" elections and political radicalism were constantly increasing. In order to put a stop to this, a military putsch was staged in 1935. The

Return of the King

monarchy was re-introduced, and from 1936 until 1940 Greece was under the military dictatorship of the general Metaxas, supported by the King. The divided parties were helpless to act against it.

The Greek monarchy was able to survive the occupation by the Italians and Germans. The Communists fought the right-wing Governments from 1936–1949 in a large-scale partisan war. Foreign military help was once more required (Great Britain and U.S.) to end this conflict. In 1950, 45 parties contested the parliamentary seats; in 1951, only 9 parties were left. The right wing had been united by the "Hellenic Collective Movement", whereas the left wing had formed the "Uniform Democratic Left" under communist leadership. There was also a "Centre Coalition", which succeeded in gaining a very narrow majority in Parliament; but this party was itself so divided that it soon proved incapable of governing. New elections were held in 1952, this time according to the majority system. These elections were fought less on the strength of programmes and more on the personalities of the two leaders: the right-wing leader of the "Hellenic Collective Movement" Marshal Papagos and the outstanding figure of the Centre, General Plastiras. Papagos won, and

Right-wing Government

with him began eleven years of right-wing rule. He died in 1955. Karamanlis succeeded him with the support of King Constantine. After consolidating his position, he founded the "National Radical Union" which was intended to comprise the old representatives of the Collective Union and also various members of the Centre Union. The old Centre, the Liberals and the collective groups of the left faded from the political arena. It was only in the 1960's that the Centre Union regained its political stature; this was after the Governments led by Karamanlis had succeeded in initiating a certain economic upturn in the country without, however, consolidating on this by a strengthening of the democratic base. The assassination of the left-wing delegate Lambrakis in 1963 caused a grave domestic crisis. In May of the same year Karamanlis resigned, having fallen out with the

Military dictatorship

Monarch over differences of opinion regarding a state visit to England. In the following elections, the Centre Union gained the relative majority and formed a new Government under Papandreou; Karamanlis left the country on 9th December, 1963, and designated Kanellopoulos as his successor. Internal quarrels caused disruption within the new Government. In July 1965, Papandreou was virtually dismissed by the King. The three following Governments of the Centre, which each only lasted a few weeks, were only able to survive through the support of the National Radical Union. Stephanopoulos, a member of the Centre Party, then succeeded in sustaining a Government until April. At the King's wish, he was succeeded on 4th April by Kanellopoulos who immediately began working towards holding new elections. However, on 21st April (2 days before the campaign was due to begin) a coup d'état was staged by a group of officers.

The new authoritarian dictatorship forcibly removed all traces of Greek parliamentarianism. Ideologically, it opposed the corrupt rule of the parties and a degenerate parliamentarianism. But it soon became evident that the military was neither capable of governing the country properly, nor of implementing the urgently needed social and economic reforms. In 1974, the military resigned their political powers following American pressure; and the longest dictatorship since the country's independence came to an end.

Karamanlis returned to power and his first move was to eradicate all political connections with the Army. Parallel to this he held the first free elections in November 1974 and emerged as the decisive victor.

The Parties

After the end of the military dictatorship, Karamanlis founded the "New Democracy" (Nea Dimokratia). This was supposed to document his separation from the National Radical Union; yet the new party consisted largely of remnants of that Union. The New Democracy regards itself as a party of the people and the political centre. In the 1975 elections, it obtained 54.4% of the votes cast and had a two-thirds majority in Parliament.

New Democracy

The former Centre Union under Papandreou and the more social-democratic "Movement of New Political Forces" joined to form the complex "Centre Union/New Forces" led by the Liberal intellectual Mavros; it gained 20.4% of the votes and 60 parliamentary seats, and thus became the second-largest political group in Greece.

Centre Union

The Panhellenic Socialist Movement (PASOK) concentrated its efforts mainly on the younger voters and the intelligentsia. This movement was founded by Papandreou jr; it is openly anti-American. With only 13.5% of votes and 12 parliamentary seats, it is not yet a significant political force.

PASOK

The United Left is still further left on the political spectrum. For a long time it was considered a substitute organisation for the activities of the prohibited Communist Party. Today it unites the following parties: the Moscow-orientated Communist Party in exile, the Greek Communist Party that was prohibited for a long time, and its sympathiser organisation called the "United Democratic Left". In the elections the United Left won 9.4% of the votes, but only obtained 8 parliamentary seats. At present it has no political significance.

Communists

183

There are further splinter parties which should be mentioned. One of them is the "National Democratic Union" led by Petros Garoufalias, a supporter of the Army. The Union has Fascist elements; but with only 1.1% of the votes, failed to win a parliamentary seat. Another splinter group is the Maoist "Revolutionary Communist Movement" which put forward some candidates in the elections but did not achieve a 1% vote share.

The re-installed Greek democracy appears to be functioning well on a formal level. The second election after the abolition of the military dictatorship may be mentioned to prove this point. In the elections held in November 1977, the Prime Minister Konstantin Karamanlis' party "New Democracy" failed to maintain its two-thirds majority. On 28th November, a new Government under Karamanlis was sworn in.

Results of the Parliamentary Elections

Out of the 6,389,255 people entitled to vote, 5,129,884 valid votes were counted; 18.7% abstained from voting. Below is a comparison between the 1974 and 1977 election results:

	1974		1977	
	Percentage of votes	Seats	Percentage of votes	Seats
New Democracy	54.37	220	41.85	173
Centre Union	20.42	60	11.95	15
Panhellenic Socialist Movement (PASOK)	13.58	12	25.33	92
Alliance	9.45	8	2.72	2
Communist Party of Greece ("Abroad")	—	—	9.36	11
National Democratic Union	1.10	—	6.82	5
Neo-Liberals	—	—	1.08	2
EKKE (Maoists)	0.02	—	0.23	—
Popular Democratic Union (Left Wing)	—	—	0.43	—
Various Independents	0.06	—	0.46	—
		300		300

Karamanlis' New Democracy retained a majority despite major losses. The socialist PASOK under the leadership of Andreas Papandreou had the greatest increase in votes (it campaigns against Greece's full membership of the European Community and for the removal of all American and Western military bases according to the motto: "Greece for the Greeks"). PASOK's increase in votes was at the expense of the liberal Centre Union, led by the former acting Prime Minister and Foreign

184

Minister Georgios Mavros. (The Centre Union believes in a closer rapport between Greece and all block-free states, and for an end to cooperation with the USA.) On 27th November, Mavros resigned as Chairman of the Centre Union. The Communist Party (which before only had 4 seats within the Alliance) won 11 seats and thus became a parliamentary party. The right-wing National Front, led by the former Prime Minister Stafanos Stephanopoulos, took 5 seats; it had only been founded on 7th October, 1977 and its sole public support was the newspaper Eleftheros Kosmos. The Front calls for the liberation of the leaders of the military regime who have been in prison since 1975.

Future Prospects

At present, the new Greek democracy is largely in the hands of the old party leaders' elite. The mood of euphoria following a return to democracy after 10 years of military dictatorship has mostly vanished. Large-scale reforms of social structure seem unlikely in the near future, and only the next years will show whether a genuinely democratic rule can be established in Greece.

Portugal

HERBERT MAIER

Historical Development

Monarchy

In 1820, Portugal took the first steps towards establishing a constitutional monarchy. However, the following years brought little progress in the development of the constitution. The reason was that until 1910 the Portuguese monarchy enjoyed extensive prerogatives which hampered the development of strong party groups. The monarchy finally allowed a constitutional dictatorship under Joao Francos (from 1907–1910) which was set up to overcome grave domestic crises.

Republic

Following a bloodless revolution, Portugal was declared a republic on 5th October, 1910. At the same time, a genuine parliamentary system was introduced which copied the then French Republic. It took only a few years for this newly introduced parliamentarianism to degenerate to such an extent that it lost public support. Between 1911 and 1926, 8 Presidents and 24 Governments followed each other in quick succession. A military coup d'état finally put an end to the obvious bankruptcy of the State. On 28th May, 1926, General Gomez da Costa seized political power. The generals failed to put forward a suitable concept for the re-structuring of the state, and their Finance Minister Salazar was soon able to take over. Closely connected with Portugal's Catholic circles, he was committed to the idea of a "corporate State" which had begun to emerge during the military Government. He became Prime Minister in 1932.

Salazar regime

Salazar was head of the authoritarian Government in Portugal for more than 40 years. The authoritarian structures were gradually extended and consolidated politically and constitutionally, helped by the creation of special political organisations (National Union and secret police). The National Union was a mass organisation which, supported by the Catholic church and high military officials, had replaced the parties. Considerable restrictions on the right to vote served to perpetuate the authoritarian regime. After 1961, only about 15% of the entire Portuguese adult population was entitled to vote; the principle of secret ballots was repeatedly violated by the use of ballot papers of different colours and sizes; and the corporate voting power of the second chamber brought further limitations.

Authoritarian system

Salazar held the post of Prime Minister until 1968. The only other political institutions were the President of State and the two-chamber Parliament: both without any significant influence. After Salazar's death in 1970, his successor Caetano attempted some moderate reforms; they were less aimed at a democratisation process and more at the full realisation of the initially planned corporate political system (Estado Nuovo). The National Union (of which only the name

186

had remained) became the "National Popular Action Group" (Accao Nacional Popular). Its rival groups, the United Democratic Election Commission, the Democratic Election Commission and the Monarchist Cause, were allowed to fight a limited election campaign. However, they were dissolved once the elections to the National Assembly were over.

Social and Economic Problems

The Salazar/Caetano regime was characterised by an extremely tight control on the economy. The economist Salazar painstakingly issued directives for virtually everything and tried to model national affairs on his own almost ascetic way of life. This led to the preservation of vast latefundia in the possession of a few rich families. These familes at the same time dominated the Portuguese banking system and the most important industrial and service businesses. They made no attempts to phase in rationalised industrialisation. Instead, their policy was that of paying the lowest possible wages and moving their capital abroad. This resulted in extreme social inequality, massive unemployment and the lowest increase in income in Europe. The large-scale tax evasions of the rich did not allow the State to take the urgently needed steps to improve the country's infra-structure. The educational system was underdeveloped to such an extent that even in 1940 only every other Portuguese had attended school; and as late as 1970 school attendance was limited to four years. Today about 30% of the adult population are still illiterate.

The situation was made all the more grave by the steadily increasing costs of the defense and preservation of Portuguese colonial property. The military budget finally absorbed almost half of all Portuguese public expenditure.

It was self-evident that in these circumstances the Government was unable to plan or realise any improvements in the agrarian sector. Agricultural production levels fell so low that basic foodstuffs had to be bought with expensive foreign currency. The miserable conditions of the rural population led to a massive migration from the country to the more or less industrialised coastal regions between Porto and Lisbon. This resulted in an increase in unemployment which finally triggered off large-scale emigration. In 1960, an average 40,000 Portuguese emigrated per year; by 1970, the number had risen to about 200,000 and was still growing. Altogether more than 2 million Portuguese emigrated during the authoritarian regime. Today, Portugal has a population of about 9 million.

The Military Putsch

The Caetano Government attempted to improve the situation; after 1970, for example, the Gross National Product increased by 5 to 6% per annum. Yet the colonial war in Angola and other areas necessitated considerable military expansion. The Army was even forced to accept declared critics of the regime to maintain a sufficient level of officers. Army officials were keenly aware that the colonial empire would inevitably fall; but the Caetano Government did not dare to change

187

to a policy of de-colonialisation. In February 1974 the Vice-Chief of the General Staff, Antonio de Spinola expressed the beliefs of the military forces in his book "Portugal and the Future" which caused a sensation. Spinola stated that it was impossible to win the guerilla wars in the colonial territories and that it was consequently no longer morally or ideologically justifiable to bleed the young generation of Portugal. The Chief of General Staff, Francisco Costa Gomes and many high-ranking officers were in agreement with what he said. Even before the book was published, a "Captains' Movement" had been formed which went a good deal further than the Caetano Government in its proposed political measures.

On 15th March, 1974 about 200 people attempted a putsch in a small garrison. When it was suppressed by the Government, all supporters of the "Captains' Movement" as well as other opponents of the regime set up a consolidated front in reaction to the secret police's rather brutal treatment of suspected conspirators as well as completely innocent people. On 25th April, the "Junta of National Salvation" led by General Spinola, took over political power. Caetano was forced to resign, and the Junta was supported by the jubilant population of the capital Lisbon.

By 15th May, a provisional Government had been installed and a date fixed for free universal elections. The Prime Minister Carlos da Palma was the head of the new provisional Government which was composed of Socialists, Social Democrats, Liberals and Communists — a potentially explosive mixture. The armed forces (MFA — Movimento das Forcas Armadas) retained political power.

The first Government under Palma Carlos resigned because of insurmountable difficulties with the Communists. The military forces worked towards the appointment of Colonel Vasco Goncalves as Prime Minister, although the then President of State Spinola was strictly opposed to this. De Palma's intentions were in practice reversed as Goncalves proved to be extremely pro-Communist. When Spinola tried to stabilise his position by mobilising Liberal forces, the political left at once reacted and forced the Junta and the MFA to decide against Spinola. The crisis of the first provisional Government manifested itself in July 1975. In September of the same year Spinola resigned from office; in March of the following year he was deprived of all political power and had to leave Portugal under suspicion of plotting a counter-revolution. The power of the extreme left in the Government and in the military forces reached its climax at this time. State and private media were under their control; businesses were undermined by left-wing extremists; and regional assemblies provided them with a broad basis for controlling local administration.

Towards a New Party System

When Spinola had finally been robbed of all power, the MFA was confronted with a new problem. The elections to the constituent assembly were supposed to take place on 25th April, 1975. Despite the interference of the Communist Party under Alvaro Cunhal, the military was ultimately in favour of holding the elections as planned. This was indicative of the course later followed by the MFA in which the more moderate forces (that is, the socialist and social democrat elements) were dominant. A large number of parties fought the elections of 25th April. They may be divided as follows:

The extreme left consists of the Communists (PCP) and about 10 small groups of the radical left. In the first free elections, they managed to win about 28% of the votes cast. It is a striking fact that the Communists gained less than half of that figure: they won 12.5% of the vote, whereas the remaining groups polled about 15.5%. The left-wing groups enjoy their greatest support in the country's industrial belt; that is, around Lisbon, Beja and Evora as well as in the region of the Alentejo with its large estates. The radical left fights for extensive land reform and appropriation without compensation. The ultimate objective is an absolute collective system of agricultural production. On the industrial front the introduction of a systematised economy is planned.

The Socialist Party of Portugal under its leader Mario Soares emerged as the real dominating force in the elections to the constituent assembly, polling 37.9% of the votes. The party may be compared programmatically to the German Social Democrat Party during the Empire and the Weimar Republic. It differs fundamentally from the Communists, since it chooses the "hard path" of reform, supported by a broad majority of the population, and rejects revolution and radical theory. The first minority Cabinet under Soares produced a programme of economic austerity and rejected any coalition with the Communists.

Portugal's Social Democrats are slightly to the right of the Socialists. In the elections to the constituent assembly, they won 26.4% of the votes as the "Democratic People's Party" (PPD); in the two following elections they called themselves the "Social Democrat Party" (PSD) and succeeded in retaining their vote percentage in the parliamentary elections. They differ from the Socialists in that their objectives are more modest and moderate; they are more pragmatic than ideological; and they correspond rather closely to the middle-European type of "people's party".

The Democratic Social Centre occupies the right wing of the political spectrum; it is similar to the German Christian Democrats. The supporters of this party come from the strictly Catholic groups of Portugal's population which approve of extended democracy but do not necessarily support large-scale economic and social changes. With only 7.7% of votes at the elections, the party did not do quite as well as the party leaders might have expected. The party generally tolerates the Socialist minority Government under Soares, or else forms the opposition together with the Communists (as in the case of land reform). Exactly one year after the elections to the constituent assembly, the first parliamentary elections were held on 25th April, 1976. The Socialists maintained their lead with 35%, the Social Democrats did well with 24%, the Christian Democrats doubled their percentage to 15.9%, and the Communists achieved a slight increase to 14.6%.

In December 1977, the minority Government of Mario Soares suffered a severe blow. After 16 months in office, the Government was faced with a no-confidence vote: the Socialists were defeated by 159 to 100. Soares was unable to go through with his stringent economic programme which was the condition for a $750 million

Extreme Left

Socialists

Social Democrats

Middle-class groups

Minority Government under Soares

189

loan from the International Monetary Fund. However, Portugal's relative domestic stability was demonstrated by the fact that the President of State Eanes, despite the grave political crisis, paid a long-planned oficial visit to the Federal Republic of Germany. The Social Democrats and the Centre offered their support to Soares for a further coalition Government. Astonishingly enough, Soares then formed a new Government which included the more Conservative Centre. At present the Government has 143 out of the 243 parliamentary seats. The new Government programme made no mention of social and political reforms. Instead, it announced a restriction on private consumption, import cut-backs, and tax increases. Wage increases were not to exceed the 20% limit; in view of the present 30% rate of inflation, this meant a decrease in real income. The Government also aimed at Portugal's accession to the European Community.

Government coalition with the political right

The coalition broke up at the end of July 1978; Soares was dismissed by the President of State, Eanes. Yet Soares is still considered the strongest political figure in Portugal.

Outlook

Revolution or reform?

In Portugal, the structures of the corporate system were abolished during the revolution. National party, para-military movements and youth organisations disappeared. The population is still restless; and it remains to be seen whether the elections of 25th April, 1976, and the presidential elections of July 1976 have brought a certain peace. Because of the anti-Communist attitude of the PSP and PSD, a popular front policy seems unlikely; in the same way, a Conservative democracy under the dominance of the Christian Democrats is out of the question. A consolidation of the political situation is possible as long as the military forces tolerate and support the present development. On the surface, the parties have attained a structural framework but it is certainly too early to speak of a genuine stability. One has to consider that about a quarter of the population is interested in radical socialist politics; and one cannot be sure whether the new democratic institutions have found such a degree of acceptance that even the politically weaker groups will continue to support them.

Spain

HERBERT MAIER

Historical Background

The Spain of the post-Franco era has clearly tried to resume the course of previous constitutional development and political tradition. Towards the end of the 19th century, a constitutional monarchy had been implemented with a corresponding constitution. The Spanish involvement in the 1898 war with the Americans (which led to the loss of Cuba and the Philippines as spheres of influence) and the Spanish-Moroccan war of 1921/23 exhausted the Spanish State both economically and politically. The monarchy could only survive by setting up a military dictatorship under General Primo de Rivera. His successor, General Berenguer, caused such conflict that Spain was finally declared a republic.

The new republican system was essentially a parliamentary system with distinct political secularization. The Jesuit order was suppressed, the property of the Church confiscated, and the political and public rights of the Church restricted. This dominance of rather left-wing forces provoked strong right-wing opposition: together with the Liberal right-wing they succeeded in the 1933 elections in winning a majority in the "Cortes", the Spanish Parliament. The division into two opposed camps had assumed such proportions that the Government was virtually unable to operate. This facilitated the 1936 military uprising under the Spanish General Francesco Franco, and resulted in the bloody Civil War of 1936–1939. The General emerged victorious due to foreign military support from Fascist Italy and the National Socialist German Reich. From then on until his death (1975), Franco was dictator of Spain.

The republican system

Civil War

Since King Juan Carlos came to power, Franco's dictatorship, which lasted almost forty years, has undergone significant modifications. Immediately after his accession, King Juan Carlos changed the political course towards a representative democratic system. This is partly the result of the King's deliberate decision to bring Spain in line with the other constitutional democratic monarchies in Europe; but it must also be seen as an adjustment to new social and economic structures in Spanish society.

King Juan Carlos' politics

Stages in the Democratisation of Spain[1]

The first phase on the path towards democracy was the dissolution and "detachment" from the previous authoritarian political system. This was caused by the political leader's death.

Even in Franco's lifetime, however, the process of democratisation had been

Phase I: Detachment

191

initiated by Carlos Arias Navarro who tried to steer a cautious Liberal course following the violent death of his predecessor, Luis Carrero Blanco. On Franco's death, Navarro became Head of State and was able to concentrate fully on the realisation of his aims. The reformist groups of the former Government camp were then able to carry through the necessary steps towards liberalisation by out-voting the right wing of the Francoist movement.

**Phase II:
Preparation for
the transition**

The second phase was the new formation of the political elite. The first post-Franco Government under Carlos Arias Navarro included among others the reformist politicians Manuel Fraga Iribarne and Jose Maria de Arellza. Their political reforms envisaged more freedom and rights for the citizen, extended rights of assembly, and a reform of all existing parliamentary institutions aiming at greater representation and participation. On the whole, however, these were simply improvements to the existing political system. In April 1976, Navarro presented a programme of reform which envisaged a two-chamber system and a constitutional court of law. Furthermore, a time schedule was to be fixed for the holding of elections and the revision of existing electoral laws. A constitutional commission was formed; unfortunately, the activities of this commission were intentionally blocked by people opposed to reform. Although Navarro had the political power to do so, he was not willing to simply overrule these opponents and therefore had to resign.

**Phase III:
Transformation**

So began the third phase: its starting-point was Adolfo Suarez' accession to power in July 1976. He succeeded in forming a well-balanced Government which was not afraid of tackling the anti-reformists. An extensive amnesty was issued in August, aimed particularly at political prisoners. Professors who had been dismissed by Franco were again accepted by the Universities of Salamanca and Madrid. A Liberal military officer was appointed as the new Minister of Defence. He was also given the post of Vice-President to appease the military forces. Now events followed in quick succession. In January 1977, the "National Movement" (Movimento Nacional) which had comprised the older Fascist and Conservative political elite, was dissolved. The institutional reform was introduced on 4th January by the King in the "Law on Political Reform"; this Bill had been passed by the Cortes in November of the

Reform Bill

previous year and ratified in December by a referendum. 77.4% of the electorate had voted; of those, 94.2% voted in favour of the Reform Bill, 2.6% against and 3% abstained.

It has to be pointed out that the Bill did not go beyond the framework of the old Franco constitution and, from a purely legal point of view, did not violate the constitutional law of the authoritarian regime. It is true that the democratic opposition in Spain had called for a constituent assembly to establish a clear break with the old political system; but they had been too weak to force their demand through. The Suarez Government showed itself open to democratic change, and it no longer seemed necessary to make such a public demonstration.

The era of the corporate State had come to an end. Spain no longer wanted the socially classified representation of the "Cortes"; instead there was an acknowledgement of the principle of the people's sovereignty and the creation of the parliamentary organs based on general and direct elections. An essential condition for this was the establishing of a system of competing political parties.

It is worth noting that the transformation of the political system had been initiated by part of the old political elite from the authoritarian Franco State; this group had managed to dispossess the anti-reformists and reactionaries of their power, or at least to "neutralise" them for a while. The admission of parties in free competition created a basis for the pluralism essential to a democratic system. The parties were all formally registered.

The subsequent phases can be regarded as the "beginning of a democratic system" and the "consolidation of the democratic system". The former began with the elections of 15th June, 1977. Nineteen months after Franco's death, Spain had completed the transition to democracy. It now remains to be seen whether Spain is able to consolidate its position. The most pressing political problem is the settlement of the Spanish nationality problem. Up to now, the inhabitants of Castile, Galicia, the Basque country and of Catalonia have been prevented by the Spanish Central Government from realising their regional demands and wishes. A genuinely democratic State will have to take the various local interests into consideration and proceed in a way which protects the ethnic features of the individual regions and at the same time does not lead to insular attitudes.

Phases IV and V: Democratisation

Economic and Social Conditions

During the 1950's the economic development of Spain gave cause for concern. The growth of the Gross National Product per head of the population was well below that of comparable people's democracies (Poland, Yugoslavia) and that of Italy, another relatively underdeveloped country. However, since 1960 economic growth has rapidly accelerated at a rate which even exceeds that of Japan. Apart from the dramatic increase particularly in industrial production, Spain benefits financially from the fact that Spanish "guest-workers" (in Germany, for example) send all or part of their wages home, and tourism brings further foreign currency into the country.

Problems of growth

The social progress which should have gone hand in hand with economic advance is lacking in Spain. In the agrarian sector we find the greatest discrepancy in land distribution in the whole of Europe. The economy is dominated by some major banks, owned by a financial oligarchy of large landowners and aristocrats. The workers had lost all political power in the Franco era; their organisations, the trade unions, were suppressed. Only now is a proper representation of the workers' interests gradually beginning again. The general educational system is relatively poorly developed: in 1960, 13% of the adult population were still illiterate.

Social problems

Apart from the imbalance in the vertical social stratification, horizontal divisions play an important part in Spanish society and in the political system as a whole. Regional groups seeking political autonomy are to be found in Catalonia, the Basque region, Galicia and even in Castile. Franco's consistent policy of assimilation was in reality a failure; contrary to his intentions, it strengthened the bond between the various socio-ethnic groups and stimulated further efforts towards independence.

Regionalism

Possible solutions to this problem would appear to be either a radical separatism which excludes individual ethnic groups from the body of the State; or alternatively the gradual abolition of the centralism which has resulted from Franco's dictatorship.

Autonomy

A first step in this direction was the reinstatement of the Catalonian Generalidad (= a "general committee of Catalonia" with independent Government functions) at the end of September 1977. This committee was authorised to "put a Catalonian stamp" on financial affairs, jurisdiction, administration and cultural affairs on the condition of not endangering the unity of Spain. About 17% of the Spanish electorate live in Catalonia. At the moment, the left-wing forces possess a narrow majority. In October of the same year, formal negotiations began concerning the autonomy of the Basque provinces and Galicia.

The Party System

Variety of parties

The present party system comprises a multitude of political parties. According to the party register of 10th May, 1977, there are more than 250 different parties. In the elections of 15th June certain new structures became evident; and it seems generally safe to assume that a multi-party system of about 10–15 parties will evolve in Spain. A party system of only three or three and a half parties, as predicted by J.J. Linz, still seems a long way off.

Development

Historically, one can distinguish three groups of parties: (1) parties which existed before Franco, (2) parties which were founded during the Franco regime, and (3) parties which established themselves after Franco's death during the transition from an authoritarian regime to a democratic political system. The parties may be classified on the usual right-left spectrum.

Parties before Franco

The Socialist Workers' Party (PSOE = Partido Socialista Obrero Espanol) and the Communists (PCE = Partido Communista Espanol) date back to the era before Franco, that is, to the time of the 2nd Spanish Republic. During the Franco regime, they led a difficult existence underground and made their public political appearances as a party in exile. In the Spanish Civil War, they suffered severe losses among their leading figures, as both parties were at the centre of the Republican opposition against General Franco. Two other parties can look back on a long tradition. They are the PNV (= Partido Nacionalista Vasco), the Basque party which forms part of the Christian Democrat camp, and the Catalonian wing of the Communists, the PSUC (= Partit Socialista Unificat de Catalunya).

Franco Era

Two main political groups of the Franco regime can be distinguished: (1) the party groups which supported the authoritarian system, and (2) their political opposition.

Opposition groups

As far as the latter are concerned, the following groups have to be mentioned: (a) The Monarchists were originally to be found in the Falange camp; they became opposed to the system because of Franco's hesitation over the monarchy question. (b) Some dissidents from the national camp did not approve of Franco's politics. For example, dissidents who pleaded for a democratic, but not a Marxist socialist

194

society formed the Partido Social Democratica, which occupied a middle position in the party spectrum. (c) The Socialists did not wish to follow the directives of the exiled PSOE, as they regarded the latter's political concepts as too theoretical. They later produced the PSP (= Partido Socialista Popular). (d) Of the Christian Democrat groups, the Federacion Popular Democratica (FPD) was founded in 1958 as Democracia Social Christiana (DSC). The party was basically Monarchist and decidedly anti-Communist. The other Christian Democrat group worth mentioning is the Izquierda Democratica (ID) which from the beginning enjoyed good relations with all other opposition forces and showed itself relatively open to the underground Communist movement.

Groups faithful to the system

On the side of the regime, there were no parties in the proper sense as only the Falange movement was officially permitted. This Fascist mass movement was founded in 1933 by Primo de Rivera; during the Franco era it managed to penetrate the Spanish executive to a considerable extent. From the 1960's , the movement was split up into various groups. Outside the Falange, the Catholic organisation "Opus Dei" gained a certain influence through its cooperation with the regime.

New foundations after Franco's death

Further parties were founded during the post-Franco period of transition, some of which should be mentioned here. For example, the Partido Popular (PP) of Pio Cabanillas, a former Minister for Information who had become a dissident. Also the Centro Democratico which was organised by Adolfo Suarez to unite the Conservative and Liberal groups which were calling for democratic reform. They later became the Union del Centro. By contrast, a Francoist wing consisting of former ministers under the leadership of Manuel Fraga Iribirne initiated the Alianza Popular (AP = Popular Alliance). Initially, it showed reformist tendencies but today, due to the rapid changes in the Spanish political system, it belongs to the reactionary wing which is opposed to the new system.

Contemporary party system

The following table gives a breakdown of the party system at the time of the elections of June 15th, 1977:[2]

Block/Coalition	Associated Parties	Leading Politicians
Extreme Right (National Alliance of 18th July)	Fuerza Nueva	Blas Pinar
	Falange Espanola de las JONS	Nemesio Fernandez-Cuesta
	Ex-Combattants	Jose Antonio Giron
Alianza Popular	Reforma Democratica	Manuel Fraga Iribarne
	Union Nacional Espanola	G. Fernandez de la Mora
	Union del Pueblo Espanol	Cruz Marinez
	Democracia Social	Licinio de la Fuente
	Accion Democratica Espanola	Federico Silva Munoz
	Accion Regional	Laureano Lopez Rodo
Centro Democratico/ Union del Centro	Partido Popular	Pio Cabanillas Gallas
	Partido Democrata Cristiano	Fernando Alvarez de Miranda
	Federacion Partidos	Joaquin Guarrigues Walker
	Democratas Liberales	Enrique Larroque

Block/Coalition	Associated Parties	Leading Politicians
Christian Democrat Equipe of the Spanish State	Partido Liberal	
	Partido Democrata Popular	Ignacio Camunas
	Partido Social Democrata	Francisco Fernandez Ordonez
	Union Democrata Cristiana	Jesus Barros de Lis
	Federacion Popular Democratica	Jose M. a Gil-Robles
	Union Democratica de Cataluna	Anton Canyellas
	Union Democratica del Pais Valenciano	Alberto Ruiz Monrabal
	Partido Popular Gallego	Fernando Garcia Agudin
	Partido Nationalista Vasco	Julio Jauregui
	Izquierda Democratica	Joaquin Ruiz Jimenez
Social Democrat Alliance	Partido Socialista Democratico Espanol	Antonio Garcia Lopez
	Reforma Social Espanola	Manuel Canarero
	Partido Socialista Obrero Espanol (PSOE historico)	Manuel Murillo
	Federacion Socialdemocrata	Jose Ramon Lasuen
Socialist Union	Partido Socialista Obrero Espanol (PSOE)	Felipe Gonzalez
	Partido Socialista Popular	Enrique Tierno Galvan
	Federacion de Partidos Socialistas	Regionale Führer
Communists	Partido Communista Espanol	Santiago Carrillo
	Partido Socialista Unificado Catalan	Gregorio Lopez Raimundo

It is significant that the two right-wing blocks do not call themselves "party" under the old tradition of the Moviemento. On the basis of their political programme, they belong to those parties opposed to the system, whereas, or perhaps because, their supporters enjoyed considerable protection during the Franco era.

The Elections of 15th June, 1977

Right to vote

The new franchise law is based on the principles laid down in 1907.
1) Every Spaniard over 21 years of age possesses the active and passive right to vote.
2) Members of the Cabinet, high Civil Servants and members of the armed forces are excluded from voting.
3) All accepted political parties have free access to all mass media and may use public buildings for election meetings.

196

4) For the first time, the elections will be conducted in secret in voting booths.

5) Expenses incurred by parties and candidates during the elections will be refunded in proportion to the percentage of votes polled.

6) Each province delegates four representatives to the Senate who are chosen according to the majority system. The delegates are elected according to the system of proportional representation; each province is allocated a minimum number of seats, and the less populated rural provinces are given special consideration.

7) A party has to poll at least 3% of votes in order to be able to delegate a representative.

Election results

The Socialist Workers' Party (PSOE) emerged as the strongest single party in the elections with 28.6% of all votes. In spite of this, the Centre Union was the outright winner. Under the leadership of Adolfo Suarez, this party alliance won 31.1% of the votes. The alliance benefited further from the system of distribution of seats in Parliament and the Senate, as votes cast in rural areas (where the Centre Union is particularly popular) count more than others. In this way, the Union won 165 out of 350 parliamentary seats; whereas the Socialists, who polled 2.5% less votes, only obtained 118 seats. The Communists lagged far behind with 9.4%; the neo-Francoist Popular Alliance polled just 8.5%. The latter results demonstrate the unpopularity of the old political system and its representatives. The extreme right is no longer represented in the new institutional framework, whereas the Basque left wing, the independent Catalonian Centre and the Independent Aragonian Centre were able to secure one seat each in Parliament. The most important objective of the old and new Suarez Government is the creation of a new democratic constitution for Spain.

Notes

[1] The division into phases was taken from: Carlos Huneeus a. Dieter Nohlen : Der Regimewechsel in Spanien. In: "Die Buerger im Staat", Heft 2, 1977.

[2] Also taken from Huneeus/Nohlen, ibid, p.99. Some additions by the author.

IV. Comparison of National Party Systems in Europe

THEO STAMMEN

Individuality of national party systems

Constant features

The preceding sections aimed at presenting an individual picture of each national party system as it evolved under the prevailing historical, social and political conditions.

In this section these individual forms are systematically compared to consider whether certain constants or similarities can be detected. Such features might be an important basis for the creation of a uniform European party system.

1. Historical Conditions

The origin of parties in Europe

It has already been mentioned in the introduction that the various European political parties have followed an almost parallel course of development. This was due to the historical, political, ideological and social similarities in Europe; it is therefore not surprising that the various parties share a number of common features. This applies particularly to the Continental European parties. The British parties are somewhat of an exception in that they date back to the 17th century and the evolution of a functioning two-party system occurred during the 18th century, that is, during the period *before* the American and French Revolutions. The modern "face" of British politics only developed during the 19th century.

One may generally state that modern political parties evolved in Europe as late as the 19th century. They took shape at a time when the whole of Europe was experiencing a phase of total upheaval which may be seen politically as a consequence of the French Revolution, and economically and socially as a result of the Industrial Revolution.

a) Political Crises towards the End of the 18th Century

American & French Revolutions

Political movements

The following factors were most important to the emergence of political parties at that time. First of all, it is safe to assume that the formation of political parties in Europe was connected with a general *crisis of the political systems*. There were countless signs of this in the late 18th century, most dramatically expressed in the American and French Revolutions. It was ultimately a *crisis of legitimacy* for the old political order. The "Age of Enlightenment" and the French Revolution brought with them new political thinking which exerted considerable influence on the formation and differentiation of parties during the 19th and 20th century: Liberalism, Conservatism, Christian democracy, Radicalism, Socialism. These

198

ideologies may be regarded as common European phenomena in that they initiated new political movements, although obviously they assumed different national forms. If one considers this *common ideological root* of the European parties, one can understand why even today the profiles of the individual national party systems, and in particular the *party spectrum*, bear strong resemblances.

b) Middle Classes/Working Class

The process of economic and social development in the various European countries also contains marked similarities. The modern middle-class society evolved with its corresponding capitalist production process; then the social **Social** question arose with the advent of the working class and its struggle with the **question** established powers in State and society. These movements have produced comparable party developments which are mirrored in the close links between social classes and parties: middle-class (Liberal and Conservative) parties versus workers' parties (Social Democrat or Socialist; later also Communist).

c) Development of Democracy

The dominating form of constitution was first of all constitutional and later that of **Formation** parliamentary monarchy; in this system, parliaments together with their parlia- **of party** mentary delegate groupings gained increasingly in importance and initiated the **organisations** (at first parliamentary) formation of parties. This was followed by democratic development which manifested itself in the series of electoral reforms in the 19th century; these reforms necessitated extra-parliamentary party organisations to enable the mass of new voters to continually participate in the political process.

2. Social Conditions

a) Structural Conformities

The sections on the national party systems in Europe were aimed at elucidating the **Social** specific social (that is, social-structural, economic and cultural) conditions of the **development** individual party systems. One can see a significant number of structural conformities or similarities which are of importance with regard to the formation of European parties.

First of all, it may be stated that in comparison with non-European developing **Industrial** countries, all the European countries considered in this study have reached a **society** similar social, economic and cultural level of development. This is particularly true for the countries in Northern, Western and Middle Europe (perhaps with the exception of Ireland). It does not apply to the same extent to Southern Europe: Spain and Portugal, in particular, have a lower social and economic level of development as a result of their authoritarian regimes; and Greece and the southern part of Italy are also less developed for different internal reasons.

Otherwise the European countries can be classified as modern industrial societies which are characterised by largely analogous socio-structural conditions (class structure, social stratification) and highly dynamic social change. The social conditions in turn determine the differentiation of parties.

b) The Inherent Tension Between "Capital and Labour"

Economic
development

It is true that the Western European countries differ considerably as to their level of economic development; as their economic efficiency and productivity vary considerably. However, compared with the economic systems of the socialist world, all Western European countries ultimately correspond to *one* general type ("the capitalist economy"), which allows variation. On the basis of these economic structures, all the European countries considered in this book suffer from similar tensions between "capital and labour", that is, between the organised interests of workers and employers. This tension is reflected in party-political differentiation and the division of class-structured parties.

c) Cultural Background

The cultural background which influenced European party formation and which is strongly traditional does not vary very much in the countries studied, at least not regionally. For example, in all the Continental European countries the structure and social influence of religious denominations has had a strong and lasting effect on party structure.

We can see then how the social conditions of the European nations have created similarities in the national party systems and consequently the parties themselves. These conformities and similarities may be regarded as favourable prerequisites for the creation of all-European parties.

3. Political Conditions

Political
systems

Structural equivalents can be observed in the *political* sector even more so than in the social sector. The most general political condition of a party system is the structure of the given political system. The political systems of the European countries studied all follow the same tradition; they can all be classified under the term "Western liberal-constitutional democracy". This sufficiently characterises the general political framework which emerged in most of these countries as early as the 19th century; in a few countries – such as Portugal and Spain – it has replaced long-standing autocratic regimes only very recently.

Constituent
elements

The essential elements of this general type of political structure are that:
- it is based on a pluralist society and a corresponding social understanding;
- the (usually written) constitution acknowledges individual basic rights that existed before the State was founded and that are now guaranteed by the State;
- it is founded on the democratic principle of the people's sovereignty, that

200

political power is distributed for the purposes of limitation and control and the execution of political power is subject to examination and limitation.
— the people's political participation is safeguarded both through the direct election of Parliaments (representatives of the people) within the framework of a representative constitution, and through the appointment of Governments for a fixed period of time.

a) Variants in the Distribution of Power

The above general stipulations allow for a whole series of variants; one of the most obvious is the distinction between the various forms of parliamentary or presidential political systems.

Variants

With the exception of the French V Republic and Switzerland, it is true of all the countries studied that they have developed parliamentary systems in which a particularly close interplay between Parliament and Government exists (integration of powers). A closer look reveals that, apart from the British (original) model of the parliamentary system, modified versions are to be found in Western Europe. As a rule, the main difference lies in the varying distribution of power between Government and Parliament. The British type and its more faithful copies (West Germany) are now referred to as a "prime ministerial" or "chancellor" democracy — indicating the influence of the political leader. The more common Continental European version of parliamentary system, which is generally characterised by a multi-party form with the corresponding complexities of majority and coalition, suffers from a relative weakness and instability of Government and dominance of Parliament.

Parliamentary systems

By contrast, the French V Republic (after 1958) represents quite a special type of political system, where the position of the President vis-a-vis Parliament and the Government is extremely powerful. K. Loewenstein calls this "neo-presidentialism". Switzerland has a directorial system (which was taken from the 1795 Constitution of the French Revolution and is now unique). The directorial system with its particular historic and structural features can be classified as a presidential system.

Neo-presidentialism

Directorial system

b) The Emergence of Similar Party Structures

The fundamental structural similarities between most of the European political systems (as parliamentary systems) are mirrored in the similarity of status and function of the political parties and the structure of the party systems. As a rule, this finds its expression in equivalent forms of political interaction (for example, in the formation of coalitions). The party systems are normally of a pluralistic nature, containing two or more parties.

Similar party systems

Apart from these general conditions, the national party systems are influenced by more specific political determinants of which the electoral systems are doubtlessly the most important. One can state that in Europe (in those countries studied) the system of proportional representation is predominant; only Great Britain (relative

Electoral systems

majority system), France (absolute majority system) and the Federal Republic of Germany (personalised system of proportional representation with a minimum vote requirement) are the exceptions. The system of proportional representation is favourable to multi-party systems; this is corroborated by the evidence of most European nations. Multi-party systems are certainly predominant — apart from Great Britain (for the most part a two-party system) and West Germany (three party system). They create complicated and difficult conditions for interactions between parties, particularly in forming coalitions and Governments.

It can be assumed (and further analysis tends to confirm this) that political conditions in particular have long-lasting effects on the emergence of similar European party structures; so preparing the way for the formation of transnational European parties.

4. Constant Features of the National Party Systems in Europe

Attention can now be turned to those *constant features* of the national party systems which are important to the formation of transnational European parties.

Bearing in mind the concept of a future uniform European party system, the country descriptions in Part II can be considered from two general viewpoints:

Profile of the European party system

a) *Profiles of the National Party Systems*. The valid question is: can the integration of the individual national party systems lead to any conclusions on the probable profile of the future uniform European party system?

Quantitative distribution

b) *Quantitative representation or strength* of the individual party groups in Europe. The valid question here is: can the strength of the party groups in the future European party system be predicted on the basis of the parties' quantitative strength in the national party systems?

a) The Profile of the European Party System

European party spectrum

In order to be able to make any statements on the profile of a future European party system, a general party classification scheme is required. Such a scheme is not modelled on a single national party system, but gives equal consideration to all the European party systems studied.

Using the classic right-left classification scheme, the following party-political spectrum can be established. This "mould" is filled differently in the various countries, but it can house practically all the parties that exist in Europe.

1. Ethnic and regional minorities.
2. Extreme right-wing parties.
3. Conservatives.
4. Conservative-Liberals.
5. Christian Democrats.
6. Centre/Agrarian parties.
7. Radical-Liberals.
8. Social Democrats.

9. Independent Socialists.

10. Communists and associated groups.

If we try to fit the parties of the national party systems into this party-political right-left classification scheme (see figure below), we arrive at two kinds of conclusion. Firstly, some insight is obtained into the party spectrum of an individual country. Secondly, and this is more important for our purposes, the scheme reveals the general topography of the European party landscape.

Europe's Political Spectrum

(% of votes polled in the 1974 elections)

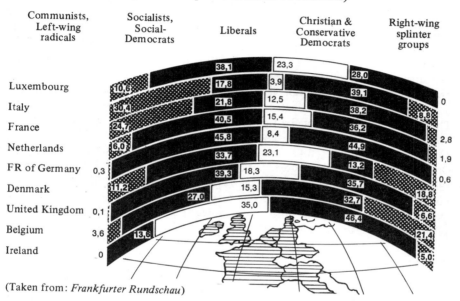

(Taken from: *Frankfurter Rundschau*)

An interesting picture of equivalents and non-equivalents between the national party systems and their elements (the parties) emerges from the above figure. It is easy to see whether a given national party is an isolated phenomenon (based on unique national factors) which only occurs in one party system, or whether such a party represents a national variant of a more general type of party found in other countries.

It is parties of the latter kind which will be of significance to a future European party system. The table shows certain "density zones" which indicate a disposition towards all-European parties: for example, in the case of the Communists, the Social Democrats, the Liberals, the Christian Democrats and, less clearly, the Conservatives. It is therefore to be expected that those political parties which play an active part in several or even all European countries will be the main contributors to the formation of transnational European parties.

Trend towards formation of European parties

Without wanting to draw premature conclusions, one can predict from these party constellations a rough profile of the future European party system. The nucleus of the European party system will consist of Social Democrats, Liberals and Christian Democrats; the Communists will establish themselves on the left wing, with the Conservatives on the right.

b) The Quantitative Ratios of Strength in the European Party System

The above classification scheme does not enable us to make any concrete statements on the ratios of strength of the various parties in a future European party system. The analysis of the individual systems has shown that the Liberals, for example, vary considerably in strength from one country to another; this applies equally to the other national parties. Furthermore, the party-political ratios of strength rarely remain constant over a long period of time. The future of the individual European party groups (a question which is of particular importance for the first direct elections to the European Parliament) has been estimated by projecting the national election results since the end of the 2nd World War onto a common (European) denominator and analysing them (see following figure).

The temporal dimension of the figure does not only enable us to make statements on certain quantitative ratios among the European parties, but also to give an assessment of probable future ratios of strength in the European party system. One can predict the ratios before those parties which will presumably play a leading role in a European party system: the Christian Democrats, the Liberals and the Social Democrats. It seems safe to assume that the Social Democrats and Christian Democrats will each get a third of the votes (parliamentary seats), whereas the Liberals will probably poll less than 10%.

5. Summary

This second part of our study was aimed at exploring the *national* conditions for the development of a *European* party system.

This was done in two steps. A section each was devoted to the presentation of the individual party systems of the nine EC countries and other Western European countries. It was intended to elucidate the individual particularities of the national party systems against their historic, social and political background.

Secondly, the national party systems were systematically compared in order to find out whether (and if so, which) *constant features* exist in the national party systems which might favour the emergence of a uniform European party system based on European parties.

We must now corroborate these assertions with fact. For it is only by examining more closely the already existing *transnational* connections between the national parties that one can make reasonably reliable statements on the configuration of a future European party system after the first direct elections to the European Parliament.

% of Votes Polled by the Political Parties in Europe 1946-1975

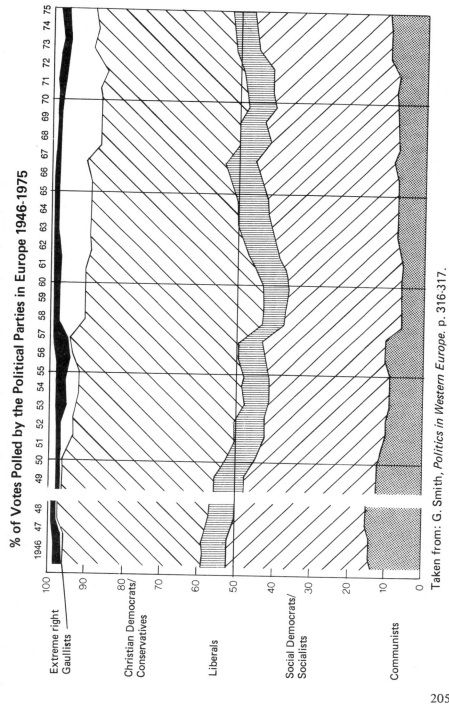

Taken from: G. Smith, *Politics in Western Europe*. p. 316-317.

205

Part III: Transnational Party Relationships in Europe.

THEO STAMMEN

I. Introduction

In the preceding part of our study we saw a number of similarities between the national parties and party systems in Europe. The historical, social and political factors which give rise to these may be regarded as *conditions* favourable to transnational European parties, but not more. **Existing party connections**

Genuine European parties will only emerge as a result of direct transnational relationships between national parties of similar or identical political beliefs.

Do such transnational connections already exist? If so, what is their nature, and how far advanced are they at present? Can they already be regarded as the beginnings of genuine European parties? These are the questions which require examination. **European politics**

It is necessary to distinguish between various levels of relations and treat them individually.

1. The first level is that of the *institutional* integration of national parties in transnational entities. An example of this are the *parliamentary groups* of the European Parliament. **Parliamentary groups**

2. The second level is that of the *organisational* connections between parties (of which some are already traditional) as established through the various "Internationals" since the end of the 19th century and which have reappeared (among the middle-class parties, too) after the 2nd World War. **Parties**

Similar questions have to be considered for both levels:

a) Firstly concerning the *structure* of these institutional or organisational transnational party connections.

b) Secondly, concerning their importance in the process of forming transnational European parties on the eve of the first European direct elections in 1979.

c) Finally, concerning their further effects on the formation of European parties and a functioning European party system.

All these aspects will now be dealt with in *four steps*:

1. To start with, each level (that is, institutional and organisational) will be outlined in its essential structures and problems.

2. A section each will then be devoted to the various parliamentary groups of the European Parliament on an *institutional* level.

207

3. Returning to the *organisational* level, the transnational connections between the most important party groups in Europe will then be discussed: The Social Democrat, the Christian Democrat, the Liberal and Communist groups.

4. In the final part, a critical evaluation is made of the already existing party connections on an institutional and organisational level with regard to their importance for the emergence of European parties. This summary will provide a stepping-stone for a final question concerning the outlines of a future European party system.

II. General Synopsis of Existing Transnational Party Relationships in Europe

One firstly has to realise that a number of transnational party relationships already exist in Europe. But for this, there would have been no realistic possibility of the parties playing a proper role — analogous to their national role — in the European political process.

It is furthermore important to note that these existing connections are to a large extent "by-products" of the process of European integration and are directly relevant to the policy of unification. This has resulted in the first significant steps towards forms of transnational cooperation between parties.

These steps can be observed on the two levels we have already distinguished:

1. On the *institutional level* of the European Parliament, where, since its early days, transnational *parliamentary groups* have been actively participating in parliamentary work;

2. On the *organisational level* of transnational party relations which, based partly on tradition, have increasingly developed since the 2nd World War.

1. The "European Parliament"

Apart from the Council (of Ministers) and the Commission, a (parliamentary) Assembly was one of the basic institutions of the European Communities. (Initially of the European Coal and Steel Community (1952), and later of the Euratom and the European Economic Community (1957). All relevant treaties contain the identical clause that the Assembly shall consist of "representatives of the peoples of the States brought together in the Community" and that these delegates "shall be designated by the respective Parliaments from among their members in accordance with the procedure laid down by each Member State".

a) Parliamentary Parties were always "Political"

Right from the beginning, transnational party connections (at first in the Assembly of the European Coal and Steel Community, later in the joint Assembly of the three European Communities) took the form of *parliamentary groups*. The delegates

208

to the Assembly of the CSC, which had been founded in 1952 as the first of the three European Communities, did not form national delegations but political groups. Some of these parliamentary units were transnational from the very beginning in as much as they included delegates from various EC countries.

When in 1957 the Assemblies of the three European Communities (European Coal and Steel Community, Euratom and European Economic Community) merged into *one*, namely the "European Parliament", the division and organisation into parliamentary groups was retained.

The *charter* of the European Parliament contains the following regulations on parliamentary groups (Article 36):

"1. The delegates may form parliamentary groups in accordance with their political beliefs.

2. A parliamentary group is officially formed as soon as the President of the Parliament has been informed of its foundation; the declaration has to contain its official name, the signatures of its members and the composition of the group's executive committee.

3. The declaration of foundation is published in the *Gazette of the European Communities*.

4. No one person may be registered on the lists of more than one parliamentary group.

5. A minimum of 14 members is required for the formation of a parliamentary group. It is possible to form a parliamentary group consisting of at least 10 members if they come from at least three different member countries."

Originally, three parliamentary groups with transnational features existed in the European Parliament: the Christian Democrat, the Socialist and the Liberal (and Allies). There were also some independent delegates.

The Liberals not only accepted members of Liberal parties but also groups such as the Italian Monarchists and French Gaullists. They grew to a considerable size but suffered internal instability and disharmony. In 1963, the French Gaullists left this parliamentary group when, after the Algerian crisis, de Gaulle's anti-European policy became more pronounced. Until 1965, the Gaullists did not belong to any parliamentary group; when they finally had 15 members, they formed a group of their own. The "European Democratic Union" however, consisted only of French members. The situation changed with the extension of the European Economic Community, that is, the accession of Great Britain, Ireland and Denmark in January 1973. The members of the Irish "Fianna Fail Party" joined the Gaullists, as their political opponents, the "Fine Gael Party", had already become a member of the Christian Democrat parliamentary group. A later addition to the "European Democrat Union" was the only representative of the Danish Progress Party. The parliamentary group became transnational and changed its name to the "Parliamentary Group of the European Democrats for Progress".

b) The Communists

In 1969 seven Italian Communists and two allied independent left-wingers entered the European Parliament. With other Communists from France, Denmark and the Netherlands, they formed a parliamentary group in the European Parliament in October 1973 under the name of the "Communists and Allies Group".

The "European Conservative Parliamentary Group", consisting of British and Danish Conservatives, also came into being in 1973. Although to an extent related to the Christian Democrats, the two groups have not merged because of their ideological differences.

There are today only a few members of the European Parliament who are unattached to these parliamentary groups. There are two members of Italy's national right wing, some representatives of particular regional parties (such as two members of the Walloon Collective Movement) and one member of the Scottish National Party. At present, they have no power in the European Parliament; but in future, in a larger and directly elected European Parliament, these regional parties may take on a considerable significance.

c) At present 6 Parliamentary Parties in the European Parliament

There are now 6 parliamentary groups in the European Parliament. Each group has more or less distinct transnational features; that is, they have developed transnational forms of cooperation between national party groups to a varying extent.

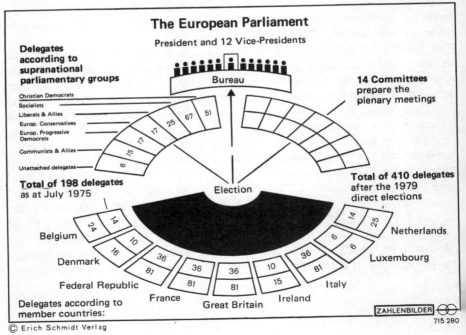

The European Parliament

President and 12 Vice-Presidents

Delegates according to supranational parliamentary groups

Christian Democrats
Socialists
Liberals & Allies
Europ. Conservatives
Europ. Progressive Democrats
Communists & Allies
Unattached delegates

Bureau

14 Committees prepare the plenary meetings

Total of 198 delegates as at July 1975

Total of 410 delegates after the 1979 direct elections

Election

Delegates according to member countries:

Belgium · Denmark · Federal Republic · France · Great Britain · Ireland · Italy · Luxembourg · Netherlands

ZAHLENBILDER
715 280

organisation were usually related to general, sometimes global party alliances, and were regarded as their regional sections.

c) Organisations

In this section the existing transnational party relationships and the organisational forms they take, are examined. It can be assumed that at present at least three relatively established organisational structures exist among:
(1) Social Democrats and Socialists, (2) Christian Democrats, and (3) Liberals.
1. In 1974, the Social Democrats and Socialists of the European Community formed the "Union of Social Democratic Parties in the European Community". The Union, which comprises 10 parties from all 9 member countries of the EC, regards itself as a regional sub-section of the Socialist International.
2. In 1976, the Christian Democrats founded in Luxembourg a "European People's Party – Federation of the Christian Democrat Parties in the European Community". Its members are Christian Democrat parties from 7 EC countries.
3. Also in 1976, the Liberals founded in Stuttgart the "Federation of Liberal and Democratic Parties of the European Community". So far, 14 parties from 8 EC countries have joined as members.
As far as the Conservatives are concerned, the "European Democratic Union" (EDU) was founded in April 1978, but does not represent a specific party alliance in the framework of the European Community.

III. European Parliamentary Groups

As mentioned earlier, at present the European Parliament consists of 6 parliamentary groups with distinct transnational features. These groups are examined more closely, on a structural level, in this section and consideration is given to their role in the decision-making process of the European Parliament. It is then possible to evaluate the contribution that these groups can make towards the development of transnational political parties in Europe.
The political role of the parliamentary groups in the European Parliament depends ultimately on the status of the European Parliament itself in the overall context of the European institutions (Council of Ministers, Commission, Parliament, Court of Justice). It has already been pointed out that the European Parliament is not yet able to play a proper role in the political process of the European Community (that is, interrelating with the Council of Ministers and the Commission) that might be compared to the role of national Parliaments. The European Parliament enjoys at present only limited powers, and there has been constant lobbying for an extension to its authority. The development of transnational cooperation between national parties was certainly made easier by the fact that the European Parliament did not possess the power to make important political decisions on its own. Such decisions might easily have become the cause of polarisation and confrontation between

2. The Organisational Aspects of Transnational Party Relationships in Europe

Transnational cooperation between national parties and the organisational form they take are based on different traditions.

As far as the (Social Democrat and Communist) workers' parties were concerned, the concept of internationalism (that is, cooperation beyond national boundaries) figured in their theoretical and actual programmes and resulted in the 1st and 2nd Internationals of 1864 and 1889. By contrast, the middle-class parties (Liberal, Conservative and others), took the national state as the "natural" frame for their theoretical and practical party-political activities up to the 20th century. As a result, no transnational party connections developed.

a) Different Starting Points

19th ct: Workers' movement and inter-nationalisation

The workers' movements of the 19th century (including the workers' parties as well as the trade unions) regarded as their primary objectives the liberation of the working man from the suppression and alienation that go hand in hand with capitalism. The movement held the firm belief that these objectives could only be attained by an international strategy, as the capitalist system of production was in itself an international phenomenon.

The non-socialist parties, on the other hand, identified with the nationally organised political systems until well into the 20th century. Immediately after the 1st World War, only individuals within the Christian Democrat movement (such as the Italian Luigi Sturzo) began to realise the necessity of international cooperation between parties of similar political orientation. On this basis, the first congress of Christian Democrat parties was held as early as 1925.

The 2nd World War and all its after-effects cast doubt on the validity and significance of the principle of the national state, particularly in Europe. It was only then, and under the pressure of the new East-West conflict, that the non-socialist parties took the initiative on European cooperation. It is a well known fact that the connections between the Christian Democrat parties in Europe in particular furthered and influenced the European policy of unification in its early stages.

b) New Forms of Cooperation

New Inter-nationals for all parties

Initially, there was a tendency to develop far-reaching, mostly world-wide "platforms" of cooperation between parties: corresponding "Internationals" were founded, congresses were held and manifestos issued whose high level of abstraction was inversely related to their practical political importance.

It soon became clear to those involved that international cooperation between political parties can only have practical consequences and success if it is practised in a regional context clearly defined by concrete problems and tasks. This led in almost all party-political camps to forms of transnational party cooperation which were geared to the specific problems of European integration. These new forms of

212

organisation were usually related to general, sometimes global party alliances, and were regarded as their regional sections.

c) Organisations

In this section the existing transnational party relationships and the organisational forms they take, are examined. It can be assumed that at present at least three relatively established organisational structures exist among:
(1) Social Democrats and Socialists, (2) Christian Democrats, and (3) Liberals.
1. In 1974, the Social Democrats and Socialists of the European Community formed the "Union of Social Democratic Parties in the European Community". The Union, which comprises 10 parties from all 9 member countries of the EC, regards itself as a regional sub-section of the Socialist International.
2. In 1976, the Christian Democrats founded in Luxembourg a "European People's Party — Federation of the Christian Democrat Parties in the European Community". Its members are Christian Democrat parties from 7 EC countries.
3. Also in 1976, the Liberals founded in Stuttgart the "Federation of Liberal and Democratic Parties of the European Community". So far, 14 parties from 8 EC countries have joined as members.
As far as the Conservatives are concerned, the "European Democratic Union" (EDU) was founded in April 1978, but does not represent a specific party alliance in the framework of the European Community.

III. European Parliamentary Groups

As mentioned earlier, at present the European Parliament consists of 6 parliamentary groups with distinct transnational features. These groups are examined more closely, on a structural level, in this section and consideration is given to their role in the decision-making process of the European Parliament. It is then possible to evaluate the contribution that these groups can make towards the development of transnational political parties in Europe.
The political role of the parliamentary groups in the European Parliament depends ultimately on the status of the European Parliament itself in the overall context of the European institutions (Council of Ministers, Commission, Parliament, Court of Justice). It has already been pointed out that the European Parliament is not yet able to play a proper role in the political process of the European Community (that is, interrelating with the Council of Ministers and the Commission) that might be compared to the role of national Parliaments. The European Parliament enjoys at present only limited powers, and there has been constant lobbying for an extension to its authority. The development of transnational cooperation between national parties was certainly made easier by the fact that the European Parliament did not possess the power to make important political decisions on its own. Such decisions might easily have become the cause of polarisation and confrontation between

different *national* viewpoints in the Parliament.

1. Parliamentary Groups in National Parliaments

Parliamentary groups functioning as political agents are well-known to us from our experience of national Parliaments, such as the German "Bundestag". As defined by the statutes ($10) of the "Bundestag", parliamentary groups are "factions of at least five out of every hundred members of the Bundestag who belong to the same party or to such parties which do not compete with each other for reasons of similar political objectives". Opinions differ on the legal status of parliamentary groups. Sometimes they are acknowledged as parliamentary organs; but mostly they qualify as unincorporated unions (coming under the civil law). They are also called "agents", and it is emphasised that "it is more fitting to regard parliamentary groups as constitutional entities *sui generis" (Handbook of German Parliamentarianism*, p. 149).

There is general agreement, however, on the political significance of parliamentary groups in contemporary Parliaments. These groups are essential elements of parliamentary activity which alone make it possible to cope rationally and sensibly with the complicated procedures of parliamentary deliberation and decision. Individual party delegates are integrated into functioning units that are vital to a proper cooperation between parties and Parliament. For these reasons, parliamentary parties today are generally acknowledged as parliamentary groups whose legal status as well as composition and rights are laid down in the statutes of the individual Parliaments.

2. Transnational Parliamentary Groups in the European Parliament

The parliamentary groups in the European Parliament are basically analogous to those in the national Parliaments; the statutes of the European Parliament contain norms for their structure and scope of activity. However, it is important to note that the parliamentary groups in the European Parliament do *not* consist of the members of *one* party (as is usually the case in the national Parliaments), but of various national parties which have merged into a parliamentary entity. This creates a *transnational* character to these groups, and at the same time cause them a number of practical and organisational problems.

Before we look at the individual parliamentary parties in detail, I should like to make a few general remarks on the status and function of these groups in the European Parliament.

3. Similarity of Activity

It may be generally stated that the 6 parliamentary groups in the European Parliament exert a decisive influence on the practical work of Parliament, as occurs on a national level. This becomes clear from various parliamentary customs, now firmly established, and from the procedural rules fixed in the statutes.

- Important debates in the European Parliament are as a rule opened by official spokesmen for the parliamentary groups (Stat. art. 31.2.2). Statutory norms
- The parliamentary groups are represented through their Chairmen in the enlarged presidency of the European Parliament; they thus gain immediate influence in the planning and structuring of parliamentary schedules and procedures (Stat. art. 12.1.1 and art. 28).
- It is furthermore important that appointments of committee leaders are distributed proportionately among the parliamentary groups according to their size.
- The parliamentary groups also designate those persons who are to report on the work of the committees before the plenum of the Parliament.
- Finally, the parliamentary groups are in a position to decisively influence the (annual) election of the President and the Vice-Presidents of the Parliament. Originally, the strongest parliamentary group appointed the President. Since 1962, his election has been decided through agreements between the groups and group coalitions.

4. Bridging Opposed National Viewpoints

It frequently occurs that in their internal sessions and discussions the individual parliamentary groups achieve genuine compromise between conflicting viewpoints of their member countries. This integrative effect can be regarded as an essential contribution towards the development of transnational European parties. In fact, cooperation between various national parties has been practised over a considerable period of time at parliamentary group level. This does not, of course, apply to the same extent to all parliamentary parties, as we have already seen. Transnational cooperation

The balancing interaction of the national parties frequently settles differences of opinion between the parliamentary groups of the European Parliament. As a result, parliamentary resolutions are often founded on a broad consensus between the parliamentary groups. The cooperation between parliamentary groups in the European Parliament has been likened to the "concordance" model of parliamentary settlement of conflicts, in contrast to the "competition" model that predominates in most of the national Parliaments (K.H. Nassmacher: *Demokratisierung der Europäischen Gemeinschaft*, 1972, p. 138 ff).

5. The Importance of Unity

It must be realised that the European Parliament, as it has little real power, is compelled to present a united front to the other institutions of the European Community, particularly the Council of Ministers which is the most powerful organ. The Parliament also has to actively promote European integration, and this requires that opinions and decisions in the parliamentary groups of the European Parliament are arrived at in an amicable way. Need for unity

A quotation from R. Bieber well sums up the importance of the parliamentary groups: "Today, the parliamentary parties represent the decisive elements of power in the (European) Parliament. However, the coherence and authority of a parliamentary party may not be judged by national criteria; in particular, the breadth of the joint political basis varies considerably". (R. Bieber: *Organe de erweiterten Europaischen Gemeinschaften: Das Parlament*, 1974, p. 143).

Despite the relatively intense and extensive cooperation between them, the parliamentary parties in the European Parliament must be considered as independent agents, and it is their individual features that we shall now examine.

IV. Presentation of Individual Parliamentary Groups

1. The Socialist Group

When the British Labour Party abandoned its boycott of the European Parliament and accepted the allocated seats, the Socialist parliamentary group became the strongest in the European Parliament, overtaking the Christian Democrats. At present, the Socialist group is composed as follows:

List of members

Great Britain:	Labour Party	Lab.GB	17
Germany:	Sozialdemokratische Partei Deutschlands	SPD	18
France:	Parti Socialiste	PS	6
	Mouvement des Radicaux de Gauche	RG	2
Italy:	Partito Socialista Italiano	PSI	5
	Partito Socialista Democratico Italiano	PSDI	1
Netherlands:	Partij van de Arbeid	PvdA	4
	Demokraten '66	D'66	1
Belgium:	Parti Socialiste Belge	PSB	3
	Belgische Socialistische Partij	BSP	1
Denmark:	Socialdemocratiet	S	3
Ireland:	Labour	Lab.IR	2
Luxembourg:	Parti Ouvrier Socialiste Luxembourgeois	POSL	2

Unity

The Socialist parliamentary group is the only one which comprises parties from all EC countries. The rapid growth (at present 63 members from 14 parties of 9 countries) has significantly affected the group character.

During the initial phase of European integration, the Social Democrat parties had all been in opposition in the six founding countries of the EC. They were thus unable to exert any significant influence on their Governments' decisions concerning European politics. After the foundation of the European Communities, however, the common Socialist parliamentary group in the European Assembly afforded them an important platform for voicing their opinions.

The Socialist group had to put up a united front in the Parliament to make full use of their position, and so developed "in the European Parliament into the politically

216

most coherent multi-national group with the best structured and differentiated organisation" (*Zusammenarbeit der Parteien in Westeuropa*, p. 175). A developed and efficient organisation as well as a homogeneous attitude towards parliamentary work was typical of the Socialist group from the very beginning.

It may also have been part of proven Socialist party tradition to build a stable and competent organisation for the parliamentary group. Two leading political organs in the group should be mentioned: on the one hand, the plenum which makes the most important decisions and has the essential role of integrating conflicting national viewpoints and forming an actionable strategy; and on the other hand, the parliamentary group's executive office. There are also internal institutions for the preparation of parliamentary work and intra-party voting. **Organisation**

The importance of the parliamentary group committees is twofold: they function as decision-making bodies in the various sectors of European politics; and they also serve to prepare the parliamentary group as a whole for the plenary debates.

The committees concern themselves continuously with political aspects that are of special importance: "Political questions and foreign affairs; economic and agrarian questions; finance, legal and budgetary matters; social problems and the environment." (*Zusammenarbeit der Parteien in Westeuropa*, p. 186).

A separate secretariat functions as an ancillary organ in all administrative matters; it also acts as a co-ordination office (founded in 1958) for the Socialist parties of the EC countries. In this dual capacity, it ensures an effective cooperation of the Socialist parliamentary group with the "Union of the Social Democrat Parties of the European Community".

In contrast to the other large parties in the European Parliament, the Socialist group has attempted since the early 1960's to establish a firm link with the transnational connections forged through the Socialist International. Its efforts to coordinate its policies on these two levels have meant "that, apart from its relatively united grouping in the European Parliament, the Socialist parliamentary group has been able to stimulate the cooperation of the Socialist Parties outside the Parliament". (*Zusammenarbeit der Parteien in Westeuropa*, p. 183).

The expansion of the European Community in 1973 was not entirely positive for the Socialist parliamentary group. In practical terms, there was the addition of further Socialist parties from the three new member countries. As the British Labour Party at first refused to send delegates to the European Parliament, the only new members of the Socialist group were the representatives of the Irish Labour Party and the Danish Socialdemocratiet. When the British Labour Party abandoned its boycott in 1975, the Socialist group became the strongest in the European Parliament. At the same time, however, much of its fundamental harmony was lost. **Role of the Labour party**

Today the Socialist parliamentary group is faced with "the conflict between the more North European Social Democrat parties with their pragmatic strategy of a social people's party, and the South European Socialist parties with their orthodox attitude of class war". This conflict was recently exemplified by a heated controversy over the cooperation between Socialist and Communist parties on a national **Conflict** and transnational level. The British Labour Party has brought the issue of pro- and anti-European Community into the parliamentary group; "this issue has already more than once proved an obstacle to group unanimity on decisions on integration policy". (Bangemann/Bieber: *Direktwahl*, p. 82)

2. The Christian Democrat Group

Apart from the Socialist and the Liberal parliamentary groups, the Christian Democrat group is among the oldest in the European Parliament. The first Christian Democrat parliamentary group was formed in 1953 in the "Consultative Assembly" of the European Coal and Steel Community. It then almost gained an absolute majority with 38 out of a total of 78 seats.

This was a period when the Christian Democrats were the governing parties and their distinguished leaders A. de Gasperi (Italy), R. Schuman (France) and K. Adenauer (Germany) took the decisive initiatives and decisions for the foundation of the European Communities and for the integration of Western Europe.

Until the British Labour Party abandoned its boycott, the Christian Democrat parliamentary group remained the largest and as such the dominating political force in the European Parliament. This was partly due to the fact that its members held fundamentally similar views on European integration and so initiated practical steps in that direction.

Composition

Before Great Britain, Ireland and Denmark joined the European Community, all 6 EC countries were represented in the Christian Democrat group with one or more parties. After the 2nd World War, the Christian Democrat parties had developed in almost all West European countries to become the dominant political force. At first, the Christian Democrat parties of the larger countries (Italy, France and Germany) played a corresponding role in European politics; but the party groups of the BENELUX countries also fought hard for European unification. In the 1960's, the French Christian Democrats, who were mostly organised in the MRP, lost almost all their importance and severely weakened French representation in the European Parliament.

Programme

Despite their common Christian basis, the European Christian Democrat parties differ considerably. Some are more right-wing, some are more socially and trade union orientated; as a rule, corresponding wings exist in all the national parties.

These sectional differences obviously have their effects on the stability of the European parliamentary group. It was partly the reason why the Christian Democrat parties did not form a joint group with the (British and Danish) Conservatives. The Christian Democrat parliamentary group laid down specific terms of membership, listing the Christian Democrat parties of the EC countries and insisting on adherence to basic Christian values (in contrast to the Liberal parliamentary group for example). Parties such as the Conservatives which did not wish to commit themselves in this way were not allowed to enter the parliamentary group. This held even if their political objectives, especially concerning European politics, were largely identical with those of the Christian Democrats; at the most, an informal cooperation was possible.

The Christian Democrat parliamentary group needed a well-developed organisation because of its large membership, and from the very beginning. Its organisation corresponded largely to that of the Socialist group on a structural level, but initially did not have the latter's homogeneity and efficiency. In the Christian Democrat group, the meetings of the parliamentary group are the centre of the political process. They "weigh possible differences in interests, filter national and ideological contrasts and achieve a compromise, ... The meetings serve to provide general information for the individual members. Thus the leaders of the parliamentary groups who are members of the Enlarged Bureau report on decisions taken by this body; the committee spokesmen report on the activities of the parliamentary committees. Basically, however, the meetings are dependent on the parliamentary agenda. The number of delegates taking part in the meetings varies according to the subject matter of parliamentary debate at that time" (N. Gresch: "Die supranationalen Fraktionen im Europaischen Parlament", in: *Zeitschrift für Parlamentsfragen*, 1976, p. 190 ff, here: p. 196/197).

The ultimate purpose of these sessions is to integrate the various parties and nationalities into the parliamentary group.

The parliamentary group leaders are of utmost importance to the strategy and life of the group. The Christian Democrat parliamentary group possesses the largest executive committee. It is subdivided into an inner (Chairman, two vice-Chairmen, and 7 members as spokesmen for the national delegations) and a *general* committee. The latter consists of 8 additional members who all hold offices in the parliamentary group (members of the parliamentary bureau, Chairmen of committees, and former parliamentary Presidents). The practical parliamentary work and its preparation and discussion within the parliamentary group all take place in the committees and study conferences of the parliamentary group. The committees have evolved parallel to the parliamentary committees. On the one hand, they help to prepare group opinion on the issues to be dealt with in the committees of the European Parliament; on the other hand, they inform the group on the activities and results of the committees and provide an information base for plenary debates and resolutions.

The teams of the Christian Democrat groups are concerned also with fundamental and long-term political subjects and problems. Over the past years, the following teams have been active: regional policy, financial policy, agricultural policy, development policy and future policy.

Extraordinary sessions of the entire parliamentary group, which as a rule take place twice annually in the member countries, are regarded as study days or conferences. On these occasions, basic problems of European politics are discussed in extenso, and furthermore the sessions are intended as a personal contact with the specific regional problems of the country in which the conference takes place.

As in the Socialist group, the secretariat of the Christian Democrat group is responsible for all the group's administrative matters: organisation of the group's

Organisation

Role of the leaders

Procedure

activities, public relations and preservation of contacts (for example with the transnational party organisations of the Christian Democrats in Europe).

At the time of writing, the Christian Democrat group comprises 52 members from the following parties and countries:

Belgium:	Parti Social Chrétien	PSC	2
	Christelijke Volkspartij	CVP	4
Germany:	Christlich-Demokratische Union	CDU	12
	Christlich-Soziale Union	CSU	4
France	Centre Démocratie et Progrès	CDP	2
	Réformateurs et Démocrats Sociaux	RDS	2
Ireland:	Fine Gael	FG	3
Italy:	Democrazia Christiana	DC	13
	Südtiroler Volkspartei	SVP	2
Luxembourg:	Parti Chrétien-Social	PCS	2
Netherlands:	Katholieke Volkspartij	KVP	3
	Christelijke Historische Union	CHU	1
	Anti-Revolutionaire Partij	ARP	1

3. Liberal and Democrat Group

Compared with the Socialist and the Christian Democrat parliamentary groups, the "Liberal and Democrat Group" has had the most difficulties in evolving a common means of organisation and programme.

Heteroeneity

Until recently, the Liberal group was officially called "Liberal and Allies Group"; this name is already indicative of the fact that, in the early days of the European Parliament, the Liberal group conceived of itself more as a "resting-place for delegates ranging from the Centre to the Right rather than as a parliamentary representative of Liberal politics". (Bangemann/Bieber: *Die Direktwahl*, p. 83). It attracted groups and individuals who wanted neither to belong to the Socialist nor to the Christian Democrat parliamentary groups. As a result the traditionally Liberal element was for a long time in the minority. For a while the French Gaullists and Italian Monarchists belonged to this group, and it became the second-largest (after the Christian Democrats) in the European Parliament from 1958 to 1963. However, its size (1959: 41 members) destroyed internal balance and harmony, and the heterogeneous composition of the group forced the abandonment of ideology and discussion of a common programme.

Greater homogeneity

Only gradually did a genuine Liberal group develop with a relatively balanced structure and at the same time greater political scope in the European Parliament, and, this development necessarily reduced the size of the group.

The development and consolidation was achieved in various stages. The break with the French Gaullists was the first significant event. It was connected with the anti-European course which de Gaulle steered in the early 1960's and which his party in the European Parliament had to follow.

220

The generally pro-European attitude which, despite all party-political and national differences, had until then existed in the European Parliament was suddenly put in question; and cooperation with the Gaullists in one parliamentary group was made impossible. The result of this conflict was the withdrawal of the Gaullists from the Liberal group in 1963.

Right-wing
borderline

Equally significant, but for different reasons, was the withdrawal of the only member of the Italian Monarchist Party in 1973. It was caused by a refusal to admit the newly elected representative of the Italian Neo-Fascists into the Liberal group. The Italian Monarchist resigned in protest. The importance of this was that for the first time in the history of the Liberal parliamentary group a specific united position on ideology and on a programme was adopted. Both events have increased the homogeneity of the Liberal group and strengthened it considerably.

The Liberals also benefited, in a two-fold way from the accession of Great Britain, Ireland and Denmark (1973) to the European Community. First of all, quantitatively; for it was joined by three new parties: two Danish Liberal parties and the British Liberal Party. Second, qualitatively; for with these new parties the genuinely Liberal element finally gained the upper hand in the parliamentary group.

Finally, more recently, the foundation of the "Federation of Liberal and Democratic Parties of the European Community" (1976) — (to be discussed later) — has contributed towards the integration of the Liberal parties in the European Parliament into a united and effective group.

The "Liberal and Democrat Group" (the new name corresponds directly to the "Federation of the Liberal and Democrat Parties") has 27 members which represent 14 parties from 8 EC countries (only Ireland is still not represented):

France:	Mouvement des Radicaux de Gauche	RG	1
	Réformateurs et Démocrats Sociaux	RDS	1
	Républicains Indépendants	RI	6
	Républicains Indépendants d'Action Sociale	RIAS	1
	Réformateurs, Centristes et Démocrats Sociaux	RCDS	1
Denmark:	Venstre Landforbund	VL	3
	Det Radikale Venstre Landforbund	RVL	1
Germany:	Freie Demokratische Partei	FDP	3
Netherlands:	Volkspartij voor Vrijheid en Democratie	VVD	3
Belgium:	Parti de la Liberté et du Progrès	PLP	1
	Partij voor Vrijheid en Vooruitgang	PVV	1
Luxembourg:	Parti Démocratique	PD	2
Great Britain:	Liberal Party	Lib.	1
Italy:	Partito Liberale Italiano	PLI	1
	Partito Republicano Italiano	PRI	1

It is a striking fact that the member parties of the Liberal parliamentary group are on the whole very small; 10 of them are only represented by a single delegate. This, of course, makes it more difficult for the group to present a united front to the

Problems
of size

European Parliament. The party organisation is less well developed than that of the Socialist and Christian Democrat parliamentary groups. The Liberal group does not have any committees; rather working groups and study conferences. These have so far only been held on an *ad hoc* basis and "have made hardly any attempts at long-term political planning" (N. Gresch, *Die supranationalen Fraktionen*, ibid, p. 200). Three topical issues have been discussed so far: "Trade Unions and Co-Determination in Europe; European Institutions; A European Defence Policy". The Liberal group also has a secretariat which deals with general internal matters. Until now it has not concerned itself with relations between the Liberal parties within the European Community but this may well change following the foundation of the "Liberal Federation". The Liberal group uses its study conferences to understand and deal with the more general and fundamental problems of European politics and the individual European regions.

4. European Progressive Democrats

The remaining three parliamentary groups of the European Parliament differ considerably from those discussed so far. First of all, they are much smaller: with 17 members each, they just meet the minimum number of delegates required in the statutes of the European Parliament for the formation of independent parliamentary groups (15 members). Also, they are all much newer: they were founded after the accession of Great Britain, Ireland and Denmark to the European Community in 1973. Finally, and this is the most important difference, their transnational character is considerably less pronounced. They contain only a few parties from a small number of member countries.

A good example of these features is the "Group of European Progressive Democrats" which we shall examine first.

This group came into existence in 1973 when the French Gaullists joined the Irish Fianna Fail Party. A little later, the only member of the Danish Progressive Party in the European Parliament joined as well.

Role of the Gaullists

It has already been mentioned that the French Gaullists (UDR) had belonged as an "Allies group" to the Liberal parliamentary group from 1958 (the year that General de Gaulle came back to power and the V Republic was founded in France) until 1963. Because of their size and political unity, they had formed a unit within the parliamentary group. The controversy over de Gaulle's European policy had finally led to the withdrawal of the Gaullists from the Liberal group. In 1965, with 15 delegates in the European Parliament, they reached the required minimum and founded an independent group. Consisting only of parliamentarians of one party from one country, the "European Democratic Union" was rather untypical; in the de Gaulle era it became the mouthpiece of his European policies in the European Parliament.

After the French elections in 1973, the Gaullists no longer had the necessary number of delegates for the constitution of a group of their own. They were forced to seek partners, and it so happened that the representatives of the Irish

Fianna Fail Party which was new in the European Parliament had not yet committed themselves to a particular group. Together with the Irish delegates of the Fianna Fail and a representative of the Danish Progress Party, the Gaullists formed a parliamentary group called "European Progressive Democrats". It had 17 members from the following national parties:

France:	Gaullists	RPR	11
Ireland:	Fianna Fail	FF	5
Denmark:	Fremskridtspartiet	FRP	1

The French Gaullists are still in the majority; only a few parties and countries are involved and the group has few transnational features. The fact that the representatives of these particular parties have united to form a parliamentary group is more the result of a chance party configuration in the 1973 European Parliament than that of a clear party-political option. There is no fundamental agreement between the Gaullists and the Irish Republicans on policy which might justify their cooperation.

5. European Conservative Group

Until the expansion of the European Community (1973) no Conservative parliamentary group had existed in the European Parliament. It was only with the accession of Great Britain and Denmark that traditional Conservative parties entered the Parliament and were faced with the problem of fitting into the existing parliamentary groups.

One might have assumed that these new parties would have tried to join the already existing large group of the Christian Democrats as they largely agree on political objectives, particularly concerning European policies. The reasons for the failure of such a coalition have to be looked for in the conflicting ideologies of the partners. The left wing of the Christian Democrats was principally opposed to a union with the Conservatives. The Conservatives from Northern Europe, on the other hand, were reluctant to join a group whose programme constantly mentioned a "Christian conception of man and society" and "Christian principles" as its political base. The British Conservatives may have feared that they would not have been able to play an effective and independent part in the European Parliament if attached to a group which was dominated by the Italian Christian Democrats and the German CDU/CSU.

Special role of the Conservatives

So the union never took place; instead, a separate Conservative parliamentary group was founded. At first it contained 20 members from three parties (two Danish and one British party). Since then the number of delegates has sunk to 17, and the group is composed as follows:

Great Britain:	Conservative Party	Cons.	16
Denmark:	Centrumsdemokrater	CD	1

The British Conservatives quite clearly enjoy an overwhelming majority. Despite the one Danish member, the parliamentary group cannot be called truly trans-national. The fact that the group is almost solely composed of British members has often meant that it has spoken purely for national interests, particularly on matters of European agrarian policy.

On a more general parliamentary level, however, a relatively close but officially informal cooperation between the Conservative group and the Christian Democrat group has developed since 1973. One of the by-products of the first European direct elections may be a closer nexus between the Conservatives and the Christian Democrats.

6. The Communist and Allies Group

The third and last small parliamentary group is that of the "Communist and Allies". It is one of the very new groups: founded in 1973, it now has 17 members.

One has to be aware that there have been Communist delegates in the European Parliament since 1969. At that time, the Italian Parliament changed its views on Communists as national representatives in the European Parliament: they were no longer excluded. Seven members of Italy's Communist Party (KPI) and two associated independent left-wingers entered the European Parliament.

The Communists also benefited from the expansion of the Community, although only to a moderate degree; they were joined by a member of the Danish Socialist People's Party. After the French elections in March 1973, four members of the French Communist Party (KPF) were sent as delegates to the European Parliament. So by the summer of 1973, the number of Communists and related groups had increased to 14.

In October of the same year, the statutes of the European Parliament were altered; Article 36 now stipulated that "a parliamentary group (can be) ..... formed with at least 10 delegates if they come from at least three different member countries". The Communists and related groups thus acquired the status of a parliamentary group in the European Parliament with the corresponding rights of representation. For a while the group was also joined by a member of the Dutch Communist Party.

In the 1976 Italian parliamentary elections, the Communists gained a considerable number of votes; their number in the European Parliament increased to 11 members. At present, the Communist group consists of 17 members which represent four parties from three countries as follows:

Italy:	Partito Communista Italiano	PCI	11
	Independente di Sinistra	Ind.Sin	1
France:	Parti Communiste Français	PCF	4
Denmark:	Socialistik Folkepartei	SFP	1

The Italian Communists are clearly in the majority in this parliamentary group.

224

They were the first West European Communist party to abandon its totally negative and deprecatory attitude towards the EC (regarded as an institution of the Cold War and of NATO imperialism). Since the end of the 1960's, they have sought to maintain a realistic but critical attitude towards the EC and its institutions. In this way they have interpreted their role in the European Parliament as that of a conservative opposition, seeking further developments along the lines of Communist democratisation; and they have acted accordingly in the plenum and committees of the European Parliament. They were for some time in favour of holding European direct elections; although in January 1973, when the matter was voted on in the European Parliament, they abstained for practical political reasons.

By contrast, the French Communists have adhered much longer to their negative **Obstructions** attitude towards the European Community. The reasons were partly Marxist, partly national (analogous to the French Gaullists). The French Communists have only recently changed their standpoint in a way similar to that of the Italian Communists, but as yet not quite so advanced.

It is interesting to note that the French and the Italian Communists have both sent a member of their Central Committee as leading delegate to the European Parliament (Gustave Ansart; Giorgio Amendola). This indicates clearly that they now value their presence there relatively highly.

There has been a recent rapprochement between the KPI and KPF on a "Euro- **Differences** Communist" level. Nevertheless it would be premature to say that the Communist group of the European Parliament represents a united and homogenous unit. It is not so much that it contains so-called "Allies" groups; but there are still differences on European politics between the Italian and French Communists. It is for this reason that the Communist group in the European Parliament still has to be regarded as a "difficult group". (K.H. Buck: "Die Haltung der KPI und KPF gegenüber Direktwahl und Funktionen des Europaparlaments", in: *Zeitschrift für Parlamentsfragen*, 1976, p. 209f).

7. Delegates Without Attachment to a Parliamentary Group

By far the majority of the delegates in the European Parliament are included in the six groups studied. In the old Parliament, there were five delegates without attachment to any particular group; a brief outline of their political positions is given below.

Two of these five delegates belong to the Italian "Democrazia nazionale", a right- **Outsiders** wing union of the Neo-Fascists and the remaining Monarchists. It has already been pointed out that for some time the Italian Monarchists were a member of the Liberal (and Allies) group; in 1973, they withdrew from this group when a newly elected Neo-Fascist was refused admission. Since that time, the two Italian delegates have represented a politically insignificant splinter group in the European Parliament.

More interestingly and perhaps more importantly for the future party developments in Europe are the other three unattached delegates. Two of the three belong to the Belgian "Front Démocratique des Francophones – Rassemblement Wallon" (FDF-RW), the third delegate is a member of the Scottish National Party (ŚNP). Both are regional parties whose importance has greatly increased in various European countries. It would be wrong to underestimate the importance of such parties in **Regionalism** the first direct European elections, for: "In a directly elected Parliament, which represents all strata of the population and as such all regional elements through an increased number of representatives, these representatives might possibly unite, unless the classic parliamentary groups show themselves more open to regional concerns within the European Community in order to avoid fragmentation." (A. Kohler, in: *Das Parlament*, No. 49, 4.12.1976, p. 10). It is astonishing that, in an age of increasing transnational connections, there is a continually growing emphasis on regionalisation.

Literature

M. Bangemann/R. Bieber: Die Direktwahl – Sackgasse oder Chance, 1976
R. Bieber: Organe der erweiterten Europäischen Gemeinschaften: Das Parlament, 1974
European Parliament (Ed.): Bulletin 1977/78: List of Members, June 1977
J. Fitzmaurice: The Party Groups in the European Parliament, 1975
A. Jüttner/H.J. Liese: Taschenbuch der europäischen Parteien und Wahlen, 1977
Zeitschrift für Parlamentsfragen, Heft 2, 1976
Zusammenarbeit der Parteien in Westeuropa, 1976
"Das Parlament", Special edition (No. 49, 4.12.1976)

V. Transnational Party Relationships

The previous part was devoted to the presentation of the *institutional* party connections as they have resulted from the cooperation between the transnational parliamentary groups of the European Parliament. The following pages are concerned with the description of the *organisational* connections between the European parties in the form of party alliances and federations.

Development Organisational connections have only really developed over the past few years. It is true that transnational party connections in the form of the various "Internationals" or analogous groupings existed before the 2nd World War; as a rule, however, they were conceived of as world-wide phenomena without any effective organisation.

There has, therefore, been a good deal of inter-party activity aimed at developing genuine European parties. These new transnational party connections are of particular interest; but consideration is given to other informal and formal party connections that have existed since the end of the 2nd World War and that can be seen as the precursors of transnational groups.

Here, as always, it is the main concern to examine whether and, how far these transnational connections between European parties can be considered as a platform for the formation of genuine European parties and a corresponding European party system.

Union of Social Democrat Parties in the European Community

Member Parties:

BSP/PSB (Belgium); Socialdemocratiet (Denmark); SPD (Federal Republic of Germany); PS (France); Labour (Ireland); PSDI and PSI (Italy); LSAP/ POSL (Luxembourg); PvdA (Netherlands); Labour (United Kingdom); Social democratic and Labour Party (Northern Ireland).

Organisations with Observer Status:

Study groups of the Social Democrat Women;
European Young Socialists;
Commission of the Socialist Teachers in the European Community;
Northern Ireland Labour Party (NILP);
Partido Socialista (PS — Portugal);
Partido Socialista Obrero Espanol (PSOE);
Israeli Workers' Party.

Secretariat:

Brussels and Luxembourg

Organs:

— Executive Committee
— Congress

Study Groups: (for the direct elections to the EP and its Presidents)
— Foreign Affairs (Bruno Friedrich)
— Economic Policy (Michel Rocard)
— Social Policy (Lionello Levi-Sandri)
— Democracy and Institutions (Schelto Patijn)

1. Socialist and Social Democrat Parties

HERBERT MAIER

HERBERT MAIER

Necessity of cooperation

Transnational cooperation between Social Democrat and Socialist parties has always featured in their programmes. Today, at a time when national solutions are often no longer satisfactory for reasons of various economic, political and social interdependencies, cooperation has become essential. European integration and the creation of new European institutions has put a new stamp on the old internationalist movement of socialism. On the one hand, industry and commerce can operate within the EC under uniform conditions. Their social counterpart, however, the trade unions and the working-class parties, are not united in the same way. They can only be active on a national level and are thus put at a disadvantage.

The 2nd International

2nd International

After the 2nd World War, the first step towards establishing cooperation between the Social Democrat parties was the holding of the 2nd International which was intended to continue where the 1st International (1889-1914) had left off. At a conference in Frankfurt from 30th June — 3rd July 1951, Socialist parties from 30 countries all over the world issued a joint declaration on the tasks and objectives of democratic socialism. The starting point of this declaration was the sharp and clear rejection of all capitalist systems; the commitment to a social order based on social justice, welfare, freedom and world peace; and a clear separation from communism and its totalitarian tendencies.

Although the formal Frankfurt statement of intent conveyed an impression of homogeneity and a uniform ideology, it was of little practical importance politically. As a rule, the individual parties' political activities were determined more by their own national phenomena and the party's status in the political system than by declarations of intent on an international level. The situation was further complicated by the impending split of Europe's Socialist parties into Marxist socialist and people's parties.

Structural problems

At the same time, structural difficulties arose for several reasons. As the Socialist International comprised parties from all over the world, there was an inherent heterogeneity. This was frequently marked by a collision of national interests, as, for example, in the case of the Israeli, Egyptian or Syrian Socialists who bring their specific conflicts into the International. The International will therefore scarcely be able to operate as an instrument for the solution of practical political problems; instead, its function will be restricted to the exchange of opinions and

228

the exposure of general social problems.

A closer form of cooperation would at least require a minimal geographical proximity of the parties and mutual economic and cultural relations without deep divisions. The European Community fulfils these conditions *par excellence*. However, it still lacks one important ingredient: the parliamentary power of a supranational legislature. Political parties have the general function of working out political objectives and political programmes and striving for real political power in the framework of a competitive system. The European Community has up to now lacked a corresponding organ, a voice of supranational opinion; the elections to the European Parliament certainly represent an important step in this direction. The Assembly of the European Coal and Steel Community, the Assembly of the West European Union and the European Parliament have been able to take over this role on a provisional basis, so becoming a significant element in the development of transnational party connections in Europe.

The Socialist and Social Democrat parties in Europe benefited from their relatively homogeneous ideology which provided an initial framework for cooperation. The institutions mentioned in the preceding paragraph necessitated forms of cooperation which were rather narrowly based on parliamentary activity, and which resulted at first only in the formation of Socialist and Social Democrat parliamentary groups. Of these the Socialist group is today the most important in the European Parliament. However, the necessary link between the parliamentary groups and the individual national parties was missing.

Following the initiative of the Socialist parliamentary group, a conference of the Socialist parties in the then European Steel and Coal Community was called in 1957. The Federal Republic of Germany was represented by the German Social Democrat Party (SPD), France by the "Section Française de l'Internationale" (today PSF: "Parti Socialiste Française"), Belgium by the "Parti Socialiste Belge" (PSB), Holland by the "Partij van de Arbeid" (PvdA), Luxembourg by the "Parti Ouvrier Socialiste Luxembourgeois" (POSL) and Italy by the "Partito Socialista Democratico Italiano" (PSDI). In cases where one country possessed more than one Socialist party, only the party with membership of the 2nd International attended. The conference was aimed at establishing a common platform for public action and developing joint concepts for the impending European Economic Community.

"Link Bureau" for the Socialists of the EC Countries

Those Socialist parties that had convened in Luxembourg assured the Socialist parliamentary group of their support. To establish permanent contact between the parties, they decided to found a "Link Bureau" which was to meet at least twice a year, and which would have one permanent representative from each party. The quick agreement among the parties in Luxembourg was ultimately a result of the German Social Democrats' change of opinion on the European question. Until the late 1950's, they had adopted a sceptical view on Western integration and the

229

"little Europe" of the capitalist countries. At the Luxembourg conference, the constitution of the European Economic Community was regarded as unfavourable to the development of a socialist European Community, but it was finally accepted that it would not rule it out altogether.

The newly established "Link Bureau" illustrated its close ties with the Socialist parliamentary group through the fact that the group's executive committee became a permanent part of the Bureau; at the same time, there was a strong bond between the Bureau's and the group's secretariat. The Luxembourg conference was to meet every two years as the "Congress of the Social Democrat Parties in the European Community". The rapid development of economic integration soon led to more frequent meetings. Between 1958 and 1960 the conferences were mainly concerned with the drafting of a joint agrarian programme. At the 5th Congress in 1962, a "Common Action Programme for the Social Democrat Parties in the European Community" was passed.

The general crisis of the EEC in the mid-1960's resulted in a break-down of Congress work. Nevertheless the primary objectives were not totally forgotten. The Socialist parties were in favour of a single body, that is, a fusion of the three treaties (ECSC, EEC and Euratom); called for uniform institutions; and demanded the direct election of the European Parliament. Furthermore, the EEC was to be extended to those countries which, politically and economically, were in a position to honour the treaties of Paris and Rome. Foreign affairs, defence and cultural policies were to be transferred as quickly as possible to the European Community. In 1971, the Congress met again for the first time in five years. This 8th Congress was dominated by the problem of creating a supranational structure of all European Social Democrat forces. The Dutch Socialist Alfred Mozer was responsible for drawing up a report with suggestions for forms of future cooperation. As a minor reform, the "Link Bureau" changed its name to "Bureau of the Social Democrat Parties in the Community" in order to indicate more clearly that the cooperation should not be restricted to the Socialist parliamentary group but developed towards a supranational party body.

"Union of the Socialist Parties in the European Community"

New approaches

Mozer presented his paper at the 9th Congress in April 1973. The paper was not discussed during the conference itself, but referred to the individual national parties for debate. In autumn 1973, a team from Holland, Denmark, France and Germany began to draft a resolution concerning the restructuring of cooperation between the Socialist parties in the Community. They envisaged transforming the "Bureau" into a "Union of the Socialist Parties in the European Community" which was to have the authority to make binding decisions even for the national parties.

On 5th April, 1974 the Union was constituted in Luxembourg; the cooperation between the parties entered a new phase. Wilhelm Dröscher,[1] a member of the executive committee of the German SPD, became the Union's Chairman, his deputy

230

was the former Vice-President of the EC Commission, Sicco Mansholt. The Union's major task was seen as elaborating joint statements for the direct elections, as well as the development of transnational decision procedures for the definition of the Union's own powers.

In the meantime a Union office was opened in Brussels. The Union contains 10 Social Democrat or Socialist parties of which 7 share Government responsibility. The Federal Republic of Germany, France, Italy and Great Britain send 18 delegates each from their corresponding parties, Belgium and the Netherlands send 7 each, Denmark and Ireland send 5 each, and Luxembourg sends 3 delegates. In addition to that, every country which belongs to the Union sends 2 delegates, and there are also a certain number of party delegates from the European Parliament. It can be considered as a weakness in the Union that the individual delegates may not act independently and only subject to a party conference: they are essentially links to the various party executive committees.

Reasons for the Slow Development

Despite the Union, international cooperation on a party level has only developed very slowly and hesitantly. There are several reasons for this: **Obstacles**

1. A close alliance of Socialist parties and the creation of a genuine supranational decision-making committee involves a loss of power for the existing party élites.
2. The larger Socialist parties have to accept considerable limitations on their freedom of political action. This restriction applies in particular to the SPD and the British Labour party.
3. Fundamental political differences between the individual Socialist and Social Democrat parties have not yet been overcome. The national parties are highly individualistic and there are significant differences of understanding on the nature of a socialist economy, particularly on the subject of co-determination.
4. There are still considerable regional differences in the political attitudes and activities of the various parties' supporters. This goes hand in hand with a broad spectrum of political objectives and plans which include both radical concepts and moderate suggestions for reform; for the moment, it seems impossible to establish a clear political line by means of majority decisions in the common European party body of the Socialists.

Objectives of European Socialist Politics

Despite the difficulties and problems mentioned, the following objectives of European Socialists are apparent:

1. A desire for social equality, and the support of long-term projects in European countries to bring this about. **Basic programme**
2. Support through the EC for Third World countries in order to support their economic and social development.
3. Securing full employment within the EC and the elimination of regional econo-

mic differences.

4. Educational policies which bring about equal opportunity.

5. The improvement and conservation of the environment.

6. The democratisation of the European economy, and the development of uniform and socially balanced financial policies.

Apart from the formal level of party connections discussed so far, we naturally have to consider the informal cooperation that exists. A good deal of information is fed through the parties' contact committees. They collect information, and forward it to their own party as well as to their contact party. The committees also prepare meetings of the party Chairmen. Such meetings are usually devoted to the discussion of important topical issues. Various contact circles can be distinguished: there are the Socialist parties of Switzerland, Austria, Finland and Sweden : in other words, parties from the neutral countries in Europe. Another group consists of the Social Democrats from West Germany, the Scandinavian countries as well as Great Britain and Austria. Close cooperation between the Scandinavian parties is of particular importance. Of importance also are regional conferences which meet formally under the auspices of the 2nd International. In the Alpine area, for example, a group was formed of German Social Democrats, Austrian Socialists, Swiss and Italians. The main topics of these regional conferences have been the problems of "guest workers", regional trade and transport connections, questions of large-scale area planning and support for the borderland regions. In addition an international youth organisation of the Socialist parties exists; but, politically, it is of little importance.

Connections only at the Highest Party Level

It is a striking fact that these informal connections between the Socialist and Social Democrat parties are restricted to the higher party levels. They are only rarely formalised in party statutes. Essentially they are an exchange of insider information which can be of great importance for the parties concerned, but leaves the party base completely unaffected.

The parties' tasks

It is left to the parties' executive committees to either draw political conclusions from the information obtained or to simply file it away. It seems probable that the development of a "European Social Democrat Party" is unlikely in the near future. The individual national parties are confronted with far too weighty problems of their own; and in those countries where Socialist or Social Democrat parties share Governmental power, policies will continue to be dependent on the domestic constrictions of the political system.

The difficulties in cooperation can be highlighted by the position in the Federal Republic of Germany. If a strong CDU/CSU opposition makes the fight against Communism its central political objective, it is not possible for the governing Social Democrats, who are also committed to this, to take a different line. This being so, a uniform Socialist Party of Europe would not be able to brush the problem under the carpet by means of a majority decision. It is probable that various strong wings would develop; ultimately, the consensus between the parties might be so small that the party would be put in a situation of permanent instability. To take another example: the French Socialists who have chosen the posture of popular front and alliance with communist policies in the pursuit of political power cannot be prevented from doing so by a supranational decision. As we have seen in the description of the party systems of the various European countries, the national Socialist parties are frequently split internally into distinct wings. This could lead to bizarre coalitions on a supranational level.

Common Election Platform

Transnational cooperation is mutually dependent on the development of European integration in general. An adjustment of political structures and economic situations in all EC countries will be a prerequisite for further cooperation. At the same time, the individual national parties will have to discuss European problems on a broader basis within their own units. The German SPD has already made a first step in this direction: at their party conference in Hanover in 1973, they decided to form a European commission which was supposed to work out an overall conception of Social Democrat European politics by 1975. Important from an organisational point of view, this commission included the party's executive committee and delegates from the various party districts.

The Socialist and Social Democrat parties have further succeeded in drafting a joint **Election** election platform which was passed on 6th June 1977, in Luxembourg under the **platform** title "Social Democrats on the Path to Europe — An Election Platform". A further reciprocal effect may be expected from the fact that national Governments increasingly transfer decision-making powers to European bodies. As intra-state processes diminish, the parties will have to become more open to transnational cooperation if they wish to maintain their political influence.

European People's Party (EPP) — Federation of Christian Democrat Parties in the EC

Founder Members:
CVP/PSC (Belgium); CDU/CSU (Federal Republic of Germany); CDS (France); Fine Gael (Ireland); DC, Südtiroler Volkspartei (Italy); PCS (Luxembourg); ARP, CHU, KVP (Netherlands); CD Group of the European Parliament.

Seat of the Party:
Brussels

Organs:
- Congress
- Political Bureau
- Executive Committee

Committees:
Programme commission (responsible for the elaboration of a programme for the European elections).

2. Christian Democrat Parties

RAINER KUNZ

Cooperation between the various Christian Democrat parties developed relatively late. The very first steps were taken in the 1920's by the "Partito Populare Italiano" under their founder Luigi Sturzo who tried to enter into cooperation with the German Centre and the Bavarian People's Party. These relations remained tenuous and were not formalised.[1] The developments in Germany and Italy following the rise to power of the Fascists and National Socialists soon put a stop to the activities of the Christian Democrat parties, and a new beginning was only possible after the end of the 2nd World War. In 1945, Christian Democrat parties were founded or re-established in almost all European countries, and they quickly realised the advantages and necessity of transnational cooperation. To begin with, personal contacts were established between the leading politicians; for example, in 1946/47 meetings were arranged between politicians such as Bidault, Hurdes, Piccioni, Serrarens, Sassen and Holzapfel[2]. In the course of these meetings, the idea of closer formalised cooperation between the European Christian Democrat parties began to take shape. The Swiss Conservative Christian Social Party[3] lent considerable support to this development, as it was the only Christian party in Europe whose party apparatus had not been affected by the war. In 1947, the MRP deputy Robert Bichet[4] founded an organisation of the Christian Democrat parties in Europe, called "Nouvelles Equipes Internationales" (NEI). The NEI regarded itself as an umbrella organisation for the European Christian Democrat parties, concentrating on the exchange of experiences and ideas. The member parties retained absolute independence in their political work. The statutes of the organisation envisaged the possibility of corporate membership of entire parties, as well as the membership of so-called national "équipes". These "équipes" were groups of Christian Democrat politicians of various nationalities who belonged to parties which were not corporate members of the NEI.[5] Apart from the executive committee, a number of commissions and special committees were formed in order to deal with specific areas: the organisation programme; the coordination of parliamentary work; East/West problems; cultural affairs; economic and social problems; and youth problems. The latter committee failed to meet the expectations of the various parties' youth organisations, and the NEI was extended in 1951. It was joined by the "Union des Jeunes Démocrates Chrétiens" which functioned as the mother organisation for all youth groups and whose structure of special committees and commissions corresponded to that of the NEI. These first contacts between Christian Democrat parties in Europe were

Marginal notes: **Development of cooperation** · **Foundation of the NEI** · **Membership** · **Organisation** · **Youth organisation**

235

subsequently extended in two ways. The Christian Democrat parties of the East European countries had been involved in the foundation of the NEI. Later, after the Communist Governments had either robbed them of all political power or banned them in their own countries, emigrant East European Christian Democrat politicians formed the "Christian Democrat Union of Central Europe" (CDUCE) which had its headquarters in New York. The organisation was primarily concerned with questions relating to East European Communism and the possibilities of democratising the political systems in Eastern Europe. The Union's links with the NEI remained intact in as much as NEI's executive committee always included representatives of the CDUCE. At the World Congress of Christian Democrat parties in 1961 in Chile, the interest of non-European Christian Democrat parties, and in particular that of the Latin-American parties, led to the foundation of the "World Union of Christian Democrats". The large regional organisations NEI, CDUCE and the "Organisación demócrata cristiana de America Latina" (ODCA), the Union of the Latin-American Christian Democrat parties, joined as members. The World Union provides the organisational framework for international contacts between Christian Democrat parties on a world-wide scale.

Cooperation of Christian Democrats in Europe

The "World Union of Christian Democrats" soon realised the limitations of functional cooperation on such a vast scale. The divergence of individual party-political objectives, party social structure, share of governmental responsibility, and the political and social environment made a close nexus impossible.[6] The activities of the Union were therefore rather erratic: it organised meetings and congresses, and arranged talks between leading Christian Democrat politicians. On the European level, however, cooperation between Christian Democrat parties seems to be continually increasing. The European policy of unification has been the primary reason for this development. Above all, the European Parliament with its Christian Democrat group[7] forced the parties into closer cooperation. The NEI revised its constitution to meet these changes. The organisation's declared commitment is now to an active policy of European cooperation. The new name "European Union of Christian Democrats" (EUCD) also emphasises this fresh line. The EUCD succeeded in winning over almost all European Christian Democrat parties as members. They are at present[8]:

Belgium:	Christelijke Volkspartij
	Parti Social-Chrétien
Federal Republic of Germany:	Christlich-Demokratische Union
	Christlich-Soziale Union
France:	Union centriste des démocrates de progrès
Ireland:	Fine Gael
Italy:	Democrazia cristiana
	Südtiroler Volkspartei

236

CDUCE

World Union of Christian Democrats

Work of the Union

EUCD

Member parties

Luxembourg:	Parti chrétien social
Malta:	Partit Nazzjonalista
Netherlands:	Anti-revolutionaire partij
	Christelijk Historische Unie
	Katholike Volkspartij
Austria:	Österreichische Volkspartei
Portugal:	Centro Democratico y Social
San Marino:	Partito Democratico Christiano Sammarinese
Switzerland:	Christlich-demokratische Volkspartei der Schweiz
	Parti démocrate-chrétien suisse
	Partito democratico-cristiano popolare svizzero

The following organisations are members of the EUCD:

Associated organisations

— European Union of Young Christian Democrats
— Union of Christian Democrat Women
— European Union of Christian Democrat Workers

Objectives of the EUCD

The objectives of the European Christian Democrats were laid down in their "Manifesto of the Christian Democrats in Europe" issued in 1976. It contains the following principles:

— the personal freedom of development in a peaceful and pluralistic society;
— freedom, equal opportunity, social justice and solidarity;
— the application of democratic methods in the realisation of all political concepts[9]

EPP

In order to plan for the direct election of the future European Parliaments, the executive committee of the EUCD set up a study group which, over the past years, worked on the problems of founding a European Christian Democrat party. In February 1976, it presented a draft constitution for a "European People's Party" which was conceived of as a federation of the Christian Democrat parties within the European Community. After various alterations, the draft was finally accepted in April 1976 by the Political Committee of the EUCD. Among the founder members of this new European party are the Christian Democrat parties of Belgium, the Federal Republic of Germany, France, Ireland, Italy, Luxembourg and the Netherlands. In March 1978, the member countries of the EPP passed the "Political Programme of the EPP".[10]

Also in 1976, efforts were made to interest the European Conservative parties, such as the French Gaullists and the British Conservatives which had joined neither EUCD nor the newly founded European People's Party, in a formalised coopera-tion. First talks on the foundation of such an organisation took place in March 1977 in Munich, during a meeting of advisers on international cooperation from the non-socialist parties of Scandinavia, Great Britain, Portugal and Austria. In April 1978, 10 Conservative and Christian Democrat parties of Western Europe, among them the German Union parties, united to form the "European Democratic Union" (EDU). The Chairman of the Austrian People's Party, Taus, was elected as its leader.[11]

EDU

Difficulties in reaching agreement on European political issues does not only apply

Consensus

to the two camps of the Christian Democrat and Conservative parties. A closer look at the various Christian Democrat parties in Europe reveals differences which necessarily create disagreement over joint policy decisions. However, such differences are concerned in the main with detail, and as such are not too important. The Christian Democrat parties are generally in agreement over political development and are both in favour of increasing European political cooperation. It is

Ideology

typical of the European Christian Democrat parties' ideologies that they have detached themselves from their previously strong link with Christian social ethics. This applies to the parties' declared programmes as well as to their political activity. Today, the parties are committed to the idea of a Christian society. This modification to original ideology has had a twofold benefit. It has solved the problems with which the parties were faced before the 2nd World War in countries with a denominationally mixed population.[12] While the detachment from the Church has given the parties greater autonomy in their political activities. Once these ties had been severed, the Christian Democrat parties were able to open themselves to all strata and groups of the population. This acquisition of political autonomy is the main explanation for the enormous increase in votes for the Christian parties in the post-war period.

Basic
Christian
attitude

The basic Christian principle that all parties have in common today is the preservation of man's dignity.[13] The interests of the individual are not regarded as an absolute entity; rather they are embedded in the interests of the community. In this way, the Christian Democrat *Weltanschauung* seeks a feasible middle course between individualism and collectivism. The political consequences are the

Political
consequences

tendencies already mentioned: the creation of larger communities through international integration, and at the same time decentralisation within the community. It remains to be seen how far this delicately balanced ideology is suited to propaganda battles, particularly against socialism.

European
politics

The European Christian Democrat parties are unanimously in favour of working towards a united Europe. As early as 1945 a first group had campaigned for the unification of Europe: a group of French MRP delegates under the leadership of Bichet had chosen as their political motto: "Unir l'Europe pour construire la paix". In the years following 1945, the desire for peace was accentuated by the desire for mutual support and cooperation. The conditions in the European countries were mostly catastrophic. In many countries, the Christian Democrat parties had sole political responsibility for the first time, and consequently they were interested in exchanging their experiences and coordinating their policies. The threat that the countries of the Communist camp posed to Europe and the corresponding desire for security among the European countries increased the willingness to cooperate. This was reinforced by a wish to express European political interests on an equal footing with the large political powers; this presupposed the unification of Europe.

Different
interests

Basic agreement on ideological matters and overriding political objectives does not, of course, prevent the emergence of particular interests which have to be balanced against each other. The fact that rights of national sovereignty could

238

not be interfered with, together with questions on currency, prices, capital growth and worker co-determination constantly created new problems for which solutions could only be found after lengthy negotiations or which are still unresolved. These sort of problems will continue to arise even if the EPP is firmly established in a European Parliament. The individual Christian Democrat parties differ too widely in the way they have to consider the interests of their voters, potential coalition partners in national Parliaments, and the political and social system of their country as a whole. So far, differences of this kind have only resulted in a slowing down of the development of joint Christian Democrat political activities; it has not been brought to a stand-still. It may be assumed that this will also be true of their joint parliamentary or governmental activity on a European scale.

Notes

[1] The Italian de Gasperi was also involved in these preparations. When the Fascists came to power, Sturzo went into exile in Great Britain. During the war, he continued in his efforts with the European politicians in exile; however, without making any real results.

[2] Of particular importance were the so-called "Geneva talks" which were arranged by Swiss politicians, sometimes by Bidault.

[3] The party's Secretary General at the time, Martin Rosenberg, was a fervent advocate of the idea of cooperation between the Christian parties in Europe.

[4] He was also the first Secretary General of NEI.

[5] For example, the British "equipe" which, until the 1960's, was composed of Conservative and Labour politicians; also the Belgian "equipe" which consisted of members of the Christian People's Party – the party as such only became an official member in the 1960's.

[6] It was also attempted without success to initiate regular contacts (for example, discussion groups) with the Socialist International and the World Union of Liberal Parties.

[7] A separate chapter is devoted to the Christian Democrat parliamentary group in the European Parliament.

[8] As at December 1976. Changes have occurred as the party prohibition was lifted in Spain and several Spanish parties are officially applying for membership.

[9] "Manifesto of the Christian Democrats in Europe", p. 3. See: Part V.

[10] Reprinted in Part V.

[11] 8 further parties participated in the founding session as observers. The Christian Democrats from Belgium, Italy, Luxembourg and the Netherlands, who were responsible for the refusal to admit the British Conservatives into the EPP, are not members of the EDU. They argue, according to the Chairman Taus, that the term "conservative" has negative connotations in their countries, and consequently these Christian Democrats refuse to cooperate with the Conservatives in the EDU.

[12] Denominational Christian Democrat parties still exist in the Netherlands. Christian Democrat parties in countries with one major denomination naturally tend to represent that sector; this is well illustrated by the Italian Christian Democrats' attitude towards divorce legislation.

[13] "Manifesto of the Christian Democrats in Europe", p. 3.

Federation of Liberal and Democrat Parties in the European Community

Member Parties:

Belgium:
1. Partij voor Vrijheid en Vooruitgang (PPV — Flemish)
2. Parti de la Liberté et du Progrès (PLP — Walloon)
3. Parti Libéral (PL — Brussels)

Denmark:
4. Venstres Landsorganisation (V)
5. Det Radikale Venstres Landsforbund (RV)

Federal Republic of Germany:
6. Freie Demokratische Partei (FDP)

France:
7. Mouvement (also: Force Nationale) des Républicains Indépendants (MRI or FNRI)
8. Mouvement des Radicaux de Gauche
9. Parti Radical-Socialiste

Great Britain:
10. Liberal Party Organisation

Italy:
11. Partito Liberale Italiano (PLI)
12. Partito Republicano Italiano (PRI)

Luxembourg:
13. Parti Démocratique (PD)

Netherlands:
14. Volkspartij voor Vrijheid en Democratie (VVO)

Organs: — Congress (annually)
— Executive Committee (meets at least 4 times a year)

Secretariat: Brussels

3. Liberal Parties

THEO STAMMEN

Historical Summary

It was mentioned earlier that until the end of the 2nd World War, non-socialist parties in Europe were not particularly interested in transnational party relationships; the prevailing attitude was that party-political interaction and activity should be limited to individual countries. Despite the existence of the League of Nations, a real stimulus for party connections beyond the national frontiers (analogous to the various "Internationals" of the workers' parties) was missing. The nations and their Governments were considered as the only legitimate political agents between different countries.

Such an attitude was also typical of the *Liberal parties* in Europe: they often contained a strong national element. It thus proved difficult to establish transnational connections.

In post-war Europe, there was a fresh assessment and evaluation of international political relations and cooperation at all levels (politics, economy, culture). This change of attitude was brought about by the political upheaval following the 2nd World War, and the rejection of nationalism as a political model. This new attitude was reflected by all the parties. The Liberal parties decided on principle to contri-. bute actively and positively to European unification. **Changed circumstances after 1945**

Apart from the West German FDP's opposition to the ratification of the Rome Treaties, one can say that Liberal parties have generally supported European integration in the various sectors (European Coal and Steel Community, EEC, Euratom). The Liberal parties in the new member countries Great Britain and Denmark have committed themselves with particular intensity and consistency. **The Liberals' attitude towards Europe**

The "Liberal International"

The Liberal parties' changed attitude towards international politics in general and European politics in particular resulted in the development of international cooperation between the Liberal parties.

In 1947, the "Liberal World Union" was founded, the name later being changed to "Liberal International". The Oxford "Liberal Manifesto" (1947) has remained its programme up to today. **"Liberal International" (1947)**

This Liberal International is not only a union of the Liberal parties of the EC countries (with the exception of Ireland); it also includes other European and non-

European countries. It further contains the Liberal parliamentary groups of the European Parliament and the Consultative Assembly of the European Council; the Liberal group of the West European Union; and the representatives of Liberals in exile from Eastern-bloc countries.

European politics

This party union has its roots in the countries of Europe. It is therefore not surprising that questions of European politics and European integration have always dominated the annual congresses of the Liberal International. This bias is so strong that, mainly due to the personal efforts of the Belgian Roger Motz, an additional "Liberal Movement for a United Europe" was founded in 1952. Later, in 1972, it was integrated into the Liberal International as a regional group.

Expansion of the EC

The Liberal International repeatedly made its presence felt with initiatives towards European integration: for example, at the 1967 congress in Oxford, it called for an expansion of the European Community. At the Munich congress in 1969, it spoke for the first time in favour of European direct elections. Finally, at the 1972 Paris congress, it demanded a strengthening of the rights of the European Parliament and the holding of direct elections on a proportional representation basis by 1980. Furthermore, it was suggested that a federation of the Liberal parties of the EC countries be established with a permanent secretariat.

Federation of Liberals

Following this initiative, the statutes for the Federation were drawn up and accepted in 1974 in Florence. The Berlin congress in 1975 provided the Liberal leaders with an opportunity of formally resolving to set up the Federation in 1976; they further announced the preparation of a Liberal European election programme for 1977.

The Federation of Liberal parties was clearly necessary to coordinate Liberal politics within the European Community. The Liberal International had much too loose an organisational structure, and contained a wide-ranging field of national interests, many of which lay outside Europe.

The Federation of Liberal and Democrat Parties in the European Community (FLIDPEC)

Foundation in Stuttgart (1976)

The Federation of Liberal parties was officially founded during the Stuttgart congress of March 26th/27th, 1976. For any one conversant with the history of European liberalism, particularly of the 20th century, it is amazing that it was Liberals who achieved the foundation of the *first* European party. It is also significant that the initiative did not stem from the Liberal group in the European Parliament, but from the Liberal International and meetings of party leaders. As we have already seen, the European parliamentary group did not only include "Liberal" parties in the strict sense but also so-called "Allies". The statutes of the Liberal International, however, contain more precise criteria for membership.

Objectives

The foundation of the Federation of Liberal parties in 1976 was directly connected with the first European direct elections. The letter of invitation to the founding conference in Stuttgart, signed by G. Thorn (Luxembourg, President of the Liberal International) and H.D. Genscher (Federal Chairman of the FDP), emphasises the challenge presented by these elections:

"In 1978, all citizens of the European Community will directly elect their Parliament for the first time. The Liberal parties in the EC have to face this challenge. The citizens of the European Community expect of the Liberals that they will take decisive steps towards a European Union and that they will present a united and independent front in the first direct elections to the European Parliament."

A similar line is taken in the statutes of the Federation (revised in Stuttgart) as well as in the "Stuttgart Declaration". According to Art. 2.2 of the statutes, the member parties are obliged "to support the universal direct elections to the European Parliament in order to strengthen the democratic character of the European Community". **Statutes**

And in the Stuttgart Declaration, the undersigned "welcome" the fact "that the first direct elections to the European Parliament will be held in 1978". They "have therefore decided to found a Federation of the Liberal parties in the European Community", of which this is the "Action Programme". **"Stuttgart Declaration"**

From the 9 EC countries, 14 parties had been invited to Stuttgart: three Belgian parties, two Danish parties, one German, three French, two Italian, and one party each from Luxembourg, the Netherlands and Great Britain. The Liberal group of the European Parliament, the Liberal International and other transnational Liberal organisations also took part. Of these 14 parties, 9 joined the newly founded Federation at the onset, the rest taking some time to make the decision. Only Ireland is not represented. **Members**

The Liberal group in the European Parliament, formerly known officially as the "Liberal and Allies Group" changed its name to the "Liberal and Democrat Group". By doing so, it made it clear that from now on it was to be regarded as the parliamentary group of the Liberal Federation in the European Parliament.

Between March and November 1976, that is, between the founding congress in Stuttgart and the first congress of the Liberal Federation in The Hague (5–7 November, 1976), altogether 14 parties from 8 EC countries joined the Federation. The first congress was important for the election of the President and the executive committee of the Federation (as was to be expected, Gaston Thorn from Luxembourg became President; the German Hans-Dietrich Genscher and the Dutchman Hans de Coster were elected as Vice-Presidents); and also for the further discussion of the Federation's programme.

By spring 1977, a central programme commission headed by the German Martin Bangemann had drafted a comprehensive programme, which was accepted in April 1978 by the executive committee and referred to the national member parties for further and final deliberation. The German FDP, for example, debated and finally accepted this draft by their federal committee in September 1977.

At the Federation's second congress (it had in the meantime decided to use the initials "ELD" short for "European Liberal Democrats") in Brussels (18–20 November 1977), the programme for the impending election campaign for the first direct elections was finally resolved.

Organisation of the Federation

Organisation
according to
the statutes

Criteria of
membership

It is interesting to note the founding conference in Stuttgart did not simply copy the 1974 statutes drafted and accepted by the Liberal International, but finally accepted a revised version. This would indicate that the Federation wished to establish itself as a new and independent organisation. This attitude is reflected even more clearly in the new regulations concerning membership. The statutes of the Liberal International stipulated: "Membership of the Federation is open to all political parties from those countries in the European Community which belong to the Liberal International or which have signed the Oxford Manifesto of 1947 and the Oxford Declaration of 1967. They have to support membership of the European Community, and the strengthening of the democracy of the Community by direct elections to the European Parliament".

This passage was revised as follows: "Membership of the Federation is open to all those political parties in the European Community which acknowledge the statutes and political programmes resolved by the Federation congresses".

This wording stresses the Federation's autonomy particularly in relation to the Liberal International. Members are no longer pledged to the declarations and manifestos of the International, which are necessarily vague and non-committal; but rather to the Federation's programmes which have been specifically designed for the European Community.

Organs of the
federation

The main organs of the Federation are the *Congress*, the *Executive Committee* and the *Secretary General*.

1. Congress

The Congress consists mainly of delegates from the member parties. It was originally intended that their number should correspond to the number of members from the individual EC countries in the European Parliament. This would have meant that the four large countries would have had 36 delegates each, the Netherlands and Belgium 14 each, Denmark 10 and Luxembourg 6 delegates. This, however, proved problematic as well as unfair, because it did not do justice to the size of the national parties and national election results. In Stuttgart a solution was found which takes the national election results into account. Article 22 reads: "The Congress consists of the following members:

1a) 6 Representatives from each country. In the case of countries with more than one member party, the representation is divided in proportion to the number of votes polled by each party in the last national general election that took place at least two months prior to the Congress.

1b) The number of representatives for each member party is fixed according to the following proportions (with the number of votes polled by that party in the last general national elections):

— one representative for every 100,000 votes (or nearest figure) for a total of up to 3 million votes;

— one representative for every 250,000 votes (or nearest figure) for a total of between 3 and 5 million votes;

— one representative for every 500,000 votes (or nearest figure) for a total of over

244

5 million votes."

The same article further specifies who the other members of the Congress shall be:
2. "The members of the Liberal and Allies group in the European Parliament and the Liberal members of the Commission of the European Communities (if they belong to one of the member parties) are by rights members of the Congress.
3. 10 representatives appointed by a federation of Liberal youth organisations in the countries of the Community."

The Congress, which meets once a year, elects the President of the Federation and 12 members of the Executive Committee (for a term of 2 years).

2. Executive Committee

The Executive Committee consists of: the Presidents, "12 members who are appointed by their respective parties in accordance with the criteria valid for the European Communities Commissions; 12 members who are chosen by the Congress according to the same criteria for a term of two years; the Chairman of the Liberal and Allies group in the European Parliament; those members of the Commission of the European Communities who belong to a member party; a member appointed by a federation of Liberal youth organisations from the countries in the Community, who should at the same time belong to a member party of the Federation of Liberal parties" (Article 13 of the statutes).

The Executive Committee, which should meet at least four times per year, elects from its ranks two Vice-Presidents, a treasurer and the Secretary General whose primary task it is (according to Art. 30ff) to support the other organs of the Federation. The Executive Committee is authorised, for the period between Congresses, "to speak and act in the name of the Federation in all areas for which the Federation is responsible" (Article 17). It is also responsible for the nomination of candidates for the European direct elections: "When direct elections to the European Parliament are held, the list of accepted candidates from each country shall be drawn up by the individual national member parties in consultation with the Committee" (Article 17, paragraph 2).

Powers of decision making

1. Congress

It is important that the organs of the Federation can make binding decisions. Article 26 specifies:

"The Congress can:
1. take decisions concerning all matters within the scope of the treaties for the foundation of the European Communities, and that are connected with political cooperation in the European Community;
2. decide on all other matters which, according to the unanimous opinion of its members, lie within its powers;
3. deliberate on all suggestions presented by a member party or one of its representatives, and comment on these suggestions;
4. consider the Executive Committee's report and debate it, if it so wishes;
5. consider reports of the Liberal and Allies group in the European Parliament;
6. make alterations in the statutes and rules of procedure;
7. address recommendations to the Liberal and Allies group in the European Parliament."

2. Executive Committee

With regard to the Executive Committee, Article 16 specifies: "The Committee's decisions shall be ratified by a majority of the voting members. There shall be no vote if less than 12 members are present."

It is thus clear that the organs of the Federation have a good deal more power than those of the International, and give the Federation a strong international bias.

Finally, it is interesting to note how the statutes define the relationship between the Federation and the Liberal group in the European Parliament. It has already been mentioned that the Chairman of the parliamentary group is a member of the Executive Committee and that all members of the parliamentary group, if they belong to a member party of the Federation, are also members of the Federation Congress.

Article 10 of the statutes specifies:

"The Federation is represented in the European Parliament by the Liberal and Allies group. Elected or appointed members of the European Parliament who belong to a member party of the Federation, are members of the Liberal and Allies group."

This Article constitutes a kind of reciprocal relationship between the Federation and the parliamentary group. The first paragraph illustrates a relatively close representative relationship; the second paragraph emphasises the link between the members of the Federation and the parliamentary group which is solely responsible for the representation of Liberal interests in the European Parliament. This has in fact already been put into practice: after the Italian Republicans had joined the Liberal Federation, a member of this party withdrew from the Socialist group in the European Parliament and joined the Liberal group.

Obviously, time will tell what sort of influence the Federation can exert on the parliamentary group. We shall have to wait until after the first direct elections when the Federation has properly established itself.

Federation Programme

The European Liberals are well ahead of the other main parties in the preparation of a transnational programme.

They benefited from the fact that they had already formulated their programme under the auspices of the Liberal International in the Oxford Manifesto (1947) and in the Oxford Declaration (1967). Furthermore, there were no fundamental differences or tensions on European policies among the Federation members.

It was therefore not surprising that the founding congress in Stuttgart in 1976 issued the "Stuttgart Declaration" as its first policy statement. The Liberal concept of the future shape of Europe was propounded, with special emphasis on human and civil rights as well as the necessity for a free democratic constitution for a European Union. The declaration also contains details on a joint European economic and foreign policy.

As far as the first direct elections were concerned, the Liberal Federation did not think the Stuttgart Declaration sufficient. At their congress in Rome (March/April 1977), they drafted a comprehensive programme specifically designed "for

246

the direct elections to the European Parliament in 1978". Throughout 1977, the national Liberal parties considered the draft and finally, at the general convention of the European Liberals in Brussels (18–20 November 1977) brought out their "Programme for Europe".

This comprehensive programme deals with the following subject areas: (1) human and civil rights, (2) European institutions, (3) social policies, (4) education and culture, (5) a policy for the environment, (6) regional policies, (7) economic principles, (8) economic and currency union, (9) energy policy, (10) small and medium-sized businesses, (11) transport policy, (12) agrarian policy, (13) foreign policy and security, and (14) policies of cooperation and development. The programme has been published in *two* versions: firstly, as "Papers of the election programme of the Federation of European Liberal Democrats", and later as a detailed and comprehensive "Programme for Europe". **Subject areas**

The Liberals' *Programme for Europe* is characterised by a surprising degree of agreement on objectives. This indicates that the "Federation of Liberal and Democrat Parties in the European Community" is no longer a loosely-knit group of national parties. It possesses a considerable degree of homogeneity which will make it a strong political force in the European party system. Against this background, the words of the President of the Liberal Federation, the Luxembourg Minister of State Gaston Thorn, may be seen as a realistic summary of the Liberals' future in Europe:

Gaston Thorn
"It is our belief that the Federation has clarified Liberal thinking and so made its policies more convincing. We are tolerant; we reject all forms of sectarianism; and we know how to overcome nationalist conflicts: all this enables us to lay the foundation stone for an election programme and to cooperate with all those political forces which, like us, are willing to unconditionally acknowledge and defend the fundamental values of a Liberal democracy. We are prepared to take up our position on the political chess board. The public, which regards the Socialist forces with a certain scepticism and which is equally unconvinced by the Conservatives, expects different ideas, a different style, a different ideal. We would make a mistake by not fulfilling these expectations, for Europe belongs to the party or group which knows how to seize this opportunity. The Liberals have provided the basis; the Federation will now act for them."
(Quoted from: *Das Parlament*, No. 49, 4.12.1976, p. 10).

No Ideological Conflict

Although Liberals do not have any traditions of transnational party relationships and, although they began to form a European party relatively late, they have made rapid progress in a short time. At present, the "Federation of the Liberal and Democrat Parties in the European Community" is the most advanced with regard to its organisation and programme.

One of the reasons for such a development may be the fact that the Liberal parties are usually smaller parties. In their national party systems, where they often function

247

as the decisive weight in the balance of power, they have entered a variety of different coalitions and have therefore developed a comparatively greater flexibility and capacity for cooperation. Now they are reaping the benefit on a European scale. It is also important to note that no genuine policy or ideological differences exist between the Liberal parties; they have achieved a full consensus on European policies. The following statement of FDP politician Martin Bangemann sums up the situation: "The foundation of the Federation of Liberal and Democrat parties to further their cooperation in the European Community and in the direct elections to the European Parliament has provided the Liberal parties with a basis for effective Liberal politics." (Bangemann/Bieber: *Die Direktwahl*, 1976, p. 95).

Selected Literature

Bangemann, M./Bieber, R.: Die Direktwahl — Sackgasse oder Chance für Europa, 1976, p. 86 ff.

Zusammenarbeit der Parteien in Westeuropa, 1976, (See: *Ficker/Fischer-Dieskau, Ch./Krenzler, H.G.:* Die Zusammenarbeit der Liberalen Parteien in Westeuropa — auf dem Wege zur Föderation, p. 13 ff.).

Federation of the European Liberal Democrats (Ed.): Congress Brüssels 1977 (18.–20. Nov. 1977), 1978.

4. Communist Parties

HEINZ RAUSCH

Three Forms of Communism

For decades, the term "Communist party" was clearly defined. It referred to those parties which accepted the historical authority of the Communist Party of the Soviet Union (CPSU) and, in individual countries, represented the Marxism/Leninism defined by Moscow. With the "tripartition of Marxism" (Wolfgang Leonhard) into Soviet Marxism, Maoism and Reformist Communism the ideological and political unity of the Soviet block came to an end. The range of "Communist" parties has considerably increased. In the Federal Republic of Germany, for example, the situation is somewhat confusing with the official German Communist Party (DKP), the various Maoist groups, the Trotskyist International and other splinter movements.[1] We shall limit our definition of "Communist party" to the more orthodox Moscow-style groups, even though some of the Western parties established their own path towards Socialism at the Berlin conference of Communist parties in June 1976. Following the events in Prague in 1968, these parties had already rejected the so-called Breshnev doctrine of limited sovereignty.

"Euro-Communism"

The somewhat misleading term "Euro-Communism" has been coined for these parties; it is mainly applied to the groups of Italy, France and Spain, and more recently also to Great Britain. These parties aim at harmonising Communism with Western democratic concepts. Common features are the rejection of dictatorship; the principle of a representative democracy; the use of elections as the sole means for a change in power; and the emphasis on the freedom of the individual. By contrast, the CPSU and its closely related governing parties are committed to the idea of "proletarian internationalism". According to this theory, there is only *one* Communism, based on the principles of Marx, Engels and Lenin. This kind of Communism can only fulfil its historic function if it acts as a unity. Any "special" kind of Communism which follows an independent or national course is ruled out.[2]

The Soviet Union fights for the "protection of Marxism/Leninism from dogmatism and revisionism"[3]: this attitude conceals the concept of only *one* leading force. For historical, political and ideological reasons, only the Soviet Communist Party can fill this role. That much at least becomes clear in the discussion of Santiago

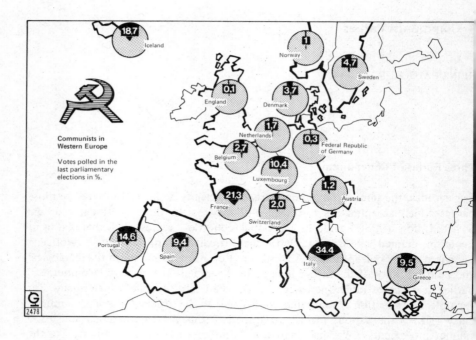

Communists in
Western Europe

Votes polled in the
last parliamentary
elections in %.

Carrillo's (leader of the Spanish Communist Party) provocative book on *Euro-Communism and State*[4]; the book was condemned by the Soviet journal Nowoje Wremja[5].

Carrillo is right in always putting "Euro-Communism" in inverted commas, as he is not concerned with Europe but with a more "humane" kind of Communism. Carrillo flatly rejects the kind of Communism practised in the Soviet Union. In his view, the proletarian state has never been achieved there; still less can the contemporary Western constitutional state be envisaged within the doctrine of Lenin. This is why Carrillo puts forward an objective and not a programme by pointing out: "The political system of Western Europe — Parliament, party pluralism, separation of powers, decentralisation, observance of human rights — is principally right and will be even more efficient with a Socialist economic structure". This statement with its implicit renunciation of essentially Marxist/Leninist principles is certainly not shared by all "Euro-Communists".

Significantly, pro-Soviet forces have been active in Italy's Communist Party for some time, and Berlinguer has repeatedly made it clear that criticism of the Soviet Union does not mean renunciation. Nevertheless Carrillo's move should not be underestimated. The French Communist Party, the most Stalinist of all West European groups, now has to convincingly prove its change-over to "Euro-Communism".

Moscow's counter-attack leads one to conclude that the limited acknowledgement

Objectives of "Euro-Communism"

Counter-attack of the CPSU

250

of national positions at the 1976 conference of European Communist parties in Berlin was only a ploy to win.time. For a while, the phrases "Socialist solidarity" and "international cooperation" replaced "proletarian internationalism" in the communiqué, only as a means of later attacking "Euro-Communism" as an anti-Soviet off-shoot of Imperialism. A hard-fought battle of ideological leadership seems likely. The CPSU has already often adopted the tactic of breaking up the weakest link in the chain, the French Communist Party.

Process of Change or a New Form?

Moscow is clearly watching the "Euro-Communist" movement carefully. The same anxiety has also spread to Western Europe, for one has to ask whether "Euro-Communism" represents a genuine process of change within Communism or is merely a new form, leading to world-wide Communism. Developments in countries with strong Communist Parties (for example, the "historic compromise" in Italy between the Italian Communist Party and the Christian Democrats and the growth of the French popular front movement) demand an answer to this question. It is striking that former members of Communist parties are the ones to acknowledge **Supporters** and approve of the changes, particularly if they themselves have turned their back on Stalinism because of reformist-Communist measures and objectives. Milovan Djilas for example, a harsh critic of the "new class" of bureaucrats and technocrats in Communist regimes, regards "Euro-Communism" as a new opportunity for free and pluralist Socialism.[6] His statements have been echoed by Wolfgang Leonard[7]. At the other end of the scale are the philosophical and practical reservations of **Critics** Leszek Kolakowski[8] and the scepticism of some politicians. Wilhelm Dröscher, the late chairman of the Union of Social Democrat Parties in the EC, rejects the idea of cooperation with the Communists, distinguishing between whether a "party is democratic or whether it merely governs in a democratic way". It is indeed difficult to believe that plurality and democracy rule within the party when the French Communist Party Congress *unanimously* rejects the dictatorship of the proletariate, a principle which it had equally unanimously supported previously.[9] Is this not a sign of the "democratic centralism" of orthodox doctrine which even the Spanish Communist Party, at present the standard bearer of "Euro-Communism", laid down as inalienable principle in its election programme for June 1977? However, democracy within a party and a State is founded on the freedom (of the individual and of groups) of expression. An acknowledgement of human rights and democratic conventions remains purely superficial as long as a party does not tolerate different opinions and oppositional behaviour.

Take-over of Power as a Test

Henry Kissinger, the former American Foreign Minister and professor of political sciences, analyses the situation in the same way.[10] He asks: can we trust the statements of the "Euro-Communists"? Once the take-over of power has happened,

251

will they carry out their promises? Would the transition to the kind of Socialism they aim at be irrevocable?

His reservations are founded on historical facts. So far, Communist parties have given little cause to believe that they would keep their promises once they had come to power and taken over Government. (Iceland, Finland and Portugal cannot really be cited as counter-examples; in these countries, the Communist parties played only minor roles in coalition Governments and were far removed from Soviet territory; in the case of Finland different Soviet interests had to be considered).

In all European countries which came under Communist influence following the 2nd World War, the national Communist party leaders each stated their willingness to support parliamentary democracy and the multi-party system. In Poland, Gomulka said as early as January 1946 that the dictatorship of the proletariate could not be and was not an essential element of Polish Government. The "Euro-Communists'" condemnation of the principle can be interpreted as a tactical move, for it has now been eliminated from the Soviet constitution, being regarded as outdated.

The Need for Scepticism

One's approach to "Euro-Communism" depends on a sceptical or an optimistic political attitude, and on whether trust or distrust of statements of intent determine political behaviour. According to the German Foreign Minister Genscher for example, the activities of the Soviet Union refute the "myth of the alleged independence of Euro-Communism"; in reality it is only a "form of world-Communism which has been adapted to the circumstances and is therefore particularly dangerous".[11]

It would certainly be wrong simply to adopt a hostile attitude towards the West European Communist parties which try to detach themselves from the Soviet Union and its faults. As regards the Federal Republic of Germany, however, it has to be admitted that its reactions stem from historical experience and are therefore more understandable. Nothing would be more dangerous than underestimation and nothing more fatal than a blanket rejection of the "Euro-Communists", which would drive them back into the powerful arms of the Soviet Union.

On the other hand, this ambiguity of position prevents Western Communists being acknowledged as true democratic parties. Their common objective is and remains the defeat of *capitalism*; the means to this end depend on strategy and tactics. "We believe that Lenin's statement regarding the proletariate is still fully valid: it cannot make use of the old State apparatus to exercise political power. But we also believe that the methods of acquiring power and the time required to change the political framework depend on the given historic conditions". These are the words of Luigi Longo, the former leader of the Italian Communist Party.[12] This does little to remove scepticism; as does Altiero Spinelli's (former Italian EC commissioner and present delegate of the Italian Communist Party) naive statement

252

that the nexus between the party's declarations and the interest in its political development is to a certain extent a guarantee for the honesty of the party.[13].

Scepticism remains. In Europe, the Western Communist parties could show that the change in their political thinking is more than a variation of Stalinism; that they have genuinely turned away from the "sacred" doctrine of Marxism/Leninism. Has this happened?

Soviet Union and the EC

The Soviet Union has never made a secret of its flat rejection of European cooperation. Since the foundation of the EC, the CPSU has regarded the efforts made towards European unification merely as a means of establishing an American hegemony on the Continent, with the help of the Federal Republic of Germany. This basic view, however, has not precluded ambivalent political attitudes at different times. The Soviet Union tried, for example, to play France and West Germany off against each other.[14] For a long time, the Soviets did not wish to enter into any relations with the EEC or EC. This has only recently changed. In 1972, Brezhnev acknowledged the existence of an economic group in the West, but the political significance of the EC was again played down. In 1977, a first fisheries agreement was concluded with the EC Commission in Brussels; this was the first practical acknowledgement of the Community.

Rejection on principal

All movements towards a politically united Europe go against the interests of the Soviet Union. This is why the closer bonds created by the direct elections to the European Parliament have been condemned. The *Pravda* writes: "The critics of this project (that is, the elections) stress that it means a direct isolation of the national sovereignty and independence of the West European countries. They point out that the German Federal Government which is closely linked with the United States will play a decisive role in this Parliament with the present ratios of power. This will create in Europe an atmosphere of American-West German hegemony" and in this way coordinate "the interests of the international monopolies".[15] So the Soviet Union fully retains its anti-European attitude. It was evident from the preparatory talks to a conference in Belgrade in June 1977 that this attitude may have stemmed from the partial failure of a previous conference for security and cooperation in Europe.

Against the direct elections

For a long time, the West European Communist parties modelled their attitude towards the EEC and EC on that of the Soviet Union. Following the creation of "Euro-Communism" their views have become more differentiated. Apart from the very rough division into traditionalists, reformist Communists and "opportunists" (that is, Communist parties which frequently change their kind of Communism), the dividing lines are blurred. The British Communist party, for example, rejects dictatorship of the proletariate, but at the same time rejects the EC. Similarly the French Communist Party after lengthy delays finally accepted the direct elections, but only under the condition that national sovereignty would in no way be diminished.

Attitude of West European Communist Parties

253

The Communist Parties in the 9 EC Countries

The Communist parties' view of Europe

The Communist parties of the 9 EC countries adopt the following attitude towards Europe:

— The *British* CP renounces dictatorship of the proletariate; rejects (like the majority of the Labour Party) the EC as an act of national self-abnegation and delegation of parliamentary sovereignty; and is also against direct elections, but for proportional representation (if such elections were to be held).

— The *Irish* CP with only 300 members is of little political importance. Its primary concern is the withdrawal of the English from Northern Ireland.

— The CP of the *Netherlands* abandoned its Russian line in the 1960's, mainly as a result of enormous competition from other Socialist groups. It does not acknowledge the principles of Euro-Communism, and rejects the EC as well as NATO.

— The *Belgian* CP is so small (it occupied 2 out of a total of 212 seats in the 1977 Parliament) that it is only concerned with entering into coalitions with various progressive groups.

— *Luxembourg's* CP is totally Soviet-influenced.

— The *French* CP is the sphinx of Euro-Communism. Within the EC it only accepts economic cooperation; all further delegation of sovereignty is attacked as a "crime against the French nation" (Marchais). For a long time, it was against direct elections. It welcomed the French withdrawal from NATO, and nurtures links with Gaullism, although it was allied with the Socialists in the now dissolved popular front coalition.

— The *Italian* CP is the Communist party with the most members and supporters outside the Soviet Union; it is a key figure in Euro-Communism. Following in the steps of the party's founder Gramsci, other leading figures such as Togliatti (particularly in his so-called testament of 1964), Longo and now Berlinguer have already tried to establish a rapprochement with the non-socialist parties and the Church. The Italian CP wants to contribute actively to the expansion of the EC. It was the first CP to take up seats in the European Parliament. According to its speaker for foreign affairs, Sergio Segre, the CPI regards the EC as the "prerequisite for the independence of the European countries". Even the much-maligned NATO was conditionally acknowledged in 1976 by the CP-leader Berlinguer, for it was considered a guarantee for the independence of the CPI which could prevent incidents such as the 1968 invasion of Czechoslovakia. The CPI is against a unilateral withdrawal from NATO and calls for a policy of détente which maintains a military balance between East and West.

— The *German* CP follows traditional Russian lines; it copies the German Democratic Republic in its policies.

— The *Danish* CP also belongs to the traditionalists. The party's critical wing became independent in 1969 when the long-standing Chairman Aksel Larsen resigned and founded a party of his own. It opposes the EC and NATO and any form of European integration.

254

Participation in the European Parliament

Of the parties mentioned, four are represented in the present European Parliament. They form a separate parliamentary group with 17 members under the leadership of the Italian Gorgio Amendola. However, their different attitudes makes it almost impossible to have a joint policy. The group consists of 1 member of the Danish CP, 4 members of the French CP, 11 of the Italian CP and 1 member of the Dutch CP. In addition to that, there is another member of the Italian Independent left. It was only in 1969 that the Italian CP entered the Strasburg Parliament, at first only as a group. When the French CP followed in 1973, the formation of a parliamentary group became possible. The two CPs elected members of their party élite to Parliament (Amendola for the CPI and Ansart for the CPF).

Within the European Parliament, however, the CPI and CPF differ in their political objectives.[16] Whereas the CPI has developed a European concept of its own which, among other things, mentions the strengthening of the Parliament vis-à-vis the technocrats, the CPF insists on national autonomy and is therefore opposed to any delegation of power. Such fundamental differences naturally have their repercussions on the work in the European Parliament, and the problems have not yet been properly tackled through discussion.

Apart from meetings of world Communist parties (summit conferences) or all-European CPs (for example, in 1976 in East Berlin), regional conferences have been instituted in the meantime, which initially served propaganda purposes. At the Brussels conference of the 23 Western CPs in 1974, the importance of such conferences became evident.[17] Meanwhile meetings of (three) leading "Euro-Communists" have also taken place; on these occasions, it was stressed that a new Communist movement was not intended. Nevertheless their activities represent much of what is attractive about "Euro-Communism", to the East as well as to the West. To the East, because their ideology is thereby spread further afield; to the West, because their ideas of a rapprochement are almost eagerly received.

Notes

[1] In the 1976 elections to the Bundestage, the DKP nominated candidates, also the Maoist groups of the KPD and the KBW, and the Trotskyist GIM. Further left-wing groups with candidates were: the European Workers' Party (EAP), the Independent Workers' Party (UAP) and the United Left (VL). Other than these, the following groups exist: the KPD/ML, the Communist Union (KB), the Marxist-Leninist Centre (MLZ) and a number of regional groups.

[2] *Nowoje Wremja (New Times)* according to the *Suddeutsche Zeitung* of 24.6.1977; the Bulgarian and Czechoslovak CP's had been particularly critical.

[3] According to the CP of Hungary in a comment on Euro-Communism (in: *Suddeutsche Zeitung (SZ)* of 18.2.1977).

[4] Santiago Carrillo, *Eurocomunismo y Estado*. Barcelona (Editorial Critica) 1977.

[5] Compare the defending attitude of the Spanish CP (*SZ* 25./26.6.1977), the support for the attacks from Yugoslavia (*SZ* 27.6.1977), France (*SZ* 25./26.6.1977), Italy and Greece (*SZ* 29.6.1977). Italy adopts an appeasing attitude (see *SZ* 28.6. and 30.6.1977). Violent attacks came from Czechoslovakia (*SZ* 30.6.1977), whereas Hungary mentions the respon-

sibility of each party for the Communist movement as a whole (*SZ* 1.7.1977). In the GDR, the *Neue Deutschland* reprinted the article in the *New Times* on 25.6.1977.

[6] Milovan Djilas in an interview with the ZDF (West German television channel), partly reprinted in the *Zeit* of 4.3.1977.

[7] Wolfgang Leonhard in "Pro und Contra", a West German television programme (ARD, 3.12.1976).

[8] In the *Spiegel*, No. 19, 2.5.1977.

[9] *Suddeutsche Zeitung*, 29.6.1977.

[10] Henry Kissinger, "The Peril of Eurocommunism", *Time-Europe*, 20.6.1977, p. 10f.

[11] According to the Munich *Abendzeitung* of 2.8.1976.

[12] Interview in the *Spiegel*, No. 36, 29.8.1966, p. 72.

[13] In a *Spiegel* interview 1976; see also an interview in the *Zeit* of 21.5.1976.

[14] Details in: Theo Arnold, *Europaische Integration im Spiegel der sowjetischen Politik*, in: "Grundkurs uber europaische Tragen. Perspektiven 1980". Andernach 1975, p. 57ff.

[15] See *Suddeutsche Zeitung* of 28.12.1976.

[16] For more details, see: Karl-Hermann Buck, Die Haltung von KPI und KPF gegenuber Direktwahl und Funktionen des Europa-parlaments, in: ZParl 7/1976, p. 209ff.

[17] For further details, see: Heinz Timmermann, Zwischen Weltbewegung und regionaler Kooperation – "Die Zusammenarbeit der Kommunistischen Parteien", in: *Zusammenarbeit der Parteien in Westeuropa. Auf dem Weg zu einer neuen politischen Infrastruktur*, Bonn 1976, p. 95ff: Schriftenreihe der Bundeszentrale fur politische Bildung, H. 108.

VI. Conclusions

The preceding part of our study was devoted to the already existing transnational party relationships in Europe. The question was posed as to how far transnational party connections contribute towards the formation of a European party system.

Levels of
Interaction

We saw that until now such interaction between parties has developed on two different levels: on the institutional level of the parliamentary groups in the European Parliament, and on the organisational level of party relations and federations within the European Community.

The development of institutional party cooperation in the parliamentary groups of the European Parliament preceded the formation and development of concrete and subject-minded parties. Right from the beginning of the European Communities the European parliamentarians did not organise themselves in the Assembly according to nations (as usual in international bodies), but according to supranational parliamentary groups which unite parties with identical or similar political beliefs from various countries.

Restructuring
is to be
expected

We also saw that the (at present) six parliamentary groups in the European Parliament differ with regard to their transnational nature and their internal harmony in programmatic and ideological matters. It is true to say that the formation of parliamentary groups in the European Parliament has already largely been consolidated, at least with regard to the three large groups, but it is to be expected that certain modifications and switches will take place, particularly in connection with the European direct elections in 1979 and the formation of European parties and party groups for the election campaign. This may apply above all to the Conservative camp; the two parliamentary groups of the "Conservatives" and the "European Progressive Democrats" can only with reservations be considered as genuine transnational groups, which so far have remained unparalleled by the formation of parties on the level of the European Community. It is possible, even probable, that these two groups will either merge into a single group or will ultimately, despite all political differences, join the Christian Democrats for the direct elections.

Starting
points

Disregarding possible future changes in the spectrum of parliamentary groups, one can state that firmly institutionalised forms of transnational interaction between parties have evolved at a parliamentary level since the foundation of the European Communities. This will be of great practical value for the development of a genuine European party system, which is one of the principal aims of the European Parliament. By contrast, genuine efforts towards the creation of transnational political parties within the European Community have only started in the past years, mainly in preparation for the first European direct elections.

Role of the
Liberals

At first glance it may seem surprising that the Liberal parties, renowned for their individualism, have achieved the most successful integration into a genuine European party. The Social Democrats/Socialists and the Christian Democrats have apparently found it more difficult to make the transition from theory into practice;

257

and the Communists, despite Euro-Communist movements away from Moscow's influence, have not achieved a form of efficient European cooperation. The Liberal parties have the advantage of greater flexibility, acquired in various and varied coalitions in almost all European countries. They are now reaping the benefits of this in a mutual cooperation on a European level, whereas the large Social Democrat or Christian Democrat parties with their tighter organisations and more stringent programmes have to overcome greater obstacles in their transnational cooperation. It is further worth noting that the various Conservative parties, which are represented in two separate parliamentary groups in the European Parliament, have not yet formed a concrete and politically efficient party alliance within the European Community.

Efforts towards the foundation of genuine European parties for the first European direct elections (partly as a result of the pressure imposed by the election date of June 1979) have had concrete results. One may state in conclusion that the formation of parliamentary groups in the European Parliament as well as the efforts towards the foundation of European parties are essential to a successful development of a European party system.

Part IV:
Outlines of a European Party System

THEO STAMMEN

I. Introduction

In this book it has been assumed that elections, whether in a national or transnational framework, necessarily require the involvement of political parties. National experience leaves no doubt that the very process of forming political opinion culminating in elections could not function properly without the political parties nominating candidates, issuing competitive programmes and stimulating voters. **Parties and elections**

On this theme, we were mainly concerned with the question as to whether the political parties in Europe were capable of contributing to the successful staging of the direct elections and, at the same time, towards the democratisation of the European Community.

The question has been dealt with in two ways.

(1) A study was made of the individual party systems of the European countries, with a consideration of possible transnational cooperation between parties in Europe. **National party systems**

(2) We also studied the already existing European party connections as conditions for the formation of a European party system. **Transnational party relationships**

In the final part of the book, it remains to investigate whether *the outlines of a future European party system* can be inferred from these findings.

We shall be concerned with the following aspects: (a) which European parties can be observed at present? (b) which interactions (for example, coalitions) seem possible and probable?

II. The National Party Systems in Europe

The sections on the party systems of the nine EC countries and other European countries with similar political structures and the subsequent systematic comparison of these party systems have revealed that a considerable number of structural similarities exist. Despite all the national idiosyncracies caused by historic, social, cultural, economic and political factors, we can speak of shared *constants*. The most important constants are the following: **Constants of national party systems**

259

1. Historical Constants

Constitutional
structures

The term "historical constants" subsumes structural conditions as well as processes of development, particularly during the 19th century. They occurred in almost identical fashion in the various European countries. The term refers first of all to the constitutional structures which spread in the wake of the French Revolution and copied the older British model. These structures were on the whole constitutional monarchies whose Parliaments provided the first opportunities for the formation of parliamentary groups and political parties.

Origin of
parties

As a rule, the formation of such groups was based in all countries on various political movements, such as developed similarly all over Europe in continuation of, or reaction to the ideas of the French Revolution as Liberalism, Conservatism, Radicalism, Christian Democracy, and later Socialism. Closely connected with this

Right
to vote

was the fundamental process of democratic development; in all countries the right to vote was considerably extended and thus necessitated the creation of extra-parliamentary party organisations.

Social
question
and workers'
parties

Another historical constant which applies to the whole of Europe is the process of industrialisation with all its side-effects and consequences: the social question and the fight of the working population for a say in economic, social and political matters. Everywhere trade unions and workers' parties were formed in competition to the previously dominant parties of the middle classes.

Common
features

The above factors were essentially responsible for the fact that the political, ideological and social-structural differentiation of political parties all over Europe followed a similar course. As a result, the national party systems in Europe, despite all their national idiosyncrasies, have strong common features.

2. Social and Economic Constants

In comparison with non-European countries, significant social and economic constants also became apparent in the countries studied. Similar to the historical constants, they have had formative effects on national party systems and structures. All Western European countries are modern industrial societies to varying degrees

Industrial
societies

of sophistication. Many parallels are to be found in the social structure and industrial production processes in these countries, which all affect the structure of the political parties. The standard division between non-socialist and workers'

Social
classes

parties indicates the social differentiation. The European countries under discussion have widely differing standards of living. These differences also affect the social structure, creating a moderate or more extreme pluralism.

3. Cultural Constants

Europe has always had a relatively strong cultural unity. Religious/denominational

Denominations

structures, spiritual/philosophical and social movements are all, of course, nationally individualistic; but they can on the whole be identified as variants of a general European type. This is well exemplified by the various cultural movements, Conservatism, Liberalism, Socialism, Radicalism, Christian Democracy and Communism. This constant has played a particularly important role in creating analogous conditions for the formation and differentiation of parties in the individual European countries; and has thereby laid the foundations for transnational political cooperation between them.

Cultural
movements

4. Political Constants

Finally, the constitutional heritage of the 19th century expresses itself in the contemporary political systems of the European countries and their constitutional foundations. This explains the fundamental similarities between the national political systems and the common role of the political parties within them.

Political
system

All the countries under discussion have written or unwritten constitutions founded on the acknowledgement of basic human rights and on the democratic principle of sovereignty of the people. The majority of these countries have political systems in which there is a separation of powers and a close nexus between Parliament and Government (parliamentary system).

Basic rights
and
sovereignty
of the
people

The political constants became apparent in our systematic comparison of national party systems. The evident similarities in the party system profiles doubtlessly further cooperation between political parties in Europe; for example, in the parliamentary groups of the European Parliament. They are an essential prerequisite for the formation and development of genuine European parties, and the first steps in this direction have already been taken.

Similar
party
profiles

Seen from this angle, a comparison of the national party systems in Europe permits certain conclusions as to the structure of a future European party system. It has been shown, for example, which major party-political forces and groups will be active in Europe. Most influence will lie with the Social Democrats and Socialists, the Christian Democrats and the Liberals. The smaller groups of the Communists and Conservatives will also play a role.

III. Transnational Party Relationships in Europe

The contours of a future European party system become more defined if one also considers the already existing transnational party relationships. In Part III of this book, we saw that such transnational party connections exist today on two different but related levels: firstly, on the institutional level of the parliamentary groups in the European Parliament, and secondly on the organisational level of the emerging European party federations.

1. The Parliamentary Groups of the European Parliament

The parliamentary groups of the European Parliament are particularly important to the emergence of genuine European parties, for it is in these groups that the foundation-stone of cooperation between parties from different countries has been laid. In most countries, political parties first existed as national parliamentary groups; an analogous process has occurred in Europe since the early days of European integration. The European parliamentary groups came into being much earlier than the European parties and have developed into efficient and indeed indispensable organs of the European Parliament.

This, however, does not apply to the same extent to all 6 parliamentary groups. They differ considerably in the integration of their organisation, programme and transnational cooperation. Only the three older and larger groups can really be considered as "complete" entities: the *Socialist Group* (with 63 members from 14 parties and 9 countries), the *Christian Democrat Group* (with 52 members from 13 parties and 7 countries) and the *Liberal and Democrat Group* (with 27 members from 14 parties and 8 countries.

The following groups are substantially less developed: the *European Progressive Democrats* (17 members from 3 parties and 3 countries), the *European Conservatives* (17 members from 2 parties and 2 countries) and also the *Communist and Allies* (17 members from 4 parties and 3 countries).

The membership of these latter groups is rather low, often falling below the minimum required. Furthermore, they are not genuinely supranational; they contain too few parties from too few different countries. It is also significant that these three groups do not possess the clearly-defined and established European party organisations.

This lack of cohesion could induce the two Conservative groups (the European Progressive Democrats and the European Conservatives) either to merge into one group, which would then have a much more transnational character, or else to join with the Christian Democrats.

The fact that political groups have existed in the European Parliament over a considerable period of time is not only relevant because of their contribution towards the formation and development of transnational European parties. The important factor is that these groups, as part of the European Parliament, have developed and tested a multitude of forms of practical political cooperation and interaction (*between* and *within* groups). The short- and long-term coalition behaviour which has evolved between the parliamentary groups in the European Parliament will certainly affect the future coalition behaviour of the European parties in a directly elected European Parliament.

2. Transnational European Party Connections

In addition to the already relatively established parliamentary groups in the European Parliament, organisational connections between national parties have recently been developed. This has led in some cases to the foundation of European parties.

These newly-founded parties have a more or less reciprocal relationship with their corresponding parliamentary groups; together, they make an essential contribution towards a proper democratic development of the European Community and particularly a permanent European party system.

We have seen in Part III of this book why only recently genuine efforts have been made to form specifically *European* parties. We discovered that after the 2nd World War various transnational party connections had been established in the form of "Internationals", partly based on old traditions and partly on new ideas. However, all these Internationals were and are on a world-wide basis and their organisational structure was thus undeveloped and their programmes relatively general and non-committal. For these reasons, such groups remained ineffective on a transnational level.

The Internationals serve rather as international congresses for the exchange of opinions between parties and for the expression of declarations of intent; they do not assume the character of transnational parties.

Therefore *regional* (in our case *European*) party connections have been formed in addition to the Internationals. Because of their regional character and more developed organisational structure they have been more efficient as transnational entities.

These initiatives and activities, which over the past years (since 1974) have led to the foundation of such European parties, were the results of governmental efforts. They were keen to develop the European Community by renewing steps towards political integration, and to this end fixed the date for the first European direct elections for 1979.

It was really only under the "threat" of these direct elections requiring the existence of European parties that the three transnational European party federations were formed.

This book has shown that these three European parties have all reached different stages of development. At the moment, the "Federation of Liberals and Democrats" has attained a higher degree of transnational homogeneity and efficiency in its organisation and programme. Both the Social Democrats and Christian Democrats have to overcome major obstacles on their path to a meaningful European integration. Despite the traditional internationalism of the Communist movement, the Communists in Western Europe, the so-called "Euro-Communists", have not achieved genuine cooperation within the Community. The different national movements prevent them from doing so, both in the European Parliament and at a party level. The Conservatives, too, have failed to form a competent European organisation to represent their policies.

The mere existence of the first genuine European parties offers hope for a successful outcome to the first direct elections. However, many problems and questions remain at present unresolved; for example, the practical political cooperation between the national parties involved in the individual European parties. Here again, looking at the European parliamentary groups may provide us with a more accurate picture.

IV. Outlines of a European Party System

The results of our empirical study of the national party systems and the already existing transnational party connections, permits a *positive* answer to the initial question as to the shape of a future European party system.

Although the existing contours are very vague, a meaningful approach to a more definitive outline may be based on those structural elements which generally constitute a party system. These elements were explained in great detail in Part II of the book. It may therefore suffice at this point to repeat the definition of the term 'party system'. According to G. Lehmbruch, party systems are "the regular interactions of parties in a political system".

Three essential factors determine a party system: (1) the *parties*, (2) the political *system*, and (3) the regular *interactions* between the parties.

Does, then, the European party system already contain these constituent factors and, if so, what is their particular form and relationship?

1. "Party"

It has been shown that two phenomena can be considered as "parties" on a European level: the parliamentary groups of the European Parliament and the first newly-founded European parties. In order to decide whether they qualify as such, we have to look at the various constituent elements of a party: a determination to occupy key positions in a given political system; a proper programme expressing an overall political conception; and a well-developed organisation.

If we apply these criteria to the present European groups (including the parliamentary groups and their work), we can at least call the Social Democrat, Christian Democrat and Liberal European party federations true parties in the sense of the above definition. It is clear that at present they do not fully comply with the criteria mentioned; but this is not a reflection of the parties alone, more of the state of the political system of the European Community. It is only now that the latter is developing a genuine democratic base.

As regards their practical effectiveness and relevance, a distinction must be made between the parliamentary groups of the European Parliament and the European parties. The parliamentary groups have already been active in the politically limited framework of the European Parliament; whereas the European parties' first major appearance will be in the context of the direct elections. Before that time there has been no democratic transnational political process in Europe in which the political parties have had an opportunity to function decisively.

2. "Political System"

Compared with the *national* political systems in Europe, the European Community has not yet fully developed into a complete political system. The supranational character of the European Community is also not fully functional in a decision-making and executive role. The Community has repeatedly suffered set-backs which have threatened to turn it into an international community of national states.

Thus, not all those political conditions which usually influence and determine the activities of political parties on a national level exist in Europe. In this context, it is of particular importance whether the present very limited powers of the European Parliament will be extended in the foreseeable future. The European Council has shown its support for this; but it is also known that some countries are opposed to an extension of the powers of the European bodies in general (and Parliament in particular) for they would ultimately be at the expense of national sovereignty.

It may be concluded that at present some of the political conditions necessary for the full development of a European party system are still lacking. This presents an immediate obstacle to the effectiveness of a European party system.

3. "Interactions"

This the most important aspect of a party system is closely related to the two factors already mentioned. It is only when they are properly established that one can expect a full range of interactions, and a fully-developed party system.

At present, interactions between transnational party units only exist within the parliamentary groups in the European Parliament.

The young European parties still have a long path ahead of them: firstly in the direct elections and then in coalitions which will probably assume considerable importance.

In order to define the various forms of interaction and cooperation more precisely, one must first quantify the groups involved.

The *number* of agents in the future European party system can be calculated relatively easily*. There will be five transnational parties or party groups: the Social Democrats, the Christian Democrats, the Liberals, the Communists and the Conservatives.

It is further probable that there will be some additional regional party groups in the European Parliament; due to their regional character, they will not become genuinely transnational parties.

As it seems unlikely that any party will gain an absolute majority, the European parties will have to enter into *coalitions*. It is interesting to consider what patterns would possibly or probably emerge.

One possible coalition pattern would be "workers' parties versus non-socialist parties", that is the Social Democrats would join the Communists in opposition to the various other parliamentary groups. Such a "popular front alliance" has long been discussed and prepared for, particularly by France and Italy. However, such a coalition does *not* seem very likely on a European level, as the North European

* See Appendix 3. The results of the direct elections are given with percentages of votes polled. This replaces the author's prognosis of the likely strength of the parties.

Social Democrat parties, and the German SPD in particular, have up to now rejected the idea. Furthermore, our analysis of Euro-Communism has shown that the Communist party group in Western Europe has not yet achieved a proper degree of uniformity. The differences between the Italian and French Communists, for example, are still far too great to make the Communist group a realistic coalition partner for the Social Democrats and Socialists.

One therefore has to look to the other four parliamentary groups for possible coalitions. Various forms of "great" coalition are conceivable: for example, an all-party coalition (without the Communists), or a coalition similar to the Great Coalition in West Germany from 1966 to 1969 between the Social Democrats and Christian Democrats. Alliances of this kind (sometimes with additional parties) are to be found in some European countries; for example, Belgium, the Netherlands and Italy. Yet the current political and ideological differences between these large party camps (well illustrated in the German Christian Democrat slogan "Freedom or Socialism") seem too great to make such a coalition likely on a European level. The most realistic and probable coalition form is the "small" coalition. There are three possible groupings. The first is a Social/Liberal coalition as exists in West Germany. The second possibility is that of coalition between Conservatives and Christian Democrats. These two groups are largely in agreement on their political concepts and aims, particularly with regard to European politics. The third possibility is that of a "non-socialist coalition" between Christian Democrats, Conservatives and Liberals. Such a coalition would doubtlessly gain the necessary majority.

All these considerations are based on the assumption that the powers of the European Parliament will be extended in the foreseeable future, so that it may function as a Parliament in a national parliamentary system.

It seems fair to conclude that a European party system *is* a realisable possibility. Nevertheless it has to be admitted that a number of essential conditions (particularly with regard to the powers of the European Parliament) are at present not sufficiently developed to provide the basis for an effective and functioning system. The *extension* of the Parliament's functions and powers is an integral part of the democratic development of the European Community. In the long run, the success of direct elections will depend on the speed with which this can be achieved.

Part V: Documentation

Document I

From: Treaty on the Foundation of the European Economic Community (EEC)
(of March 25, 1957)

Part Five. Institutions of the Community

Section 1. The Assembly

Article 137
Composition and Task
The Assembly, which shall consist of representatives of the peoples of the States brought together in the Community, shall exercise the advisory and supervisory powers which are conferred upon it by this Treaty.

Article 138
Designation and Number of Delegates
1. The Assembly shall consist of delegates who shall be designated by the respective Parliaments from among their members in accordance with the procedure laid down by each Member state.
2. The number of these delegates shall be as follows:

Belgium	4
Germany	36
France	36
Italy	36
Luxembourg	6
Netherlands	14

3. The Assembly shall draw up proposals for elections by direct universal suffrage in accordance with a uniform procedure in all Member States.
The Council shall, acting unanimously, lay down the appropriate provisions which it shall recommend to Member States for adoption in accordance with the respective constitutional requirements.

Article 139
Ordinary and Extraordinary Session
The Assembly shall hold an annual session. It shall meet, without requiring to be convened, on the second Tuesday in March.
The Assembly may meet in extraordinary session at the request of a majority of its members or at the request of the Council or of the Commission.

Article 140
President, Commission and Council
The Assembly shall elect its President and its officers from among its members.
Members of the Commission may attend all meetings and shall, at their request, be heard on behalf of the Commission.
The Commission shall reply orally or in writing to questions put to it by the Assembly or by its members.
The Council shall be heard by the Assembly in accordance with the conditions laid down by the Council in its rules of procedure.

Article 141
Votes and Quorum
Save as otherwise provided in this Treaty, the Assembly shall act by an absolute majority of the votes cast.
The rules of procedure shall determine the quorum.

Article 142
Rules of Procedure, Proceedings
The Assembly shall adopt its rules of procedure, acting by a majority of its members.
The proceedings of the Assembly shall be published in the manner laid down in its rules of procedure.

Article 143
Discussion of the Annual General Report
The Assembly shall discuss in open session the annual general report submitted to it by the Commission.

Article 144
Motion of Censure on the Activities of the Commission
If a motion of censure on the activities of the Commission is tabled before it, the Assembly shall not vote thereon until at least three days after the motion has been tabled and only by open vote.
If the motion of censure is carried by a two-thirds majority of the votes cast, representing a majority of the members of the Assembly, the members of the Commission shall resign as a body. They shall continue to deal with current business until they are replace in accordance with Article 158.

Document II
From: Convention on Certain Institutions Common to the European Communities (1957)

Section I. The Assembly

Article 1
The powers and jurisdiction which the Treaty establishing the European Economic Community and the Treaty establishing the European Atomic Energy Community confer upon the Assembly shall be exercised, in accordance with those Treaties, by a single Assembly composed and designated as provided in Article 138 of the Treaty establishing the European Economic Community and in Article 108 of the Treaty establishing the European Atomic Energy Community.

Article 2
1. Upon taking up its duties, the single Assembly referred to in Article 1 shall take the place of the Common Assembly provided for in Article 21 of the Treaty establishing the European Coal and Steel Community. It shall exercise the powers and jurisdiction conferred upon the Common Assembly by that Treaty in accordance with the provisions thereof.
2. To this end, Article 21 of the Treaty establishing the European Coal and Steel Community shall be repealed on the date when the single Assembly referred to in Article 1 takes up its duties, and the following provisions substituted therefor:

"Article 21
1. The Assembly shall consist of delegates who shall be designated by the respective Parliaments from among their members in accordance with the procedure laid down by each Member State.
2. The number of these delegates shall be as follows:

Germany	36
Belgium	14
France	36
Italy	36
Luxembourg	6
Netherlands	14

3. The Assembly shall draw up proposals for elections by direct universal suffrage in accordance with a uniform procedure in all Member States.
The Council shall, acting unanimously, lay down the appropriate provisions, which it shall recommend to Member States for adoption in accordance with their respective constitutional requirements."

Document III

Draft Convention on the election of the European Parliament by direct universal suffrage (adopted by the European Parliament on May 17, 1960) (abridged)

The European Parliament

believing that the time has come to associate the peoples directly in the building of Europe; conscious of the fact that a Parliament elected by direct universal suffrage is a key factor in the unification of Europe;

in execution of the mandate delivered to it by the Treaties setting up the European Communities;

approves the following

DRAFT CONVENTION

giving effect to Article 21,3 of the Treaty setting up the European Coal and Steel Community, Article 138,3 of the Treaty setting up the European Economic Community, and Article 108,3 of the Treaty setting up the European Atomic Energy Community on the election of the European Parliament by direct universal suffrage. The Special Council of Ministers of the European Coal and Steel Community,

The Council of the European Economic Community,

The Council of the European Atomic Energy Community,

resolved to take the freely expressed will of the peoples of the member States of the European Communities as the basis of the mission entrusted to the European Parliament;

anxious to enhance the representative character of the European Parliament;

having regard to Article 21 of the Treaty setting up the European Coal and Steel Community;

having regard to Article 138 of the Treaty setting up the European Economic Community;

having regard to Article 108 of the Treaty setting up the European Atomic Energy Community;

having regard to the draft prepared by the European Parliament and adopted by it on 17 May 1960;

have drawn up the following provisions which they recommend their member States to adopt:

The elected Parliament

Article 1

The representatives of the peoples in the European Parliament shall be elected by direct universal suffrage.

Article 2

The number of representatives elected in each member State shall be as follows:

Belgium	42
France	108
Germany (Fed. Rep.)	108
Italy	108
Luxembourg	18
Netherlands	42

Article 3

During a transitional period, one third of these representatives shall be elected by the Parliaments from among their own members, in accordance with a procedure that ensures that the political parties are fairly represented.

Article 4

The transitional period shall begin on the day this Convention comes into force.

The date of its expiry shall be fixed by the European Parliament. This shall not be earlier than the end of the third stage of the establishment of the Common Market, as defined in Article 8 of the Treaty setting up the European Economic Community, nor later than the expiry of the legislative period during which that third stage comes to an end.

Article 5

1. Representatives shall be elected for a term of five years.

The mandate of the representatives elected by the Parliaments shall, however, end with the loss of the national parliamentary mandate or at the end of the period for which they have been elected by their national Parliaments. Any representative whose mandate ends in this way shall remain in office until the mandate of his successor has been confirmed in the European Parliament.

2. The five-year legislative period shall begin at the opening of the first session following each election.

Article 6

Representatives shall vote on an individual and personal basis. They shall accept neither instructions nor any binding mandate.

Article 7

During the transitional period, membership of the European Parliament shall be compatible with membership of a Parliament.

The European Parliament shall decide whether these mandates are to remain compatible after the end of the transitional period.

Article 8

1. During the transitional period:

(a) The office of representative in the European Parliament shall be incompatible with that of:

member of the Government of a member State;

member of the High Authority of the European Coal and Steel Community, of the Commission of the European Economic Community or of the Commission of the European Atomic Energy Community;

judge, advocate-general or registrar at the Court of Justice of the European Communities;

member of the Consultative Committee of the European Coal and Steel Community or member of the Economic and Social Committee of the European Economic Community and of the European Atomic Energy Community;

auditor, as provided for in Article 78 of the Treaty setting up the European Coal and Steel Community, or members of the supervisory committee of auditors provided for in Article 206 of the Treaty setting up the European Economic Community and Article 180 of the Treaty setting up the European Atomic Energy Community;

member of the committees or other bodies established under the Treaties setting up the European Coal and Steel Community, the European Economic Community and the European Atomic Energy Community for the purpose of managing the Communities' funds or carrying out a direct administrative task;

member of the Board of Directors, Management Committee or staff of the European Investment Bank;

official or other servant in the active employment of the institutions of the European Communities or of the specialized bodies attached to them.

Representatives of the European Parliment appointed, in the course of a legislative period, to any of the offices mentioned above shall be replaced under the terms of Article 17.

(b) Each member State shall determine whether, and to what extent, the incompatibilities laid down by its laws with regard to the exercise of a national parliamentary mandate shall apply to the exercise of a mandate in the European Parliament.

2. The European Parliament shall decide on the system of incompatibilities to be adopted after the end of the transitional period.

The electoral system
Article 9
The European Parliament shall lay down the provisions governing the election of representatives after the end of the transitional period provided for in Article 4, in accordance with as uniform a procedure as possible.

Until these provisions comes into force, the electoral system shall, subject to the terms of the present Convention, fall within the competence of each member State.

Article 13
The constitutional provisions governing the admission of political parties to elections in each member State shall apply to elections to the European Parliament.

Article 14
Elections to the European Parliament shall be held on the same day in all six member States; the date shall be fixed so that national elections do not coincide with those for the European Parliament.

Any member State may, however, on grounds of tradition or geographical conditions, decide to hold the elections one day earlier or later than the fixed date or to spread them over all three days.

Article 18
Candidates or lists that secure not less than ten per cent of the votes cast by the electorate in the constituency in which they have stood for election, shall be entitled to a refund of certain election expenses.

The necessary credits shall be entered in the European Parliament's budget to enable such refunds to be made in accordance with a procedure to be fixed beforehand by its Bureau.

Document IV
Draft Convention introducing "Elections to the European Parliament by direct universal suffrage"
("PATIJN Report")
of 14 January, 1975

A. Motion for a resolution on the adoption of a draft convention introducing elections to the European Parliament by direct universal suffrage

Chapter I

The European Parliament
— having regard to the report of its Political Affairs Committee (Doc. 368/74),
— reaffirms its conviction that the process of European unification cannot succeed without the direct participation of the peoples affected;
— therefore considers a European Parliament elected by direct universal suffrage as an indispensable element in achieving further progress towards integration and establishing a better equilibrium between the Community institutions on a democratic basis,
— in pursuance of the task assigned to it by the Treaties establishing the European Communities,
— having regard to the need to adapt the draft convention of 1960 to the changed circumstances as they now exist,
— replaces the draft convention it adopted on 17 May 1960 by the following

Draft Convention
on the election of members of the European Parliament by direct universal suffrage
'The Council of the European Communities,
— resolved to take the freely expressed will of the peoples of the Member States of the European Communities as the justification for the mission entrusted to the European Parliament;
— anxious to emphasize the representative character of the European Parliament by the election of its members by direct universal suffrage;
— having regard to Articles 21(3) and 96 of the Treaty establishing the European Coal and Steel Community;
— having regard to Articles 138(3) and 236 of the Treaty establishing the European Economic Community;
— having regard to Articles 108(3) and 204 of the Treaty establishing the European Atomic Energy Community;
— having regard to the draft prepared by the European Parliament and adopted by it on 14 January, 1975;
has drawn up the following provisions which it recommends the Member States to adopt:

Chapter I
General provisions
Article 1
The representatives of the peoples in the European Parliament shall be elected by direct universal suffrage.

Article 2
1. The number of representatives elected in each Member State shall be as follows:

Belgium	23
Denmark	17
France	65
Germany (FR)	71
Ireland	13
Italy	66
Luxembourg	6
Netherlands	27
United Kingdom	67
	355

2. The Parliament, the Commission or the Government of any Member State may propose to the Council changes in the number of members provided for in paragraph 1.
Amendments to this convention shall be made pursuant to the procedure provided for in Article 14 of this Convention.

Article 3
1. Representatives shall be elected for a term of five years.
2. The five-year legislative period shall begin at the opening of the first session following each election.

Article 4
1. Representatives shall vote on an individual and personal basis. They shall accept neither instructions nor any binding mandate.
2. National legislation shall ensure that the representatives receive the same guarantees as to independence, indemnity and immunity as their counterparts in the national Parliaments.

Article 5
Membership of the European Parliament shall be compatible with membership of a Parliament of a Member State.

Article 6
1. The office of representative in the European Parliament shall be incompatible with that of:
— member of the Government of a Member State;

- member of the Commission of the European Communities;
- judge, advocate-general or registrar at the Court of Justice of the European Communities;
- member of the Court of Auditors of the European Communities;
- member of the Consultative Committee of the European Coal and Steel Community or member of the Economic and Social Committee of the European Economic Community and of the European Atomic Energy Community;
- member of committees or other bodies set up in pursuance of the Treaties establishing the European Coal and Steel Community, the European Economic Community and the European Atomic Energy Community for the purpose of managing the Communities' funds or carrying out a permanent and direct administrative task;
- member of the Board of Directors, Management Committee or staff of the European Investment Bank;
- active official or servant of the institutions of the European Communities or of the specialized bodies attached to them.

2. Subject to the entry into force of special rules pursuant to Article 7(1) of this Convention, the provisions of each Member State relating to incompatibility with a national parliamentary mandate shall be applied.

3. Representatives of the European Parliament appointed, in the course of a legislative period, to any of the offices mentioned above shall be replaced under the terms of Article 12.

Chapter II
Electoral system

Article 7
1. The European Parliament shall draw up a proposal for a uniform electoral system by 1980 at the latest. The Council shall unanimously lay down the appropriate provisions, which it shall recommend to the Member States for adoption in accordance with their constitutional requirements.
2. Pending the entry into force of this uniform electoral system and subject to the other provisions of this Convention, the electoral system shall fall within the competence of each Member State.

Article 8
The provisions governing the admission of political parties to elections in each Member State shall apply to elections to the European Parliament.

Article 9
1. Elections to the European Parliament shall be held on the same day in all Member States.
2. Any Member State may, however, decide to hold the elections one day earlier or later than the fixed date or to spread them over two consecutive days including that day.

3. The Council shall make arrangements in accordance with the procedure laid down in Article 14, to ensure that the election results are declared at one and the same time.

Article 10
1. Elections to the European Parliament shall be held not later than one month before the end of each legislative period.
2. The European Parliament shall sit automatically on the first Tuesday following an interval of one month from the last day of the elections.
3. The outgoing European Parliament shall remain in office until the first sitting of the new Parliament.

Article 11
Pending the entry into force of the uniform electoral system to be adopted in accordance with Article 7(1), the European Parliament shall verify the credentials of representatives and rule on any disputes that may arise in this connection.

Article 12
Pending the entry into force of the uniform electoral system to be adopted in accordance with Article 7(1) and subject to the other provisions of this Convention, the Member States shall lay down appropriate procedures for filling any seat which falls vacant during a legislative period.

Chapter III
Transitional and final provisions

Article 13
1. Subject to the provisions of Article 9, the first elections to the European Parliament shall be held not later than the first Sunday of May, 1980.
2. The exact date of subsequent elections shall be fixed, taking account of Articles 3, 9 and 10, in accordance with the procedure laid down in Article 14.

Article 14
Should reference be made to the procedure laid down in this Article or should it appear that further measures are required to implement direct elections to the European Parliament in accordance with this Convention and if the necessary powers are not provided, the Council shall, acting unanimously on a proposal from the European Parliament and with its approval, make the appropriate provisions. The Council shall consult the Commission before making its decision.

Article 15
1. The following provisions stand repealed by the present Convention:
Article 21(3) of the Treaty establishing the European Coal and Steel Community,
Article 138(3) of the Treaty establishing the European Economic Community, and
Article 108(3) of the Treaty establishing the European Atomic Energy Community.

2. Article 21 (1 and 2) of the ECSC Treaty, Article 138 (1 and 2) of the EEC Treaty, and Article 108 (1 and 2) of the EAEC Treaty shall be repealed on the date fixed in Article 10(2).

Article 16
This Convention is drawn up in the Danish, Dutch, English, French, German and Italian languages, all six texts being equally authentic.

Article 17
1. This Convention shall be ratified by the Member States in accordance with their respective constitutional requirements.
2. The instruments of ratification shall be deposited with the Government of the Italian Republic, which shall inform the signatory States and the institutions of the European Communities when this has been done.
3. This Convention shall enter into force on the day the instrument of ratification is deposited by the last signatory State to carry out this formality.

II

The European Parliament
— instructs its Political Affairs Committee to establish appropriate contacts with the Council and the Member States with a view to securing the early adoption of the draft convention;
— urges the Council to establish the appropriate contacts with the European Parliament immediately if, in its opinion, changes should be made to the draft convention;
— instructs its Political Affairs Committee to bring forward a supplementary report when modifications of the draft Convention appear to be necessary;
— instructs its Political Affairs Committee immediately to carry out the necessary preliminary work for the introduction of a European electoral system;
— instructs its President to forward this resolution, together with the draft convention and the report of its committee, to the Council and Commission of the European Communities and to the Parliaments and Governments of the Member States;

Document V
Decision and Act of the EC Council
"Concerning the election of the representatives of the Assembly by direct universal suffrage"
of 20 September, 1976

Decision

The Council
composed of the representatives of the Member States and acting unanimously,
— having regard to Article 21(3) of the Treaty establishing the European Coal and Steel Community,
— having regard to Article 138(3) of the Treaty establishing the European Economic Community,
— having regard to Article 108(3) of the Treaty establishing the European Atomic Energy Community,
— having regard to the proposal from the Assembly,
— intending to give effect to the conclusions of the European Council in Rome on 1 and 2 December 1975, that the election of the Assembly should be held on a single date within the period May/June 1978,
— has laid down the provisions annexed to this Decision which it recommends to the Member States for adoption in accordance with their respective constitutional requirements.
The Decision and the provisions annexed hereto shall be published in the Official Journal of the European Communities.
The Member States shall notify the Secretary-General of the Council of the European Communities without delay of the completion of the procedures necessary in accordance with their respective constitutional requirements for the adoption of the provisions annexed to this Decision.
The Decision shall enter into force on the day of its publication in the Official Journal of the European Communities.
Done at Brussels on the twentieth day of December in the year one thousand nine hundred and seventy-six.
For the Council
The President of the European Communities.

Act concerning the election of the representatives of the Assembly by direct universal suffrage

Article 1
The representatives in the Assembly of the peoples of the States brought together in the Community shall be elected by direct universal suffrage.

Article 2
The number of representatives elected in each Member State shall be as follows:

Belgium	24
Denmark	16
Germany	81
France	81
Ireland	15
Italy	81
Luxembourg	6
Netherlands	25
United Kingdom	81

Article 3
1. Representatives shall be elected for a term of five years.
2. This five-year period shall begin at the opening of the first session following each election. It may be extended or curtailed pursuant to the second subparagraph of Article 10(2).
3. The term of office of each representative shall begin and end at the same time as the period referred to in paragraph 2.

Article 4
1. Representatives shall vote on an individual and personal basis. They shall not be bound by any instructions and shall not receive a binding mandate.
2. Representatives shall enjoy the privileges and immunities applicable to members of the Assembly by virtue of the Protocol on the privileges and immunities of the European Communities annexed to the Treaty establishing a single Council and a single Commission of the European Communities.

Article 5
The office of representative in the Assembly shall be compatible with membership of the Parliament of a Member State.

Article 6
1. The office of representative in the Assembly shall be incompatible with that of:
— member of the Government of a Member State,
— member of the Commission of the European Communities,
— Judge, Advocate-General or Registrar of the Court of Justice of the European Communities,
— member of the Court of Auditors of the European Communities,
— member of the Consultative Committee of the European Coal and Steel Community or member of the Economic and Social Committee of the European Economic Community and of the European Atomic Energy Community.
— member of committees or other bodies set up pursuant to the Treaties establishing the European Coal and Steel Community, the European Economic Community and the European Atomic Energy Community for the

purpose of managing the Communities' funds or carrying out a permanent direct administrative task,
- member of the Board of Directors, Management Committee or staff of the European Investment Bank,
- active official or servant of the institutions of the European Communities or of the specialized bodies attached to them.

2. In addition, each Member State may, in the circumstances provided for in Article 7 (2), lay down rules at national level relating to incompatibility.

3. Representatives in the Assembly to whom paragraphs 1 and 2 become applicable in the course of the five-year period referred to in Article 3 shall be replaced in accordance with Article 12.

Article 7

1. Pursuant to Article 21 (3) of the Treaty establishing the European Coal and Steel Community, Article 138 (3) of the Treaty establishing the European Economic Community and 108 (3) of the Treaty establishing the European Atomic Energy Community, the Assembly shall draw up a proposal for a uniform electoral procedure.

2. Pending the entry into force of a uniform electoral procedure and subject to the other provisions of this Act, the electoral procedure shall be governed in each Member State by its national provisions.

Article 8

No one may vote more than once in any election of representatives to the Assembly.

Article 9

1. Elections to the Assembly shall be held on the date fixed by each Member State; for all Member States this date shall fall within the same period starting on a Thursday morning and ending on the following Sunday.

2. The counting of votes may not begin until after the close of polling in the Member State whose electors are the last to vote within the period referred to in paragraph 1.

3. If a Member State adopts a double ballot system for elections to the Assembly, the first ballot must take place during the period referred to in paragraph 1.

Article 10

1. The Council, acting unanimously after consulting the Assembly, shall determine the period referred to in Article 9 (1) for the first elections.

2. Subsequent elections shall take place in the corresponding period in the last year of the five-year period referred to in Article 3.

Should it prove impossible to hold the elections in the Community during that period, the Council acting unanimously shall, after consulting the Assembly, determine another period which shall be not more than one month before or one month after the period fixed pursuant to the preceding subparagraph.

3. Without prejudice to Article 22 of the Treaty establishing the European Coal and Steel Community, Article 139 of the Treaty establishing the European Economic Community and Article 109 of the Treaty establishing the European Atomic Energy Community, the Assembly shall meet, without requiring to be convened, on the first Tuesday after expiry of an interval of one month from the end of the period referred to in Article 9 (1).

4. The powers of the outgoing Assembly shall cease upon the opening of the first sitting of the new Assembly.

Article 11

Pending the entry into force of the uniform electoral procedure referred to in Article 7 (1), the Assembly shall verify the credentials of representatives. For this purpose it shall take note of the results declared officially by the Member States and shall rule on any disputes which may arise out of the provisions of this Act other than those arising out of the national provisions to which the Act refers.

Article 12

1. Pending the entry into force of the uniform electoral procedure referred to in Article 7 (1) and subject to the other provisions of this Act, each Member State shall lay down appropriate procedures for filling any seat which falls vacant during the five-year term of office referred to in Article 3 for the remainder of that period.

2. Where a seat falls vacant pursuant to national provisions in force in a Member State, the latter shall inform the Assembly, which shall take note of that fact.

In all other cases, the Assembly shall establish that there is a vacancy and inform the Member State thereof.

Article 13

Should it appear necessary to adopt measures to implement this Act, the Council, acting unanimously on a proposal from the Assembly after consulting the Commission, shall adopt such measures after endeavouring to reach agreement with the Assembly in a conciliation committee consisting of the Council and representatives of the Assembly.

Article 14

Article 21 (1) and (2) of the Treaty establishing the European Coal and Steel Community, Article 138 (1) and (2) of the Treaty establishing the European Economic Community and Article 108 (1) and (2) of the Treaty establishing the European Atomic Energy Community shall lapse on the date of the sitting held in accordance with Article 10 (3) by the first Assembly elected pursuant to this Act.

Article 15

This Act is drawn up in the Danish, Dutch, English, French, German, Irish and Italian languages, all the texts being equally authentic.

Annexes I to III shall form an integral part of this Act.
A declaration by the Government of the Federal Republic of Germany is attached hereto.

Article 16

The provisions of this Act shall enter into force on the first day of the month following that during which the last of the notifications referred to in the Decision is received.

Done at Brussels on the twentieth day of September in the year one thousand nine hundred and seventy-six.

Annex I

The Danish authorities may decide on the dates on which the election of members to the Assembly shall take place in Greenland.

Annex II

The United Kingdom will apply the provisions of this Act only in respect of the United Kingdom.

Annex III

Declaration on Article 13

As regards the procedure to be followed by the Conciliation Committee, it is agreed to have recourse to the provisions of paragraphs 5, 6 and 7 of the procedure laid down in the joint declaration of the European Parliament, the Council and the Commission of 4 March 1975 (1).

Declaration by the Government of the Federal Republic of Germany

The Government of the Federal Republic of Germany declares that the Act concerning the election of the members of the European Parliament by direct universal suffrage shall equally apply to Land Berlin.
In consideration of the rights and responsibilities of France, the United Kingdom of Great Britain and Northern Ireland, and the United States of America, the Berlin House of Deputies will elect representatives to those seats within the quota of the Federal Republic of Germany that fall to Land Berlin.

Section 2 : Documents relating to the political parties

1. The Social Democrat Parties

Document I
Appeal to the Electorate (Europa 79)

On 12 January 1979 the eleven Socialist parties of the nine countries of the European Community, meeting in Brussels for the Xth Congress, unanimously adopted an Appeal to European electors for the first elections by direct universal suffrage to the European Parliament. In this Message, the Socialists present the joint proposals they undertake to defend in each country and in the European Parliament if you elect them.

Appeal to the European Electorate
For the first time in history, the citizens of nine European countries, representing a single electorate of some 140 million voters, will directly elect their representatives to the Assembly of the European Community (the European Parliament).
For democratic Socialists, these elections are not an end in themselves. They are to be considered as an additional means to promote progress towards a society freed from oppression and exploitation. We share a common goal of a new world order based on democratic Socialist principles. Thus the voters will have the opportunity of directly influencing progress in that direction.
In shaping this European Community, the logic of the capitalist market system, namely the pursuit of private commercial and financial interests, has for too long prevailed over the search for commonly defined social and human objectives. Obviously a directly elected European Parliament will not automatically solve all the challenging problems of our times. Each country will have to continue to introduce indispensable social and economic changes by its own efforts and with its own means, including legislation. But we are deeply convinced that action undertaken in common could, in various fields, accelerate the progress towards these goals to the greater benefit of each of them.
Our parties have inherited different experiences down the years. They operate in countries where the level of economic development, the intensity of social struggle, cultural traditions, awareness of social problems and the interplay of internal political alliances profoundly differ. Yet we share a common goal of a more human and egalitarian Europe for all our citizens.
We note with concern:
- the inability of our present social structure to solve the grave problem of unemployment;
- a trend towards less equality and solidarity as seen in the ever-widening gulf between the rich and the poor throughout the world and within the European Community;
- that uncontrolled growth in production and consumption, especially in the wealthier regions of the world, is being achieved at the

cost of exhausting and polluting the environment, and of declining living and working conditions for millions of workers — something which Socialists cannot permit.
Therefore, the democratic Socialist parties herewith present the following commonly agreed principles:
- to ensure the right to work for all and in particular for youth;
- to bring economic and social development under democratic control;
- to fight pollution;
- to end discrimination, in particular against women;
- to protect the consumer;
- to promote peace, security and cooperation;
- to extend and defend human rights and civil liberties.

Ensuring the Right to Work
Unemployment results from the crisis of the present economic system. It increases inequality among individuals, it limits women's rights to work, it demoralizes young people unable to find a job, it contributes to despair and disillusionment in society.
Socialists will seek to ensure that all members of the European Community contribute to the solution of the problems of underemployment through reorientation and better control of the economy as well as through more active employment and education policies. The market economy will not lead automatically to social justice. Until such times as there is real economic democracy, living and working conditions cannot become more humane. The demand of the Conservatives for the subordination of labour to capital must be rejected. In particular Socialists shall strive to ensure that further economic growth will benefit those with the lowest incomes.
The right to work is and will remain one of the basic aims of Socialism. It is a fundamental human right for men and women. The principle tasks of the European Community and its member countries must therefore be to combat unemployment. In this connection Socialists place greatest emphasis not only on a policy of full employment but also on a policy aimed at creating better working conditions.
Our fight for a society in which available resources are distributed fairly demands that we shape and guide social and economic development. The conventional economic policy instruments have proved inadequate; an active employment policy and the planning of the economy will be necessary to reduce unemployment. We also seek a fairer distribution of available work with an important place being

277

given to a shorter working day, a 35-hour working week, and a systematic policy of vocational training and retraining. Here we must take particular account of those groups which face the greatest difficulties on the labour market; young people, women, older workers, the disabled and foreign workers.

The best way to achieve these conditions is through common policies agreed between the main industrial nations. Such policies can be achieved only in close cooperation with all trade union organisations, particularly the European Trade Union Confederation. The ETUC must be more involved at Community level in the preparation of, and the procedure for, making decisions. Our parties also intend to work out their proposals, where possible, in collaboration with the trade union movement.

We realize that the fight against unemployment also requires longer-term structural reforms and economic planning involving a key role in certain sectors for public enterprises.

Keeping Economic and Social Developments under Democratic Control

Economic policy must be based on a type of economic growth more respectful of human needs, avoiding the waste of scarce natural resources, the pollution of the environment, and promoting solidarity between regions. To meet these demands, we call for close scientific and technological cooperation between countries in order to modernize older industries and to create new ones. We advocate structural reforms, economic planning and effective controls on multinational undertakings and major industrial and financial groups. Steps will be taken to guide investment, particularly in the branches of industry with a strong international involvement. More means than at present available should be provided for regional and social policies aiming at reducing the big inequalities between regions and groups of the population. Therefore, we shall strive:

- to create efficient and democratic economic structures and economic stability;
- to ensure the democratisation of industry at all levels in way adapted to the specific circumstances of each individual country and in cooperation with the trade union organisations;
- to ensure public control of big industrial and financial concentrations and multinational companies;
- to develop workers' cooperatives and similar publicly useful companies;
- to stimulate small and medium-sized firms.

The Common Agricultural Policy must be adapted so as to achieve a better balance between production and consumption, more stable prices and an equitable development of agricultural incomes through greater efficiency and better structural policies. The consumer interest must be taken fully into account in the evolution of the C.A.P.

Fighting Pollution

The combined efforts of the countries of the European Community should be given a strong lead to ensure that a worldwide effort will be made to maintain ecological balance.

The improvement of the quality of life in the cities and the countryside and the fight against pollution cannot be limited to the boundaries of one single country. Only close cooperation among our countries can provide the required protection for the people through commonly agreed and implemented measures.

Concerning energy, we propose:

- that an effective programme should be set up by the European Community for energy saving and the development of alternative sources of energy;
- that no further development and use of nuclear energy will be acceptable unless control and management is in public hands and unless clearly effective safeguards are provided against dangers to public safety, health and the environment.

Ending Discrimination, in particular against Women

Socialism stands for equality and rejects all discrimination based on sex, race, religion and political and philosophical opinions. This means that we reject exclusion from government service solely on the grounds of political beliefs. Equality also means special protection for the old, the handicapped and social outcasts. Men and women should be in a position to make their mark to the same extent on the development of society at all levels, at work and at home, in public and private life.

Similar conditions for men and women should be required for access to education, to the labour market, to social benefits, to public life, etc.

In order to reach these goals we particularly stress that:

- the content of education should be modified in order to meet the needs of women;
- institutions taking care of children should be accessible to all;
- a general spirit of tolerance and comradeship should be actively promoted throughout the European Community.

Protecting the Consumer

In our consumption-orientated society special care should be given to the protection of the consumer against aggressive and misleading publicity and the abuse of goods detrimental to the health of the individual and which encourage the waste of valuable resources. Collective needs are often disregarded in the pursuit of increased consumption of useless products encouraged by the interests of producers and advertisers.

We therefore propose:

- to favour objective information and the right to counteract misleading publicity;
- to encourage democratic consumers' associa-

tions and to reinforce their rights to introduce legal actions against abuse by producers;
— to enlarge the responsibility of producers for the quality of the goods that they produce.

Promoting Peace, Security and Cooperation

Freedom, justice and solidarity are not only principles applicable in our different countries but are also our guidelines for the new economic world order that we are seeking to establish. Socialists in Europe will therefore contribute to the pursuit of detente between East and West.

We are working for the full implementation of the Helsinki agreements and for worldwide peace and security. In the meantime, the maximum effort should be made to halt the arms race, especially in the nuclear field, and to bring sales of arms under international control. Satisfactory measures must be found to prevent the proliferation of nuclear weapons. Socialists will not be a party to the supply of arms to fascist or racist regimes.

In the medium and long-term the prosperous countries will have to accept a slower increase in their material affluence in order to overcome the North-South conflict. Only if Europe proves its active solidarity with the poorer regions of the world will it be in a position to contribute effectively to a lasting peace.

This is why we should also intensify European cooperation with the developing countries. The basic principles of this cooperation are the following:
— commitment of the Community to the overall advancement of the developing countries;
— full recognition of the independence of the developing countries and their right to freedom from intervention, whether politically or commercially motivated;
— greater benefit to the developing countries through trade relations;
— scientific and technical cooperation designed to benefit everyone;
— the conclusion of an agreement on joint action with a view to imposing at world level, effective and equitable rules for the monetary system and economic transactions.

The Lome Convention is to be welcomed as an important step in the right direction. But much remains to be done in the field of development assistance and cooperation.

Our programme in this field can be summarized briefly as follows:

Aid should be concentrated on the poorest countries and on those countries that follow a social policy aiming at the improvement of the conditions of the poorest sections of their population;

Official development aid with no strings attached should be increased up to 1% of the GNP of the European Community;

The Community should extend its financial aid to non-associated developing countries;

The UNCTAD IV integrated programme on raw materials should be encouraged;

The European Community should adopt and implement the UN Charter on economic rights and obligations of states.

Extending and Defending Human Rights and Civil Liberties

Human rights derive from the most basic human needs. The message which Socialists are seeking to propagate is that the only sure approach to the attainment of basic human rights lies in the creation of a free and democratic political, economic and social system. The promotion of human rights must be genuine and in no sense an instrument of political advantage.

Therefore we will demand in the Community's Assembly (the European Parliament):
— that all the Member States of the Community implement in full the European Convention on Human Rights;
— that the European Community should be in the frontline of the fight for the realisation of human rights throughout the world.

As far as the rights of the citizens of the Community are concerned we will strive for:

The eradication of all legal and political discrimination affecting citizens of each country wherever they may live in the Community;

Fundamental economic and social rights should be part of these Community rights, including the right to work. All discrimination against foreigners must be eliminated.

The highest standards of political and legal rights should be extended to all Community citizens.

We welcome the re-establishment of democracy in Greece, Spain and Portugal; we strongly support the accession of these countries to the Community. Moreover, we believe that democratic Europe has an urgent responsibility to contribute to the strengthening of democracy in these countries and must demonstrate its solidarity with the working people of the countries concerned.

We know that the economic and social structures of these countries and the particular products concerned make it necessary to have certain arrangements for adaptation and an appropriate timetable of transitional periods, in order to respect the legitimate interests of all people — both in the Community and in Greece, Portugal and Spain. The enlargement of the Community must become a source of new strength and dynamism for Europe.

We do not see the European Community as an end in itself. Neither can it be considered as the whole of Europe. The tendency to use the word 'Europe' as a description of the Community is to be deplored since it obscures the fact that the majority of European states and peoples are not part of the Community. We believe that in fighting for international Socialism we go beyond the confines of the Community.

The directly elected European Parliament must initially develop within the framework of the existing treaties. We recognize that any further transfer of powers from national governments to the Community institutions or from national parliaments to the European Parliament can take place only with the clear and direct assent of the national governments and parliaments.

In each of the nine countries belonging to the Community the democratic Socialists represent an important and coherent political force.

All these proposals have been approved by the democratic Socialist parties of the European Community. In each of these countries we will defend them.

The progressive policies of the Socialist parties are now more relevant than ever to the needs of Europe's people since it is manifest that capitalism cannot solve the problems which exist.

Work for the solution of today's problems must proceed at both national and Community level and can be facilitated by actions based on closer European cooperation.

For successful action in the interests of all the people, the voice of the Socialist Movement must be strong, in the directly elected European Parliament and in the parliaments of the Member States.

Document II
Political Declaration (Party Leaders' Conference, 23-24th June 1978 in Brussels)

We, the Socialist parties of the European Community are committed to the pursuit of the common goals of freedom, social justice, equality and harmonious economic development.

Our parties have inherited different experiences down the years. They operate in countries where the level of economic development, the intensity of social struggle, cultural traditions, awareness of social problems and the interplay of internal political alliances profoundly differ, yet we share a common goal of a more human and egalitarian Europe for all our citizens, as part of a new international order based on democratic socialist principles.

Our drawing more closely together in Europe is quite compatible with respect for each other's individuality.

Throughout Europe, it is the Socialists who, in the cause of human welfare, are battling to eradicate injustice and inequality, and to ensure a harmonious development of society.

In the European Community, the most important objective for Socialists is the liberation of the individual from every form of dependence, exploitation and need and the giving of more power and rights to each individual.

To achieve this objective we must change the economic and social structures in our countries. We realize that whilst each country can by itself do much towards this end, joint action between us in some fields can accelerate our progress. After twenty years of existence, the Community must now advance to a new phase in which the emphasis — in policy and in action — will be changed from the dictates of commercial interest to the pursuit of humane and cooperative goals. The first phase of the life of the Community has ended with only free trade achieved but with little regional and social balance.

We note with concern:
- the inability of our present social structure to solve the grave problem of unemployment;
- a trend towards less equality and solidarity as seen in the ever-widening gulf between the rich and the poor throughout the world and within the European Community;
- that uncontrolled growth in production and consumption, especially in the wealthier regions of the world, is being achieved at the cost of exhausting and polluting the environment, and of declining living and working conditions for millions of workers — something which Socialists cannot permit.

We accept that our duty to posterity, and to the millions of people living in dire poverty, compels us to accept restrictions in the use we make of the world's natural resources and to work for a better distribution of wealth, both within the Community and between the Community and the Third World.

Our fight for a society in which available resources are distributed fairly demands that we shape and guide social and economic development. The conventional economic policy instruments have proved inadequate; an active employment policy and the planning of the economy will be necessary to reduce unemployment. We also seek a fairer distribution of available work, with an important place being given to a shorter working span, a shorter working week, and a systematic policy of vocational training and retraining. Here we must take particular account of those groups which face the greatest difficulties on the labour market; young people, women, older workers and foreign workers.

We believe that the best way to achieve these conditions is through a common policy agreed between the main industrial nations. This common policy can be achieved only in close cooperation with all Trade Union organisations, particularly the ETUC. Our parties emphasize the growing role that the ETUC has to play in defending the personal and material interests of the working people of Europe and in achieving social progress and the democratisation of the economy. The ETUC must be more involved in the preparation of, and the procedure for, making decisions. Our parties also intend to work out their own proposals in close collaboration with the Trade Union movement and to encourage every possible step towards greater freedom for the workers of Europe.

In addition to reducing unemployment, an improvement in working conditions is urgently required. The third industrial revolution has been accompanied by great technological progress, but also by an increase in the scale and concentration of economic power, producing massive and impersonal production units which make individual workers and consumers feel insignificant and powerless. Increasing mechanisation and mass production mean that work is rarely geared to the aptitudes and wishes of the individual worker. Inhuman working conditions lead to alienation, increasing absenteeism and inefficiency. The traditional small and medium-sized undertakings are often unable to keep up with the large undertakings and are threatened with extinction. We oppose this trend. Therefore we shall campaign for:
- increased responsibility for workers within the enterprise. Democracy within industry and the economy as a whole should be developed in forms appropriate to each country and in cooperation with trade unions.
- democratic control of major industrial concentrations and multinational concerns: respect for competition rules, checking transfers of profits, greater control of the movement of capital and the allocation of investment.
- active encouragement of small and medium sized enterprises, and development of workers cooperatives, and similar social instruments.

The Socialist parties therefore undertake to strive for an economic policy aimed at establishing
- Full employment

- Stability
- A fairer distribution of income and wealth
- An effective and democratic economic structure
- Economic democracy
- Improved social security
- Better living and working conditions
- Improved educational opportunities.

The right to work is and will remain one of the basic aims of Socialism. It is a fundamental human right for men and women. The principal tasks of the European Community and its member countries must therefore be to combat unemployment and to ensure full employment. In this connection Socialists place greatest emphasis not only on a policy of full employment but also on a policy aimed at creating better working conditions.

Socialists therefore advocate humane and harmonious growth, which means that innovation, investment and the creation and location of jobs will take account of the need for a balanced society, particularly with regard to the environment.

We Socialists will continue to strive for a more equitable distribution of income and wealth. We note with particular concern that efforts to assist the development of the Community's less-favoured regions have made little headway.

We therefore demand a clear and vigorous regional policy designed to reduce differences in living standards between the various regions in the Community. At the same time we demand an effective social policy capable of removing the many inequalities between groups of citizens in our countries.

Democratic Socialism stands for an equitable educational system which offers equal opportunities and maximum possibilities of development for all. In Europe we want a social expenditure policy which will ensure that everyone, irrespective of social background, sex or age, can avail himself of opportunities for continuing education throughout his life.

The exhaustion of raw materials and the dangers of environmental pollution are most alarming. Only a worldwide effort can enable the nations to implement a policy designed to maintain the ecological balance and save raw materials; Europe should give a lead in this direction.

Of great importance here will be a Community energy conservation programme, together with a Community effort to develop alternative energy sources. We recognize that the further development and use of nuclear energy can be considered only if there is public ownership and control to ensure adequate safeguards against security and environmental hazards.

We welcome the re-establishment of democracy in Greece, Spain and Portugal; we strongly support the accession of these countries to the Community. Moreover we believe that democratic Europe has an urgent responsibility to contribute to the strengthening of democracy in these countries and must demonstrate its solidarity with the working people of the countries concerned.

We know that the economic and social structures of these countries and the particular products concerned make it necessary to have certain arrangements for adaptation and an appropriate timetable of transitional periods, in order to respect the legitimate interests of all people — both in the Community and in Greece, Portugal and Spain.

The enlargement of the Community must become a source of new strength and dynamism for Europe.

Europe should see itself as a force for peace. In our view, social progress based on freedom and a sense of responsibility within and outside the Community are possible only if we remain at peace. We wish to contribute towards this end and therefore support the policy of detente between East and West. Our aim is to work towards a situation in which European peace becomes a reality.

Europe has failed to achieve an organized peace — for the mere absence of war does not constitute a secure peace. We therefore support a policy consciously aimed at preventing war. We want to see a policy of detente between the power blocs.

The Socialist parties in Europe are the best guarantee that in future, the renunciation of the use of force, stability, cooperation and the non proliferation of nuclear weapons will remain the basic principles of international politics.

We spare no effort to achieve the renunciation of violence at regional and world level. Freedom, justice and solidarity are not only principles ruling the way of life of our countries but also a reliable guide for the international order that we are striving for.

With regard to the present military balance in the world and developments in the field of armaments technology, negotiations on arms control are becoming more and more important. The arms race must be stopped, as it swallows up huge resources and could endanger strategic stability through the increasing development of new weapons technology. The policy of limiting and reducing arms must be so conceived as to make it possible to stop the arms race spiral.

As regards our relations with Eastern Europe, we favour a policy of detente and cooperation as set out in the Final Act of the Helsinki Agreement. This first effort at cooperation between East and West in Europe since the Second World War includes practical plans for cooperation in the economic field as well as in science and human relations. These plans can become a reality only if the true spirit of the Helsinki agreement, including the area of human rights, is supported by all signatories.

Only a Europe which declares itself in solidarity with the world's poor can make a genuine contribution to peace. In the medium and long term the prosperous countries will have to accept a slower increase in their material affluence in order to overcome the North-South conflict.

This is why we would also intensify European cooperation with the developing countries. The

success achieved so far — in particular through the Lome agreement — shows that we are on the right path towards further progress. The basic principles of this cooperation are the following:
— commitment of the Community to the overall advancement of the developing countries;
— full recognition of the independence of the developing countries and their right to freedom from intervention, whether politically or commercially motivated;
— greater benefit to the developing countries through trade relations;
— scientific and technical cooperation designed to benefit everyone;
— the conclusion of an agreement on joint action with a view to imposing at world level, effective and equitable rules for the monetary system and economic transactions.

We attach the highest importance to the preservation and protection of human rights and civil liberties within the Community. In particular, we abhor and will strongly oppose any discrimination on grounds of sex, colour, ethnic origin or religious belief. The Community countries must implement fully the provisions of the European Convention of Human Rights. At the same time, the Community should be in the forefront of the struggle for human rights throughout the world and, wherever possible, should use its influence to support this struggle. We want a democratic Europe. Because we are convinced that the conditions in which we live and which we can expect in the future, require increasing responsibility on the part of government, we consider it absolutely essential that government bodies should be openly and publicly accountable to the people. Responsibilities should be devolved to smaller administrative units. We are against the uncontrolled and uncontrollable exercise of power. This applies also to the business world.

In the direct elections to the European Parliament to be held in 1979, the citizens of Europe must make their choice for or against a policy which is consistently geared to the equitable distribution of income, knowledge and power.

The directly elected European Parliament must initially develop within the framework of the existing treaties. We recognize that any further transfer of powers from national governments to the Community institutions or from national parliaments to the European Parliament can take place only with the clear and direct assent of the national governments and parliaments.

The year of the first European elections has dawned. The progressive policies of the Socialist Parties are now more relevant than ever to the need of Europe's people since it is manifest that capitalism cannot solve the problems which exist. Work for the solution of today's problems must proceed at both national and Community level and can be facilitated by actions based on closer European cooperation.

For successful action in the interests of all the people the voice of the Socialist Movement must be strong, in the directly elected European Parliament and in the Parliaments of the Member States.

We want to build a Europe in which every individual can live in peace and in freedom. Democracy and Socialism are for the citizens of Europe, the guarantee of peace and freedom.

Document III
Rules of Procedure of the Confederation of Socialist Parties of the European Community

1. The cooperation between the parties in the European Community which are members of the Socialist International is based on the provisions of the statutes of the Socialist International pertaining to regional cooperation between members.

2. The purpose of such cooperation is to strengthen inter-party relations and, in particular, to define joint, freely agreed positions in problems raised by the existence of the European Community.

3. The cooperation between the parties in the Confederation of Socialist Parties of the European Community is mainly conducted through the following bodies:
a. The Bureau
b. The Congress

4. The president of the Confederation is elected for a period of two years by the Congress on proposal of the Bureau.

5. The Bureau consists of two members from each affiliated party and the President of the Socialist Group. Each party, including the Socialist Group, has one vote. Member parties appoint their own representatives and specify the duration of their term of office.
The following are also members of the Bureau in a consultative capacity:
a. the members of the Bureau of the Socialist Group of the European Parliament;
b. the socialist members of the Commission of the European Parliament;
c. a representative appointed by the Bureau of the Socialist International;
d. a representative appointed by the Socialist Group of the Consultative Assembly of the Council of Europe.
The Bureau may invite the chairman or general secretaries of affiliated parties to attend particular meetings or may invite other socialist parties and organisations to send observers to its meetings.

6. The Bureau appoints:
a. up to four vice-presidents for a period of two years from among its members;
b. a general secretary;
c. two auditors.

7. The main tasks of the Bureau comprise:
a. discussing matters arising in connection with the activities of the European Community;
b. making recommendations to the affiliated parties;
c. organising the exchange of information between member parties;
d. convening Congresses, fixing their agenda and deciding where they are to be held;
e. executing the decisions of Congress;
f. calling extraordinary meetings;
g. approving the budget and fixing membership dues.

8. The Bureau can set up permanent or ad-hoc working groups and confer consultative status on certain organisations.

9. The decisions of the Bureau are taken by majority voting (except for the procedure foreseen under Article 13).
Any modification of the rules of procedure requires a majority of two-thirds of the Bureau.

10. The Bureau may publicly define its position on current matters falling within its field of competence. Positions so defined shall be submitted to the affiliated parties and shall bind them only if subsequently approved by them.
Positions to be published on behalf of the affiliated parties shall be submitted to them before publication. Amendments of the affiliated parties shall be forwarded to the Bureau, which shall take them into account.

11. The Bureau meets at least four times a year.
Any affiliated party or the Bureau of the Socialist Group of the European Parliament or the Bureau of the Socialist International may request a meeting of the Bureau.

12. The Congress consists of:
a. 18 delegates each from the Federal Republic of Germany, France, Italy (1), and the United Kingdom;
7 delegates each from Belgium and the Netherlands;
5 delegates each from Denmark and Ireland;
3 delegates from Luxembourg;
b. the members of the Bureau;
c. a number of delegates equal to the number of deputies in the European Parliament belonging to each party.
Those invited to Congress to participate in a consultative capacity are:
a. the members of the Socialist Group of the European Parliament;
b. representatives of member parties of the Socialist International;
c. representatives of the Socialist Group of the Consultative Assembly of the Council of Europe.
The Bureau may invite other representatives from other organisations and individual persons to attend the Congress.

13. The Congress can adopt with a simple majority recommendation to the parties.
A party which considers itself unable to implement a recommendation is to indicate the reasons to the Bureau.
Acting on an unanimous proposal of the Bureau, the Congress can adopt a decision binding on parties. Such a decision requires a two-thirds majority of Congress.
A proposal for a decision which obtains a majority short of a two-thirds majority is transformed into a recommendation.

14. Congress decisions and the list of Congress documents are forwarded to the Bureau of the Socialist International and the European socialist parties.

(1) 9 delegates each for the PSDI and PSI.

2. The Christian Democrat Parties

Document I
Political Programme of the European People's Party

Our Guidelines for Europe

Only by joint action can Europe safeguard its own personality (its own identity), its right of self-determination, and hence its ideals of freedom, solidarity, justice, peace and democracy.

In a federation, Europe will achieve this unity and safeguard its diversity.

The European Union must be a community in which all the forces of democracy find freedom of expression and in the formulation of which such forces can actively participate.

Europe must remain open to the world and make its own essential contribution to the fight against hunger, poverty and violence and to the achievement of justice and true peace in freedom.

Our Concept of Man

Our policy is based on a concept of man which is characterised by the fundamental Christian values and finds its expression in the inalienable and inviolable dignity and freedom of man — in equality, in diversity, in the struggle of self-realisation and in the awareness of the imperfection of man.

Man is dependent on the community for his development and cannot therefore attain to self-realisation unless he bears responsibility for himself and for others. The cornerstones of our society — freedom, justice, solidarity, pluralism and openness — all have their place in this personal concept of man.

In accordance with this philosophy, we confirm the value of the family, which is the mainstay of our society, which is particularly suitable as a means of furthering the development of each of its members and which is a crucial element in the education of children.

We will safeguard human rights and basic freedoms as a foundation for the development of the individual and for the establishment of a just society.

We also advocate the creation of conditions which will make it possible for everyone in our modern society to benefit fully from these human rights and basic freedoms, and in particular the right to a minimum income, to treatment in the event of illness, to work, to equal pay for equal work, to strike, to a healthy environment, to accommodation and to access to educational establishments and objective information.

The solidarity which we are striving to achieve represents a bond between all men and women. It is a prerequisite for community life. Solidarity finds expression in rights and duties.

In this spirit we are ready to fight against injustice, discrimination and poverty. The social problems of inequality between social groups, regions and countries can be solved only by a European policy of solidarity and by structural change.

Pluralist democracy is the form of government which best corresponds to our concept of a modern society based on partnership.

We also believe that political power should be decentralised wherever possible.

Europe in the World

Only if Europe is united will it be strong enough to further effectively the cause of freedom, solidarity, peace and justice for the peoples of the world.

Only if Europe is united will it be able to make a real contribution as a motive force behind progress and international social justice, to the creation of a new world order.

Only if Europe is united will it be strong enough to fulfil its responsibilities, to look after its legitimate interests in the world, to assert itself against the threat of military action and to safeguard its future existence as a free and sovereign power.

We have a duty to defend human rights, basic freedoms, and the rights of peoples. Unless these rights and freedoms are respected, true peace is impossible.

We will overcome the division of Europe by peaceful means. The right of self-determination of all European peoples, including the German people, remains for us a principle of European policy.

We firmly advocate effective and lasting detente on a balanced reciprocal basis. The furtherance of human, political, economic and cultural relations between the peoples of East and West contributes to the credibility of detente and is thus an important factor in the maintenance of peace.

Considerable importance attaches to mutual balanced and controlled troop and arms limitation, particularly in view of the growing military potential of Eastern Europe.

European security is based on the Atlantic Alliance which must be equal to the task. The Member States of the European Community should draw up a common security policy. (This concerns only those EEP parties from countries which are signatories to the Treaty).

We will cooperate on the formulation of a comprehensive new development and growth strategy in which the developing countries will participate on a basis of equality.

The industrialised countries — including the Community — must phase in their contributions to development aid at the agreed level (at present at least 0,7% of the gross national product). Steps must be taken to ensure that the funds available are allocated primarily to the poorest nations.

The European Community's Policy

Economic development is not an end in itself. It centres on mankind. Its aim must be to improve living conditions for everyone and to protect the natural and cultural surroundings.

As a basic prerequisite, the efficiency of the social market economy must be maintained. In this system social responsibility finds its expression in active solidarity. It transcends capitalism and collectivism. It ensures a maximum of co-determination and co-responsibility, the development of personality, property and prosperity and social security for everyone.

Although a solution to the problems of economic and monetary policy can only be sought at world level in the framework of international agreements, such a solution nevertheless calls, at Community level, for the immediate definition of the objectives to be pursued on a joint basis, particularly in the following fields:

— the fight for full employment, particularly for young people;
— the fight against inflation;
— the creation of a climate favourable to investment;
— the facilitation of the necessary structural changes within undertakings and at sectoral level;
— the promotion of the free movement of workers;
— the promotion of energy and research policies;
— the promotion of structural and regional policy, accompanied by a harmonized and active social policy.

In the longer term, it will be necessary to make Economic and Monetary Union a reality. This is one of the most important prerequisites for the maintenance, consolidation and further development of the Community's achievements.

As part of our basic philosophy, we believe that social policy should stimulate initiatives to benefit the weakest, unorganised groups of the population, in particular the handicapped and the old.

Social policy must contribute to the achievement of equality between men and women and in particular the realisation of the principle of equal pay for equal work.

Partnership and solidarity should guarantee justice for everyone and at the same time ensure that our economic system is more efficient. The Christian-Democrat option is based on freedom and justice and not on capitalism without a social face or on collectivism.

We will promote at European level:

— the creation of a Charter on the rights of workers;
— worker participation at shop-floor, plant and undertaking level, particularly by means of balanced representation on boards of directors and work councils in European limited companies;
— greater participation in property formation with a view to a more balanced distribution;
— freedom of movement and more mobility for workers based on free choice and not imposed by the social differences between favoured and less favoured regions of the Community;
— measures for migrant workers, relating in particular to their accommodation, professional training, social, political and cultural integration, and the education of their children.

With a view to ensuring that the individual can rediscover the value of his work — and this applies to both manual and non-manual work — we are fighting for the further "humanisation" of living and working conditions, in particular by minimising monotonous and production-line work and by reducing night shifts and Sunday shifts.

Social policy must recognise, promote and safeguard the importance of the family in a free democratic society. We are in favour of a policy which enhances the cohesion of the family, strengthens its educational capacity, protects the life of unborn babies and furthers the personal development of children. A social policy with these aims must ensure that large families also have incomes which are sufficient for the upbringing and education of their children.

This policy must enable men and women to discharge their responsibilities in the family, at work and in society, on a basis of equality.

The European Community's structural and regional policy measures must be considerably intensified. In this connection, regional, national and Community measures must be brought together to form a coherent whole.

In the common agricultural policy, efforts centre in particular on:

— the safeguarding of what has already been achieved especially in eliminating monetary difficulties;
— the correction of imbalances on the agricultural market by means of an appropriate price and structural policy; viz., the operation of forms of intervention with a more balanced effect to ensure to all beneficiaries guarantees which, while differentiated, would be comparable in their effects;
— the further extension of existing market regulations;
— the use of regional policy measures in areas with natural disadvantages;
— the intensification of measures to improve agricultural and sales structures.

The energy crisis has made a common energy policy essential. Such a policy must form part of the Community's foreign and external economic policy.

High priority must be given to Community environmental policy. The main aim of this policy should be the adoption of Community minimum norms on emissions in order to prevent distortions of competition between undertakings and to afford the same protection to all citizens of Europe.

We advocate measures to protect health, in particular as regards the purchase of foodstuffs and medicines, and measures to ensure that technical equipment can be operated safely, as well as the harmonisation of current national legal provisions in the Community, based on the most advanced legislation.

The Community's Institutional Framework

The unity of Europe must be based on the determination of its peoples.

In the transitional period leading up to Political Union and Economic and Monetary Union, it is crucially important for the Community to move towards the establishment of a single Community decision-making centre, the true partner of which will be the democratically elected European Parliament.

We expect the directly elected and democratically legitimated Parliament to provide a new constitutional and institutional impetus for the achievement of European Union and progress towards a European federation, the ultimate political aim of unification.

Youth must take an active part in the construction of Europe. Recognised European organisations must be listened to by the Community institutions when their interests are involved.

To this end,

— the existing Treaties must be applied in full and maximum use must be made of their potential;
— the authority and powers of the European Parliament and Commission, principal guarantors of the interests of the Community, must be developed;
— the Council should apply the practice of majority decisions on Community matters in accordance with the Treaty.

Our Goal: A United Europe

For us, the European Union, as described in the Tindemans Report and formally proclaimed by the Heads of State or Government meeting the European Council, will represent an important step towards European unification.

We are firmly committed to the final political objective of European unification, that is the transformation of the European Union into a "unique" European federation of the type described, many years ago, by Robert Schuman in his declaration of May 9, 1950.

This Europe will not be able to manifest its capacity or dynamic and unequivocal action until the necessary institutions have been created.

— a directly elected European Parliament which gives expression to the free will of the people;
— a Chamber of States, which represents the legitimate interests of the Member States;
— a European Government, which is willing and able to govern effectively.

287

3. The Liberal Parties

Document I
Stuttgart Declaration (adopted on March 26, 1976)

The democratic parties in the European Community based on liberal principles
— resolved to protect and to promote the rights and freedoms of the individual.
— desiring to make possible for all citizens of Europe a decent life in a free society.
— believing that peace, freedom and prosperity in Europe can best be assured if the European Community progresses towards a European Union,
— welcoming the decision to hold the first direct elections to the European Parliament in 1978,
have therefore decided to establish a federation of liberal and democratic parties in the European Community, based on the following platform:
1. The supreme task of the European Union must be to guarantee human, civil and political rights on the European level. We therefore call for:
— a bill of human rights and fundamental freedoms, directly applicable throughout the European Community, to be drawn up by the first directly elected European Parliament.
— the right of every citizen to appeal to the European Court of Justic when his civil rights are impaired by decisions of the Community institutions.
— the abolition of remaining administrative restrictions within the European Community on the free movement of persons, goods, services and capital.
2. The European Union needs a free democratic constitution based on the principles of division of powers, majority voting and the protection of minorities. We therefore call for:
— increased powers and legislative responsibilities for the European Parliament in all questions within the competence of the European Community, including political co-operation,
— election of the European Parliament according to the principles of proportional representation.
— accountability of the European Commission to the European Parliament and the Council of Ministers,
— an endeavour on the part of the Council to increasingly take decisions by majority vote.
— protection of the legitimate interests of the regions and minorities in the Member States of the European Community in such a way as to ensure that the diversity of Europe is preserved,
— the greatest possible recourse to the Economic and Social Committee and to the Standing Committee on Employment, with a particular view to securing at the level of the Community the participation of workers in the management, control and profits of undertakings.

3. The European Union must assure steady and balanced economic growth, thus creating for its citizens the conditions for effective social protection in the vicissitudes of life. This can no longer be done on a national level. We therefore call for:
— the Member States and the institutions of the European Community to make practical progress along the road towards economic and monetary union, for example through an ever greater harmonization of their economic and financial policies and of their currencies, including the creation of a joint central bank, and by increasingly holding their resources in common,
— promotion of free competition within a free market system and its protection from abuse by monopolies and cartels, as well as from the excessive influence of public enterprise, by allowing private firms all the room necessary to form themselves into genuine instruments of democracy and progress in the context of a coordinated economy, with a view to ensuring optimal economic growth and sufficient resources to provide effective help for the socially disadvantaged,
— the redistribution of wealth both by use of the Social Fund to reduce inequalities between individuals and the Regional Development Fund to reduce inequalities between Regions,
— development of the Common Agricultural Policy in ways which both benefit consumers and encourage efficient farming,
— further progress towards common environmental and energy policies.
4. The European Union needs a common foreign policy covering both the external relations of the European Community and the European Political Co-operation and designed to serve the freedom and security of Europe and peace in the world, side by side with our partners in the Atlantic Alliance, notably the United States, and in the United Nations. We therefore call for:
— the development of the closest possible ties also with Western European countries which are not members of the European Community
— the further expansion along the lines of the Lome Convention of co-operation between the European Community and the Third World in the context of a balanced development of the world economy,
— active participation by the Member States of the European Community in all efforts to establish stability and peace in the Mediterranean region and in the Middle East,
— the European Community to speak with one voice particularly in its relations with the countries of Eastern Europe and the Soviet Union.

5. The European Union must be founded on the common conviction that the freedom of the individual, equal opportunities for all and the free competition of ideas and parties are indispensable elements of a democratic society. We therefore:
— welcome the accession to or association with the European Community and in future the European Union of every European State whose constitution and policy is in conformity with these principles,
— are willing to co-operate within the European Community with all political groups which are ready without reservation to accept and defend the fundamental values of liberal democracy.

Document II
Declaration

Believing that the European Community was created to benefit the individual citizens of Europe as well as the peace and prosperity of our continent, the Federation of Liberal Parties of the European Community calls on all its supporters to work for the following as aims of the European Community on the basis of the objectives set by the Rome Treaty:
1. The creation of a European citizenship and the right of every citizen to appeal to the European Court when her/his rights are affected by the decisions of the Community;
2. The abolition of all restrictions at the frontiers of the Member States of the Community for its citizens:
3. Direct elections by a proportional system to the European Parliament in May 1978;
4. The establishment of legislative power in the European Parliament for all matters that are the responsibility of the Community.
5. The welcome to the Community of other European States where liberal democracy is established and where they are willing to accept the principles on which the Community is based;
6. The bringing within the framework of the Community institutions of all forms — and especially the meetings of the European Council — of political co-operation between its nine Member States;
7. The recognition that the well-being of the Community requires a generous recognition of its duty to promote trade with and provide assistance for, the nations of the Third World, of which the Lome Agreement is only the beginning;
8. The development of the system of free enterprise, safeguarded against the abuse of cartels, as the best means for providing greater prosperity for all to accomplish social reforms and of providing help for the needy;
9. The acceptance of the responsibility of the Community to protect the cultural and artistic heritage of its Member States and their natural resources from waste and destruction;
10. The defence of the rights and interests of the regions and minorities of the Member States in all their variety so that our Community may reflect unity in diversity and not the sterile uniformity which illiberal systems seek to impose.

Document III
Statutes and Rules of Procedure of the Federation of Liberal and
Democratic Parties of the European Community (Stuttgart, 26-27 March, 1976)

Preamble

We, citizens of Member States of the European Community, believing that its closer unity depends on the development of democratic political institutions and that the liberty and progress of man requires both the closer co-operation of European democracies and the use of liberal institutions in international relations, resolve to form a federation of political parties to promote these ends.

Introduction to the competence of the Federation
Chapter I
Article 1

The purpose of the Federation shall be to bring together the parties of the countries of the Community who, within the framework of Liberal ideals, wish to contribute to the creation of a European Union.

Article 2

To fulfil this purpose the Federation will:
1. seek a common position on all the important problems affecting the Community;
2. undertake to support elections to the European Parliament by universal suffrage, with a view to strengthening the democratic character of the European Community;
3. inform the public and involve it in the construction of a united and liberal Europe.

Membership
Chapter II
Article 3

Membership of the Federation is open to all political parties of the European Community who accept the Statutes and the policy programmes as agreed by the Congresses of the Federation.

Article 4

The parties founding the Federation are the following:
- Germany
- Belgium
- Denmark
- France
- Italy
- Luxembourg
- Netherlands
- United Kingdom.

Any other party complying with the provisions of Article 3 may submit an application for membership to the Secretary-General who will refer it for decision to the Executive Committee. The Executive Committee must unanimously agree to accept the application for membership. When the Executive Committee is unable to reach a decision, then it should be put before the Congress, who will make the decision according to the normal voting procedure.

Article 5

The Federation will be financed by contributions of the member parts in proportions and amounts agreed by the Executive Committee.

Article 6

Any member party of the Federation may withdraw by notifying its decision to the Secretary-General. Notice shall take effect at the end of the current year if it has been given within the first nine months of the year and at the end of the next year if given during the last three months.

Article 7

Any member party of the Federation which no longer complies with the provisions of Articles 1 and 3 may be asked by the Executive Committee to withdraw. If this request is ignored, the Committee may decide that the member concerned has ceased to belong to the Federation from a date fixed by the Committee. The contributions paid by the member concerned will be refunded proportionally. The member concerned has the right to appeal to the next Congress for a ruling.

Article 8

If a member fails to meet its financial obligations, the Executive Committee may suspend its right of representation on the Committee and the Congress until it has fulfilled the said obligations.

General Provisions
Chapter III
Article 9

The organs of the Federation shall be:
— the Congress
— the Executive Committee
These two organs shall be assisted by the General Secretariat.

Article 10

The Federation is represented in the European Parliament by the Liberal Group.
Members of the European Parliament, elected or nominated, and belonging to one of the member parties of the Federation will be members of the Liberal Group.

Article 11

The registered office and the secretariat of the Federation shall be at Brussels.

Article 12

The official languages of the Federation are the official languages of the European Community. The working languages are the same as those of the European Community: French, English, German.

Executive Committee
Chapter IV
Article 13

The Executive Committee comprises:
- the President of the Federation, as its Chairman;
- twelve members appointed by their respective parties in accordance with the criteria adopted for the allocation by nationality of the members of the Commission of the European Communities;
- twelve members elected by the Congress for a period of two years according to the same criteria;
- the chairman of the Liberal Group of the European Parliament;
- the members of the Commission of the European Communities who belong to a member party;
- one member appointed by a Federation of Liberal Youth organisations of the countries of the Community. He should belong to a member party of the Federation of Liberal Parties.

(N.B. If an Irish party adheres to the Federation, Ireland will be entitled to one representative appointed by the party and one elected by the Congress.)

Article 14

The Committee shall appoint two Vice-Presidents from among its members. The Committee shall appoint the Treasurer and the Secretary-General.

Article 15

The Committee shall meet at least four times a year at a place and date chosen by the majority of its members.

Article 16

The Committee shall reach decisions by a majority of the members present and voting. No vote will be taken unless there is a quorum of twelve members present.

Article 17

Between meetings of the Congress, the Committee will be empowered to speak and act on behalf of the Federation in all spheres of the latter's jurisdiction.

When there are direct elections to the European Parliament, the list of approved candidates from each country will be drawn up by the national member parties after consultation with the Committee.

Article 18

The Committee may set up advisory or technical committees for any purpose it thinks fit.

Article 19

The Committee shall adopt its own rules of procedure.

Article 20

At the meeting of the Congress, the Committee shall submit a report on its activities.

Congress
Chapter V
Article 21

The member parties of the Federation which have been designated as the national parties fulfilling the criteria of Article 3, will meet annually in a Congress.

Article 22

The Congress shall consist of the following members:

1. (a) Six representatives from each country. In the case of a country where there is more than one member party these representatives shall be allocated to each party as far as possible in proportion to the number of votes cast for each party at the last national general election, held at least two months before the Congress.

(b) For each member party, a number of representatives based on the following relationship to the number of votes, cast for that party at the last national general election:
- one representative for each 100.000 votes or a major part thereof up to three million votes;
- one representative for each 250.000 votes or a major part thereof between three and five million votes;
- one representative for each 500.000 votes or a major part thereof exceeding five million votes.

2. The members of the Liberal Group of the European Parliament and the Liberal members of the Commission of the European Communities (provided in both cases they belong to one of the member parties) shall automatically be members of the Congress.

3. Ten representatives nominated by a Federation of Liberal Youth organisations of the countries of the Community.

N.B. The Executive Committee shall be responsible for defining the liberal votes taking into consideration the different national electoral systems.

Article 23

1. A 2/3 (two thirds) majority of members voting and present is needed.
2. No vote will be taken unless there is a quorum of 100 persons present.
3. The member parties may also nominate substitutes to a maximum of half of the number of their designated representation.
4. Each member has the right to one vote.
5. In the case of absence, 1/4 + 1 of the representatives from each delegation have the right to two votes.

Article 24

The Congress shall hold an annual meeting in one of the countries of the Community.

The party/parties in whose country the Congress is being held will provide the Chairman of the Congress.

Article 25

The Congress will elect the President of the Federation. He shall serve for two years, after which he is eligible for re-election but may not serve for more than six years in total.

The Congress shall elect 12 members to serve on the Executive Committee for a period of two years.

Article 26

The Congress can:

1. make decisions on all matters within the competence of the Treaties establishing the European Communities and on matters regarding political co-operation of the European Community;

2. decide on all other matters which the members have unanimously recognised as falling within its competence;

3. deliberate on all proposals submitted to it by a member party or one of its representatives and may deliver an opinion on such proposals;

4. receive the report of the Executive Committee and debate it if it so desires;

5. receive reports from the Liberal Group of the European Parliament;

6. have powers to make amendments to the constitution;

7. make recommendations to the Liberal Group of the European Parliament.

Article 27

Each member party and the Liberal Group of the European Parliament will have the right to place items on the agenda of both the Executive Committee and the Congress.

Article 28

The Congress may set up committees to examine any matters within its competence as defined in Article 26.

Article 29

The debates of the Congress shall be published. The Congress may decide to publish the debates in full or in part.

Secretariat
Chapter VI
Article 30

1. The Federation shall be assisted by a Secretary-General appointed by the Executive Committee.

2. The Secretary-General must be a national of one of the Member States of the Community. He must be a member of a party affiliated to the Federation.

3. The Secretary-General shall head a secretariat, the composition and organisation of which shall be determined by the Executive Committee.

Article 31

The Secretary-General shall be assisted in the exercise of his functions by the national parties.

Article 32

The Secretary-General shall be responsible to the Executive Committee and the Congress.

Article 33

The Secretary-General may not be gainfully employed by a Government, be a member of a national Parliament, or engage in work incompatible with his duties.

Article 34

1. The Secretary-General shall organise the meetings of the Federation and arrange for publicity.

2. He shall attend the annual conferences of the member parties of the Federation and, if asked, shall report to them on the work of the Federation.

3. He shall maintain contacts between the parties of the Federation.

4. He shall arrange for publicity to be given to the work of the Federation and any member party.

Rules of Procedure

I. Congress

1. The Congress shall be held once a year.

2. The Executive Committee shall determine the date and the duration of the Congress.

3. The Executive Committee shall fix the place of the Congress in one of the Member States of the Community.

II. Agenda of the Congress

1. The Executive Committee shall draw up the agenda.

2. Items on the agenda may be placed by: member parties, the Liberal Group in the European Parliament and the Executive Committee.

3. Items for inclusion must be submitted not less than ten weeks prior to Congress.

4. The agenda will be sent to all members of the Congress not less than six weeks prior to Congress.

5. Alterations to the agenda to allow for emergency debates shall be at the discretion of the President of the Federation.

6. The Minutes of the previous Congress, the Annual Report of the Executive, the Annual Report of the Liberal Group in the European Parliament, the Budget and any other relevant items will be sent out at the same time as the agenda.

III. Representation at the Congress

1. A list of representatives and substitutes shall be sent by each member party to the Secretary General at least two weeks prior to Congress.

2. Any verification of credentials will be carried out, if required, by the Executive Committee

IV. Elections

1. The President of the Federation shall be elected by the Congress to serve for two years.
2. The voting procedure will be the Alternative Vote system.
3. The ballot will be secret.
4. No person may serve as President for more than a total of six years.
5. Each member party may make one nomination for the presidency.
6. The Congress shall elect twelve members to serve on the Executive Committee. (There will be thirteen members when there is an Irish party).
7. The voting procedure will be the Single Transferable Vote (Quota Preferential) system. Places for each nationality will be counted and decided separately.
8. Each member party may make not more than twelve nominations. (This will be thirteen when there is an Irish party).

V. Conduct of Sessions of the Congress

1. The sessions of the Congress will be public unless the Congress decides otherwise.
2. The names of representatives who ask leave to speak will be entered in the list of speakers in the order in which their requests are received.
3. Representatives may not speak for more than five minutes.
4. Proposers of resolutions will be allowed extra time at the discretion of the Chairman.
5. No representative may speak more than twice on the same subject except by leave of the Chairman.
6. A representative who asks leave to speak for a procedural motion, in particular:

    (a) to raise a point of order.
    (b) to move the closure of a debate

    (c) to move the adjournment of a debate

shall have a prior right to do so.
7. Amendments shall relate to the text it is sought to alter.
8. Amendments shall be submitted in writing two weeks before the Congress.
9. Amendments shall be put to the vote before the text.
10. Normally the Congress will vote by a show of hands but a written ballot may be taken.
11. In all matters relating to the conduct of the Congress, the interpretation of the rules by, and the decisions of, the Chairman of the Congress shall be binding.

VI. The Executive Committee

1. The President shall direct all the activities of the Federation under the conditions laid down.
2. Should the President be absent or unable to discharge his duties he shall be replaced by one of the Vice-Presidents who shall have full powers.
3. The Executive Committee shall formulate its own rules of procedure.
4. The Executive Committee has powers to set up advisory and technical committees and to determine terms of reference and procedure.
5. In the case of dispute, the ruling by the President shall be final.

The Federation of Liberal and Democratic Parties of the European Community will act within the framework of the Liberal International, and all the activities of the Liberal International should be continued and utmost efforts be made to enlarge the scope of its activities, strengthen its organisational structure and increase continuously its political influence among states and nations.

Document IV
The Thesis of the Electoral Programme of ELD/LDE (November 1977)

Towards a democratic Europe

Human and civil rights
Thesis 1
Liberal democracy is based on the belief that every individual citizen has fundamental rights and that the supreme task of government must be to recognize and guarantee the rights and freedoms of the individual as laid down in particular in the Universal Declaration of Human Rights, and to promote the full enjoyment of these rights and freedoms.

Thesis 2
The European Union and its Member States are therefore called upon
— to strive together with the other members of the family of democratic countries, for the implementation of human and civil rights, throughout the world.
— to safeguard the full respect of human and civil rights in all legislative and administrative actions of the European Union.
— to guarantee, protect and promote human and civil rights within Member States by their own measures and, if necessary, by joint action.

Thesis 3
The Liberal and Democratic parties in the European Community call for the first directly elected European Parliament to draw up immediately a Declaration of the Union on Basic Human and Civil Rights to be ratified by the Member States. This Declaration should include the rights to life, which presupposes the abolition of the death penalty. Moreover, the State should apply criminal law — the most extreme instrument of power and the one which most radically affects citizens — only where it is necessary for the protection of the legal assets of the individual, for the defence of the constitutional state and for the preservation of an environment fit for human beings.

Thesis 4
Every citizen and resident of the Member State should be guaranteed the right to seek remedy before the European Court in Luxembourg against any legislative or administrative act promulgated or executed by the European Union's Institutions which violated individual rights as set down in the European Convention on Basic Human Rights and Fundamental Freedoms.

Thesis 5
All Member States of the European Union are urged to ratify and implement the European Convention on Human Rights in its entirety, to take steps in order to further improve the Convention and to accept the European Social Charter.

Thesis 6
At the same time, the European Union should accede to the same Convention and thereby accept the ultimate jurisdiction of the European Human Rights Commission and of the European Court of Human Rights at Strasbourg.

Thesis 7
The Liberals and Democrats call for the creation of an European passport Union and the introduction of a European passport which must also be recognized outside the European Union.

Thesis 8
The Liberal and Democratic Parties of the European Community believe that all citizens of the Member States should have the right to vote in and stand for elections to local councils in their place of residence. In the long term they believe that such citizens should have the right to vote in all public elections in the country where they live.

European Institutions
Thesis 1
The European Institutions must be given enough authority to enable them to perform their Community tasks successfully and to provide a more effective framework for the growing unit between our countries. They must be democratic so that they can serve the citizens of Europe and stimulate further development in accordance with the wishes of all its peoples.

Thesis 2
The Community's existing institutional structure is a good starting point for further development. The important thing is to define the responsibilities of the various Institutions in such a way as to achieve the correct balance while strengthening the inner driving force needed to maintain the impetus towards integration. This must be done in such a way that action is taken on the basis of treaties to expand gradually the areas at present falling within the Community's competence.

Thesis 3
The present distribution of powers between the various Institutions is out of balance — the Council has become too dominant. What is urgently needed is the correct application of the Treaties in the spirit intended by their authors and particularly the implementation of the majority principles for votes in the Council of Ministers and a strengthening of the roles of the Commission and of Parliament.

Thesis 4
The forthcoming elections are a milestone in the further development of Community Institutions. For the first time, its citizens are to be directly involved in the process leading up to European

294

Union. The greater weight and authority deriving from direct elections should spur the new Parliament to claim its rightful place with greater force.

These first elections will still be organized on a national basis. It will be the task of the newly-elected Parliament to devise a genuinely European electoral system which will guarantee fair representation to each of the political forces in the countries of the Community. In this respect, the adoption of a system based on proportional representation is indispensable.

Thesis 5
We Liberals want a European Union of free citizens, a Union within which national, regional and local powers of decision-making are placed in the context of the new European dimension and thereby are given added significance. Its internal task will be to complete the Community process of integration and unification, on the twin foundations of liberal democracy and human rights. In the world at large, it must stand for the principles on which it itself is founded — peace, freedom, individual responsibility and social justice. In this way, it will be able to play a role in the world of which every European citizen may be proud.

Thesis 6
The institutions of the Union should be the logical continuation and conclusion of the development that we advocate. Capacity to reach decisions has to go hand in hand with plurality, fair distribution of powers and "checks and balances".

This is our view of the kind of European Union we want and the institutions with which it should be provided. It will be the great task of the elected Parliament to draw up a Treaty to this effect and to press for its speedy ratification by all Member States.

Towards a Liberal Society

Social policy
Thesis 1
Liberals believe in both individual and social responsibility.

Thesis 2
Liberal social security policy guarantees freedom and security and safeguards individual rights, by providing the means of living that individuals cannot provide for themselves.

Thesis 3
In a Liberal and Democratic society the individual will be defended against any abuse of great social, economic or political power. This must include the protection of those without collectively organised power and hence the influence to defend their interests through negotiation. It is our duty to defend the common interest of all citizens and the responsibility of Parliament therein.

Thesis 5
Unemployment among young people represents a serious problem for the development of our society. A European policy to eliminate unemployment among the young is therefore of prime importance. The Liberals and Democrats believe it essential that young people should receive competent professional training permitting them to undertake productive activities. The nature of training must be modified in such a way as to make young people flexible so that they can continue the training process in the course of their lives.

Thesis 6
To stimulate the commitment of young people to the creation of a European Union a Community youth policy is of major importance. It must aim at helping young people find their proper place in our society.

Thesis 7
Liberals and Democrats demand a redistribution of roles between men and women. Both attitudes and legislation must be changed in order that women, who have long been the objects of discrimination, should obtain the equality to which they are entitled. The beneficial result for society as a whole would be a redistribution of roles between men and women in the sense of a sharing of responsibility between equal partners. More specifically Liberals therefore demand.

Thesis 8
Liberalism itself is based on the ideas of fighting for peoples rights either as individuals or as minorities, therefore it has most to offer the minorities of Europe, both because we believe in the rights and welfare of all people and because we desire a free and diverse society.

Thesis 9
The European Union should have a common consumer protection policy.
The main aims of this policy should be the right of:
— protection of health and safety
— protection of economic interests
— redress
— complete information
— representation.

Thesis 10
We stand for the right of employees to participate in the responsibility for the running, stability and development of the enterprise in which they work and to acquire a financial interest therein.

Thesis 11
The European measures of social security developed at Community level should be more than a simple addition to national systems. They should develop a distinct role of their own, especially in the structural field. We believe, however, that social policy should never become

an exclusive Community policy, since the major task of the Community is better harmonisation of the different social security systems within it.

Thesis 12
The European Community should assure throughout its area the freedom of movement of its citizens, whatever their occupation. It must have special care and responsibility for those who are working outside their own country, for both citizens of Community countries and migrant workers who come to work from outside the Community.

Cultural policy
Thesis 1
The right to education is one of the most basic rights. Liberals have pioneered and always fought for it. Everyone should have access to education throughout his life.

Thesis 2
A Community educational policy should stimulate citizen's appreciation of and interest in their fellow European cultures and encourage educational innovation.

Thesis 3
European educational and training policies should encourage greater association between the various national systems.

Thesis 4
The Liberals and Democrats call for the creation of a European Sports Council consisting of the competent members of the governments of the Member States and of representatives of the central bodies of national sports organisations.

Environmental policy
Thesis 1
It is essential to have a Community policy for the environment, to ensure that it develops in accord with liberal principles and enables citizens of Member States to enjoy the highest possible quality of life. This calls for harmonious interaction between man and his environment and between the various components of this environment.

Thesis 2
The European environmental policy should pay particular attention to the need to combat and prevent transfrontier environmental pollution.

Thesis 3
Environmental protection takes priority over the profit motive. Those who cause pollution should pay to repair the damage.

Thesis 4
One of the great riches of the Community is the diversity of Europe's natural, historical, architectural and cultural heritage.

Thesis 5
Thinking about our economic future should incorporate social and ecological factors. Growth cannot be an end in itself. Technology must remain the means and not the end. Economic decisions must be assessed on the basis of their effect on the environment.

Thesis 6
The lack of a real policy for developing energy resources in the past has meant that today we have to rely more and more on nuclear power, and this presents a real danger to humanity. We must find an answer without resorting to extreme solutions that are usually determined by passion instead of reason.

Thesis 7
Farming methods are the main influence on the natural environment and we must recognise and encourage those methods which retain an ecological balance — if necessary by financial incentives. Community forestry policy must also recognise this objective.

Thesis 8
Every citizen must be allowed his say in determining the quality of life, and to do this he should be kept fully informed. Each generation must recognise its responsibility in laying the foundations for the quality of life for succeeding generations.

Thesis 9
A Community environment policy must include the power to intervene in cases of potential danger. In these circumstances the Community must be able to activate the powers of various bodies set up to intervene politically, administratively and financially. We need joint European procedures for approving infrastructure projects and regional planning proposals which concern several Member States. The Community should also formulate Community-wide minimum standards of quality.

Thesis 10
Worldwide cooperation is needed to develop universal protection of the environment.

Thesis 11
Worldwide cooperation must be in the form of an international code for the environment binding on everyone. Developing countries must be encouraged to work out their own growth strategy within this code.

Regional policy
Thesis 1
We consider an effective regional policy to be an essential part of the European Union we are seeking to create. But we recognise the complexity of needs and aspirations which characterise the many different regions of Europe.

Thesis 2
Decentralisation of political power is a fundamental principle of the structure of government and of regional policy.

Thesis 3
Europe's cultural diversity is its true character and its strength.

Thesis 4
European Union offers a new chance to many regions in Europe.

Thesis 5
Within a European Union all areas must have true equality of opportunity — this should be a high priority.

Thesis 6
We recognise the particular problems of those regions which are peripheral in the area of the European Community.

Thesis 7
Present Community regional policy is unsatisfactory — the Community must have the means to advance regional policies throughout the Community.

National governments should not be permitted to reduce their own financial aid to regions because of EEC aid.

Thesis 8
Regional authorities should have direct access to all Community Institutions for the exchange of information and mutual consultation.

Thesis 9
Steps must be taken to achieve effective coordination of regional economic policies, transport policies, energy policies, regional planning and landscape conservation measures by means of transfrontier institutional and administrative integration. The Community should have a special concern for cooperation between frontier regions.

Thesis 10
The Community Institutions should pay increasing attention to the major questions of regional planning; there is a need for a judicious balance in regional structure-plans between different sectors of employment, communications, use of available land and cooperation between regions, particularly in dealing with ecological effects across frontiers.

Thesis 11
The Liberals and Democrats call for the abolition of administrative restrictions at the internal frontiers of the Community. Within the European Community people should immediately be able to move freely and without hindrance throughout its territory. Frontier formalities should be abolished so as to make the Community a visible reality to the millions of travellers crossing its internal borders every day.

Thesis 12
The Community policy should not discourage regional coherence extending beyond the frontiers of the European Union. On the contrary, it should promote such coherence.

Towards a liberal economy

Principles of economic policy
Thesis 1
The main objectives of our modern economic and monetary policy are to ensure steady and balanced growth and the restoration and safeguarding of full employment. As well due accent should be given to the quality of life and to the interests of the consumer and not only to quantitative figures.

This policy thus should create the conditions for the effective social protection of all citizens in the vicissitudes of life. In the present situation, with a relative shortage and correspondingly high cost of energy, raw materials and foodstuffs and with increasing conflicts between minorities, social groups and regions, the achievement of these objectives becomes more difficult. These factors lead also to a growing tendency of injustice, parasitism and to the development of greater privileges and poverty, which distort the working of a free and modern market economy, thereby endangering the maintenance of an open and pluralistic society. To counter these dangers the Liberals and Democrats believe we have to rely on both the dynamism of private enterprise and the overall democratic management of the economy through flexible planning in which the social partners should participate and including guidelines on prices and wages. Moreover Liberals and Democrats take the view that a democracy confined to matters of the state is not sufficient. They therefore call for a system of maximum and equal participation of all citizens in the decisions concerning the division of tasks in the economic field.

Thesis 2
Our aim is the redistribution of wealth in Europe.

Thesis 3
We also aim to redistribute wealth in the world.

Thesis 4
The structural changes in industry which are the inevitable product of technological progress create problems which require a concerted approach at Community level. Policies to deal with these problems may require selective public intervention but this must aim to create viable enterprises in competitive market conditions. Liberals cannot accept that public money should be pumped into industries, whether old or new, with no hope of economic viability.

Thesis 5
We consider the fight against unemployment of fundamental importance for the preservation of democratic liberties. Full employment throughout the EEC remains our ultimate objective, but

we recognise that technological developments and increasing competition from countries outside the Community constitute serious handicaps. The creation of new (and the expansion of existing) industries and enterprises must be actively pursued in the Community in order to reduce structural unemployment and to provide work, especially for the young.

Thesis 6
The aims of economic and social policy in Europe can no longer be achieved at national level: political and economic unification are complementary.

Economic and Monetary Union
Thesis 1
We need an Economic and Monetary Union — EMU. Only with EMU can the Member States of the European Community overcome together the economic and social crisis that they all share. This means a determined effort to achieve parallel economic development in all Community countries, and to achieve economic integration in the widest sense of the term.

Thesis 2
Progress towards EMU requires strengthening of the revenue-raising role of the Community.

Thesis 3
Progress towards EMU requires strengthening of the role of the Community in sharing revenues but we emphasize the need for thrift in Community expenditure.

Thesis 4
Progress towards EMU means that the Community must increase its responsibilities towards the Third World.

Thesis 5
Progress towards EMU requires new initiatives and new ways of developing Community policy and expenditure in other areas where there is a clear need for the Community budget and Parliament.

Thesis 6
Progress towards EMU requires new arrangements in monetary affairs;
- the maintenance of flexible exchange rates until the introduction of a standard European currency;
- an increase in the powers of the European Monetary Fund and the gradual pooling of the currency reserves;
- an increase in reciprocal credits conditional on greater cooperation;
- the introduction of a European currency in parallel with national currencies.

Thesis 7
The Community should "speak with one voice" to the world in economic and monetary affairs.

Thesis 8
An attempt should be made to achieve further progress towards EMU in particular in connection with the harmonisation of competition, economic affairs, taxation, finance, currency matters and social policy. The realisation of EMU is essential if we are to protect the existing achievements of the Community.

Energy policy
Thesis 1
The energy policy of the European Community can determine the nature of the society in which we and future generations will live. It should not only guarantee greater independence with respect to our energy supplies but it should also ensure that present and future generations are exposed neither to environmental pollution nor to any situation in which peace is threatened as a result of the spread of dangerous technologies. The contribution of nuclear energy will have to be examined. Our scientific knowledge about nuclear energy will have to be broadened and more research into alternative sources of energy is needed. Liberals and Democrats believe the Community has a key role to play in this area. We intend to secure the Community's energy supplies in order to enable it to face challenges of the future.

Thesis 2
The sharp increase in energy prices together with the limited availability of energy resources represent a challenge which can jeopardize our prosperity and our well-being. We should strive to supply all consumers with a sufficient quantity of energy at reasonable prices. Rational planning to secure optimum utilization of the energy available to us will be necessary. As it will not be possible to maintain fully the free choice of energy options available in the past, competition in the use of the various energy sources will to a certain extent be weakened. It is the task of the liberal policy to avert any undesirable economic development which might thereby ensue.

Thesis 3
Liberals and Democrats feel that too great a concentration of power over energy supplies, whether in public or private hands, is dangerous, because of economic, bureaucratic and political implications. Competition must be maintained between the various sources of energy supplies.

Thesis 4
Liberals and Democrats are concerned about the consequences of the energy crisis for the present generation. The energy requirement of future generations could be in jeopardy unless agreement is reached at once on measures to secure continued supplies.

Thesis 5
Joint action in the field of energy is essential within the Community. Harmonious relations with other countries must be established and

maintained, whether they are consumers or producers, taking into account the worldwide political and economic implications of energy problems.

Thesis 6
Community energy policy should strive for the most rational use of existing resources. The main objective must be to reduce Europe's dependence on outside supply. An important contribution is the war on waste, which yields savings that will not affect the standard of living.

Thesis 7
Liberals and Democrats believe energy from nuclear fission can provide a necessary, but temporary answer to the growing demand for energy. Yet, it is dangerous and for the moment too unpredictable as an alternative to cover future power requirements. We are fully aware of the problems connected with the spread of nuclear power. All available know-how should be utilized in a research programme, aiming on the one hand, to solve the problems involving the reprocessing of radioactive waste, on the other hand, the development of alternative energy sources, including forms of nuclear energy which are completely safe and not detrimental to the environment. Meantime though, authorisation to build new nuclear power stations in individual Member States of the E.C. is irresponsible unless arrangements are made in the Member States concerned for:
— the safe disposal of highly active waste;
— safe and technically sound intermediate storage;
Liberals and Democrats do not call for the existing nuclear power stations to be closed down.
Because of the uncertainty surrounding future energy consumption and the development of alternative energy sources, we would reserve the right to opt at a later stage for nuclear energy to cover residual demand without committing ourselves irrevocably to this policy at the present stage.

Thesis 8
The Community policy on raw materials other than energy sources should primarily aim at diversifying the present sources of raw material supply by improved exploitation of the earth's surface, the economical use of raw materials and the recovery of raw materials from waste and other products.

Small and medium-sized businesses
Thesis 1
Because of their productivity and their effect on employment, small and medium-sized undertakings are a vital element in the economic life of the Member States of the European Communities.

Thesis 2
We are deeply convinced of the need to promote the development of small and medium-sized businesses for both political and economic reasons. They guarantee an active market, economic pluralism and the presence of independent economic forces: they are free from the bureaucratic practices of state-owned industries and the general tendency to bureaucracy of large companies. Small and medium-sized businesses produce trained people in management and skilled people for the workforce; in fighting unemployment they develop better human relationships; they are essential for the spread of economic power which is linked with the spread of political power. They are an essential element of the social free market economy which is the basic aim of the Federation of Liberal and Democratic Parties of the E.C.

Thesis 3
Liberals and Democrats demand the implementation of a programme to aid small and medium-sized businesses in the Community. The main points of the programme should be:
a. coordination of national policies;
b. development of Economic and Monetary Union;
c. proper application of the rules of competition
d. harmonized, more flexible and simplified taxation policy;
e. credit policy measures to counteract the disadvantages involved in financing small and medium-sized undertakings;
f. adjustment of certain aspects of social policy to reflect the economic situation of small and medium-sized companies;
g. promotion of training and protection of entrepreneurs;
h. easier access to research; encouragement of joint research by small and medium-sized firms;
i. harmonization and development of appropriate company law;
j. promotion of exports by small and medium-sized firms both within and outside the Community;
k. invitations to tender which do not close markets to small and medium-sized undertakings.

Agricultural policy
Thesis 1
An agricultural policy providing for sufficient food production fulfils one of mankind's basic needs. In doing so a liberal agricultural policy will at the same time ensure humane conditions of working and living in the country. It is therefore not only concerned with the technical and commercial problems of agricultural production, but has to be seen in the context of social, environmental and regional policy. It is part of an overall policy combining all these aspects into one.

Thesis 2
The Liberals are in favour of an integrated

Common Agricultural Policy replacing national policies. They believe such a policy to be an essential element of the future European Union. The smooth functioning of this policy depends critically on economic and monetary stability.

Thesis 3
The Common Agricultural Policy must bring advantages to both farmers and consumers, without loading unnecessary burdens on the European taxpayer. It must be used to help farmers modernise their farms to become more productive and competitive.

Thesis 4
The basic principles of the CAP are right. They have enabled the policy to bring stability to the agricultural economy and have avoided the inflationary effects of sharp food price rises. But the application of these principles to agricultural problems must be improved. In particular vigorous action is needed to eliminate persistent structural surplus.

Thesis 5
Agricultural policy must be developed in a way that demonstrates a responsible attitude to food supplies and production in the rest of the world. Ill-considered policy changes in one country or group of countries, can have a destabilising effect on agriculture over a wide area, European Liberals believe that the brutal fluctuations that have characterised some world markets in recent years must be avoided.

Thesis 6
While other food production has been covered by the existing CAP, fishing presents new and different problems and tasks to the Community. A continued and assured supply of fish depends on conservation and the correct management of fish stocks. Therefore the Community must have a common fishing policy aimed at conserving and increasing the resources of the seas, including measures against pollution.

Europe and the world

Foreign and security policy
Thesis 1
The European Union needs a common foreign policy. As a part of Europe, which for some time has only been an object of world politics, it must become a positive force. The pressing problems of our time can be solved only in close cooperation with other countries. We do not wish to unite Europe in order to dominate others but to make a real contribution to stability and world peace.

Thesis 2
A liberal foreign policy should be based on acting together in support of common ideals and the rule of law. In the world at large, Europe should stand for the maintenance of peace, the principles of freedom, democracy and self-determination and the right of all mankind to individual liberty, social justice and equality of opportunity.

Thesis 3
In its foreign policy the European Union must choose its priorities realistically. Cooperation within the Atlantic Alliance, detente between Eastern and Western Europe, and the North-South Dialogue are the most urgent and important tasks. The Community should follow a good neighbourhood policy towards adjacent regions. It must extend cooperation with the Western European countries which are not Member States. Moreover cooperation with the countries of the Mediterranean basin and of the Middle East should be our special concern.

Thesis 4
Foreign, security and defence policy are closely linked and must be coordinated in order to preserve peace. Our society will only be able to develop in freedom if it is protected against aggression and threats of aggression. For this reason the European Union must take security into account, develop a coherent policy, and make provision for appropriate procedures in this connection. Peace, however, is more than the mere absence of war. For this reason the European Union must work towards the establishment of mutual trust and cooperation in Europe, making armed conflict impossible. The European Union as a peacekeeping institution, must contribute to strengthen the Atlantic Alliance as well as its role within it.

Thesis 5
The European Union can and should play an important role in the difficult but necessary process of detente between East and West, and especially throughout Europe. Increased cooperation, broader contacts and growing exchanges between countries and individuals all over Europe are essential elements of peace and stability. In this connection increased efforts should be made to ensure the implementation and further development of all the measures specified in the CSCE Final Act. On this basis the European Union must adopt initiatives on disarmament (arms limitations, arms control, balanced troop reductions). The European Union should constantly work for the lowering of barriers to the free movement of people, information and ideas.

Thesis 6
The European Union must make persistent efforts to facilitate peaceful development in the countries bordering the Mediterranean, and in the Middle East, thus helping to remove the causes of chronic tension and to improve the political, economic and social situation in that area.

Thesis 7
The enlargement of the Community should be

seen not only in economic terms but also in political terms. All free and democratic countries should in time be welcome to join the Union if they so wish and provided that they fulfil the obligations of membership in particular by the organisation of free and representative elections for the European Parliament. Enlargement must not be allowed to jeopardise the steady and efficient development of the European Union. Europe must be firmly united if enlargement is to be made easier.

Thesis 8
The European Community will make every effort to urge the United Nations to perform its tasks effectively in fields such as security, freedom and social justice in the world. We therefore advocate the appointment of a UN High Commissioner for Human Rights.

Cooperation and development policy
Thesis 1
The Liberal and Democratic Parties are conscious of their responsibility to contribute to the development of the Third World. This is a prerequisite for establishing better worldwide relations and preventing the contrasts between North and South becoming more marked. A new economic order offering equal opportunities to all must be established.

Thesis 2
The European Community must make a point of helping economically backward countries by providing for appropriate development aid. It must ensure that the Community and its Member States together provide the developing countries with official aid amounting to at least 0.7% of GNP by 1983. The Liberal and Democratic parties consider that it is even more important to help developing countries increase employment as well as their trading opportunities. The market economic forms of international trade are an essential element for effective aid through trade.

Thesis 3
Economic progress in the developing countries can be helped by the right kind of investments of private capital. The Liberal and Democratic parties wish to encourage such private investments, but they feel there must be proper safeguards for both investor and recipient.

Thesis 4
The Liberal and Democratic parties resolve that, although the existence of a Western type

democracy in developing countries cannot and should not be used as a criterion when the European Community is deciding on the provision of aid, assistance should not be given to regimes which grossly and persistently violate Human Rights. However, a close watch must be kept to ensure that the aid benefits the whole population and not just a privileged group. This can best be ensured by carefully selecting the type of project to be supported.

Thesis 5
The developing countries having neither raw materials nor primary products have a greater need than the others for aid to foster activities which can guarantee their population a decent existence. The Liberal and Democratic parties consider that financial and other aid should be granted to developing countries subject to the maximum efficiency criteria. Everything must be done to avoid an increase in the debt burden of the poorest countries.

Thesis 6
The Liberal and Democrats are in favour of negotiating an international raw materials policy which pursues the following goals:
— the reduction of extreme price fluctuations in the case of specific raw materials,
— the stabilisation of revenues accruing to the emergent countries from raw material exports
— the assurance of adequate raw materials supplies to countries poor in raw materials in North and South.
— more processing of raw materials in the emergent countries as a contribution to an improved international sharing of work.

Thesis 7
Many developing countries have serious food supply problems as a result of expanding populations, insufficient domestic production and the high cost of imported food. The Liberal and Democratic parties consider that when development programmes are being drawn up, priority must be given to small scale projects and other schemes enabling food requirements to be met by means of increases in domestic agricultural production.

Thesis 8
The European Union needs a common policy of collaboration with the developing countries. Although there are no objections to a bilateral development policy on the part of individual member-states — bearing in mind the special links that certain countries have — a common development policy should be favoured.

301

Part VI: Appendices

I. Results of the 1979 Direct Elections to the European Parliament

Three out of four of those who vote in national elections voted in the first European elections.

110,967,437 people or 72.8% of the 152,366,729 who voted in the most recent national elections in their respective Member State, turned out to vote either on Thursday, 7th June or Sunday, 10th June 1979 in the first direct elections to the European Parliament.

The voters had 3,692 candidates to choose from and the 410 whom they elected met in Strasbourg for the first time on Tuesday, 17th July for their constituent session. The MEPs sit in political groups rather than as national delegations, although the rules for groups may be different now from those of the old Parliament. The rule was that 14 members were needed to form a group or 10 where members came from at least three Member States. It is now being proposed (in a report by Rudolf Luster: Doc 193/79) that the number needed to form a group should be 29 or 21 if members are from at least two Member States.

Of the 410 newly-elected MEPs, 77 served in the old European Parliament and 125 hold mandates in their national parliaments.

There are 344 men and 66 women in the European Parliament.

The following tables show how votes were cast and the seats won. The figures are taken from the Directorate-General for Information at the European Parliament in Brussels.

EUROPEAN ELECTIONS, 7th-10th June 1979
Votes, percentages and seats

	Total	Belgium	Denmark	France	Germany	Ireland	Italy	Luxembourg[2]	Netherlands	United Kingdom
Socialist	29,506,228 26.6% 111	1,274,778 23.4% 7	382,487 21.9% 3	4,763,026 23.4% 21	11,370,045 40.8% 35	193,898 14.5% 4	5,368,756 15.3% 13	(37,166) 21.7% 1	1,722,270 30.4% 9	4,393,832 32.6% 18
Christian Democrats	32,782,796 29.5% 106	2,053,865 37.7% 10	30,985 1.8% 0	(1,525,721)[1] (7.5%) 7	13,700,205 49.2% 42	443,652 33.1% 4	12,948,791 37.1% 30	(61,829) 36.1% 3	2,017,743 35.6% 10	
Conservative	6,861,580 6.2% 63		353,099 20.2% 3							6,508,481 48.4%
Communist	14,942,568 13.5% 44	145,804 2.7% 0	81,991 4.7% 1	4,153,710 20.4% 19	112,055 0.4% 0		10,343,101 29.6% 24	(8,564) 5.0% 0	97,343 1.7% 0	
Liberal Democratic Group	11,760,021 10.6% 41	885,212 16.3% 4	252,767 14.5% 3	(4,141,258)[1] (20.4%) 19	1,662,621 6.0% 4		2,164,649 6.2% 5	(48,127) 28.1% 2	914,787 16.1% 4	1,690,600 12.6% 0
European Progressive Democrats	3,867,132 3.5% 21		100,702 5.8% 1	3,301,980 16.2% 15		464,450 34.7% 5				
Others	6,173,519 5.5% 24	738,981 13.6% 3	365,760 21.0% 5	2,445,740 12.0% 0	1,002,183 3.6% 0	167,730 12.5% 5	3,845,388 10.9% 9		511,967 9.0% 2	543,693 4.1% 3
	5,073,593 4.6% 0	344,227 6.3% 0	177,287 10.1% 0			69,342 5.2% 0	306,604 0.9% 0	(15,586) 9.1% 0	403,223 7.1% 0	309,470 2.3% 0
TOTAL	110,967,437	5,442,867	1,745,078	20,331,440	27,847,109	1,339,072	34,977,289	171,272	5,667,303	13,446,076

1. UFE (Simon Veil) – list: Split between CD and L 7:19
2. In Luxembourg every voter had 6 votes so totals divided by six

European and national elections
Tentative analysis
Percentage shares of the polls

		Belgium	Denmark	France	Germany	Ireland	Italy	Luxembourg	Netherlands	United Kingdom
Turnout	EP elections	91.4	47.8	60.7	65.7	63.6	85.5	88.9	57.8	32.6
	National elections	94.6 (18.4.77)	88.9 (15.2.77)	82.8 (19.3.78)	90.7 (3.10.76)	76.9 (16.6.77)	89.9 (3-4.6.79)	90.1 (10.6.79)	87.5 (25.5.77)	76.0 (3.5.79)
Socialist	EP elections	23.4	21.9	23.4	40.8	14.5	15.3	21.7	30.4	32.6
	National elections	25.4	37.0	24.7	42.6	11.6	13.6	22.5	33.8	36.9
Christian Democrats	EP elections	37.7	1.8	7.5	49.2	33.1	37.1	36.1	35.6	
	National elections	36.3	3.4		48.6	30.5	38.9	36.4	31.9	
Conservative	EP elections		20.2							48.4
	National elections		14.9							43.9
Communist	EP elections	2.7	4.7	20.4	0.4		29.6	5.0	1.7	
	National elections	3.3	3.9	20.6	0.3		30.4	4.9	1.7	
Liberal and Democratic	EP elections	16.3	14.5	20.4	6.0		6.2	28.1	16.1	12.6
	National elections	16.3	12.0		7.9		4.9	21.9	18.0	13.8
European Progressive Democrats	EP elections		5.8	16.2		34.7				
	National elections		14.6	22.6		50.6				
Others	EP elections	19.9	31.1	12.0	3.6	17.7	11.8	9.1	16.2	6.4
	National elections	18.7	14.2	10.6	0.6	7.3	12.2	14.3	14.5	5.4

BELGIUM

Party	Electorate (European Elections): 6,800,584 — European Election 10 June 1979 (24 seats)			Electorate (General Election): 5,478,080 — General Election December 1978 (212 seats)		
	Votes	%	Seats in EP	Votes	%	National Seats
Christian Peoples Party (Flemish)	1,607,927 }	37.6	7	1,451,733	27.10	57
Christian Peoples Party (Walloon)	445,940		3	488,182	9.11	25
Socialist Party (Walloon)	698,892 }	23.3	3	523,740	11.64	32
Socialist Party (Flemish)	575,886		4	580,521	12.70	26
Liberal Party (Flemish)	512,355 }	16.2	2	} 582,426	10.87	37
Liberal Party (Walloon)	372,857		2			
SDR Rassemblement Walloon	414,412	7.6	2	—	—	—
Flemish Peoples Union	324,569	5.9	1	383,455	7.15	14
Ecologists	185,821	3.42	—	—	—	—
Communists	145,804	2.62	—	—	—	4
Others	138,404	—	—	984,792	18.38	17
Total	5,422,867	—	24	5,157,306	—	212
Invalid Votes	789,616					
Turnout	6,212,483	91.4		—	94.6	—

DENMARK

Party	Electorate (European Elections): 3,725,235 European Elections 7 June 1979 (16 seats)			Electorate (General Election): 3,542,843 General Election February 1977 (158 seats)		
	Votes	%	Seats in EP	Votes	%	National seats
Social Democrats	382,487	21.9	3	1,150,355	37.0	65
Social Liberals	56,944	3.3	–	113,330	3.6	–
Conservatives	245,309	14.1	2	263,262	8.5	15
Retsforbundet (Single tax party)	59,379	3.4	–	102,149	3.3	–
Social People's Party	81,991	4.7	1	120,357	3.9	7
Centre Democracy	107,790	6.2	1	200,347	6.4	11
Communists	–	–	–	114,022	3.7	7
Folke bevaegelsen (Anti-Market Party)	365,760	21.0	4	–	–	–
Christian People's Party	30,985	1.8	–	106,082	3.4	6
Liberals	252,767	14.5	3	371,728	12.0	21
Left Socialists	60,964	3.5	–	83,667	2.7	–
Progress Party	100,702	5.8	1	453,792	14.6	26
Siumut (Greenland)	5,118	–	1	–	–	4
Others (including Atassut)	4,654	–	–	27,206	0.9	–
Turnout	1,754,850	47.8	16	3,106,297	88.9	158

FRANCE

Party	Electorate (European Elections): 35,180,531 — European Elections 7 June 1979 (81 seats)			Electorate (General Election): 35,179,654 — General Election March 1978 (491 seats)		
	Votes	%	Seats in EP	Votes	%	Seats in EP
Socialists and Radicals of the Left	4,763,026	23.4	21	7,054,066	24.7	114
French Communist Party	4,153,710	20.4	19	5,870,340	20.5	86
Union for France in Europe	5,666,984	27.9	26			
Union for French Democracy (UDF)				6,122,180	21.4	122
Defence of interests of France in Europe (DIFE)	3,301,980	16.2	15			
Rally for the Republic				6,451,454	22.6	155
Others	2,445,740	12.0	—	3,083,022	10.8	14
Turnout	20,331,440	60.7	81	28,581,062	82.8	491

GERMANY

Party	Electorate (European Elections): 42,751,940			Electorate (General Elections): 42,058,015		
	European Elections 10 June 1979 (81 seats)			General Election 1976 (518 seats)		
	Votes	%	Seats in EP	Votes	%	Bundestag Seats
CDU (Christian Democratic Union)	10,883,085	49.2	34	14,367,302	48.6	254
CSU (Christian Social Union)	2,817,120		8	4,027,499		
SPD (Social Democrats)	11,370,045	40.8	35	16,099,019	42.6	224
FDP (Liberals)	1,662,621	6.0	4	2,995,085	7.9	40
DKP (Communists)	112,055	0.4	–	118,581	0.3	
Die Grunen (Ecologists)	893,683	3.2	–	–	–	
Others	108,500	0.4	–	215,014	0.6	
Turnout	27,847,109	65.7	81	38,165,753	90.7	518

Note: There are 3 MEPs for Berlin

IRELAND

| Party | Electorate (European Elections): 2,188,798 | | | Electorate (General Elections): 2,118,606 | | |
| | European Elections 7 June 1979 (15 seats) | | | General Election June 1977 (148 seats) | | |
	Votes	%	Seats in EP	Votes	%	National Seats
Fianna Fail	464,450	34.68	5	811,615	50.63	84
Fine Gael	443,652	33.13	4	488,767	30.49	43
Labour Party	193,898	14.48	4	186,410	11.63	17
Independent	189,499	14.15	2	116,235	7.27	4
Sinn Fein	43,943	3.28	–	27,209	1.7	–
Others	3,630	0.27	–	–	–	–
Turnout	1,339,072	63.6	15	1,630,236	76.9	148

ITALY

Party	European Elections 10 June 1979 (81 seats)			General Election 3-4 June 1979 (630 seats)		
	Electorate (European Elections): 42,193,369			Electorate (General Elections): 42,213,962		
	Votes	%	Seats in EP	Votes	%	National Seats
Christian Democracy (DC)	12,752,602	36.5	29	14,007,594	38.3	262
Italian Communist Party (PCI)	10,343,101	29.6	24	11,107,883	30.4	201
Italian Socialist Party (PSI)	3,857,436	11.0	9	3,586,256	9.8	62
Italian Social Movement (MSI)	1,907,452	5.4	4	1,924,251	5.3	30
Italian Social Democratic Party (PSDI)	1,511,320	4.3	4	1,403,873	3.8	20
Radical Party (PR)	1,282,728	3.7	3	1,259,362	3.4	18
Italian Republican Party (PRI)	895,083	2.6	2	1,106,766	3.0	16
Italian Liberal Party (PLI)	1,269,560	3.6	3	708,022	1.9	9
Democratic Party for Proletarian Unity (PDUP)	404,794	1.1	1	501,431	1.4	6
Proletarian Democracy (DP)	250,414	0.7	1	293,443	0.8	–
National Democracy (DN)	141,350	0.4	–	228,340	0.6	–
South Tyrol People's Party (SVP)	196,189	0.6	1	206,264	0.6	4
Aosta Valley Union (UV)	165,260	0.5	–	33,250	0.1	1
Others	–	–	–	135,124	0.4	1
Turnout	34,977,289	85.5	81	36,501,859	89.9	630

LUXEMBOURG

Party	Electorate (European Elections): 212,740 — European Elections 7 June 1979 (6 seats)			Electorate (General Elections): 212,740 — General Election June 1979 (59 seats)		
	Votes	%	Seats in EP	Votes	%	National Seats
Socialist Worker Party	211,097	21.7	1	737,931		14
Independent Socialists				66,907		1
Communist Party	48,738	5.0	–	177,269		2
Democratic Party	274,345	28.1	2	648,693		15
Wiert lech	–	–	–	30,271		–
Christian Social Party	351,942	36.0	3	1,049,393		24
Revolutionary Communist League	5,027	0.5	–	6,984		–
Liberal Party	5,595	0.5	–	6,143		–
Enroles de force	–	–	–	135,356		–
Socialist Democrat Party	68,310	7.0	–	181,931		1
Club of Independents	–	–	–	849		2
Turnout	965,054*	88.9	6	3,041,522	90.1	59

* In Luxembourg, voters had 6 votes each in the European election and a number equal to the seats to be filled in the National election (24 votes in the Southern constituency, 20 in the Centre, 6 in the West, and 9 in the North).

NETHERLANDS

| Party | Electorate (European Elections): 9,799,761 | | | Electorate (General Elections): 9,497,991 | | |
| | European Elections 10 June 1979 (25 seats) | | | General Election May 1977 (150 seats) | | |
	Votes	%	Seats in EP	Votes	%	National Seats
PvdA (Labour)	1,722,240	30.39	9	2,813,795	33.83	53
CDA (Christian Democrats)	2,017,743	35.61	10	2,652,280	31.89	49
VVD (Liberals)	914,787	16.14	4	1,492,691	17.95	28
D'66 (Independents)	511,967	9.03	2	452,423	5.43	8
Others	500,566	8.83	–	906,422	10.90	12
Turnout	5,667,303	57.8	25	8,317,611	87.5	150

314

UNITED KINGDOM

| Party | Electorate (European Elections): 41,559,460 | | | Electorate (General Elections): 41,093,264 | | |
| | European Elections 7 June 1979 (81 seats) | | | General Election 3 May 1979 (635 seats) | | |
	Votes	%	Seats in EP	Votes	%	Commons Seats
Conservative Party	6,508,481	48.4	60	13,697,753	43.9	337
Labour Party	4,253,210	31.6	17	11,509,524	36.9	267
Liberal Party	1,690,600	12.6	–	4,313,931	13.8	11
Scottish National Party	247,836	1.9	1	504,259	1.6	2
Plaid Cymru	83,399	0.6	–	132,544	0.4	2
Ulster Unionists	125,169	0.9	1	175,171	0.6	5
Democratic Unionist Party	170,688	1.3	1	61,625	0.2	3
Social Democratic & Labour Party	140,622	1.0	1	16,480	0.05	1
Others	226,071	1.7	–	306,938	0.8	7
Turnout	13,446,076	33.0		30,718,225	76.0	

315

II. Bibliography

General Reference Literature

Berg-Schlosser, D: *Die politischen Probleme der Dritten Welt*, 1970.

Duverger, M.: *Les Parties Politiques*, 1951.

Fenske, Hans: *Wahlrecht und Parteiensystem*, 1975.

Fenske, Hans: "Die europäischen Parteiensysteme". In: *Jahrbuch des öffentlichen Rechts*, NF 22.

Holt, St.: *Six European States*, 1970.

Jäger, W. (Ed.): *Partei und System*, 1972.

Lehmbruch, G.: "Parteiensysteme". In: *Staatslexikon der Görresgesellschaft*, Vol. 10, COL. 864.

Loewenstein, K.: *Verfassungslehre*, 1969.

Mayer-Tasch, P.C. (Ed.): *Die Verfassungen Europas*, 1975.

Naßmacher, K.H.: "Politische Systeme und politische Soziologie" *(Politikwissenschaft I)*. 1973.

Neumann, S.: *Die Parteien der Weimarer Republik*, 1932.

Neumann, S.: *Modern Political Parties*, 1967.

Ostrogorski, M.: *Democracy and the Organization of Political Parties*, 1902.

Rose, R.: *The Problem of Party Government*, 1974.

Smith, G.: *Politics in Western Europe*, 1976.

Stammen, Th.: *Regierungssysteme der Gegenwart*, 1972.

Weber, Max: *Wirtschaft und Gesellschaft*. Study edition, 1964.

Literature relating to individual countries

Andersch/Warner: *Irland*, 1973.
Andrén, N.: *Government and Politics in the Nordic Countries*, 1964.
Andrén, N.: *Modern Swedish Government*, 1961.
Alter, P.: *Die irische Nationalbewegung zwischen Parlament und Revolution*, 1971.
Bagehot, Walter: *The English Constitution*, London 1867.
Bakojannis, P.: *Militärherrschaft in Griechenland*, 1972.
Balibar, Etienne: *Uber die Diktatur des Proletariats* 1977.
Bangemann, M./Bieber, R.: *Die Direktwahl – Sackgasse oder Chance für Europa*, 1976.
Beck, R.: *Das spanische Regierungssystem*, 1975.
Beckett, J.C.: *Geschichte Irlands*, 1971.
Benedikter, H. (Ed.): *Geschichte der Republik Osterreich*, 1954.
Berchtold, K.: *Die österreichischen Parteiprogramme*, 1971.
Bergsträsser, L.: *Geschichte der politischen Parteien in Deutschland*, 1965.
Beyme, K. v.: *Vom Faschismus zur Entwicklungsdiktatur. Machtelite und Opposition in Spanien*, 1971.
Beyme, K. v.: *Das politische System Italiens*, Stuttgart 1970.
Bibes, G.: *Le système politique italien*, 1974.
Bieber, R.: "Funktion und Grundlagen direkter Wahlen zum Europäischen Parlament im Jahre 1978." In: *Zeitschrift für Parlamentsfragen* 2, 1976.
Bieber, R.: "Organe der erweiterten europäischen Gemeinschaften": *Das Parlament*, 1974.
Blondel, J.: *Demokratie in England*, 1964.
Blondel, J.: *The Government of France*, 1974.
Böll, H.: *Irisches Tagebuch*, 1957.
Bracher, U.: *Geschichte Skandinaviens*, 1968.
Bruneau, Th.C.: "Portugal auf der Suche nach seiner neuen Staatsform". In: *Europa-Archiv*, Folge 23, 1975.
Bull, E.: *Sozialgeschichte der norwegischen Demokratie*, 1969.
Castberg, F.: *Norway and the western powers*, 1958.
Chabod, F.: *Die Entstehung des neuen Italien*, 1974.
Christensen, C.A.R.: *Norwegen. Ein demokratisches Königreich*, 1962.
Chubb, B.: *The Government and Politics of Ireland*, 1971.
Cullen, L.M.: *An Economic History of Ireland since 1660*, 1972.
Dahrendorf, R.: *Plädoyer für die Europäische Union*, 1973.
D'Estaing, Valéry Giscard: *Démocratie francaise*, 1976.
Dures, A.: *Modern Ireland*, 1973.
Eckstein, H.: *Division and Cohesion in Democracy. A Study of Norway*, 1966.
Ehrmann, H.W.: *Das politische System Frankreichs. Eine Einführung*, 1976.
Europa-Parlament (Ed.): *Bulletin 1977/78: Mitgliedsliste*, Juni 1977.
Fetscher, I.: *Großbritannien – Gesellschaft, Staat, Ideologie*, 1968.
Finnish Political Science Association (Ed.): *Democracy in Finland. Studies in Politics and Government*, 1960.
Fischer, H. (Ed.): *Das politische System Osterreichs*, 1966.
Fitzmaurice, J.: *The Party Groups in the European Parliament*, 1975.
Flechtheim, K.O.: *Die politischen Parteien der Bundesrepublik Deutschland*, 1972.
Fusilier, R.: *Les Pays Nordiques*.
Gerhards, C./Rauch, M./Schirmbeck, S.: *Volkserziehung in Portugal – Berichte, Analysen, Dokumente*.
Goguel, F./Ziebura, G.: *Das französische Regierungssystem. Quellenbuch*, 1957.
Grabitz, E.: *Europa-Wahlrecht – die deutschen gesetzlichen Bestimmungen für die erste Direktwahl des Europäischen Parlaments*.
Gruner, E.: *Die Parteien in der Schweiz*, 1969.

318

Hallstein, W.: *Die Europäische Gemeinschaft*, 1974.

Hottinger, A.: "Die portugiesische Demokratie in der Bewährung". In: *Europa-Archiv*, Folge 15, 1976.

Hrbek, R./Keutsch, W.: *Gesellschaft und Staat in Großbritannien*, 1971.

Institut für europäische Politik: "Zusammenarbeit der Parteien in Westeuropa". Reihe Europäische Schriften Vol. 43/44. 1976.

Irving, R.E.M.: *Christian Democracy in France*, 1973.

Jennings, I.W./Ritter, G.A.: *Das britische Regierungssystem*, 1970.

Jütter, A./Liese, H.J.: *Taschenbuch der europäischen Parteien und Wahlen*, 1977.

Kempf, Udo: *Das politische System Frankreichs*, 1975.

Kogan, N.: *The Government of Italy*, 1965.

Kohler, B.: "Integration und Verflechtung durch Europäische Wahlen?" In: *Regionale Verflechtung der Bundesrepublik*, 1973.

Koskimies, E.: *The Finnish Parliament*, 1969.

Krämer, Hans R.: *Die Europäische Gemeinschaft*, 1974.

Kundloch, H.: *"Bürger wählen europäisch – 20 Fragen zur Direktwahl"*. 1975.

Kunz, R./Maier, H./Stammen, Th.: *Programme der politischen Parteien in der Bundesrepublik*, 1975.

Lagoni, R.: *Die politischen Parteien im Verfassungssystem der Republik Irland*, 1973.

Landeszentrale für politische Bildung Baden-Württemberg (Ed.): *Spanien und Portugal – Rückkehr zur Demokratie*, 1977.

Lees, J.D./Kimber, R.: *Political Parties in Modern Britain*, 1972.

Lehmbruch, G.: *Proporzdemokratie*, 1967.

Lindgren, R.E.: *Norway-Sweden*, 1959.

Linz, J.J.: "The party of Spain past and future". In: Lipset, S.M./Rokkan, S. (Ed.): *Party system and voters alignments: cross-national perspectives*. 1967.

Liphart, A.: *The politics of Accommodation, Pluralism and Democracy in the Netherlands*, 1968.

Loewenstein, K.: *Der britische Parlamentarismus*, 1964.

MacRae, Duncan (Jr.): *Parliament, Parties and Society in France 1946-1958*. 1967.

Mackenzie, K.R.: *British Political Parties*, 1964.

Maier, L.: *Spaniens Weg zur Demokratie – Formen und Bedingungen der Opposition im autoritären Staat*, 1976.

Mansergh, N.: *The Irish Question 1840-1921*, 1965.

McKenzie, R.T.: *Politische Parteien in England*, 1961.

Meynaud, J.: *Bericht über die Abschaffung der Demokratie in Griechenland*, 1969.

Miller, K.E.: *Government and Politics in Denmark*, 1968.

Mintzel, A.: *Die CSU – Anatomie einer konservativen Partei*, 1975.

Mintzel, A.: *Geschichte der CSU*, Opladen, 1977.

Mitterand, Francois: *La paille et le grain*, Paris 1975.

Mohler, Armin: *Die Fünfte Republik. Was steht hinter de Gaulle*, 1961.

Naßmacher, K.-H.: *Das österreichische Regierungssystem*, 1968.

Nawrath, A.: *Norway*, 1965.

Nousiainen, J.: *The Finnish political system*, 1971.

Nyholm, P.: *Parliament, Government and Multi-Dimensional Party Relations in Finland*, 1972.

Peyrefitte, Alain: *Was wird aus Frankreich*, Berlin 1977.

Pickles, D.: *The Government and Politics of France*, Vol. I, II, 1972.

Pivot, S.: *Norvege*, 1965.

Pöhle, M.: "Direktwahl des europäischen Parlaments: ein Ablenkungsmanöver? Zehn skeptische Thesen zu den möglichen Wirkungen." In: *Zeitschrift für Parlamentsfragen* 2, 1976.

Raschke, Joachim: *Organisierter Konflikt in westeuropäischen Parteien*, Opladen 1977.

Raschke, Joachim (ed.): *Die politischen Parteien in Westeuropa*, Reinbek/Hamburg 1978.

Rass, H.H.: *Großbritannien – eine politische Landeskunde*, 1972.

Röhring, H.H./Sontheimer, K. (Ed.): *Handbuch des deutschen Parlamentarismus*, 1970.

Rosenbaum, P.: *Italien 1976 – Christdemokraten mit Kommunisten*, 1976.

Rump, E.: *Nationalismus und Sozialismus in Irland*, 1959.

Runge, Chr.: *Einführung in das Recht der europäischen Gemeinschaften*, 1975.

Rustow, D.A.: *The Politics of Compromise. A Study of Parties and Cabinet Government in Sweden*, 1969.

Scandinavian Political Studies, Various years.

Schumann, K.: *Das Regierungssystem der Schweiz*, 1977.

Senell, R.: *Politische, wirtschaftliche und gesellschaftliche Strukturen Belgiens*, 1970.

Setzer, H.: *Wahlsystem und Parteienentwicklung in England*, 1973.

Siegfried, André: *Frankreichs Vierte Republik*, Stuttgart 1959.

Stacey, Frank: *The Government of Modern Britain*, 1969.

Stacey, F.: *British Government – 1966 to 1975*, 1975.

Staritz, D. (Ed.): *Das Parteiensystem der Bundesrepublik*, 1976.

Steiner, J. (Ed.): *Das politische System der Schweiz*, 1971.

Sternberger, D. u. a.: *Die Wahl der Parlamente*, Vol. I, II, 1969.

Storing, J.A.: *Norwegian Democracy*, 1963.

Tindemans, L.: "Bericht an den Europäischen Rat." In: Jüttner/Liese: *Taschenbuch der europäischen Wahlen und Parteien*, 1977.

Valen, H./Katz, D.: *Political Parties in Norway. A Community Study*, 1967.

Vinde, P.: *Swedish Government Administration*, 1971.

Wallace, M.: *A Short History of Ireland*, 1973.

Weil, G.L.: *The Benelux-Nations.: The Politics of Small Country Democrates*, 1970.

Young, A.B.: *Der Entwicklungsprozeß der politischen Parteien in Osterreich*, 1970. (Dissertation).

Ziebura, G.: *Die V. Republik. Frankreichs neues Regierungssystem*, 1960.

Ziebura, G. (Ed.): *Beiträge zur allgemeinen Parteienlehre*.

III. List of abbreviations for the European parties in the EC

Belgium

BSP	Belgische Socialistische Partij
PSB	Parti socialiste belge
CVP	Christelijke Volkspartij
PSC	Parti social-chrétien
FDF	Front démocratique des franco-
RW	phones – Rassemblement wallon
PVV	Partij voor vrijheid en vooruitgang
PLP	Parti de la liberté et du progrès

Federal Republic of Germany

CDU	Christlich-Demokratische Union
CSU	Christlich-Soziale Union
FDP	Freie Demokratische Partei
SPD	Sozialdemokratische Partei Deutschlands

Denmark

CD	Centrum-Demokraterne
FRP	Fremskridtspartiet
KF	Det konservative folkeparti
RV	Det Radikale venstre
S	Socialdemokratiet
SF	Socialistisk folkeparti
V	Venstre, Danmarks liberale parti

France

GD	Gauche démocratique
PCF	Parti communiste français
PS	Parti socialiste
RCDS	Réformateurs des centristes et démocrates sociaux
RG	Mouvement des radicaux de gauche
RDS	Réformateurs et démocrates sociaux
RI	Républicains indépendants
RIAS	Républicains indépendants d'action sociale
UCDP	Union centriste des démocrates de progrès
RPR	Rassemblement pour la République
MRP	Mouvement Republicain Populaire

Ireland

FF	Fianna Fail Party
FG	Fine Gael Party
Lab.	Labour Party

Italy

DC	Democrazia Cristiana
Ind. Sin.	Indipendenti di Sinistra
Man.	Manifesto
MPL	Movimento Politico Lavoratori
MSI/DN	Movimento Sociale Italiano – Destra Nazionale
PC	Partito Comunista (marxista leninista italiano)
PCI	Partito Comunista Italiano
PLI	Partito Liberale Italiano
PRI	Partito Republicano Italiano
PSI	Partito Socialista Italiano
PSDI	Partito Socialista Democratico Italiano
PSIUP	Partito Socialista Italiano di Unità Proletaria
SVP/ PPST	Südtiroler Volkspartei/ Partito Popolare SudTirolese

Luxembourg

LPL	Liberal Partei Lötzeburg
LCR	Parti Communiste Révolutionnaire
PC	Parti Communiste
PD	Parti Démocratique
PCS	Parti Chrétien Social
POSL	Parti Ouvrier Socialiste Luxembourgeois
PSD	Parti Social Démocrate

Netherlands

ARP	Anti-Revolutionaire Partij
BP	Boerenpartij
CHU	Christelijk Historische Unie
CPN	Communistische Partij Nederland
D'66	Demokraten 66
DS'70	Demokraten Socialisten '70
GVP	Gereformeerd Politiek Verband
KPN	Katholieke Partij Nederland
KVP	Katholieke Volkspartij
PPR	Politieke Partij Radikalen
PSP	Pacifistische Socialistische Partij
SGP	Staatskundig Gereformeerde Partij
PvdA	Partij van de Arbeid
VVD	Volkspartij voor Vrijheid en Democratie

Great Britain

Cons.	Conservative and Unionist Party
Lab.	Labour Party
Lib.	Liberal Party
SNP	Scottish National Party